Judaism and Christianity

The Brill Reference Library of Judaism

Editors
Alan J. Avery-Peck (College of the Holy Cross)
William Scott Green (University of Miami)

Editorial Board
David Aaron (Hebrew Union College-Jewish Institute
of Religion, Cincinnati)
Herbert Basser (Queen's University)
Bruce D. Chilton (Bard College)
José Faur (Netanya College)
Neil Gillman (Jewish Theological Seminary of America)
Mayer I. Gruber (Ben-Gurion University of the Negev)
Ithamar Gruenwald (Tel Aviv University)
Maurice-Ruben Hayoun (University of Geneva)
Arkady Kovelman (Moscow State University)
David Kraemer (Jewish Theological Seminary of America)
Baruch A. Levine (New York University)
Allan Nadler (Drew University)
Jacob Neusner (Bard College)
Maren Niehoff (Hebrew University of Jerusalem)
Gary G. Porton (University of Illinois)
Aviezer Ravitzky (Hebrew University of Jerusalem)
Dov Schwartz (Bar Ilan University)
Günter Stemberger (University of Vienna)
Michael E. Stone (Hebrew University of Jerusalem)
Elliot Wolfson (New York University)

VOLUME 28

Judaism and Christianity

New Directions for Dialogue and Understanding

Edited by

Alan J. Avery-Peck

and

Jacob Neusner

BRILL

LEIDEN • BOSTON
2009

This book is printed on acid-free paper.

Library of Congress Cataloging-in-Publication Data

Judaism and Christianity : new directions for dialogue and understanding / edited by Alan J. Avery-Peck and Jacob Neusner. — 1st ed.
  p. cm. — (Brill reference library of Judaism, ISSN 1571-5000; v. 28)
  Includes bibliographical references and index.
  ISBN 978-90-04-17938-7 (hard cover : alk. paper)
  1. Judaism—Relations—Christianity—History. 2. Christianity and other religions—Judaism—History. I. Avery-Peck, Alan J. (Alan Jeffery), 1953- II. Neusner, Jacob, 1932- III. Title. IV. Series.

  BM535.J823 2009
  296.3'96—dc22

2009030132

ISSN 1571-5000
ISBN 978 90 04 17938 7

© Copyright 2009 by Koninklijke Brill NV, Leiden, The Netherlands.
Koninklijke Brill NV incorporates the imprints Brill, Hotei Publishing, IDC Publishers, Martinus Nijhoff Publishers and VSP.

All rights reserved. No part of this publication may be reproduced, translated, stored in a retrieval system, or transmitted in any form or by any means, electronic, mechanical, photocopying, recording or otherwise, without prior written permission from the publisher.

Authorization to photocopy items for internal or personal use is granted by Brill provided that the appropriate fees are paid directly to The Copyright Clearance Center, 222 Rosewood Drive, Suite 910, Danvers, MA 01923, USA.
Fees are subject to change.

PRINTED IN THE NETHERLANDS

CONTENTS

Preface vii

INTRODUCTION

Renewing Religious Disputation in Quest
of Theological Truth 3
Jacob Neusner

THE FIRST CENTURIES

Mosaics as Midrash: The Zodiacs of the Ancient
Synagogues and the Conflict between Judaism
and Christianity 11
Yaffa Englard

Judaic Social Teaching in Christian
and Pagan Context 29
Jacob Neusner

Planting Christian Trees in Jewish Soil 61
Herbert W. Basser

Rabbinic Texts in the Exegesis of the New Testament 83
Miguel Pérez Fernández

Christianity, Diaspora Judaism, and Roman Crisis 109
Robert M. Price

THE MEDIEVAL PERIOD

Newton, Maimonidean 127
José Faur

Moslem, Christian, and Jewish Cultural Interaction
in Sefardic Talmudic Interpretation 163
Daniel Boyarin

Don Quixote—Talmudist and *Mucho Más* 197
José Faur

THE MODERN PERIOD

Torah and Culture: H. Richard Niebuhr's *Christ and Culture* after Fifty Years: A Judaic Response 217
Jacob Neusner

Five Types of Judaism? Reflections on the Inner Logic of Judaism as Revealed by Niebuhr's Phenomenological Typology 243
Evan M. Zuesse

The Agenda of *Dabru Emet* 265
Jon D. Levenson

Index of Names 293
Index of Ancient Sources 295

PREFACE

This volume treats the interrelationship between Judaism and Christianity from the first centuries and into modern times, paying particular attention to these faiths' social, cultural, and theological interactions. While the essays collected here concern diverse ways in which the history and traditions of Judaism shed light on Christianity, and vice versa, the volume as a whole emerges out of and supports a single thesis. This is the idea articulated most directly by the collection's opening and closing chapters, Jacob Neusner's statement on "Renewing Religious Disputation in Quest of Theological Truth" and Jon Levenson's critical essay "The Agenda of *Dabru Emet*." While reflecting on distinct aspects of interfaith dialogue as it has taken shape especially in the past half century, Professors Neusner and Levenson share a perspective that has been lost in the recent trend towards asserting that what Jews and Christians share is much more important than any unique elements of belief that stand between them.

By contrast to this common perception of contemporary interfaith dialogue, Professors Levenson and Neusner argue that the interests of each community and of interfaith understanding overall are better served by a different approach entirely. Professor Neusner in particular argues that Jews and Christians must approach each other on the foundation of a clear perception of their own faith's beliefs and world-view. On this basis, they must be prepared to engage the other in serious debate over the elements of faith and theology that distinguish each community. Such debate takes seriously the place of reason in shaping religious beliefs, and it acknowledges that to maintain and take seriously the convictions that define us as Jews or Christians necessitates arguing what we believe to be true and why. Interfaith dialogue, as Professor Neusner notes, thus must emerge from debate rather than negotiation, and, to be meaningful, it must recognize that the distinctive world-views that separate religions are neither trivial nor meaningless. By knowing and debating what we believe, we do justice to and secure our own theological convictions and, at the same time, illuminate our relationship with those who hold otherwise. In serious and honest debate we take seriously and show respect for the other, even if it is an other with whom we do not ultimately agree.

A foundation of the debate that must comprise interfaith dialogue is knowledge of how Judaism and Christianity historically have related to each other and interacted in shaping each other's theologies and world-views. It is to this aspect of Jewish-Christian dialogue that the essays collected here contribute. At stake are issues ranging from the formation of Jewish and Christian ideology in the context of Roman paganism to the ways in which Christian culture and theology of the medieval and modern periods form a backdrop to the creation of Jewish identity. While the historical periods and the issues covered are diverse, the result of these essays read as a group is to suggest the importance of our recognition of the close development of Judaism and Christianity. We see in these essays how the two faiths related to each other as they evolved in shared historical and cultural contexts, even as each maintained its own distinctive ideologies and beliefs.

The editors with to thank the authors of the essays collected here for sharing them with the readership of the *Review of Rabbinic Judaism*, in which they first appeared, and for allowing them to be reprinted here. Since its founding (as *The Annual of Rabbinic Judaism*) in 1998, the *Review of Rabbinic Judaism* has remained the only journal dedicated to examining Rabbinic Judaism in all of its historical periods and aspects, as representative of a fundamentally unitary religious phenomenon from its beginning and to the present. Authors such as those whose work is collected here have immeasurably advanced our comprehension of the Rabbinic tradition, and the editors thank them for sharing their best work with us. Our thanks go as well to our editors at Brill, Michiel Klein Swormink and now Jennifer Pavelko, who supported the creation of the *Review of Rabbinic Judaism* and who encouraged the production of this volume. Their interest in and dedication to the study of Judaism, and the gratification they clearly take in results such as are represented here, makes our work with them a source of great satisfaction.

The Editors

Alan J. Avery Peck
Kraft-Hiatt Professor in Judaic Studies
College of the Holy Cross
Worcester, Massachusetts

Jacob Neusner
Distinguished Service Professor of the History
and Theology of Judaism
Senior Fellow of the Institute of Advanced Theology
Bard College
Annandale-Upon-Hudson, New York

INTRODUCTION

RENEWING RELIGIOUS DISPUTATION IN QUEST OF THEOLOGICAL TRUTH

Jacob Neusner
Bard College

In ancient[1] and medieval times disputations concerning propositions of religious truth defined the purpose of dialogue between religions, particularly Judaism and Christianity. Judaism made its case vigorously, amassing rigorous arguments built upon the facts of Scripture common to both parties to the debate.[2] Imaginary narratives, such as Judah ha-Levi's *Kuzari*, constructed a dialogue among Judaism, Christianity, and Islam, a dialogue conducted by a king who sought the true religion for his kingdom.[3] Judaism won the disputation before the king of the Khazars, at least in Judah Halevi's formulation. But Christianity no less aggressively sought debate-partners, confident of the outcome of the confrontation. Such debates attested to the common faith of both parties in the integrity of reason and in the facticity of shared Scriptures.

Disputation went out of style when religions lost their confidence in the power of reason to establish theological truth. Then, as in Lessing's *Nathan the Wise*, religions were made to affirm a truth in common, and the differences between religions were dismissed as trivial and unimportant. An American president was quoted as saying, "It doesn't matter what you believe as long as you're a good man." Then disputations between religions lost their urgency. The heritage of the Enlightenment with its indifference to the truth-claims of religion fostered religious toleration and reciprocal respect in place

---

[1] My contribution to the study of the Judaeo-Christian disputations of late antiquity is *Aphrahat and Judaism. The Christian-Jewish Argument in Fourth Century Iran* (Leiden, 1971; reprint: Atlanta, 1999). See also *Judaism and Christianity in the Age of Constantine. Issues of the Initial Confrontation* (Chicago, 1987; paperback edition: 2007).

[2] See Hyam Maccoby, ed. and trans., *Judaism on Trial: Jewish-Christian Disputations in the Middle Ages* (Rutherford and London, 1982); and David Berger, *The Jewish-Christian Debate in the High Middle Ages: A Critical Edition of the Nizzahon Vetus with an Introduction, Translation, and Commentary* (Philadelphia, 1979; reprint: Northvale, 1996).

[3] Judah ha-Levi, *The Kuzari: In Defense of the Despised Faith*; translated and annotated by N. Daniel Korobkin (Northvale, 1998).

of religious confrontation and claims to know God. Religions emerged as obstacles to the good order of society. For the past two centuries Judaeo-Christian dialogue served as the medium of a politics of social conciliation, not religious inquiry into the convictions of the other. Negotiation took the place of debate, and to lay claim upon truth in behalf of one's own religion violated the rules of good conduct.

An opportunity to renew the rigorous disputation of medieval times presented itself with the advent of Pope John XXIII and Vatican II. Two new facts opened the way to a renewed debate about religious truth. First, the Pope signaled the desire of Catholic Christianity to bring about a reconciliation between Jews and Christians in the aftermath of the Holocaust. He expressed respect for Judaism. Second, Vatican II began the work of formulating a Catholic theology of Judaism and other religions, an enterprise realized for Christianity in Pope John Paul II's *Threshold of Hope*. The counterpart for a Judaic theology of world religions is British Chief Rabbi Jonathan Sacks's *Dignity of Difference*.[4] In that context I undertook a systematic critique of the Judaeo-Christian dialogue as practiced in the late nineteenth and twentieth centuries[5] and an experiment in redefining the rules of engagement.[6] That experiment deliberately imitated the medieval disputation in its engagement with the claims of theological truth of Judaism and Christianity.

In *A Rabbi Talks with Jesus* I undertook to take seriously the claim of Jesus to fulfill the Torah and weigh that claim in the balance against the teachings of other rabbis—a colloquium of sages of

---

[4] *The Dignity of Difference: How to Avoid the Clash of Civilizations* (London and New York, 2002).

[5] *Jews and Christians: The Myth of a Common Tradition* (New York and London, 1990; reprint: Binghamton, 2001; reprint: Eugene, 2003). See also *Telling Tales: Making Sense of Christian and Judaic Nonsense. The Urgency and Basis for Judaeo-Christian Dialogue* (Louisville, 1993).

[6] *A Rabbi Talks with Jesus. An Intermillennial, Interfaith Exchange* (New York, 1993: Doubleday. Jewish Book Club Main Selection, February, 1993. Paperback edition: New York, 1994: Image Books. Second edition Montreal and Kingston, 2000: McGill-Queen's University Press. And Ithaca, 2000: Cornell University Press. Second printing, 2001. Book of the Month Club selection, 2002. Italian translation: *Disputa immaginaria tra un rabbino e Gesus: Quale maestro seguire?* (Casale Monferrato, 1996: Redizioni Piemme). Swedish translation: *En rabbin medtalar med Jesus* (Stockholm, 1996: Verbum). German translation: *Ein Rabbi Spricht mit Jesus. Ein jüdisch-christlicher Dialogue* (Munich, 1997: Claudius Verlag). Polish translation under contract. Russian translation: *Rabbi beseduet s Yisusom* (Moskva, Mosty Kul'tury, 2007, translated by Boris Dynin. Moscow, 2006: Gesher Publishing Co.).

the Torah. I explain in a very straight-forward and unapologetic way why, if I had been in the Land of Israel in the first century and present at the Sermon on the Mount, I would not have joined the circle of Jesus' disciples. I would have dissented, I hope courteously, I am sure with solid reason and argument and fact. If I heard what he said in the Sermon on the Mount, for good and substantive reasons I would not have become one of his disciples. That is difficult for people to imagine, since it is hard to think of words more deeply etched into our civilization and its deepest affirmations than the teachings of the Sermon on the Mount and other pronouncements of Jesus. But, then, it also is hard to imagine hearing those words for the first time, as something surprising and demanding, not as mere clichés of culture. That is precisely what I proposed to do in my conversation with Jesus: listen and argue. To hear religious teachings as if for the first time and to respond to them in surprise and wonder—that is the reward of religious disputation in our own day.

I wrote the book to shed some light on why, while Christians believe in Jesus Christ and the good news of his rule in the kingdom of Heaven, Jews believe in the Torah of Moses and form on earth and in their own flesh God's kingdom of priests and the holy people. And that belief requires faithful Jews to enter a dissent at the teachings of Jesus, on the grounds that those teachings at important points contradict the Torah. Where Jesus diverges from the revelation by God to Moses at Mount Sinai that is the Torah, he is wrong, and Moses is right. In setting forth the grounds to this unapologetic dissent, I mean to foster religious dialogue among believers, Christian and Jewish alike. For a long time, Jews have praised Jesus as a rabbi, a Jew like us really; but to Christian faith in Jesus Christ, that affirmation is monumentally irrelevant. And for their part, Christians have praised Judaism as the religion from which Jesus came, and to us, that is hardly a vivid compliment.

We have avoided meeting head on the points of substantial difference between us, not only in response to the person and claims of Jesus, but especially, in addressing his teachings. He claimed to reform and to improve, "You have heard it said . . . but I say . . . ." We maintain, and I argued in my book, that the Torah was and is perfect and beyond improvement, and the Judaism built upon the Torah and the prophets and writings, the originally-oral parts of the Torah written down in the Mishnah, Talmuds, and Midrash—that Judaism was and remains God's will for humanity. By that criterion

I proposed to set forth a Jewish dissent to some important teachings of Jesus. It is a gesture of respect for Christians and honor for their faith. For we can argue only if we take one another seriously. And we can enter into dialogue only if we honor both ourselves and the other. In my imaginary disputation I treat Jesus with respect, but I also mean to argue with him about things he says.

What's at stake here? If I succeed in creating a vivid portrait of the dispute, Christians see the choices Jesus made and will find renewal for their faith in Jesus Christ—but also respect Judaism. I underscore the choices both Judaism and Christianity confront in the shared Scriptures. Christians will understand Christianity when they acknowledge the choices it has made, and so too Jews, Judaism. I mean to explain to Christians why I believe in Judaism, and that ought to help Christians identify the critical convictions that bring them to Church every Sunday. Jews will strengthen their commitment to the Torah of Moses—but also respect Christianity. I want Jews to understand why Judaism demands assent—"the All-Merciful seeks the heart," "the Torah was given only to purify the human heart." Both Jews and Christians should find in *A Rabbi Talks with Jesus* the reason to affirm, because each party will locate there the very points on which the difference between Judaism and Christianity rests.

What makes me so certain of that outcome? Because, I believe, when each side understands in the same way the issues that divide the two, and both with solid reason affirm their respective truths, then all may love and worship God in peace—knowing that it really is the one and the same God whom together they serve—in difference. So it is a religious book about religious difference: an argument about God.

My goal is to help Christians become better Christians, because they may come to a clearer account of what they affirm in their faith, and to help Jews become better Jews, because they will realize there—so I hope—that God's Torah is the way (not only our way, but the way) to love and serve the one God, creator of heaven and earth, who called us to serve and sanctify God's Name. My point is simple. By the truth of the Torah, much that Jesus said is wrong. By the criterion of the Torah, Israel's religion in the time of Jesus was authentic and faithful, not requiring reform or renewal, demanding only faith and loyalty to God and the sanctification of life through carrying out God's will. And there is an authentic Christian reply to be set forth. It is fully exposed in Pope Benedict XVI's reply to *A Rabbi Talks with Jesus* in his *Jesus of Nazareth* Chapter Four, on the sermon on the Mount.

Do I then propose that, after they have read my book, Christians reexamine their convictions about Christianity? Not at all. Christian faith finds a legion of reasons for believing in Jesus Christ (not merely that Jesus was and is Christ); all I argue is, maybe so, but not because he fulfilled the Torah or sustained the Torah or conformed to the Torah; not because he improved on the Torah. By that criterion, I should not have followed him then, and I should not counsel anyone to follow him now. But, of course, Christian faith has never found troubling the fact of its own autonomy: not a mere continuation and reform of the prior faith, Judaism (always represented as corrupt and venal and hopeless anyhow), but a new beginning. So this argument—set forth on a level playing field—should not trouble the faithful. And I don't mean it to. But if Christians take seriously the claim that the criterion of Matthew is valid—not to destroy but to fulfill—then I do think Christians may well have to reconsider the Torah ("Judaism" in secular language): Sinai calls, the Torah tells us how God wants us to be.

The Pope in his book addresses the question of the historical Jesus. So one may wonder, Do I mean, then, to set forth an argument of Jewish apologetics that consists in the rather tired claim, yes to the historical Jesus, no to the Christ of Christianity? For not a few apologists for Judaism (including Christian apologists for Judaism) distinguish between the Jesus who lived and taught, whom they honor and revere, from the Christ whom the Church (so they say) invented. They will maintain that the apostle, Paul, invented Christianity; Jesus, for his part, taught only truth, which, as believers in Judaism, we can affirm. I take a different path altogether. I am not interested in what happened later on; I want to know, how, if I were there, standing at the foot of the mountain where Jesus said the words that came to be called "the Sermon on the Mount," I would have responded. I found the fundamental affirmations of a fully exposed Christianity in the Sermon on the Mount, and so does the Pope.

The Jesus Christ of fully articulated Christianity is realized in the Sermon on the Mount. The Jesus with whom I compose my argument is not the pre-determined historical Jesus of a scholar's studious imagination, and that is for a simple reason: those fabricated historical figures are too many and diverse for an argument. Moreover, I don't see how religious people can differ about what confronts them only in scholarly works. When Jews open the New Testament, they assume they are hearing from the Jesus Christ of Christianity, and when Christians open the same book, they surely take the same view. That is not to say the historical Jesus is not a presence within and behind the Gospels; it is only to affirm that the Gospels as we read them portray Jesus to most of us who propose to know him. I write for believing Christians and faithful Jews; for them, Jesus is known through the Gospels. I address one of those Gospels.

When my publisher asked for suggestions of colleagues to be asked to recommend the book, I suggested Chief Rabbi Jonathan Sacks and then Cardinal Joseph Ratzinger. Rabbi Sacks had long impressed me by his astute and well crafted theological writings, the leading contemporary apologist for Judaism. I had admired Cardinal Ratzinger's writings on the historical Jesus and had written to him to say so. His willingness to confront the issues of truth, not just the politics of doctrine, struck me as courageous and constructive. Both responded with generous comments.

But now His Holiness has taken a step further and has answered my critique in a creative exercise of exegesis and theology. In his *Jesus of Nazareth*, the Judaeo-Christian disputation enters a new age. We are able to meet one another in a forthright exercise of reason and criticism. The challenges of Sinai bring us together for the renewal of a two thousand year old tradition of religious debate in the service of God's truth.

THE FIRST CENTURIES

MOSAICS AS MIDRASH:
THE ZODIACS OF THE ANCIENT SYNAGOGUES AND THE CONFLICT BETWEEN JUDAISM AND CHRISTIANITY*

Yaffa Englard

For more than fifty years, the mosaic floors of ancient synagogues have engendered extensive discussion. There is broad agreement that the panels portraying an architectural facade, seven-branched candelabras, and other ritual symbols express a longing for the rebuilding of the Temple and the renewal of the divine service. The zodiac, with Helios at its center, found in five synagogues from the fourth to sixth century[1] is a riddle to this day. It has been suggested that it may be a consequence of pagan influence on non-Rabbinic, "Hellenistic" Jews[2] or evidence of belief in evil spirits, black magic, and astrology among the Jews of the land of Israel.[3] Alternatively, it is even seen as evidence that some Jews worshiped Helios as a minor deity.[4] By contrast, most scholars try to place the synagogue zodiacs within a Jewish context, as either connected with the Hebrew calendar,[5] as representing a liturgical calendar that served annual ceremonies performed by the community,[6] or as a metaphor for the sun or for

---

* Reprinted from *Review of Rabbinic Judaism* 6:2-3, 2004, pp. 189–214. This article elaborates a lecture delivered at the Congress of Jewish Studies in Jerusalem in the summer of 1997 and an article published in Hebrew in *Cathedra Quarterly* 98, December, 2000.

[1] Hammat Tiberias, Beth Alpha, Na'aran, Ussefiyeh, and Sepphoris, where the depiction of the sun disc replaces Helios. A zodiac was present in the synagogue at Susiya, too, but it was covered by another mosaic. R. Hachlili, *Ancient Jewish Art and Archeology, the Land of Israel* (Leiden, 1988), p. 305; Z. Ilan, *Ancient Synagogues in Israel* (Tel Aviv, 1991) (Hebrew), p. 315.

[2] E.R. Goodenough, *Jewish Symbols in the Greco-Roman Period* (New York, 1953), vol. 8, pp. 214–218; vol. 1, pp. 3–6; vol. 14, pp. 7–8, 26–27.

[3] E.L. Sukenik, *Ancient Synagogues in Palestine and Greece* (London, 1934), pp. 64–67.

[4] L.A. Roussin, "Helios in the Synagogue: Did Some Ancient Jews Worship the Sun God?" in *Biblical Archaeology Review* 27/2, March/April 2001, pp. 53–56.

[5] M. Avi-Yonah, *Art in Ancient Palestine* (Jerusalem, 1981), pp. 396–397 (Hebrew). A.G. Sternberg finds a link with the publication of the intercalary method by Nasi Hillel in the second century: *The Zodiac of Tiberias* (Tiberias, 1972), pp. 72–87 (Hebrew).

[6] R. Hachlili, "The Zodiac in Ancient Jewish Art, Representation and Significance," in *BASOR* 228 (1977), p. 76.

God's Omnipotence. Foerster maintains that the zodiac, with Helios at its center symbolizing the sun, represents the sanctity and blessing inherent in the divine order of the universe. It is a visual manifestation of liturgical poems praising the God of Israel and the laws by which God governs creation. In this view, the mosaics served as a kind of substitute for the prayer books that the worshipers did not possess.[7]

Weiss and Netzer believe that the figure of Helios in the synagogue mosaics is an allegorical symbol of God's omnipotence. God, the true ruler of the world, remembers his promise to Abraham on Mount Moriah and recalls the Temple he will rebuild at that place in the future.[8] Weiss has no answer, however, to the question, "Why would Jews display in their synagogues a Greek zodiac adapted to the Hebrew months, and why would they choose to use a metaphor for God's omnipotence involving a Greek god?"[9]

I wish to suggest a different ideological significance to the zodiac and to the entire iconographic array. The depiction of the Aqedah in the mosaics at Beth Alpha and Sepphoris functioned as a reminder to the worshipers of Abraham's strength in "trial." Abraham's vocation to become the progenitor of a great nation was supposed to be realized through Isaac, his son. Even so, when Abraham was commanded to sacrifice Isaac and all hope for the fulfillment of God's promise appeared lost, he did not hesitate. Abraham was ready to obey God's will, and he thus demonstrated perfect loyalty and faith.[10]

---

[7] G. Foerster, "The Zodiac in Ancient Synagogues and Its Place in Jewish Thought and Literature," in *Eretz-Israel* 19 (1987), pp. 231–232 (Hebrew). A similar idea was presented earlier by Y. Yahalom, "The Zodiac in the Early *Piyyut* in Eretz-Israel," in *Jerusalem Studies in Hebrew Literature* 9 (1986), pp. 314–315 (Hebrew).

[8] Z. Weiss and E. Netzer, *Promise and Redemption: A Synagogue Mosaic from Sepphoris* (Jerusalem, 1996), pp. 36–39.

[9] Z. Weiss, "The Sepphoris Synagogue Mosaics" in *Biblical Archaeology Review* 26/5, September/October 2000, pp. 48–61, 70.

[10] This is in contrast to the almost uniform view that depictions of the Aqedah in synagogue mosaics are a symbol of God's promise to Abraham and are associated with the subject of redemption. This is first by virtue of God's oath to Abraham at Gen. 22:16. Second, it is on account of the identification of the place of the binding of Isaac with Mount Moriah, on which, according to tradition, the Temple was built and where it is to be rebuilt with the advent of the redemption. In the view of Weiss and Netzer, the sacrificial service too (in particular, the two sheep of the daily offering in the pavement of Sepphoris) was intended to remind God of his promise to Abraham that he would be with his progeny in the future and would save them from any calamity (*Promise and Redemption*, p. 39).

To the members of the congregations, the unique composition of the zodiac in the synagogues represented a witness to the everlasting covenant God made with David, the people of Israel, and the priests. The purpose of the figurative mosaics in the synagogues should be understood in the setting of the conflict between Judaism and Christianity in the first centuries C.E.

I. *The Significance of the Zodiac*

The zodiac as represented in the synagogue is unique. Each of the items from which it is composed is known from pagan culture, but the whole appears only in the synagogues.[11] Note particularly that, in the synagogue mosaics, a moon and a star or stars accompany the sun god. This display is most rare in the portrayals of Helios outside the synagogues.[12]

In an examination of the meaning of the synagogue mosaics, one must ask two fundamental questions: First, what associations were aroused in the synagogue goers by the visual forms comprising the zodiac and, second, what was the purpose of the figurative mosaics in the synagogues?

Foerster's argument that the zodiac is "an attempt to describe the divine heavenly order, the regularity in the courses of the sun

---

M. Schapiro suggested that the story of the binding of Isaac symbolizes God's salvation for his elect and/or his covenant with Abraham. See "Ancient Mosaics in Israel: Late Antique Art—Pagan, Jewish, Christian," in his *Late Antique, Early Christian and Mediaeval Art* (New York, 1978), p. 28. But the primary message of the story of the binding is not the promise made at the second revelation of the angel of God at the end of the story. This promise had been made to Abraham in the story of the "covenant between the pieces" (Gen. 15) and in the story of the circumcision (Gen. 17), where it is a major theme.

[11] Hachlili, op. cit., p. 65; Weiss and Netzer, op. cit., p. 28.

[12] G. Foerster, "Representations of the Zodiac in Ancient Synagogues and Their Iconographic Sources," in *Eretz-Israel* 18, 1985, p. 391, n. 100 (Hebrew), opposes this view because he found isolated examples (mainly on gems) in which the moon and/or a star can be found beside Helios. These are negligible, however, compared with the wealth of instances in which Helios is not accompanied by the moon and a star. See C. Letta, "Helios/Sol," in *Lexicon Iconographicum Mythologiae Classicae* (Zurich, 1988), vol. 4/2, pp. 366–384. It is also doubtful whether the depiction on the shield of Constantine is a good parallel (Foerster, op. cit., p. 388), because Helios holds a whip and torch in his left hand. This seems to reflect the influence of depictions of the Heliopolitanic gods, sometimes seen with a torch in hand and beside them the moon and/or a star. See Y. Hajjar, "Heliopolitani Dei," in *Lexicon Iconographicum Mythologiae Classicae*, vol. 4/1, pp. 573–577; vol. 4/2, p. 361.

and the moon,"[13] is reasonable. Yet this regularity, in the synagogue context, seems to have eschatological significance. The zodiac is accordingly a factor linking the depiction of the binding of Isaac, demonstrating absolute faith in God and the withstanding of trial, with the subject of "redemption," as expressed in the portrayal of the architectural facade, the candelabras, the ritual vessels, and other eschatological symbols.[14] Heavenly bodies, the sun, the moon, and the stars, are displayed on the zodiac as witnesses to the eternity of the covenant between God and the people of Israel and the house of David.

The depiction of Helios in the quadriga may be seen as the adoption of a popular image and its conversion to Judaism[15] for the purposes of Jewish society, with the addition of the moon and stars. For the Jews, by this period, Helios had become a symbol or a metaphor for the sun.[16] This transformation was made possible

---

[13] Foerster, "Representations," p. 388.

[14] On the eschatological significance of the lion and ox located on either side of the dedicatory inscription in the entrance to the nave in the Beth Alpha synagogue, see M. Bregman, "The Riddle of the Ram in Genesis 22: Jewish-Christian Contacts in Late Antiquity," in F. Manns, ed., *The Sacrifice of Isaac in the Three Monotheistic Religions* (Jerusalem, 1995), p. 140, n. 47.

[15] "In a world of religious syncretism, images and their meanings were sometimes conflated, each religion giving a specific meaning to images used in common;" B. Narkis, "Representational Art," in R. Weitzman, ed., *Age of Spirituality* (New York, 1979), p. 370. According to Stern, "a fundamental distinction existed in rabbinic halakhah as well as in the pagan, Greco-Roman world, between worshipped and non-worshipped images. Non-worshipped, ornamental images such as those in synagogues, although representing mythological or 'pagan' motifs, were never considered idolatrous" (S. Stern, "Figurative Art and Halakha in the Mishnaic-Talmudic Period" in *Zion* 61, 1996, pp. 397–419 (Hebrew)). By the last quarter of the eighth century B.C.E, Hezekiah adopted the two-winged scarab and the two-winged sun disk with six rays as royal emblems. These icons were borrowed from Egyptian or Phoenician iconography laden with symbolic content. See M. Lubetski, "King Hezekiah's Seal Revisited," in *Biblical Archaeology Review* 27/4 July/August 2001, pp. 44–47, and R. Deuthsch, "Lasting Impressions," in *Biblical Archaeology Review* 28/4 July/August 2002, pp. 50–54.

[16] H. Mack, "The Unique Character of the Zippori Synagogue Mosaic and Eretz Israel Midrashim," in *Cathedra* 88 (1988), pp. 39–56 (Hebrew), assumes that the ideas of the "Book of Secrets," which ascribes independent powers to the sun and describes ritual and magic ceremonies in connection with the sun, had some influence in the cities of Israel in late Roman and early Byzantine times (p. 54). In his view, the rabbis of Sepphoris were acquainted with the world of magic emanating from the Book of Secrets and its like and were therefore very careful not to depict any anthropomorphism of God on the floor of their synagogue. But the fact that they refrained from showing the sun in the form of Helios/Sol in Sepphoris does not prove that in the other synagogues the presentation of

partly in light of Ps. 19:6-7, which, in a poetic allegory, describes the sun as a strong man wanting "to run a race" "from the end of the heaven" to "the ends of it."[17]

The eschatological dimension to the zodiac arises from God's promise to David that his house and his throne will endure forever. This promise was first expressed through Nathan, in God's name: "I will set up your seed after you . . . and I will establish his kingdom . . . and I will make firm the throne of his kingdom for ever. I will be his father and he will be my son. . . . And your house and your kingdom will be established for ever before you: your throne shall be firm for ever" (2 Sam. 7:12-16).[18]

This promise was anchored in a written and preserved covenant, as stated in David's final words: "For he has made with me an everlasting covenant, ordered in all things and sure" (2 Sam. 23:5). This covenant is not subject to violation, because "the Lord swore in truth to David: he will not turn from it" (Ps. 132:11, 89:4-5). To emphasize the eternity of the covenant between God and the house of David, the Psalmist likens it to the existence of the orders of creation and the infinity of the heavens, the sun, and the moon, which abide for ever (Ps. 89:29-38):

> I will keep my truth[19] with him for evermore, and my covenant shall stand fast with him. His seed also will I make to endure for ever, and his throne like the days of *heaven*. . . . I will not utterly take my steadfast love from him, nor suffer my faithfulness to fail. My covenant I will not break, nor alter that which has issued from my lips. Once I have sworn by my holiness that I will not fail unto David, his seed shall endure for ever, and his throne shall be like the *sun* before me. It shall be established for ever like the *moon*, and a witness in the *sky* is sure. Sela.

Helios/Sol was anything more for the congregation than the use of an artistic convention for a symbolic representation of the sun. See also M. Dothan, "The Figure of Sol Invictus in the Mosaic of Hammath-Tiberias," in H.Z. Hirschberg, ed., *All the Land of Naphtali* (Jerusalem, 1967), pp. 130–134 (Hebrew).

[17] This poetic allegory is also based on early mythological perceptions. See A. Weiser, *The Psalms* (London, 1962), pp. 199–200.

[18] In these verses, Nathan speaks in the first person in God's name, so the version *lephanekha*, "before you" (v. 16) combined with "for ever" is strange. The Septuagint rendering "before me" is preferable. Presumably, the corruption in the Masoretic text is due to dittography. Cf., H.P. Smith, *The Books of Samuel* (Edinburgh, 1977), pp. 301–302.

[19] The term *hesed* expressed contractual relations. M. Weinfeld, "'*Habrit Vehachesed*'– 'Bond and Grace'—Covenantal Expressions in the Bible and in the Ancient World: A Common Heritage," in *Leshonenu* 37 (1971–1972), pp. 90–91 (Hebrew).

Similarly, Ps. 72 compares the eternity of the rule of the house of David to the sun and the moon. "May they fear you[20] (*yira'ukha*) as long as the *sun* and *moon* endure, throughout all generations . . . let the righteous flourish; and let there be abundance of peace till the *moon* is no more" (5-7); "May his name endure forever; may his name continue as long as the *sun*" (17). These words imply that the sun and the moon are proof, renewed daily, of the very existence of God's oath that the house of David will endure forever and that its reign will never end.

In Jeremiah, correspondingly, we find the sun, the moon, and the stars as witnesses of the new covenant between God and his people. This future covenant is different from the covenant at Sinai, which the people violated, in that it is not subject to infringement. It is written on the hearts of the people of Israel and therefore stands forever like the days of heaven: "Thus says the Lord, who gives the *sun* for a light by day, and the ordinances of the *moon* and of the *stars* for a light by night. . . . If those ordinances depart from before me, says the Lord, then the seed of Israel also shall cease from being a nation before me for ever" (Jer. 31:34-36).

In another chapter, the prophet links the eternity of the reign of the house of David over Israel to the service of "the Levites, the priests" in the Temple. He emphasizes that the validity of God's covenant with David and with the Levites resembles the validity of the orders of creation (33:20-21):

> If you can break my covenant with the day, and my covenant with the night, and that there should not be day and night in their season; then also my covenant may be broken with David my servant, that he should not have a son to reign upon his throne; and with the Levites the priests, my ministers.

---

[20] Rashi and other traditional commentators understood *yira'ukha* as referring to God. But the object of this word is the king. The Septuagint's rendering, "and he shall continue" is preferable, as it reflects the Hebrew form *veya'arikh*. The difference from the Masoretic text is due to the transposition of two letters. The meaning of the verse is that the king will prolong his days like the sun and like the moon throughout the generations. Cf., A. Weiser, op. cit., pp. 500–501; C.A. Briggs and E.G. Briggs, *Psalms* (Edinburgh, 1907), vol. 2, pp. 131, 133–134, 138. *'im* in the sense of *kemo* is frequent in the Bible: see Ps. 28:1, Job 9:26. The word *lephanay* also has the sense of *kemo*, see 1 Sam. 1:16, Job 4:19. According to Justin, these verses are evidence of the eternity of Jesus: St. Justin Martyr, *The Writings of St. Justin Martyr, the Dialogue with Trypho* (*The Fathers of the Church*, vol. 16) (Washington, 1948), pp. 198–199.

Centuries later, Ben Sirah (45:15) in the same spirit describes the right of Aaron and his descendants to eternal priesthood: "And it became for him an eternal covenant, and for his seed, as long as the *heavens* endure."

The four seasons that appear in the synagogue mosaics as a frame for the zodiac are not mentioned among the witnesses to the validity of the covenant. They may be understood as a result of the constancy of the appearance of the sun and the moon, day and night. The seasons, however, seem to be intended to remind the Jewish onlooker of the creator's decision after the flood, namely, that never again would the regularity of the divine order be infringed, and that all variations in nature would succeed in order. "While the earth remains, seed time and harvest, and cold and heat, and summer and winter, and day and night shall not cease" (Gen. 8:22). According to some of the Rabbinic schools, six seasons of the year are mentioned here.[21] But in the Jerusalem Targum (Pseudo-Jonathan) to this verse[22] four seasons are listed: "As long as the earth endures, sowing *in the season of Tishre*, and harvest *in the season of Nisan*, cold *in the season of Tebet*, and heat *in the season of Tammuz*, summer and winter, day and night, shall not cease." Likewise in

---

[21] "Rabban Simeon b. Gamaliel says in the name of R. Meir, and so would R. Simeon b. Menasya say as well: The second half of Tishre, Marheshavan, and the first half of Kislev is the planting season. The second half of Kislev, Tebet, and the first half of Shevat is the winter season. The second half of Shevat, Adar, and the first half of Nisan is the cold season. The second half of Nisan, Iyar, and the first half of Sivan is the harvest season. The second half of Sivan, Tammuz, and the first half of Ab is the summer season. The second half of Ab, Elul, and the first half of Tishre is the hot season" (B. B.M. 106b). The same version with a difference in the speakers appears at T. Ta. 1:7, and with slight differences also at Gen. Rabbah 34, 11. By contrast, at Gen. Rabbah 13, 12, only four seasons are listed, and in a different context. As for the debate over the meaning of the word *tequfah*, whether it defines a period of time or the solstice or the equinox, see Gad B. Sarfatti, "*Tequfah* in the Sepphoris Mosaic," in *Leshonénu* 49 (1995), p. 353 (Hebrew).

[22] A. Shinan, "Pseudo-Jonathan Targum: Its Nature and Date," in *Proceedings of the Ninth World Congress of Jewish Studies* 9 (A) (1985), pp. 109–115, argues for an evident dependence of Targum Jonathan on Pirqe d'R. Eliezer and accordingly advances the date of the final form of this translation to the seventh or eighth century. But the source of the interpretive tradition of the four periods in Gen. 8:22 may be an early tradition of sages that was not perpetuated in the Rabbinic literature but found expression in later times in Targum Jonathan and Pirqe d'R. Eliezer in parallel.

Pirqe d'R. Eliezer 88: "Seed is the season of Tishre; harvest is the season of Nisan; cold is the season of Tebet; and heat is the season of Tammuz. Summer in its time and winter in its time." These are the seasons that appear in all the displays of the zodiac in the synagogues.

Thus, at the center of the zodiac are the witnesses to the covenant that ensure its eternity, and in the four outside corners are the seasons, calling to mind God's decision that these witnesses, which are part of the divine order, will never cease.

The tradition of an everlasting covenant with the house of David is also expressed in post-biblical literature. It can be found in Ben Sirah,[23] Maccabees,[24] and the messianic interpretations of Gen. 49:10 and 2 Sam. 7:11 from Qumran.[25] Echoes of these can be seen in the *Amidah* in the benediction "Speedily cause the offspring of thy servant David, to flourish. . . . Blessed are you, O Lord, who causes salvation to flourish."[26]

The tradition that regards the sun, moon, and stars as witnesses to the existence of the covenant with the house of David was so deeply rooted among the people that Judah the Patriarch asked Hiyya to inform him of the new moon's appearance and its sanctification with the password "David, king of Israel, is alive and well" (B. R.H. 25a). This formulation exists to this day and is recited with every blessing on the new moon. The sun and the moon as witnesses to the covenant are mentioned in diverse forms in the midrashic literature,

---

[23] "And he lifted up his horn for ever. . . . Also he gave him the decree of the kingdom, and established his throne over Israel," Ben Sirah 47:11.

[24] "David, for being merciful, inherited the throne of a kingdom for ever and ever," 1 Macc. 2:57.

[25] J.M. Allegro, "Further Messianic References in Qumran Literature," in *Journal of Biblical Literature* 85 (1956), pp. 174–187: "I will set up your seed after you, and I will establish his royal throne [for eve]r. I [will be] to him as a father, and he will be to me as a son. His is the shoot of David, who will arise with the Interpreter of the Law, who [...] in Zi[on (?) in the l]ast days; as is written, And I will raise up the tabernacle of David that is fallen. That is the tabernacle of David which is falle[n and after]-wards he will arise to save Israel" (pp. 176–177). This fragment was published a second time in J.M. Allegro, *Qumran Cave 4*, (4Q158-4Q186), vol. V (Oxford, 1968), pp. 53–54.

[26] Translation: P. Birnbaum, *Daily Prayer Book* (New York, 1969). On the connection between the Amidah and the Bible, see M. Weinfeld, "The Biblical Roots of the Standing Prayer on the Sabbath and Festivals," in *Tarbiz* 65 (1995–1996), pp. 547–560 (Hebrew).

in the Targums, and in liturgical poetry. Midrash Rabbah to Lamentations states:

> Remember your creator: Remember who created you while his selection of you still endures; while the covenant of the priesthood still endures . . . while the covenant with the kingship of the house of David still endures . . . while the covenant with Jerusalem still endures. . . . Before the *sun* is darkened (Ecc. 12:2)—for the kingship of the house of David, of which it is written, "And his throne as the *sun* before me" (Ps. 89:37).[27]

The same idea is found in Targum Jonathan to Is. 60:20: "Your *sun* shall no more go down," which identifies the setting of the sun with the ending of the kingdom: "Your kingdom shall no more cease, nor your glory pass away".

In the piyyut for the night of the Ninth of Ab that opens "Then in our sin,"[28] the poet describes the witnesses to the covenant, the sun, the moon, and the stars, in hiding and in mourning after the destruction of Jerusalem. When the covenant between God and his people, his priests, and the house of David seems to have been violated, the witnesses to the covenant temporarily disappear: "The sun darkened and the moon grew gloomy and the stars and zodiac signs gathered in their radiance." The piyyut then lists the zodiac signs that mourn the destruction: "Aries was the first to weep. . . . Taurus emitted a wail. . . . Gemini seemed broken because the blood of brothers had been shed like water. Cancer wished to fall to earth. . . ," and so on. Here in one piyyut we have, with the exception of the seasons, the entire zodiac.

The swearing of oaths with the sun as a witness was apparently practiced among the Jews over a prolonged period. This is attested by Bar Qappara and Zeira (Y. Ned. 1:2, 37a) and, later, by Maimonides: "If anyone swears by the heavens, the earth, the sun . . . this is no oath."[29] Also, "Greek and Hellenistic contracts and the oath of

---

[27] Lam. Rabbah, Proem 23, S. Buber edition, pp. 16–17. Buber, p. 5, dates this Midrash to the fourth century, that is, after the Jerusalem Talmud was arranged but before the Babylonian Talmud.

[28] D. Goldschmidt, *Order of Lamentations for the Ninth of Av* (Jerusalem, 1968), p. 11 (Hebrew).

[29] *The Code of Maimonides*, Book Six, trans. B.D. Klein (New Haven and London, 1962), chap. 12, p. 51. S. Liberman, *Greek and Hellenism in Jewish Palestine* (Jerusalem, 1962), pp. 105, 106, 107, and n. 173.

allegiance to the emperor open . . . with a list of the witnesses of Zeus, earth, and sun."[30] In the fourth century, the emperor Julian evokes Zeus and Helios as witnesses in his oath *"isto megas Helios"* ("be my witness great Helios").[31]

To summarize, the sun as witness to a contract or oath was known in the Jewish community in the land of Israel from the Bible, which had a central role in synagogue ritual. It was also familiar in the context of the constantly crystallizing midrashic literature, from liturgical poetry, and from what was customary among common people as well as among the Greek and Roman rulers of the land.

The zodiac with the sun at the center, accompanied by the moon, a star or stars, and around it the seasons of the year, thus symbolized the witnesses to the eternal covenant between God and his people, his messiah, and his priests, as expressed in the Bible and in Rabbinic literature. The formal array was adopted from the Hellenistic-Roman culture[32] and might also have originated in the Ancient Near East. But the Jewish significance was original, because heavenly bodies had by then undergone a process of de-mythologization. The sun and the moon were part of God's works in creation and bore witness that the covenant that "the Lord made . . . with Abraham saying to your seed have I given this land" (Gen. 15:18) was vigorous and robust. It was endorsed by an everlasting covenant between God and Abraham's descendants and between God and his messiah of the house of David. The heavens, the sun, the moon, and the stars, the day and the night, were witnesses to the covenant. For as long as these existed, the Jews could be certain that God's promise would be fulfilled and that on the appointed day the kingdom of the house of David would be re-established, the Temple would be rebuilt, and the Lord's service in it would be renewed.

---

[30] M. Weinfeld, "The Loyalty Oath in the Ancient Near East," in J.C. Greenfield and M. Weinfeld, eds., *Shnaton, An Annual for Biblical and Ancient Near Eastern Studies* (Jerusalem, 1975), p. 69 (Hebrew).

[31] *The Works of Emperor Julian*, trans. W.C. Wright (London, 1961), vol. 3, p. 22. On *"isto"* in the sense of witnessing (seeing), see also Liddell and Scott, *An Intermediate Greek-English Lexicon*, 7th ed. (Oxford, 1996), p. 227, *eido (B), the imperat. in protestation, *"isto Zeus autos"* = be Zeus *my witness*.

[32] Sun (as a divinity) drawn in a chariot with horses is known in a Jerusalem rite at the end of the First Temple period. See their removal from the Temple in the reform of Josiah, 2 Kgs. 23:11.

II. *The Purpose of the Mosaic Floors*

The purpose of the mosaic floors and the part they played in the life of the community, as well as the significance of the iconographic plan, should apparently be sought in the context of the relations between Judaism and the ever stronger Christianity in the land of Israel. Christianity, whose source lay in Judaism, adopted the Jewish world of concepts and used it in its claim to be the heir of the biblical people of Israel (Rom. 9:10-13). As early as the second century, Justin Martyr argued that the Jews had no part in the Scriptures, because their stubbornness prevented them from understanding them correctly. Only Christians were capable of comprehending the texts properly, so ownership of Scripture passed to the Christians, who were the "true Israel."[33] Correct reading and understanding of the texts, he averred, proved that the Bible prophesied the coming of Jesus and, with his coming, the old law, which was intended for the Jews alone, became invalid before the new law intended for all human beings. The New Testament revoked the Old Testament, replacing it for all time.[34]

Words of this sort were repeated over and over again throughout the following centuries in sermons, hymns, interpretations, and theological compositions of Ephrem the Syrian, Chrysostom, Jerome, Augustine, and others. The Temple lay in ruins because the Jews had rejected Jesus and brought about his death, and he, in his death-sacrifice, annulled the laws of the Torah, the Passover offering, the sacrifices, and the tithes of the priesthood and the Levites.[35] For Christians, the destruction of the Temple and the abolition of its rites were proof of the revocation of the laws of the Torah, namely of the covenant between God and the Jews, of the death of Judaism, and the completion of its role in history.[36]

The Bible served Christians as the basis of their religious and historical arguments. They founded their claims on the Scriptures

---

[33] St. Justin Martyr, op. cit., chap. 12, p. 165; chap. 29, p. 191; chap. 123, p. 340; chap. 125, pp. 341–343. Cf., M. Hirshman, *A Rivalry of Genius, Jewish and Christian Biblical Interpretation in Late Antiquity* (New York, 1996), pp. 13–18; *The Homilies of Saint Jerome*, vol. 2 (*The Fathers of the Church*, vol. 57) (Washington, 1996), pp. 68f.

[34] Justin, ibid., chap. 11, p. 164; chap. 67, p. 256.

[35] *Ephrem the Syrian Hymns*, trans. and introduction K.E. McVey (New York, 1989), pp. 249, 254–256, 298–300.

[36] R.L. Wilken, *John Chrysostom and the Jews* (Los Angeles and London, 1983), pp. 45, 126, 136f.

themselves, and the struggle between them and the Jews centered on the interpretation of the content. Every possible verse was utilized to prove that the advent of Jesus and the destruction of the Temple were foreseen.[37] Gen. 49:10, "The staff shall not depart from Judah and the scepter from between his feet, until Shilo come," was seen as a prophecy of Jesus that had been fulfilled because, since his crucifixion, there had been no more kings in Judah. This then was proof that indeed, "the staff" had departed "from Judah and the scepter from between his feet."[38]

Dan. 9:24-27 was interpreted as a prophecy of the angel Gabriel to Daniel that, in the future, the Temple was to be destroyed absolutely and finally. This prophecy was confirmed by Jesus in Matt. 24:1-2 and in Luke 19:41-44, so the Temple could never be rebuilt. The fact that it was not re-erected from its ruins proved the truth of these words.[39]

The destruction of the Temple also had significant implications for the eternity of the house of David, because an ideological connection had been made between the building of God's house and God's promise that the progeny of David would reign for ever.[40] The destruction of the Temple thus constituted proof of annulment of the pledge of everlasting rule to the house of David.

The Jews' adherence to their religion, and the faith that the covenant between them and God was firm and strong, and that in the future they would return to Jerusalem and rebuild the Temple, sorely vexed the Church Fathers.[41] Such adherence was taken to undermine Christian claims to be the "true Israel." Not surprisingly, while Julian's efforts to restore Jerusalem to the Jews, to rebuild the Temple, and to renew sacrificial offerings in it unleashed joy and excitement among the Jews, for Christians this was a traumatic episode.[42] The re-establishment of the Temple in Jerusalem and the resumption there of the ritual

---

[37] R.S. Sarason, "The Interpretation of Jeremiah in Judaism," in I.J. Petuchowski, ed., *When Jews and Christians Meet* (Albany, 1988), pp. 99–123; St. Augustine, *The City of God*, Books 17–22 (*The Fathers of the Church*, vol. 24) (Washington, 1954), Book 17, chaps. 9, 10, 12, 16–18, 33, et al.

[38] Justin, op. cit., chap. 52, pp. 226–227; *Saint Jerome*, op. cit., pp. 62f.

[39] *Ephrem*, op. cit., pp. 232, 254f; Wilken, op. cit., p. 131.

[40] See 2 Sam. 7:13; 1 Kgs. 8:20; Pss. 2:10; 78:69-70; 132:11-17. M. Weinfeld studied this ideological affinity in *From Joshua to Josiah* (Jerusalem, 1992), pp. 100–114. I thank Dr. Ruth Fidler for drawing my attention to this.

[41] *Ephrem*, op. cit., pp. 300–305.

[42] Ibid., pp. 230–236.

demolished the ideological basis of the legality of Christianity as the heir of Judaism and of the divinity of Jesus who prophesied the final destruction of the Temple.[43] At that time, Ephrem the Syrian tried to prevent Christian converts from reverting to Judaism and interpreted such an occurrence as a trial by God to test true believers.[44]

Even after the attempt to build the Temple remained unrealized, hope to return to Jerusalem did not fade from the hearts of the Jews. Chyrsostom attests that, in his day, a generation after the death of Julian, the Jews of Antioch talked about the restoration of Jerusalem to the Jews.[45] The Jews of Antioch, and apparently of other places too, exercised great influence over the Christians. Many Christians celebrated the Jews' festivals, ceremonies, and fasts. Chrysostom's sermons were aimed at these Judaizing Christians, who constituted a danger to the Christian establishment and to the idea that Christianity was the heir of Israel.[46] The very notion of the return of the Jews to Jerusalem was a challenge to Christianity, because it attested that the covenant between God and the people of Israel, the Jews, endured. Therefore, churchmen stressed that there was no foundation for the Jews' hopes, because God had broken his covenant with them. The prophecies of consolation (Is. 35:6; 58:12; Ezek. 28:25-26; 37:8; etc.), which tell of the return of Israel to Zion and of the rebuilding of the Temple, were interpreted to accord with Christian doctrine. It was claimed, for example, that the prophecies had already been fulfilled, or referred to a spiritual experience present in the Christian Church. The interpretations of Jerome leave the impression that he was not concerned merely with interpreting the texts but was polemicizing against the beliefs and opinions of contemporary Jews, who held that the prophets' words of comfort would be realized in the future, perhaps

---

[43] Julian's wish to build the Temple in Jerusalem and to renew the ritual in it arose not out of love for the Jews but from the conflict between Christianity and Hellenism. He used the Jewish community, with its firm faith, against Christianity. Julian understood that the Temple in Jerusalem was a symbol of the legitimacy of Judaism and undermined the basis of the Christians' claim to be the heirs of Israel. He also realized that the building of the Temple would prove that Jesus' prophecy of its final destruction was false, so that Jesus was not God. By building the Temple in Jerusalem, Julian aspired to prevent the spread of Christianity. See Wilken, *Chyrsostom*, op. cit., pp. 138–144.

[44] *Ephrem*, op. cit., pp. 122–124.

[45] R.L. Wilken, "The Restoration of Israel in Biblical Prophecy: Christian and Jewish Responses in the Early Byzantine Period," in J. Neusner and E.S. Frerichs, eds., *To See Ourselves as Others See Us* (Chico, 1985), pp. 461ff.

[46] Wilken, *Chrysostom*, pp. 67–68.

the near future.⁴⁷ Augustine continued the polemic against the Jews' belief that God's promise to David, namely that his descendants would sit upon the throne for ever, had not yet been realized and against the fact that they were "dreaming up a kind of Christ of their own, one who is to have nothing to do with suffering and death." Like his forerunners, he charged the Jews with incomprehension and blindness, and like them he interpreted the texts on the covenant between God and the house of David as referring to Jesus and the Church.⁴⁸

The sages repelled this Christian onslaught in every possible way. Since the fourth century, if not earlier, they contended with the Christian claim to be the "true Israel."⁴⁹ In so doing they argued that only the Oral Law defined the "true Israel," since God concluded his covenant on both the Written and the Oral Law (Y. Pe. 2:6; Gen. Rabbah 83:5). The Christian claim that the Bible heralds both Jesus as the Son of God and his virgin birth was met with contempt and mockery. Jesus was called by the rabbis "Ben Stada" or "Ben Pandira" (the paramour of his mother) (B. San.76a; B. Shab. 104b).⁵⁰ He was accused, among other faults, of practicing magic and enticing the people of Israel to idolatry (B. San. 43a, 107b).⁵¹ The rabbis rejected the Christian interpretation of Gen. 49:10 claming that the continuation of the kings of Judah was to be found in the exilarchs in Babylonia and in the patriarchs in the land of Israel: "'The scepter will not depart from Judah'—this refers to the exilarchs of Babylon who rule over Israel with scepters; 'and a lawgiver . . .'—this refers to the descendants of Hillel who teach the Torah in public" (B. San. 5a). They did accept the destruction of Jerusalem as punishment for various sins, for example, abolition of the recitation of the Shema prayer in the morning and evening services, neglect of teaching Torah to schoolchildren, ridicule of students of the wise, and so on (B. Shab. 119b; B. Yom. 9b). For them, however, the sanctity of Jerusalem and the Temple had not dissipated with its destruction. On the contrary, the people of Israel continued to hallow them despite their ruin.

---

[47] *Saint Jerome*, op. cit., pp. 66–67; Wilken, "The Restoration," pp. 448–452.
[48] St. Augustine, op. cit., pp. 49–72, 135–136.
[49] M. Hirshman, ibid., pp. 13–22.
[50] It is of no wonder that these passages were censored in most editions of the Talmud. R.T. Herford, *Christianity in Talmud and Midrash* (London, 1903), pp. 37ff., 344ff.,
[51] I thank Dr. R. Ben-Shalom for drawing my attention to these texts. See also Herford, ibid., pp. 53ff.

The cessation of the Temple service had not reduced its status, since Judaism had accepted that worship of God in the Temple was only one mode of divine service. The Jews continued to make the pilgrimage to Jerusalem on the Ninth of Ab and perhaps on other occasions too. The inscription "And when you see this, your heart shall rejoice, and your bones shall flourish like grass," taken from a prophecy of consolation and redemption of Jerusalem (Is. 66:31), which a Jewish pilgrim carved into the southern corner of the Western Wall, probably in the fourth century, expresses a yearning combined with the real hope of the coming of the messiah.[52]

To summarize, the struggle between Christianity and Judaism concerned the validity of the laws of the Torah, the messiah, and the Temple, namely the validity of the covenant between God and the people of Israel and between God and the house of David and the priests.

Worshipers at synagogues in the land of Israel at that time, to judge by their names and the Greek dedicatory inscriptions in the synagogues, were not "a people that shall dwell alone." They were exposed to the social and cultural influences of their environment, which, from the time that Christianity was introduced as the official religion, had become largely Christian in nature. With the passage of time, Christianity in the land of Israel gathered force, Jerusalem became a Christian center, the condition of the Jews worsened, and their redemption seemed more distant than ever. In these circumstances, spiritual confusion intensified and people began to wonder whether there might be some truth in Christian doctrine after all.

The Christians' claim that God had abandoned the Jews seeped into this mood of uncertainty (Exod. Rabbah 31:10):

> When Israel was driven from Jerusalem, their enemies took them out in fetters, and the nations of the world remarked, "The Holy One, blessed be he, has no desire for this people, for it says, 'Refuse silver did men call them'" . . . for Israel was saying that there was no more hope of survival for them since God had rejected them. . . . God replied: "I will not banish Israel, even if I destroy my world," as it is said: "Thus says the Lord: If heaven above can be measured. . . ."[53]

---

[52] See Z. Safrai, *The Sanctity of Jerusalem in Desolation* (Ramat Gan, 1999), pp. 20–39 (Hebrew).

[53] Exod. Rabbah is indeed a late collection, but it contains ancient sermons and fragments of midrash. See A. Marmorstein, "Judaism and Christianity," in *Hebrew Union College Annual* X (Cincinnati, 1935), p. 238.

In this situation, the Jewish community felt the need to stress repeatedly that the God of Israel had not abandoned his people, that his covenant with them was everlasting. Not surprisingly, the community made use of every possible means to combat Christian propaganda. In the synagogues of the land of Israel, which were religious, cultural, and community centers, people worshiped, read the scriptures, studied, delivered sermons, recited liturgical poems, and also gave visual expression to their views and beliefs, as their predecessors had done in the synagogue at Dura Europos in the third century.

Serving a didactic function, art was used as a means of propagating religious (and other) messages. Christian art, for example, presents characters and stories from the Bible in their typological interpretation. Isaac, who is the fruit of a divine promise (Gal. 4:22-31), became, early on, a prefiguration of Jesus in both his birth and his binding. In the story of the binding, he symbolizes Jesus' crucifixion-sacrifice, and in this sense he appears in art already from the first centuries C.E.[54] The story of the promise made to Abraham and Sarah at the terebinths of Mamre (Gen. 18) serves as early as the fifth century as a prototype for the annunciation to Mary at S. Maria Maggiore. It appears in combination with the binding of Isaac at S. Vitale at Ravenna in the sixth century.

In contrast, the synagogue mosaics express the Jewish national religious message in various symbols: the architectural facade, the seven-branched candelabra, the shofar, the etrog, the lulav, and the *mahta* symbolized redemption and the rebuilding of the Temple. Helios, the sun in his chariot, the moon, and the stars symbolized the cosmic witnesses to the everlasting covenant God made with the people of Israel, with David, and with the priests.[55] The binding

---

[54] I. Speyart Van Woerden, "The Iconography of the Sacrifice of Abraham," in *Vigiliae Cristianae* 15 (1961), pp. 155-214.

[55] It is not impossible that the image of Helios/Sol was interpreted differently outwardly for the representatives of the rulers. In their eyes, the sun god in the synagogue might be deemed a mark of appreciation and an expression of loyalty to the emperor, who was identified with Sol Invictus. See M. Dothan, *Hammath Tiberias: Early Synagogues and the Hellenistic and Roman Remains* (Jerusalem, 1983), pp. 39-41; idem, "The Synagogues at Hammath-Tiberias," in *Qadmoniot* 1 (1968), p. 121 (Hebrew). It is inconceivable that the presentation of Helios/Sol in the synagogues was part of the cult of the emperor. Some laxity and license perhaps existed in the use of portraiture and its products; but the likeness of kings was wholly and strictly forbidden. See E.A. Urbach, "The Laws of Idolatry in the Light of Historical and Archaeological Facts in the Third Century," in *Eretz Israel* 5 (1958), p. 199 (Hebrew).

of Isaac symbolized withstanding trial. Note that in Christian art, too, there is symbolic treatment of the covenant. Thus the figure of Moses serves as a symbol of the Old Testament, and Jeremiah was a symbol of the New Testament. The two figures are placed on either side of a mosaic of the promise to Abraham and the binding of Isaac at the church of S. Vitale.

A didactic message, then, is present in the complex of depictions in the iconographic array in the mosaics (at Beth Alpha and Sepphoris it is even indicated by the caption explaining the pictures). In today's parlance, we might phrase it "a faith-awakening trip." From the entrance, down the nave, and as far as the Holy Ark the mosaic expresses a central idea, intended to fortify the faith of anyone entering the synagogue. A Jew must not despair even during the hardest hours. He must take an example from Abraham,[56] who clung to his God even at a moment when all hope seemed lost. God's demand to offer Isaac as a sacrifice was a violation of all the promises he had made to Abraham, and it may well have resulted in crisis and the absence of faith. But, even at this difficult time, Abraham did not waver in his faith nor in his adherence to his God. Because he withstood this supreme test he won a renewed promise, by oath, that his seed would be like the multitude of stars of the heavens and that he would inherit the gate of his enemy. This promise was established forever; despite the harsh reality, the Jew must not believe that a rupture ever existed between God and his people. The covenant God made with his people, with David and his house, and with the priests and the Levites is eternal and would be fulfilled when the day came. This was attested by the *heavens*, the *sun*, the *moon*, and the *stars*, and all the orders of creation. The Jew must therefore cleave to his God, and redemption would surely come.

---

[56] In the stories of the patriarch, Abraham is perceived as a model figure: in his perfect faith (Gen. 16:6; 22:1-14); in his hospitality (Gen. 18:1-8), in his demand for justice (Gen. 23-33); in his loyalty and his courage (Gen. 14). The prophets of destruction and exile recall Abraham as a heroic figure for imitation (Ezek. 33:24; Is. 51:1-3). In the sixth century B.C.E., he was perceived as an exemplary figure mainly with regard to the issue of inheriting the land. See A. Rofé, "The Betrothal of Rebekah (Genesis 24)," in *Eshel Beer-Sheva* I (1975–1976), pp. 58–59.

JUDAIC SOCIAL TEACHING IN CHRISTIAN AND PAGAN CONTEXT*

Jacob Neusner
Bard College

The social teaching of Rabbinic Judaism takes up the narrative of the Torah and recasts it into an account of the norms of Israel's social order. Its recapitulation of the Torah's story regulates relationships between Israelites and corporate Israel, among Israelites in their units of propagation and production, and between corporate Israel and the ever-present, always-sentient God. The details coalesce to yield a clear picture of an entire social order, its relationships and its points of stability and order. To treat any detail apart from its larger context is to miss its point. That point is, Rabbinic Judaism undertakes to realize in the everyday and here and now of the Jews' communal existence the imperatives set forth in the Torah for the formation of God's abode on earth.

I. *The Three Social Teachings of Rabbinic Judaism*

A brief introduction to the three parts of this study will set the stage for some preliminary comparisons, aimed at affording perspective on the Rabbinic account of Israel's social order.

In my *Social Teaching of Rabbinic Judaism* (Leiden, 2001: Brill), vols. I-III, I have identified three principal social teachings, which encompass the social thought of Rabbinic Judaism as categorically embodied by the Halakhah in norms of public conduct. They concern the principal parts of the social order, in secular language, how they are defined, how they function, how they relate and cohere. I refer to

[1] the society viewed whole and in its constituents;
[2] the relationships within the society between its principal parts; and
[3] the setting of the society in the larger context of cosmos and history.

---

* Reprinted from *Review of Rabbinic Judaism* 6:2-3, 2004, pp. 250–281.

The issue concerns how the social teachings afford recognition to the individual within the corporate society; how they mediate conflict between the smallest whole categorical aggregates of the Israelite social order; and how they embody the social results and effects of the conviction that God is everywhere present within Israelite society, through all of its transactions. Even though the documents of Rabbinic Judaism concentrate upon details, in fact, rules embody doctrines that hold together in topic and in proposition and in generative conception. In secular terms, that yields sociology, politics, and culture. But this is no secular system.

Important components of the Halakhah viewed within the Halakhic native categories contain the design of the relationships of individual to community, among the smallest social aggregates of that society; the Israelite households, among the intermediate aggregates; and between the entirety of corporate Israel and every Israelite, all together and one by one, and the ever-present God, for the largest. These three groups of native category-formations define the program. They supply its contents. They form the three teachings of Rabbinic Judaism about Israel's social order. It is a holy order, where the ubiquitous, commanding God enforces, but also is bound by, the rules he has given to shape that order. Marked by regularity and reliability, it is a society of proportion and order. It restores and maintains the stability of society partly through balances effected by man, partly through interventions on the part of God. And it is a society so constructed as to afford a place worthy of God's perpetual presence. It aims at constructing out of Israelite society a suitable abode for God.

The thesis of this entire enterprise may then be stated in a very few words. Genesis Rabbah I:1 teaches that God looked into the Torah and created the world in accord with the design he found there. The Rabbinic sages looked into the Torah and created Israel as defined by the social teaching of Rabbinic Judaism. God's was a creative reading, and so was theirs.

A. *Corporate Israel and the Individual Israelite: The Individual Finds His Being within Corporate Israel, a Whole that Exceeds the Sum of the Parts*

Rabbinic Judaism places corporate Israel at the apex of world- and social order. It is a unique social entity, because it forms a society that, as a whole, bears moral responsibility before God for its condition and conduct. No other social entity ("nation," "people") compares. That is because Israel assembled collectively at Sinai and stated unanimously, in one voice, in response to God's self-manifestation in the Torah given by God to Moses, "We shall do and we shall obey." Individuals in that context are responsible for their own actions but also for those of the community, Israel. And the entire community bears responsibility for the conduct of everyone in its midst. That is what defines its character as a moral actor, a moral entity without counterpart in humanity. That is what I mean when I say that corporate Israel forms a whole that exceeds the sum of the parts. The parts, the individuals, attain individuation only on the terms dictated by the whole, "all Israel" viewed from God's perspective. Israel defines God's stake in humanity, as Scripture's narrative makes clear.

To corporate Israel the individual Israelite is subordinated. That is for taxic reasons to begin with: the one is a genus and unique, the other is a species of a genus. Thus in the hierarchical classification of the social order, the community of Israel is primary and autonomous, the individual Israelite secondary and contingent. Addressing the priority of corporate Israel over the individual Israelite, Rabbinic Judaism must mediate between the conflicting claims of community upon individuality. When, specifically, the individual's interests intersect with those of corporate Israel, the Halakhah teaches that those of corporate Israel take priority. That accounts for the manifest policy that favors communitarian theories of stipulative proprietorship over absolute ownership. But the priority of corporate Israel, expressed in the imposition of heavy sanctions on the aberrant individual, requires explanation in its own terms. At just what turnings, for precisely what considerations, does corporate Israel find itself empowered to impose the interests of the community on the individual Israelite? The social teaching of Rabbinic Judaism evinces tolerance of individual deviation from the norm. But determinate considerations motivate the social order to intervene and sanction individual aberration.

Framing matters in this way—when the community imposes its collective will upon the individual, when not—does not mean to suggest that the system for its part even acknowledges, let alone undertakes to resolve, tension between the individual and the community. It does not address the matter in our terms. At issue for systemic construction is not finding a balance between the Israelite as an autonomous component of the social order and corporate Israel. The social teaching of

Rabbinic Judaism does not recognize the radically isolated, autonomous individual, alone before God. It is, rather, articulating the hierarchical classification that places corporate Israel at the top, the individual Israelite beneath. For—as the matter of required martyrdom to avoid the public profanation of God's name indicates—no negotiation is possible when it comes to realizing the Torah's ultimate imperative for corporate Israel. The individual Israelite, whether by choice or by birth, never can claim utter personal autonomy, only limited individuality. He has no options in the Torah but to obey or to rebel. While the social policy recognizes and values the Israelite's individuality, embodying as it does the freedom of will and the free exercise of intentionality with which everyone by nature, at creation, is endowed, the Israelite subordinates his individuality to his place within corporate Israel. To revert to the formula at the head of this sub-division: the whole not only imparts its imprint upon the parts, the whole also exceeds the sum of the parts.

B. *Between Israelites: Relationships of Balance and Stasis are to be Restored and Maintained*

The second teaching concerns resolving conflict within Israel in particular. By "Israel in particular" I refer to conflict defined in the context of corporate Israel: its public life and activities. At issue in that context is the social order that the Halakhic system conceives corporate Israel to constitute. When, therefore, in the setting of the resolution of conflict we speak of "Israel in particular," I do not mean the happenstance that two or more Jews (whether or not deemed "Israel" by the Halakhah) come into conflict. Nor do I refer to two or more Israelites in random encounters, that is, episodic narratives of contention. To register, a conflict must be designated for conflict-resolution within the categorical-structure of the Halakhic system. So I refer to two Israelites in conflict that the Halakhah deems of systemic interest, a conflict for which the Halakhah legislates.

Only those conflicts between two, or among three or more, Israelites that engage the interests of corporate Israel define the principal parts of the Halakhic categorical structure encompassing conflict-resolution. Other conflicts receive episodic attention to be sure, but that is ordinarily tangential to the main concern. It is not categorical, not comprehensive. Specifically, those conflicts in which corporate Israel recognizes no public interest—no pertinence to the commonwealth—gain only routine attention. They come to resolution, within the Halakhah, in ordinary ways. This will happen by, e.g., invoking considerations merely of generic fairness or equity. They generate the amplification of no principal category-formations. Where equity, fairness, and similar universals define outcomes without the intervention of the distinctive considerations attendant upon the participation of corporate Israel, there the system speaks in banalities. Then the differentiation between Israelite and gentile prove a systemic anomaly: a distinction where there is no important difference.

The disputes that register are those between families or households; these are the social units conflict between which is resolved in the categorical formations of the Halakhah. The Halakhah elaborately explores the contentious relationships between husband and wife or co-wives or mothers-in-law and daughters-in-law (in Ketubot, Sotah, Qiddushin, Gittin, and Yebamot for example!)—but not between brother and sister, except as to estates. The latter's relationships, furthermore, do not define, but are subordinate and tangential to, the context in which they do occur. They have to do with mainly the administration of estates and support of orphans. But the former—relationships between husband and wife—define their own categorical context(s). And these are elaborate: betrothals, marital relationships of property and personalty, and cessation of marriage through death or divorce, for example. But even here, the possibilities—issues that can have arisen in imagination—are vastly outweighed by the actualities—the problems that do predominate for exegetical attention.

Providing for the stability of the household as the building block of the social order, the Halakhah identifies those conflicts between, e.g., husband and wife, that demand attention. The Halakhic category-formations as these are unpacked will define what is important about them, and will resolve matters in a way that is not only just and equitable but that is systemically required and particular. The conception of justice and equity figures so far as it illuminates the systemic logic embodied, here as elsewhere, in the details. Then justice and equity give way, being too general to solve many critical problems.

We note in this connection the critical position in the social order assigns to oaths, which invoke God's name and presence (not to be confused with vows). Oaths, in four classifications but for a single purpose, represent exceptional media for the resolution of social conflict. The oath of the judges, the oath of testimony, and the oath of bailment all serve to introduce the criterion of truth and to exclude the exercise of force. The claimant seeks a just restoration of his property or compensation for his loss, the defendant insists upon a fair adjudication of the matter. For that purpose, words backed up not by deeds but by divine supervision serve. But contention precipitates also the remaining classes of oaths: the taking of the vain and rash oath. The rash oath involves securing credence for a preposterous allegation—one that others deny. The vain oath asks people to believe one will carry out an implausible resolve, again bearing within itself the implicit motive to secure credibility where there is none. So one way or another, the oath serves, within the Israelite polity, to engage God's participation within the transactions of man, to involve God in Israel's points of inner conflict, to ask God to impart certainty to the points of stress and strain.

The upshot is readily apparent. It is God who keeps Israel's peace. That statement should be understood in concrete, not intangible ("spiritual") terms. The concrete fact emerges from what we have learned about resolving conflict between Israel's families and households. Heaven's heavy stake in family ties, God's engagement in securing truth-telling in response to the invocation of his name—these form the foundations of Judaism's theory of the social order, its social teaching. That is not always a paramount consideration, but it is everywhere potentially present. True, conflicts that pertain to restoring and maintaining the social order come to resolution within the this-worldly media of Israelite society in all but the single instance of oaths. But that instance tells the tale. The critical teaching of the social order is, God intervenes in transactions that, in all other aspects, are guided by this-worldly rules and exchanges. That is because God is explicitly called to attest to the truth. Everywhere present, God knows the facts and "will not hold him guiltless who takes his name in vain" by swearing to the contrary. On what basis does the Halakhic system of Israel's social order confidently call upon God to resolve Israelites' own conflicts? The written Torah answers that question, specifying the character of oaths in God's name and where they pertain.

C. *God's Presence in Israel: Israel Lives in God's Ubiquitous Presence, Subject to God's Enduring Concern*

Oaths form the bridge to the third and final social teaching of Rabbinic Judaism, that Israel is to form a society worthy of God's presence. A simple fact established in Scripture and instantiated in the Halakhic system captures the palpability, the practicality, the physicality, of God's presence. Settling conflicts over ownership of a cloak or a plot of ground or an ox between Israelite householders under some circumstances requires God's direct intervention. A formula, the oath, invokes God's presence and settles the conflict over the cloak, land, or animal. That fact signals the fundamental social reality contemplated by Rabbinic Judaism: a social order in which God is ever engaged and everywhere present. As with the oath, so with much else, God dwells in Israel. His active presence affects time and space and brings about Israel's engagement both in Israel's households and in his House. That statement represents not a theological conviction alone. It also sets forth the principle of social organization that is outlined in Scripture's laws and realized and systematized in the Rabbinic Halakhah.

But God has given the rules that render his presence not disruptive but the opposite: reliable and predictable. God in Rabbinic Judaism cannot be characterized as "mysterium tremendum," intervening unpredictably and disruptively. On the contrary, the Halakhah orders and regularizes relationships with him who says, "Your thoughts are not my thoughts." With the Torah, God has made his thoughts accessible. Knowing the rules, Israel is able to think like God and abide confidently in his presence. So even in matters of sanctification, for example, of time and space and circumstance, rationality governs. That is the gift of the Halakhah. And that fact points to the question raised in this third part of my account of the social teaching of Rabbinic Judaism: how does the Halakhah embody in social norms the reality of God's presence in Israel's social order? The answer is, by revealing in the Torah the governing principles of Israel's sanctification, God has laid the foundations for Eden: an Israelite social order that is perfect and eternal.

To state the whole at the outset: the social theory of Rabbinic Judaism sees God and Israel as enlandized, their relationship as a function of location. By "enlandizement," I mean, the acts of relationship between Israel and God that take place in, and that are realized through, the situation of holy Israel within the actuality of the Land of Israel. The presence of Israel upon the Land affects the character of the Land. That presence affects, also, the character of Israel's social order, and, as Scripture makes clear, the consequence for that social order, as to the future, of Israel's conduct. That explains why the union of Israel with the Land imposes upon Israel occasions for a relationship with God that absence of Israel from the Land prevents. How Israel conducts its activities in the Land shapes Israel's relationship with God. And what matters then concerns how Israel cultivates the Land, deriving its life from the Land. God's presence among Israel in the Land permits no alternative.

Israel conditionally got, through sin lost, and by repentance regained, the Land: how many times more? Here the stabilizing power of the Torah and the sages' transformation of its cases into principles come to the fore. Moses has already stated the conditions for an enduring social order in the Land. Israel's possession of the Land is subject to the conditions of the covenant. So Israel's rendering to God what God requires as his share of the produce forms a principal expression of Israel's covenanted relationship with God, which takes place not only in, but also through, the Land. With God as landlord, Israel's social order takes shape in the Land held by Israel in the status of the sharecropper. Transactions in scarce resources—land, produce—are defined in part by the intervention of God's claim, in addition to the claims of the this-worldly participants.

God's presence in Heaven as on earth shapes not only Israel's space but also marks its division of time. One day, one occasion is differentiated from another by reason of actions God has taken, and the media of differentiation extend deep into the Israelite household. Specifically, the rhythms of life lived in correlation with the movement of certain natural bodies—the moon's months, the sun's seasons—responds to God's imperatives for occasions defined by the positioning of those bodies in the Heavens. Days, weeks, lunar months, solar seasons—all bring along their particular imperatives. That is what I mean by finding God's presence in Israel not only in space but in time.

The meeting of Israel and God is both locative, focused as it is on the Temple, and also utopian, taking place in Israelite households where they are situated. And, as a matter of fact, those very moments that find God welcoming Israel in that one place, the Temple, mark the time at which Israel in its households receives God. So encountering God *when*—not solely where—he may be found, the Israelite household matches God's House. The occasion of the arrangement of moon and solar seasons is matched by the earthly response: Israel's house is brought into alignment with God's. So eternal Israel on earth corresponds with the eternal movement of the moon and the solar seasons in Heaven, world without end. That is what the Halakhah brings into being: the realization of God's Kingdom.

II. *Rabbinic Social Teaching in Israelite Context*

The Rabbinic sages in their systematic Halakhic writings rework the Torah's narrative into the norms of the Israelite social order. Social teachings of Rabbinic Judaism convey a vision of society seen whole but also embodied in detail. They take the form of both constitutive principles for the design of a social order and casuistic instruction on public virtue of a personal sort. Encompassed are both social thought on a grand scale, on the one side, and moral theology or ethics on the other. "You [plural] shall be holy" (Lev. 19:2) addresses the entirety of society, "Love [imperative, singular] your neighbor as yourself [singular you]" (Lev. 19:18), the individual and the occasion. The former—using the plural "you" of the Hebrew—addresses the social order, the latter,—with the singular "you"—the personal attitude and condition. Teachings of a public, social character speak to the community as a working system, encompassing its parts. Those that concern social behavior, theological ethics, moral theology, and the like do not convey a vision of the whole. And the corpus of details holds together. That is the upshot of treating corporate Israel as the question, the individual Israelite as the given, within the narrative of the Rabbinic construction of the Israelite social order. That is, if, like the rest of humanity, individuals are responsible to God for their actions and attitudes, why should corporate Israel form a moral entity encompassing all Israelites and making each responsible for the actions and attitudes of all?

We have, then, to wonder whence the conception of corporate Israel as a moral actor. Why should the Rabbinic sages have constructed out of the detailed laws of ancient Israelite Scripture, such as they cite start to finish, so magnificent a vision of an entire society? My view is they learned from the Torah of Our Rabbi, Moses. Specifically, Scripture itself provokes such a mode of thinking about the whole of the social order, not only about the details, corporate conduct, not only private behavior. It fosters the notion that the parts cohere, the details work together, above all, that the conduct of society as a whole shapes the fate of individuals therein, so that each is responsible for all, and all for each. Ancient Israelite society produced in the Pentateuch a remarkably coherent account of itself, its purpose and how through a narrative of the community's story the parts fit together to attain that purpose. Scripture, then, told a single, unitary, continuous story of itself and encompassed within that narrative the entire corpus of its laws of the social order. The Pentateuch speaks of Israel as a whole and tells the story of how its social order is to realize God's plan. Rabbinic Judaism systematically states the result of profound reflection on that story and the plan it conveys—that and the determination to act upon the implications of the story and its plan.

Now the continuity of this society, which I have called "corporate Israel" to distinguish "Israel" as the people from "Israel" as the individual Israelite, is not taken for granted as a given. It is portrayed as subject to stipulations, as a conditional gift. Moses and the prophets explicitly take the condition of Israel's society as indicator of Israel's relationship with God, who expresses intense concern for that matter. That fact explains why the Rabbinic sages, in the tradition of Moses and the prophets, set forth doctrines of public policy, not merely private conduct, beginning, as we have seen, with an account of the entire society, Israel. Theirs was a vision of the whole, a perspective from afar and not only from nearby. That fact explains why this inquiry into their social teachings identifies issues of considerable dimensions. That conception, thinking about society as a whole, in its largest components, then defines what is at stake in the Judaic teaching of the social order as undertaken by the Rabbinic sages. That is, to derive from Scripture not only details but large conceptions of a social character, not only rules for the construction of that "Israel" that Moses is commanded to bring into being, but also the principles that those rules adumbrate for situations undreamed of by Moses.

Seen whole, not only in its categorical components, Judaism starts with the Hebrew Scriptures of ancient Israel. That is a judgment of the whole, not only of the parts, some of which commence in statements of Scripture, some of which do not.[1] It is a vision of

---

[1] I have worked out the entire matter in the three part work, *Scripture and the Generative Premises of the Halakhah. A Systematic Inquiry. I. Halakhah Based Principally on Scripture and Halakhic Categories Autonomous of Scripture;. II. Scripture's Topics Derivatively Amplified in the Halakhah; III. Scripture's Topics Independently Developed in the Halakhah* (Binghamton, 2000).

the whole of Scripture's account of Israel that infuses the Halakhic system, not only the stimulus of elements of that account in detail. Among the Scriptures, the Pentateuch, with its narrative formulation of the coherent design for the social order of the entire Kingdom of priests and holy people, enjoys privileged standing. Within the Pentateuchal narrative and laws, sages found the imperative to define the entirety of a social order worthy to serve as God's abode. There they identified as the moral actor in God's drama not Adam, the individual, but Israel, the corporate social entity—whether a family, as in Genesis, whether a Kingdom of priests and a whole people, as in Exodus, whether a pilgrim people engaged in a common enterprise and responsible for its own fate by reason of its covenant with God, in Deuteronomy.

That is why, following the example of Moses and building upon the revealed Scripture, the Rabbinic sages proposed to identify the rules implicit in Scripture's stories and case-law. They thought deeply about the details of the laws, amplifying and extending them by defining the principles of right action exemplified therein. But theirs, then, was the task of global organization of the data, taken out of its narrative framework and placed into the systemic one of their own devising. So they made a unique contribution to the enterprise, in the definition of the large-scale category-formations that formed of stores and cases sustained and significant principles of an abstract character. The cases and rules of Scripture and tradition were treated as exemplary, surface-indicators of a deep structure of encompassing principles. Expressing the architecture through the detailed plan only, they set forth a system of law capable of imparting shape and structure anywhere, not bound to a particular culture or circumstance, time or place. And so it has worked out for Rabbinic Judaism for two millennia.

So the upshot now is clear. The social teachings form three large statements, spinning out the imperatives of a single logic. These statements in their necessary order speak, one on the social order formed by corporate Israel in its relationship to individual Israelites, the second on relationships between Israelites, and the third on relationships between Israel's society and the ever-present, ubiquitous one and only God who has taken up residence in the people, Israel. All three relationships—between Israel and the Israelite, Israelites by households or families, and all Israel and God—are defined by the pertinent category-formations of the normative Halakhah. Now we ask, how have other heirs of Scripture responded to those same narratives and laws, and what have they made of the transformation of Adam into Israel, a single individual into an entire social order?

III. *Another Reading of the Social Imperatives of Israelite Scripture, besides the Rabbinic: Christianity as Portrayed by Troeltsch's* The Social Teaching of the Christian Churches

Rabbinic Judaism and other Judaic religious systems over time share the same Scriptures of ancient Israel with Catholic Christianity and other Christian religious systems. All Judaic and most[2] Christian heirs of Scripture participate in that common heritage of revelation. But each makes its choices, both in general terms and in detail, of those passages of Scripture that are to register. And every Judaic and Christian system for the social order draws, in addition to Scripture, upon its further authoritative writings or traditions, whether the New Testament for Christianity or the Oral Torah for Rabbinic Judaism. Comparison of a Judaic and a Christian corpus of social teaching is made possible by that common heritage of authoritative Scripture, by the differing choices made within the ancient Scriptures for defining, each its social imperative.

If, then, we treat Rabbinic Judaism as the norm, Christianity of the same age, the first six centuries, as the variable, allowing the three Rabbinic teachings of the social order to define the topics for comparison and contrast, we produce three principal issues. First, how does the social teaching of early Catholicism, as portrayed by one standard account of matters, compare with that of Rabbinic Judaism? Do we find a systematic account of the relationship between the counterpart to corporate Israel, which ought to be the social order of the Church, and the individual Christian? How does the Church propose to regulate relationships of a civil character between Christians? And how does the Christian social order prepare itself to accord an abode to God in the society and culture of Christians? These represent the counterpart issues

---

[2] Excluding certain trends in Christianity represented by Marcion, who rejected the inclusion of the Hebrew Scriptures of ancient Israel ("Old Testament") in the Christian canon.

to those we have reviewed. As we shall now see, the comparison yields no simple result, and whether or not comparison produces answers to the three encompassing questions defined by Rabbinic Judaism is not obvious at all.

An encompassing survey of Christian social thought in the first six centuries C.E., for purposes of comparison and contrast with Judaic thought on the issues of the Judaic agenda, would carry us far beyond the bounds of this simple exercise. The basic questions are,

[1] does Christianity in its orthodox, catholic statement put forth a social vision for itself that categorically corresponds to that of Rabbinic Judaism?

[2] Do we find not simply episodic doctrines on particular questions, but a general theory of the social entity formed by Christians that resembles in its basic structure the general theory of Israel embodied in the Halakhah?

I shall now show that the answers to both questions are, no. But let me begin from the beginning.

To answer those questions in a very preliminary way, we turn to a standard work on the subject. I choose, appropriately, a section of the one that inspired my lifelong interest, beginning with *A History of the Mishnaic Law*,[3] in the social description of Rabbinic Judaism out of the category-formations of the Halakhah, Ernst Troeltsch, *The Social Teaching of the Christian Churches*.[4] What I seek there is a routine, reliable representation of normative, orthodox, catholic Christian conception of the social order constituted by orthodox, catholic, Christians: "the Church." A founding figure in the study of religion and society, Troeltsch presents the formative Christian conception of social realities, and for the preliminary initiative undertaken here, that presentation will serve.[5] Troeltsch's account is at the center of matters. To his

---

[3] *A History of the Mishnaic Law of Purities, Holy Things, Women, Appointed Times, and Damages* (Leiden, 1974–1986), in forty-three volumes.

[4] Ernst Troeltsch, *The Social Teaching of the Christian Churches I-II* (New York and Evanston, 1956). Translated by Olive Wyon. With an Introduction by H. Richard Niebuhr.

[5] The scholarly literature on Troeltsch, all the more so on the problems he addresses, refines matters considerably. But I know of no more systematic and orderly account of matters, and the points important to this comparison are of such an elementary character that I deem Troeltsch on his own quite sufficient to the task.

Social Teaching, Chapter One, part iii,[6] I ask the elementary questions and require only basic facts. Here are my questions:

[1] How does Troeltsch treat the categorical program that has seemed to me native to Rabbinic Judaism and its design for Israel's social order?
[2] What perspective do we gain on the Rabbinic sages' system from the Christian alternative and the contrast it affords?

My answer is, in line with Troeltsch's account, the Rabbinic social teachings contemplate a social order that is not congruent in its basic components to that of early catholic Christianity. The differences are so fundamental that, as we shall see, Christianity yields no teachings pertinent to the generative issues that are critical to Rabbinic Judaism, and vice versa. And that is so even though we could readily find pertinent doctrines in the corpus of catholic Christianity and Rabbinic Judaism for a common agenda, questions of a domestic and economic character for example.

Then how does the Torah figure, and where has the Torah's narrative made its impact upon the social order of the Christian Church? What is astonishing is how the model of ancient Israel's Kingdom of God, valued by orthodox, catholic Christianity as much as by

---

[6] Chapter One, "The Foundations in the Early Church," deals with three topics: the Gospel, Paul, and early Catholicism. The nature of this comparison of conceptions of the social order requires a focus on the third of the three, since at interest here is not ethical theories bearing social consequences, attitudes toward the state, economics, family, or society, such as Troeltsch describes for Jesus and Paul, but a different matter altogether. It is how Christians thought of themselves as a social entity, and how they integrated attitudes toward the state, economics, family, and society into that encompassing social theory of who, and what, they were all together and all at once: the counterpart to Israel at Sinai, for example. I chose the survey of early Catholicism, because there we deal not with individual opinions, however authoritative and influential, but the collective doctrine and consciousness of the community viewed whole: "the Church." Troeltsch signals that difference. In reference to Jesus, the focus is on Jesus' main ethical idea and its sociological significance. With Paul he speaks of religious community, but at issue is theological doctrine, signaled by, among other instances, language such as the following: "Through its faith in Jesus as the Risen Lord, through the identification of Jesus with the Messiah and . . . with the universal redeeming Divine principle, through the new worship of Christ and its mystical idea of Redemption, through Baptism and the Lord's Supper as the means of becoming one with the present Exalted Christ, it has become an independent religious community, which, in ideal at least, is strictly exclusive and bound together in unity." These and comparable passages do not serve our purpose. The institutional focus of his unit on early Catholicism, by contrast, addresses issues of "Church" "state" and "society" that correspond to those we have taken up in the Halakhic framework.

Rabbinic Judaism, served not at all for the former but governed all social thought of the latter. At later times and under other circumstances, the vision of Israel conveyed by Moses in the Pentateuch would challenge important Christian communities and move them to mighty foundations—the founding of my native New England is a prime example of a Christian society modeled on Israel of old. But in the formative age of the Christianity and the Judaism subject to discussion here, that was not the case for Christianity.

Put simply: to make sense of Christianity's social teaching, we require Scripture only very rarely. Indeed, we could understand the main lines of Christian social thinking in its formative age without the map supplied by Israelite Scripture at all. But—by contrast—scarcely a line of the Rabbinic account of its Israel's social order, let alone the vision of the whole, makes sense outside of the framework of Moses' Torah. "The Church" as portrayed by Troeltsch out of the resources of orthodox Christianity simply does not form the counterpart to the Israel of which the Rabbinic sages speak. Presently, I shall show in a concrete example precisely how disparate the two entities—Church, Israel—are. Language natural for the one proves egregious, indeed, beyond all comprehending, for the other.

Let us then turn to the compatibility of the discrete category formations, the starting point for any comparative exercise. Troeltsch outlines, as topics of social teaching, such themes as "possessions, work, callings and classes, trade, the family, slavery, charity"—all topics on which Rabbinic Halakhah sets forth considerable bodies of rulings, even entire category-formations.[7] So, on the surface, the constituents of the structures to be compared do match. And yet, the basic context is so different that the details, however comparable, do not sustain comparison. Two of Troeltsch's category-formations tell the story: "the ethic of the Church which was developed out of this opposition between the Church and the world and how it bridged the gulf," and "settlement of the social problems within the Church and by the Church as a state within the state." The former of the two categories underscores the sense of separateness that characterized Christian society vis-à-vis the world beyond. The counterpart would then be the Rabbinic doctrine of Israel and the gentiles. But there is this difference. Israel regarded

---

[7] And see also my *The Economics of the Mishnah* (Chicago, 1989; reprint: Atlanta, 1998), and also *Rabbinic Political Theory: Religion and Politics in the Mishnah* (Chicago, 1991).

itself (in the Rabbinic design) as a fully-articulated society, not separate from the world, but constitutive of the social world it occupied, and utterly autonomous of any other. Its doctrine was one of separation of a working community from the inchoate world beyond. The Halakhah afforded no recognition to the legitimacy of any entity like itself, e.g., "a state within a state." Indeed, it only grudgingly and on an ad hoc basis accorded recognition to the power of the gentiles and their empires, e.g., in tractates Abodah Zarah and Tohorot.

Everything else was something else. Israel was sui generis, unique, out of phase with all other social entities, of which, as legitimate counterparts to Israel, the Rabbinic sages knew none. That is because Israel served God, and inchoate humanity, idols. There was no bridging the gulf between Israel and the realm of idolatry. The Halakhah leaves no doubt whatsoever on that score. And, along these same lines, the Israel of Rabbinic Judaism did not regard itself as "a state within the state," but as the sole state, the state of Israel, pure and simple.[8] That is to say, it accorded recognition, legitimacy, rights of bona fide negotiation, to no other entity.

The Halakhah, moreover, legislates for the people Israel as though it were that people's sole authority. The social teachings of Christianity in the formative age take account of two authorities with whom Christians engaged, Church and State. Learned by reason of its three centuries of persecution, Christianity could differentiate the sacred from the secular, the Church from the State. Such a conception lay wholly outside of the imaginative power—or the historical, social experience that was formed in consequence—of Rabbinic Judaism. I assume that is because, in its conception of Israel's past, Rabbinic Judaism found in the Scripture no picture of a subordinated or marginalized Israel, at the fringes of the nations. Rather, the Pentateuch told the story of an Israel in command of its own destiny, responsible for its fate by reason of its adherence to, or divergence from, the covenant of Sinai. Leviticus 26 and Deuteronomy 33-34 tell the story not of an excluded and persecuted community but of a self-governing, morally responsible nation—unique in humanity. Rabbinic Judaism was guided by Scripture's narrative to explain defeat by Rome, a natural enemy

---

[8] That is the Halakhic view. The Aggadic view differentiated among the nations Rome, Greece, Media, Babylonia, and knew also Egypt, Canaan, and the like. All of these attain significance only in relationship to Israel, e.g., Rome and Israel were deemed counterparts and opposites.

because it was pagan, but not persecution of the kind Christians endured from Rome. Israel was never the victim of Rome, only of its own failure.

The Rabbinic Judaic system, therefore, in its imaginative reconstruction of social reality designed the social order of not a minority settled among an encompassing majority, a state within the state, a people within a people (like Israel in Egypt) but as an autonomous social order, equivalent in standing to Rome, Greece, Media, Persia (as the standard list of the empires has it). That is why Rabbinic Judaism could in no way distinguish the realm of the sacred from the realm of the secular, the city of God from the city of man, to allude to a famous point of differentiation. It could not form a doctrine of the relationship of "Israel" to the state, because, as I said, there was from the Torah's perspective no legitimate, lawful state other than the state of, lawfully constituted by the Torah to govern, Israel.[9]

Before proceeding, let us consider principal parts of Troeltsch's "social teaching" for "early Catholicism," the age of the Rabbinic sages. Troeltsch deals in his way with the program that has guided us here: the social organizations of the state, the family, and economics, within the fundamental theory that religious ideas shape those organizations. Troeltsch's argument is outward-facing, interested as he is in "the effect on civilization of Christian-sociological principles (p. 12). But he states flatly:

> It is an actual fact of history that from the beginning all the social doctrines of Christianity have been likewise doctrines both of the State and of Society. At the same time, owing to the emphasis of Christian thought upon personality, the family is always regarded as the basis both of the State and of Society and is thus bound up with all Christian social doctrine. Once more, therefore, the conception of the "social" widens out, since in the development of a religious doctrine of fellowship the Family, the State, and the economic order of Society are combined as closely related sociological formations . . . the ultimate problem may be stated thus: How can the Church harmonize with these main forces in such a way that together they will form a unity of civilization? Thus the question of the attitude of the churches toward the social problem also includes their attitude towards the State (p. 32).

---

[9] But, as everyone knows, Rabbinic Judaism also accorded recognition to the validity of the law of the gentile Kingdoms in which Jews resided, thus "the law of the Kingdom is law." But here we speak of the Torah and its categorical effects in the Halakhah, and that is another realm of being altogether.

Here we have the model for the systemic analysis of theories of the social order: "how can the Church harmonize with these main forces . . . so that they will form a unity of civilization" is another way of asking my question, which is, how do the details fit together and work together to form a social system? But Christianity ("the Church") does not form the ground of being of the social order but only one component thereof. For in Troeltsch's language there is a single word that marks a major difference. It is "harmonize with" as against "harmonize." Harmonize is used intransitively, in harmonize with, or transitively, as "harmonize" plus a direct object.

To be clear: The question "how does the Halakhah harmonize these main forces so that they will form a unity?" would have been my way of putting matters for Rabbinic Judaism. Here, in the distinction in preferred formulations, lies a profound difference. "Harmonize with" conceives the Church as an entity apart from family, state, economic order of society—all of them autonomous of the Church, thus "Church-state relations" would follow. But natural to Rabbinic Judaism is the language, "how does the Torah harmonize—impose harmony upon—family, state, and economic order of society to form a unity?" The Torah as set forth by Moses in the Pentateuch conceives each component of the Israelite social order to cohere with all others in a cogent whole, each part harmonizing with all others to form that unity of society that Israel is to embody.

Accordingly, we find a question that the Rabbinic sages will not have framed for themselves: how can "the Church" harmonize with those main forces—family, state, economy—in such a way as to form a unity of civilization? That is because they could not imagine a "state" other than the one that they contemplated, e.g., in tractates Sanhedrin-Makkot and Horayot, meaning, the state of, embodied by Israel, whether in the land of Israel, whether not.[10]

---

[10] The Rabbinic theory of Israelite politics took for granted that Israel would form an empowered political entity, capable of self-government (perhaps within an imperial system) wherever it was located. In that sense, the state of Israel as a political entity was not enlandized or localized. And as a matter of fact, the Rabbinic documents represent the Jews of Babylonia as self-governing in a wide variety of transactions backed up by the threat of legitimate violence. The "Israel" of Babylonia was no voluntary community of co-religionists of faith but an empowered political entity, subject to superior power to be sure, with the right to inflict sanctions of property and person.

Nothing in the doctrine of the family conceived of the Israelite family outside the framework of that Israelite society that the sages designed, so that asking "the family to form a unity with the state" would have been incomprehensible. The family by definition formed an integral component of Israel. So far as the economic order of society was subject to the ordering of the state and related to the family, it too is integral to the Israelite system as a whole: an economy conducted with God as landlord and overseer.[11]

So much for the signals supplied by the diverse uses of common language. But what are we then to compare? Troeltsch asks about "the intrinsic sociological idea of Christianity and its structure and organization." He moves from sociology to Christianity: "What is the relation between this sociological structure and the 'Social'? That is the state, the economic order with its division of labor, and the family" (p. 34). Troeltsch pursues a practical program, following "the actual influence of the churches upon social phenomena." My interest, by contrast, is in the theory of things, the analysis of a system of thought concerning those same phenomena. I do not know much about the actualities of Israelite life in the time and place in which the Rabbinic sages formed their system. I do know that the Rabbinic documents do not claim people did things the way the rabbis said they should; rather, in general, they did things in their own way, sometimes in conformity with Rabbinic doctrine, sometimes not.[12] But so far as Troeltsch describes the theory, not only the reality, he proves a suitable guide for so preliminary an exercise in comparison as this one. For, to make the matter explicit, all we wish to know are Judaic and Christian ideas about the social order, with special reference to the role of Scripture in shaping those ideas.

We could then compare part to part, but, out of context, the comparison yields little perspective and no insight. So we turn to

---

[11] Volumes Two and Three of *Scripture and the Generative Premises of the Halakhah. A Systematic Inquiry*, above, n. 1, leave no doubt on that score, not to mention my *The Economics of the Mishnah*, above, n. 7.

[12] My *History of the Jews in Babylonia* (Leiden, 1965–1970), vols. I-V, contains systematic accounts of the Rabbinic sages' account of their relationships with the ordinary Israelites in their communities. These show that, in some areas, Rabbinic authority governed; in others the Rabbis portrayed a recalcitrant population, doing things as it, not the rabbis, wished.

the largest components of the social order, the principal aggregates. For Troeltsch, it is "the Church," and for Rabbinic Judaism, "Israel." The perspective of the Church upon itself, and the perspective of the Rabbinic sages upon Israel, yield two distinct angles of vision. The Church sees itself as a minority, not a free-standing, autonomous sector of humanity, not a political entity corresponding to other, comparable entities; a minority; different from the generality of humanity. The Rabbinic sages see Israel as an autonomous community, formed by God's intervention to constitute a component of humanity, a politically-empowered society, a state unto itself, sui generis among states as Israel is also sui generis among nations or peoples. Ultimately, following the prophets, the rabbis conceive that all humanity will worship the one God and so form part of that same Israel that those who eschew idolatry and worship God now constitute. That is how Scripture portrayed God's people. And that is how the Rabbinic sages viewed the Israel of whom they spoke, that corporate community so fully articulated as to yield orderly relationships, also, governing the state and individual Israelites.

So, to double back, the key to the social order, the source of coherence for the social teaching of the Christian Churches, is, for Troeltsch, and surely for the Christian social order described by him, "the Church." And that is to be differentiated from "the State." Then by that model there is no Israelite counterpart to "the Church," there is no distinguishing "Church" from legitimate "state," there is only—once more—the unique-state of Israel. That is because Israel, God's portion of humanity, encompasses both the political and the religious order corresponding to state and church in its context. Were "Israel" counterpart to "Church," we should find a comparison plausible. But it is not, so we cannot. The basic social category-formation, "Church," as distinct from "State," simply has no match in Rabbinic social categories. And though the rest—work, trade, family, slavery, possessions—may correspond to Rabbinic category-formations or sizable composites thereof, there is no foundation for comparison and contrast, other than episodic and casuistic.

A brief account of the details therefore suffices. Troeltsch opens with the Gospels, then Paul. Only with "early Catholicism (p. 89) does he reach the counterpart to the Rabbinic statement: a large, coherent religious system speaking on fundamental issues of social organization. Troeltsch explains the formation of the Church in this language:

> The sociological idea of the Gospel was based on that faith in God which arose out of the Jewish Bible and the Jewish national life, intensified and illuminated by the proclamation of the Kingdom of God, and on the incarnation of this idea in the personality of Jesus himself. When, however, . . . this new faith had severed its connection with Judaism and Jesus was no longer with his disciples, it then felt the need for something to take the place of this outward relationship; it needed an independent center of organization which would incarnate the idea at any given point of time with reference to its relation to the actual setting in which it found itself. Both aspects of the Christian faith—its individualism and its universalism—needed this independent organization in order that they might find fresh and vital forms of expression . . . (pp. 89–90).

Here, in this theory of the whole, we find the key point of departure: the Kingdom of God. We know how Israel lives in God's presence and in God's Kingdom, accepting upon itself the yoke of God's dominion and the yoke of God's commandments. What is the Christian counterpart to the entire social order formed into God's Kingdom? It is the incarnation of the Kingdom of God in the person of Jesus. The counterpart Rabbinic conception is the embodiment of the Kingdom of God in the society of Israel. The metaphor invoked by Christianity to account for the social entity constituted by Christians then is personal, that invoked by Rabbinic Judaism for the social entity constituted by Jews is public, corporate, collective.

Whatever Christianity understood by the language to which Troeltsch refers, it is not what Judaism understood by the laws of the Torah. When, in the Torah, God addressed Israel as Kingdom of priests and a holy people, when he assigned to Israel the task of serving as his witnesses, when he asked for an abode on earth for himself within Israel, he spoke of corporate Israel, beyond individual Israelites, or any one of them. God's Kingdom involved the acceptance of God's rule, detailed in the laws of the Torah, and the acceptance of the yoke of the commandments, set forth in those laws. None of this has any counterpart in any incarnate being, but solely in the entirety of the Israelite social order. So far as the Church was conceived as "the mystical body of Christ" (as Troeltsch's language implies even here), "Israel" does not compare.

So far as "Israel" forms God's abode within humanity, the Church does not compare. Troeltsch describes the formation of a social teaching for a community formed in relationship to an individual and shaped by life first in his presence and then not, in a palpable way, in his presence. Through the Halakhah, Israel always found itself in God's immediate presence, acting on that fact in countless transactions. And yet, from a certain perspective, God's abode (Israel) and Christ's body (the Church) prove remarkably congruent in conception—if not in execution.

But the conception is everything. The Church portrayed by Troeltsch emerges as a response to a circumstance, to the passage of time, to the change in the society formed by Christians. Its institutionalization is described as a matter of historical sequence. Israel, by contrast, is presented by the Rabbinic sages as eternal, atemporal, unrestricted by time, place, or circumstance. That is underscored by the execution of the governing metaphor. The Torah made little provision for the kinds of authority that the new age required; the rabbis themselves form no authorized clergy, comparable to the Christian priesthood; the politics of the community of Israel yielded no counterpart to the Church order of priests and bishops and onward. What emerged in time was "the Christian priesthood," with emphasis on a genuine tradition, secured by the bishops, and the development of the sacramental idea, which "constitutes the development of early Catholicism."

Troeltsch sees the formation of the episcopate of sacrament and tradition as a "limitation of the original sociological idea of absolute religious individualism and universalism." He says, "The religious community is now no longer bound merely to the worship of Christ, to baptism, and the Supper of the Lord, but to the Church, to tradition, to the bishop, and to the use of the sacramental means of grace through the legally appointed bishop" (p. 93). The Rabbinic sages by contrast never differentiate between religious imperatives (*misvot*) (worship of Christ, baptism) and other-than-religious institutions, traditions, and authority (Church, tradition, bishop). Their own authority is implicit, institutional only in the loosest framework. They do not differentiate between Scripture and tradition, the whole constituting the Torah of Moses. The hierarchy of learning sufficed; there was no counterpart to a bishop among the Rabbinic sages, even though some figures are represented as broadly accepted authorities, others not, the whole governed by consensus.

So the Church and Israel do not correspond at all. The Church was organized as an independent body, which formed its own "juridical constitution: she gradually founded her own system of law, the law of the Church, in which, from her own standpoint, without any consideration for the State (which until then had been the only possible source of law), she evolved her own peculiar conception of the legal relation between society and the individual, between the Church and the world" (p. 96).

> The legal subjectivity of the whole body and of the individual congregation, the sphere of authority of the bishops . . . the representation of this legal subjectivity, the rights of individuals over against this objective law, the ecclesiastical possession of property, religious institutions of charity the ecclesiastical control of sections of life which could be reached (above all, in the law of marriage), decisions affecting disputes of Christians amongst themselves and the care of morals—all this became increasingly the subject of an ecclesiastical-juridical system of thought (p. 96).

The Rabbinic sages' "Israel" emerged out of centuries of Jewish political entities; the sages could not think socially except through politics. That is why there was no counterpart to an ecclesiastical body, no distinction between state and church authority, for the sages. True, they made decisions affecting disputes of Israelites among themselves,[13] but resolving conflict was accomplished by appeal to governing principles, rules of mediation, and only rarely by force majeure, and then, in the form of the oath, it was God's.

In a word, the Rabbinic Israel formed not a state within a state, or an institution requiring state recognition, but a political entity, pure and simple—but an entity of a political character that also constituted a religious body (in the ordinary sense): a state that was also a church, a society governed by rules of sanctification and so that was also a kind of monastic community. That Israel did not seek recognition by the Roman empire, beyond the matter of political legitimacy, because that Israel saw itself as the sole legitimate public body to begin with. Rome could confer nothing; Iran could keep its distance. By contrast, out of the ecclesiastical juridical system of thought developed a system that craved recognition and that was finally recognized by the state and that in due course had to make its peace with the state. But in

---

[13] The whole of Vol. II of *Scripture and the Generative Premises of the Halakhah. A Systematic Inquiry* has shown us how that worked out.

the early Church this system was limited within its own borders and did not affect the larger social world.

> For Christianity "the world" meant "all those social institutions of life outside the Church," and the world was "denied or depreciated" (p. 110). The Christian moral law consists in directing all activity toward the ultimate goal of union with God and then expresses itself in contemplative purity of heart and in active brotherly love (p. 110) . . . . in obedience to the Church and in sacrifice for the unity of the Church . . . the destruction of the ego and self-sacrifice for others is exercised, good works are acquired, and future salvation is assured. . . . That which a man renounces he gives to the Church and by means of services of this kind . . . he secures salvation in the other world, and this again is mediated by the Church (p. 111).

For Rabbinic Judaism, this entire program will have proved exceptionally difficult to follow. That is not because Rabbinic Judaism differed, e.g., on destroying the ego and self-sacrifice for others. On the contrary, in so many words, the Sayings of the Fathers affirm both moral virtues (Tractate Abot 2:4):

> He would say, "Make his wishes into your own wishes, so that he will make your wishes into his wishes. Put aside your wishes on account of his wishes, so that he will put aside the wishes of other people in favor of your wishes."

The upshot is, a program of self-sacrifice for others, good works, and future salvation will not have surprised the Rabbinic sages, and renunciation in favor of service to others will have formed a commonplace of Rabbinic teaching on virtue.

What then is the counterpart, for Judaism, to "the Church"? If we substitute "Israel" for "Church" in Troeltsch's just cited statement we get gibberish. Thus: the Judaic moral law

> . . . consists in obedience to Israel and in sacrifice for the unity of Israel . . . the destruction of the ego and self-sacrifice for others is exercised, good works are acquired, and future salvation is assured. . . . That which a man renounces he gives to Israel and by means of services of this kind . . . he secures salvation in the other world, and this again is mediated by Israel.

How grotesque! I cannot imagine anything so incomprehensible as the notion of Israel as a focus of obedience, of sacrifice for the unity of Israel, of renouncing something and giving it to Israel, or of securing salvation mediated by Israel. None of these statements makes any sense whatsoever in the language of Rabbinic Judaism.

But there is language that does work. What if we substitute "God" for "Israel." Then: the Judaic moral law

> . . . consists in obedience to God and in sacrifice for the unity of God . . . the destruction of the ego and self-sacrifice for others is exercised, good works are acquired, and future salvation is assured. . . . That which a man renounces he gives to God and by means of services of this kind . . . he secures salvation in the other world, and this again is mediated by God.

So far as Troeltsch speaks of the Church, Rabbinic Judaism invokes God for the same declarations. I cannot imagine a more perfect statement of the Judaic moral law than this formulation, which is natural to the native category-formations of Rabbinic Judaism. Israel forms a this-worldly social entity, sui generis in humanity, bearing supernatural tasks. It is God's abode. But in the drama of humanity en route to salvation in the world to come, Israel constitutes no principal player, is not subject of obedience or recipient of sacrifice for its unity, and no one renounces anything to Israel; God is at the center of the social order, and the social order is contingent upon God's wishes and God's word.

In the Rabbinic vocabulary, it is impossible to find a category-formation that would function as does "Church" in Christianity. "Israel" does not work. "Synagogue" does not match in any way. For different reasons, "God" does not work either. But—to turn to an obvious candidate—what of "synagogue;" is it not the counterpart to "Church"? Since Christians go to Church for prayer, and Israelites to synagogue, the two institutions appear to function in the same way.

But a moment of consideration shows us that "synagogue" certainly does not work in that way. The synagogue in fact does not function like a Church, it is not a place where, uniquely, Israel meets God or conducts rites particular to that location, except for one. The Halakhah knows two principal venues for Israel's meeting with God: [1] Temple and [2] the enlandized household, that is, the household that possesses real property in the land of Israel. The Temple forms the center of service, and the offerings for the Day of Atonement, Tabernacles, and Passover define a principal interest of the Halakhah in those occasions. The enlandized household defines the matching locus for the celebration of Passover and of Tabernacles. The Halakhah of Shabbat-Erubin explicitly takes shape around the binary opposites, Temple and household; what on the

Sabbath (and, except for cooking, on festivals) one may do in the former location one may not do in the latter.

What of the synagogue—is that not a space for meeting God? The answer emerges when we ask, what do Israelites do in the synagogue, vis-à-vis God, that they do not ordinarily do elsewhere, and what defines a synagogue in time or in space? The one point at which Israel finds God in the synagogue in particular (if not uniquely) is in the declamation of the Torah. It is, specifically, in reference to the synagogue that the Halakhah provides its category-formation accommodating the rules for declaiming the Torah and—more to the point—it is in that context, and there alone, that the Halakhah further specifies other rules that govern the sanctity of the locus of the synagogue. So the synagogue finds its definition in its function; it is not a place to which Israelites go to meet God, as—the Torah indicates—the Temple is. Rather, it is utopian in the simplest sense: anywhere where ten Israelite males conduct a specified activity, the public declamation of the Torah, the function of the synagogue is carried out. That is without regard to the location of the Israelites or the character of the dedicated space, if any, that contains them. In this context, the Church and the synagogue have nothing in common; they constitute different institutions, serving different functions, in different contexts, and for different purposes.

To conclude: the pre-Constantine Church did not see itself as integral to the State or vice versa. The post-Constantine Church "was still too much concerned with the next world, still too much agitated by the heat of conflict and victory, still inwardly too detached to be able to weave ideas of that king into the inner structure of the State" (p. 145). State and Church were two

> essentially separate magnitudes: the State and the social order in general actually constitute the "world." The conception of a sinful lost world over against a Church which alone can offer redemption became more and more the governing idea in the State and the social order (p. 146).

The Rabbinic sages did not find in Scripture and tradition the notion of the alien state as legitimate and also distinct from Israel; the world they contemplated was God's, and Israel's task was to make of it God's Kingdom, as he planned from the beginning. That is the lesson Scripture taught them. The world was divided, for them, between those who know and worship the one true God, and idolaters. That is the lesson that Scripture taught them, and they took as their task the realization of that lesson in the actualities of Israel's social order. The three social teachings of Rabbinic Judaism represent the lessons that the Rabbinic sages learned from their profound reading of the Torah, both Scripture and tradition.

Here, then, we encounter God's Kingdom, not as against the world but as the fulfillment of God's plan in making the world. How did Christianity propose its counterpart? Here is Troeltsch's account:

> Christianity described herself as a basileia [Kingdom], and therefore her counterpart, the world, was also conceived as a basileia, which is plainly manifested in the Emperor, in the Imperial Law, and in the worship of the Emperor. The world becomes a "Kingdom" and it is thus the summa of the existing laws and ordinances. For a Kingdom is the support of law and order; and law and order covers the whole order of Society. The world is . . . that period in history which precedes the Return of Christ . . . the doctrine of the Old Testament was retained—that the Creation was good, but that the "world" is the result of the Fall, of the corruption of the will, and a Satanic delusion. The state also sprang from this source, and thus it comes under the uniform and essentially unchangeable principle of the "world," together with all the institutions of marriage, labor, property, slavery, law, and war . . . (p. 147).

So we have come to the center of the matter, the understanding of "Kingdom." The two heirs of Israelite Scripture part company at the notion of a Kingdom of God. That meant for Christianity the contrast between two Kingdoms, God's and Rome's, the emperor's. It entailed for Rabbinic Judaism the single, unique Kingdom of God realized by Israel in the here and now. Here the social teaching of the Christian Churches and that of Rabbinic Judaism diverge and present irreconcilable differences. If among them I had to identify the critical difference, it would be in the Christian language as formulated by Troeltsch, "the Creation was good, but that the 'world' is the result of the Fall, of the corruption of the will, and a Satanic delusion." On that language Rabbinic Judaism concurs: Creation was good and the age that followed the fall represented the result of Man's corrupt use of free will. But Rabbinic Judaism adds a sentence that Christianity omits. It concerns the Torah: the event of Sinai.

Except in the past tense Christianity does not acknowledge God's intervention to correct the consequences of Eden by his act of self-manifestation at Sinai—and Israel's act of affirmation at Sinai: "We shall do and we shall obey." To Christianity the Torah makes no difference, and to Judaism, it makes all the difference. And therein lies the real point of departure. The Rabbinic sages would have said, the departure of Christianity from the Torah, just as Tarfon has it (T. Shab. 13:5):

> A. The books of the Evangelists and the books of the *minim* they do not save from a fire. But they are allowed to burn where they are,
> B. they and the references to the Divine Name which are in them.
> D. Said R. Tarfon, "May I bury my sons, if such things come into my hands and I do not burn them, and even the references to the Divine Name which are in them.
> E. "And if someone was running after me, I should go into a temple of idolatry, but I should not go into their houses [of worship].
> F. "For idolaters do not recognize the Divinity in denying him, but these recognize the Divinity and deny him.
> G. "And about them Scripture states, 'Behind the door and the doorpost you have set up your symbol for deserting me, you have uncovered your bed' (Is. 57:8)."

What defines the context for the judgment attributed to Tarfon, who flourished at the end of the first century C.E.?

Reading from Genesis through Kings along with the Prophets as a single, unfolding and coherent narrative, the Rabbinic sages formed their social teaching in response to the Torah's account of the repair of the world under God's sovereignty through Israel's regeneration in the Torah. They took as their task the realization of God's Kingdom, as God had designed that Kingdom, and as humanity in the end of days would join itself to that Kingdom, acknowledging God's rule and accepting his dominion. That is as do all those called Israel even now. Rabbinic Judaism designed the social order in response to God's plan, set forth in the Torah, and orthodox, Catholic Christianity in the same age did not. Rabbinic Judaism tells and retells ancient Israel's Scripture's story—the Torah's story. Orthodox, Catholic Christianity tells the story of Jesus Christ. The narratives follow, each its own lines of development. They do not coincide. In a profound sense, they scarcely intersect.

IV. *Comparing the Rabbinic and the Pagan Social-Religious Structures*

If between "Church" and "Israel" we find little in common in social policy and structural definition, then what of Paganism of the same time and place? The Church as a medium of social thought and teaching is unique, with no counterpart in Judaism. We now see that it has none in Paganism either. In some ways, Paganism and Judaism are alike in that neither put forth a counterpart to the Church as the medium of salvation and the mode of realizing God's kingdom, such as Troeltsch has defined for us. But, obviously, Rabbinic Judaism and Paganism not only compare but also contrast. Paganism espoused a latitudinarian tolerance, and Rabbinic Judaism defined with great care what is required to live in God's kingdom—and how one might lose his place in the world to come.

For an account of the Pagan counterpart to Christian Church order, we follow what the great historian of pagan and Christian religion in late antiquity, Ramsay MacMullen, writes of Paganism. He contrasts the tight, hierarchical organization of Christianity with the inchoate, uninstitutionalized character of Paganism. Explaining the endurance of Paganism long after the triumph of Christianity under Constantine, he says:

> This religion had no single center, spokesman, director, or definition of itself; therefore no one point of vulnerability. Everyone was free to choose his own credo; anyone who wished could consult a priest or ignore a priest, about how best to appeal to the divine. Appeal found expression in a great variety of words, acts, and arts, which . . . had been woven into the deepest levels of daily life and culture, the secular included. . . . Not only motifs but people circulated everywhere—meaning worshipers with their religious ideas. Over the course of many hundreds of years of peaceful stirring about, the mix became constantly more complex and intimate, at least in urban settings. Variety itself became a characteristic binding together the whole fabric of religion into one whole, across space, as on the other hand, the long peace of the pax Romana had bound communities also to their past.[14]

MacMullen underscores "the variety of words, acts, and arts." Paganism survived many centuries of the Christian challenge because it had no one point of vulnerability, he argues with great effect. And so did Judaism. The tenacity of Paganism gives us a standpoint from which to see Rabbinic Judaism. Long after its formative age, that Judaism would retain the active and stubborn loyalty of the greater part of the Jewish people, and even today defines the character of Judaism for the vast majority of Jews who practice that religion in any form. But the basis for Rabbinic Judaism's power to resist the Christian and later Islamic

---

[14] Ramsay MacMullen, *Christianity and Paganism in the Fourth to Eighth Centuries* (New Haven and London, 1997), pp. 32–33.

challenge is not that it had no one point of vulnerability. It is, rather, the intangible, if not at all inchoate, character of its sustaining power, which is, its generative conviction. That is where Judaism differed from Paganism and found its point of comparison with Christianity.

For if we ask, whether Rabbinic Judaism in its formative age possessed a single center, spokesman, director, or definition of itself, the answer is self-evident: of course it did. But it did not take institutional form, as in the matter of the Church, in a priesthood and a hierarchy. Rather, the single center located itself in the Torah as expounded by the consensus of the sages, especially in the Halakhah. The counterpart to Church, priesthood, and hierarchy was embodied not in a particular man or office, but in a coherent body of ideas, represented by many men in many times and places. Rabbinic Judaism's was not a locative center: take that, and all else falls. It was utopian. And it was not a center formed by an institution. Destroy that, and all else is lost.

Its center was its books, Scripture and the oral tradition sages themselves received from Sinai and handed on to their disciples in memorized sayings or notes or in time completed documents. That is where, if asked to point us to their center, the sages of any time and place would direct our attention. That too explains why, in medieval times, Christianity time and again burned the Talmud. True, that Judaism had as its spokesman Moses (called "our rabbi") and looked to his writings in Scripture and the traditions held to commence with him for its definition. But Moses is represented as the starting point, the inner dynamics of the Torah's logic governing the articulation of the Torah. And, as history would show, Rabbinic Judaism suffered no one point of vulnerability, for to wipe out that Judaism, devastating a single center, silencing a single spokesman, would never accomplish the work, even in our own day and its singular disaster.

But unlike latitudinarian and tolerant paganism, Rabbinic Judaism, by its nature as the monotheist book-religion, found a ready definition of itself. No one was free to choose his own credo or ignore the sage's mediation in approaching the divine. A simple expression of that fact dictates how one may lose his portion in the world to come, which is, by an act of unfaith (M. San. 11:1-2):

11:1
    A. All Israelites have a share in the world to come,
    B. as it is said, "your people also shall be all righteous, they shall inherit the land forever; the branch of my planting, the work of my hands, that I may be glorified" (Is. 60:21).

C. And these are the ones who have no portion in the world to come:
D. He who says, the resurrection of the dead is a teaching which does not derive from the Torah, and the Torah does not come from Heaven; and an Epicurean.
E. R. Aqiba says, "Also: He who reads in heretical books,
F. "and he who whispers over a wound and says, 'I will put none of the diseases upon you which I have put on the Egyptians, for I am the Lord who heals you' (Exod. 15:26)."
G. Abba Saul says, "Also: He who pronounces the divine Name as it is spelled out."

11:2
A. Three kings and four ordinary folk have no portion in the world to come.
B. Three kings: Jeroboam, Ahab, and Manasseh.
C. R. Judah says, "Manasseh has a portion in the world to come,
D. "since it is said, 'And he prayed to him and he was entreated of him and heard his supplication and brought him again to Jerusalem into his kingdom' (2 Chr. 33:13)."
E. They said to him, "To his kingdom he brought him back, but to the life of the world to come he did not bring him back."
F. Four ordinary folk: Balaam, Doeg, Ahitophel, and Gehazi.

No more severe sanction than losing one's portion in the world to come, which means, giving up life eternal beyond the grave, is imaginable. That is ample proof that Rabbinic Judaism fundamentally differed from Pagan tolerance, just as the Pentateuchal narrative and prophetic teaching insisted, God could not tolerate idolatry.

Stated more broadly: a particular set of words, acts, and arts certainly did define that Judaism, excluding a broad range of the other words, acts, and arts, that Jews beyond the limits of the circle of the master and disciple valued.[15] While in centuries to come, these artifacts of religious culture would pervade the everyday life of all Israel—Jews wherever they lived—in the formative age, the sources show, tension between sages and ordinary folk attested to the particularity of Rabbinic Judaism to its circles of masters and disciples. Its faith did not represent a common consensus, nor did its practices describe ordinary behavior. The way of life was learned, and the world-view the product of particular knowledge and

---

[15] For a contrary view, see Menachem Kellner, *Must a Jew Believe Anything?* (Littman Library of Jewish Civilization, 1999).

distinctive modes of thinking about and analyzing that knowledge. That is why, from the perspective of the sages and their disciples, no one was free to choose his own credo, and none could imagine ignoring the master of the Torah and his ruling. The books that portray this Judaism do not convey the portrait of variety but coherence, harmonies of rationality and uniformities of conduct in actuality. The Torah, Written as mediated by Oral, in its Halakhic embodiment, forms the counterpart to the Christian Church—law and narrative alike.

PLANTING CHRISTIAN TREES IN JEWISH SOIL[*]

Herbert W. Basser
Queen's University

PART I

Here we show how Matthew has done away with the Jewish messiah who is to redeem Israel from the Nations. In his place, he has provided a Christian messiah who is to redeem the disadvantaged and the gentiles from the Jewish leaders. This is the meaning he gives to the juxtaposition of Jesus' enthusiastic messianic procession into Jerusalem and his confrontations with the highest Jewish authorities as he enters the precincts of the city. The narrative is driven by Matthew's unique use of the term "Son of David." The Hallel Psalms (centered on Ps. 118:21), mentioning *yeshua* in the context of "salvation from foreign domination," are slightly colored by Matthew to present a thoroughly Christian model. The very term used by the Psalmist to beseech redemption from the nations—*hoshia na*—has been reworked to mean "Praise to the Son of David." Matthew uses this messianic title throughout his Gospel in scenes primarily meant to glorify Jesus over and against Jewish scholars and rulers. That having been said, we can stand utterly amazed that Matthew's literary forms, exegetical techniques, and methods of portrayal are thoroughly Jewish, thoroughly Rabbinic (if we can use that term), and thoroughly synagogual. That paradox stands at the center of Matthew 21.

Why does Matt. 21:9 identify the "one who comes" (Ps. 118:26) as the "Son of David," whereas no Gospel parallel gives this identification? My answer considers some other related conundrums. In the beginning of Jesus' entry into Jerusalem, Matt. 21:9, the crowd enthusiastically recites Ps. 118:26, "Blessed be the one who comes in the name of the Lord," while just a few chapters later in

---

[*] Reprinted from *Review of Rabbinic Judaism* 8, 2005, pp. 91–106. This article is based on two papers given at the Society of Biblical Literature Annual Meeting, San Antonio, Texas, November, 2004.

23:39 we read in surprise: "For I say to you, You will not see me from this time till you say, *Blessed be the one who comes in the name of the Lord.*" Furthermore, in Matt. 21:9 the crowds welcome Jesus, who appears to be well known, as he rides his messiah-charged animals to Jerusalem. But in the next verse, 29:10, we read, "And when he came into Jerusalem, all the town was moved, saying, Who is this?" The people in the Temple have no idea who he is until informed by the followers from the previous scene. We have two episodes viewed through an interstitiary forward movement of donkey canter, prayer cantor, then ahead backwards to old conflict scenes. Time is divided between now and future expectancy. The symbols here of reciting Psalm 118 and holding palm branches mark the ambiguity in the narrative and even in the ritual itself. Herein lies the Matthean view of sonship on either side of the threshold of the Kingdom. On one side are the Jewish verbs: people do Jewish things. On the other side are the Christian nouns: people experience Christian things. Let me deepen these motifs of chronological and eschatological time in terms of two other Jewish Temple celebrations. We will discover here how Matthew's understanding of the key scenes in chap. 21 are completely sensitive to Jewish hermeneutics.

Let us take note of Jewish rituals that look backward in order to look forward. The Passover seder rituals revolve around two poles. The first relates the Israelite experience of past slavery in Egypt. The second concerns the experience of Israel's future redemption from current persecutions. The Passover celebrates the past by anticipating the future. According to M. Pes. 10:5, the School of Shammai lumped together both of these motifs at the seder by reciting Ps. 114:1—"When Israel came out of Egypt, the children of Jacob from a people whose language was strange to them"—together with Psalm 118:26—"Blessed be the one who comes in the name of the Lord." The undivided recitation of these Psalms conflates the dual motifs. For the School of Shammai, the meal follows after the recitations and as such the paschal meal (sacrificial ritual) has messianic import. On the other hand, the School of Hillel interrupts the two halves of the Psalm recitations by the ritual Passover meal. The meal, and this is contemporary practice, simultaneously ends the Egyptian exodus suffering motif and begins the redemptive eschatology motif. The covenantal meal separating the two halves of the ceremony is the fulcrum of confluence of the themes.

An introduction (first known in writing, but apparently much older, from the *Seder of Amram Gaon*, ninth century) to the Passover *seder* is still current. This *ha-lachma anya* poem combines the two above themes: the deliverance from Egypt in the past and the future redemption in messianic times plus a mid-ritual sacrificial/feast demarcating both features: 1) Redemption from the affliction in Egypt, + 2) an invitation to partake of the Passover sacrificial/festival symbols, 3) a notice of impending redemption and return to Jerusalem. Liturgical notations, no matter the date of composition, often preserve the theological underpinnings of ancient ritual.

Another example: In the era of the Second Temple and later, holding date palm fronds expressed victory. We find palms on victory coins of the Hasmoneans. With these understandings in mind the ancient rabbis used their exegetical skills to describe the Palm-and-Psalm Sukkot ceremonies:

> Compare it to two who went before a judge. For a time, we cannot know the outcome . . . whoever emerges carrying date fronds in his hands then signals he is the victor. So it is with Israel and the nations as they pass before the Lord for judgment on the Day of Atonement: For a time, we do not know who is victorious. God told them to take palm fronds in their hands so all can know they were victorious in judgment. Thus did David say: "Then shall the trees of the wood sing for joy, before the Lord"—*when did this happen?*—"when He came to judge the earth *on* the Day of Atonement." (We note the interpolations into 1 Chron. 16:33.) So Israel waits another five days so all can know that Israel was victorious. For this reason is it written, "And you shall take for yourselves on the first day (Lev. 23:40)" (*Midrash Tanhuma* Emor 18; cf. Lev. Rabbah 30).

This is the Jewish understanding.

As for the Jewish sources, we can gain deep understanding from a late, medieval passage that situates the palm ritual with true insight. Isaac b. Moses of Vienna (thirteenth century) in his *Or Zarua*, vol. 2, *Sukka* 311, relates a well known tradition conflating Ps.118 and 1 Chr. 16. He considers it to explain a passage in the Jerusalem Talmud. He records:

> R. Samson son of Abraham [twelfth-thirteenth centuries] explained: Although the verse "We beseech Thee, O Lord, *hoshia na* [save us]! We beseech Thee" is neither the start nor finish of Psalm 118, we wave our species when we recites these words. This is because of the verse, "Then shall the trees of the wood sing for joy, before the Lord when He came to judge the earth." The verse is followed

> by the words, "O give praise to the Lord; for He is good; for His mercy endures for ever." And then by "And say ye: '*Save us*, O God of our salvation, [and gather us together and deliver us from the nations, that we may give praise unto Thy holy name, that we may triumph in Thy praise']" [1 Chr. 16:33]. This explains that the trees of the wood sing for joy by our shaking the lulav at every mention of "give praise" [Ps. 118]. For this reason do we glorify at [Ps. 118], "O give praise [to the Lord; for He is good; for His mercy endures for ever]" and [Ps. 118], "*hoshia [na]*—[save us]."

By process of metonymy, the shaking of the species during the fall celebration of Sukkot and the recitation of key phrases (glory and petition—the Rabbinic requirement for all prayer) are commonly referred to as performing "hoshanna." The day on which the ritual is performed seven times is called *Hoshanna Rabba*, i.e., *Many Hoshannas*. The word *hoshanna* as a noun is found sparingly in the Babylonian Talmud in reference to the plants used for the *hoshanna* rite and more in *Geonic* and later works in reference to specific rituals and hymns. The "hosanna" ritual combines the ideas of praising realized victories over the nations and sympathetic prayers for salvation. The mimesis of nature giving thanks as Israel supplicates for salvation makes the *hoshanna* ritual at once a celebration of an *unrealized* symbol and of the *realized* experience of an eschatological moment.

The antecedents for this kind of thinking are already found in much earlier pieces, one of which is cited by the medieval commentator. We note another early piece of evidence for palm rituals in the Second Temple era ritual of 1 Macc. 13:51. This source mentions the celebration of a finished victory in the Temple "with thanksgiving, and branches of palm trees, and with harps, and cymbals, and with viols, and hymns, and songs: because there was destroyed a great enemy out of Israel." What is missing here is the *hoshanna* request for future salvation. The motif of realized redemption is again highlighted in 2 Macc. 10:6-7:

> And they kept the eight days with gladness, as in the feast of the tabernacles, remembering that not long before they had held the feast of the tabernacles, when as they wandered in the mountains and dens like beasts. Therefore they carried branches, and fair boughs, and palms also, and sang psalms unto him that had given them good success in cleansing his place.

The medieval commentators see the meaning of *Sukkot hoshanna* victory motifs, past and future, within 1 Chronicles 16. It can be argued that this passage has always stood behind the understanding of waving palm branches as Ps. 118 was recited. Here we have a hymn reportedly sung when the liberated ark, the very throne of God, entered Jerusalem.

> [31] Let the heavens be glad, and let the earth rejoice; and let them say among the nations: "The Lord reigns." [32] Let the sea roar, and the fullness thereof; let the field exult, and all that is therein; [33] **Then shall the trees of the wood sing for joy, before the Lord, when He came to judge the earth**. [34] **O give praise to the Lord; for He is good; for His mercy endures for ever**. [35] And say ye: **"Save us, O God of our salvation,** and gather us together and *deliver us from the nations*, that **we may give praise unto Thy holy name, that we may triumph in Thy praise."** [36] Blessed be the Lord, the God of Israel, from everlasting even to everlasting. And all the people said: "Amen," and praised the Lord.

I have stressed the bold motifs here. The medieval commentators saw the passage as referring to Psalm 118 and its dual moments of *present* salvation ritual and *realized* eschatology. God is entering Jerusalem. The commentators took due notice that this hymn repeats verses already seen in Psalm 118 and as such gives the hymn both context and precise meaning.

I now want to discuss Jesus' entry into Jerusalem in the midrashic contexts of the Ark's coming to Jerusalem (where all the branches of the woods praised God) and Sukkot (where branches are waved when Psalm 118 mentions how God is praised.) The common motif in Jewish lore is Israel's victory over the nations, but there is no hint of this in the Gospels. In point of fact, I want to stress the interstitiary position of rituals acknowledging Jesus' realized messianic procession in Matthew. The passage is designed to presuppose the future eruption of the *eschaton*. The Palm-and-Psalm ritual marks the transition between the earthly ministry of Jesus and the future heavenly "redemption." The passage is not meant to occur in concrete time but in ritual time and as such it is the last public celebration of Jesus' messiahship as well as the future welcoming of Jesus in the realized *eschaton*. In this way the rituals retain their Jewish meaning, but Matthew alone shapes them in terms of Jesus' sonship. That sonship suggests the curing of the maimed and the ascendancy of the gentiles. The two most substantial cues of this break in real time have been mentioned. We noted that crowds surround Jesus and proclaim "blessed is he who comes" . . . but when he gets to Jerusalem and the scene shifts no one there knows who he is. Also, after the crowds have blessed him with branches and reciting

Psalm 118, Jesus tells his disciples they will not see him again until they will bless him with Psalm 118. These two oxymorons form the key to the entire messianic thrust of Matthew's Gospel.

What I propose is that Matthew has painted the scenarios of gradual fulfillment of prophetic signs in the pre-Easter world to lead to a sudden eruption in the appearance of the messiah in some as yet undefined reality in the post-Easter world. The Present-Now and the Invisible-Future merge and share the same stage in a moment of ritual. The records of Jewish Temple ritual and liturgy, albeit discussed in relatively late sources, show us the paradox of a realized future *eschaton* in the strangely enigmatic Psalm 118 Temple and Synagogue rituals of the now and present. The Matthean text melds these two modes together within the ritual of the crowd and the realized eschatology of the messiah-king-son's being escorted to Jerusalem. The scene is not unlike the midrashic understanding of how the Holy Ark, God's throne, had been escorted into Jerusalem. The Matthean script now follows through to the denouement. The recitation of Psalm 118 in Matthew 21 is the true end of the Gospel of Matthew even if it is not the chronological end. Matthew's Gospel lacks an ascension at the end. The end has already been addressed within the ritualized procession to the Temple.

Now that we have established the theological setting of the passages I want to examine the exegetical motifs buried deep within the texts—to be appreciated by those familiar with Jewish practice and tradition. So we examine Psalm 118, the central recitation Jewish tradition stipulates is to be accompanied by taking the species commanded in Lev. 23:40.

Psalm 118:

> [1] 'O give praise unto the Lord, for He is good, for His mercy endures for ever. . . . [21] I will give praise to You [!], for You answered me, and have become my salvation (*yeshua*). [22] The stone which the builders rejected is become the chief corner-stone. [23] This is the Lord's doing; it is marvelous in our eyes. [24] This is the day which the Lord has made; we will rejoice and be glad in it. [25] We beseech Thee, O Lord—*hoshia na*! Save us! We beseech Thee, O Lord, make us now to prosper! [26] *Blessed be the one who comes in the name of the Lord!*

We have now to parse the structure of the Psalm. Note that Ps. 118:21 ends in the word *yeshua* (= Jesus), allowing for the understanding of "I will give praise to you—Jesus." This is so since the end strophe [25] *Hoshia na*, again the Jesus root, is now able to be assimilated to

"I will give praise to you . . . i.e., Jesus, Savior." However, the form *Hoshanna*—used in the New Testament is known first in Jewish sources only from the Babylonian Talmud, where it refers to the willow branch and palm branches. Only in medieval literature do we find written evidence that Jews used the word to refer to hymns recited while the willow branches were carried around the synagogue. The ceremony was said to be in commemoration of Israelites' having carried them around the altar in the Temple while Psalm 118 was sung. In the Christian hymn, *Hoshanna* came to mean "give praise." Just as the parallel in Luke suggests. Where other Gospels read *Hosanna*, Luke reads "give glory." The use seems tied to the connection between—I will give praise . . . followed by *hoshia na (hoshanna)* in Psalm 118. The Gospels confirm the early usage of what emerges in later Jewish literature, but it is uncertain and unlikely that *Hoshann*a ever literally meant "give glory." Nevertheless, my point here stands: Jewish sources allow for the fullest appreciation of the Gospel passage.

With Psalm 118 in mind I want to progress to the subject matter at hand, the detailed understanding of the hymns accompanying Jesus' entry into Jerusalem. Matthew and Mark are framed as scriptured liturgy. They provide a hymn that begins with "Hosanna" and ends with "*Hosanna* in the highest." Here we have a typical poetic form. In Hebraic poetry of the Bible we find formal parallelisms in which the final parallel repetition expands, if even slightly, the initial thought. Thus Matthew and Mark appear as complete liturgical hymns. Luke, lacking the parallel, seems to suggest the crowds recited a part of some larger piece and either has a translation for *Hosanna* or a substitute. In all cases in the center of the hymnic frame is a rendition of Ps. 118:22.

So now we proceed to our analysis of the Gospel traditions surrounding Psalm 118 and its Jewish settings and rituals. Matthew identifies the "one who comes" before that verse is said, John does it after the verse. Luke and Mark embed the identification within the recital.

Matthew 21

8 The great crowd spread their own cloaks on the road, and others cut branches from the trees and spread them on the road.

9 And those who went before him, and those who came after, gave loud cries, saying,

Hosanna
to the Son of David:
Blessed be the one who comes in the name of the Lord:
Hosanna in the highest.

In passing, we take stock that Mark and Matthew say the crowd spread both clothes and branches for Jesus, while Luke knows only of spreading clothing. John has them holding branches. The Gospels share and differ in their accounts here and the history of transmission seems complex. It is also curious that Matthew mentions the words ". . . to the Son of David" here. *Hosanna* means "save [us], we beseech you" and is never found with "to," except in Matthew. "*Hosanna* in the highest," means "We beseech You to save us—who are in the highest. Matthew might not know what it means and may have inserted "to" believing "Hosanna" means "Give Glory to." We note Luke actually says "Give Glory" but we cannot speculate on the relationship here, if any, between the two Gospels. At any rate, this novel construction completely changes the meaning of *Hosanna* and, with it, the character of the expected Redeemer. In 21:15 he writes that "the chief priests and the scribes saw the wonders he did, and the children crying out in the Temple, '*Hosanna* to the *Son of David*!' and they became indignant." The usage is unmistakable. The children carry the Hosanna praise of the Messianic Procession scene into the Temple scene. Out of the mouth of babes the Christian healer momentarily gallops over the Priestly Redeemer. This is the last time that the words "Son of David" will be used in Matthew. At this point, *hosanna* has lost its primary messianic sense—a prayer for redemption from the Nations and their tyranny. It has now become the word of glory to welcome the Christian Messiah. And so Matt. 21:42-45 sums up Matthew's transformation of the Hallel Psalm, Psalm 118:

> Jesus says to them, Did you never see in the Writings, "The stone which the builders put on one side, the same has been made the chief stone of the building: this was the Lord's doing, and it is a wonder in our eyes." (Ps. 118:22)? For this reason I say to you, *The kingdom of God will be taken away from you, and will be given to a nation producing the fruits of it.* Any man falling on this stone will be broken, but he on whom it comes down will be crushed to dust.
>
> And when his stories came to the ears of the chief priests and the Pharisees, they saw that he was talking of them.

"Son of David" in Matthew 21 means "Universal Messiah" as it does elsewhere in Matthew when children, the disabled, and gentiles address Jesus by this term. If Universal Messiah, most likely the followers are sympathetic gentiles or marginal Jews, and the Jerusalemites are established, hostile Jews. This fits well with the Post-Easter Jesus of Matthew—make disciples of all the nations (Matt. 28:19-20 might be best rendered as Zaas suggested in an unpublished translation: "So go and teach all the gentiles, immersing them in the name of the father and the son and the holy spirit. Instructing them to keep everything I commanded you. Look, I am with you each day, until the end of the age.") The centrality of the designation "Messiah son of David" is plainly anticipated in Matt. 1:1: *The book of the birth of Jesus the Messiah, the son of David, the son of Abraham.* This line is the main genealogy, and the continuing paragraph in Matthew acts as commentary to unpack its details. This is a standard form of teaching in the Mishnah, Talmud and midrash. Concise teaching followed by detailed commentary can be seen later in this paper in the midrash of Lev. Rabbah 30:16.

John 12 renders close to the Lucan form: (12:1: Then, six days before the Passover, Jesus came to Bethany where Lazarus was, whom Jesus had made to come back from the dead . . . . 12:12: The day after, a great number of people who were there for the feast, when they had the news that Jesus was coming to Jerusalem); 12:13: Took branches of palm-trees and went out to him, crying *Blessed is the one who comes in the name of the Lord,* **the King of Israel**!

This accords somewhat with the version of Luke 19:

> 36 And while he went on his way they put their clothing down on the road in front of him.
>
> 37 And when he came near the foot of the Mountain of Olives, all the disciples with loud voices gave praise to God with joy, because of all the great works which they had seen;
>
> 38 Saying, *Blessed* **be the King** *who comes in the name of the Lord;*— peace in heaven and
>
> **glory** [peshitta: *we-shubha*, i.e., the *shevach*—sometimes a term with mystical connotations referring to God's *shekina*] **in the highest**.

For the sake of completeness let us note the treatment of the passage in Mark 11:

> 8 And a great number put down their clothing in the way; and others put down branches which they had taken from the fields.
>
> 9 And those who went in front, and those who came after, were crying out,
> **Hosanna**:
> *Blessed be the one* **who comes** *in the name of the Lord:*
> 10 *Blessed be the coming* **kingdom of our father David**:
> **Hosanna in the highest.**

That is to say that Mark is *targumic* or *pesharic* because his version cites Ps. 118:22 verbatim and follows it with the identification of the subject as the *kingdom of our father David*.

There is a further possibility. The other Gospels identify the reference in Ps. 118:9 as "King," "Davidic Kingdom," or "King of Israel," which have the best scriptural warrant. The Gospel texts themselves supply the prooftexts, for note Matt. 21:5 or Luke 19:14-15: "And Jesus saw a young ass and took his seat on it; as the Scriptures say, Have no fear, daughter of Zion: see your *King* is coming, seated on a young ass." The reference is to Zech. 9:9, "Be full of joy, O daughter of Zion; give a glad cry, O daughter of Jerusalem: see, *your king* comes to you: he is upright and has overcome; gentle and seated on an ass, on a young ass." The stated allusion is explicitly "your king." We will have to wonder why Matthew here rejects the wording suggested by his own reference to Zechariah, and we will find that Jewish sources make the same identification of the king in Zech. 9:9: Son of David.

In the Temple, if we can read our Jewish sources without regard to time frames, Hosanna hymns were recited on Sukkot, in the Fall, while holding the items commanded by Lev. 23:40. John 12:13 explicitly refers to the palm branches. The word *Hoshanna* ["O' save us"] in Ps. 118:25 came to refer to the shaking of the palm and willow branches. They were reportedly held in the hand together with myrtle branches and a citron fruit while Ps. 118:25 was sung in the Temple. The symbolism of the Sukkot species and the hymns woven about them continue to excite the poetics of Jewish ritual to the present day and a massive collection of Hosanna hymns has been preserved. The precise festival day is of no import in my view as the Jesus Entrance Procession is removed from real time narrative and reflects a distant future when the messiah will arrive in Jerusalem. The last arrival of Jesus at the Temple is the best location for the scene, whatever day it happens to be. The Passover setting is not relevant to the Entrance scene—but it is relevant to the Last Supper scene.

If the temporal setting is not relevant, Luke 19:37-38 provides the physical setting for the hymns.

> As he was now drawing near, at the descent of the Mount of Olives, the whole multitude of the disciples began to rejoice and praise God with a loud voice for all the mighty works that they had seen,— saying, "Blessed—IS THE KING—who comes in the name of the Lord!—Peace in heaven and glory in the highest!"

The post-talmudic Geonim record a tradition that on the seventh day of Sukkot the Mount of Olives was encircled by throngs holding palm branches (likely in reference to the messianic theme of Zech. 14:4). *Sefer Hasidim* (thirteenth century) chap. 630 cites Hai Gaon to the effect that after the destruction of the Temple's altar, pious Jews moved their encirclements to the Mount of Olives on *Hoshanna Rabbah*. These late traditions are given credence by the words of Luke. For Luke, as for all, the scene is out of sequence and is likely a moment from future time in a post-70 world that Jesus had never seen. When Jesus arrives in Jerusalem real time begins to move again.

We need not dismiss later sources as devoid of value to shed light on early layers of tradition. To do so would mean that the Gospels have absolutely nothing credible to say about the existence of Jesus, as they all date to times later than his alleged crucifixion. In short, it is useful to take stock that medieval and talmudic era Jews found messianic allusions in the branch and other species used that day. A medieval poem still recited on Sukkot talks about the Good News that the voice of David, God's beloved, announces at the arrival of the messianic era and alludes to Zech. 3:8: "A man has branched, Branch is his name; he is David."

Zech. 6:12 has been used to good effect: "Thus says the Lord of hosts, 'Behold, the man whose name is 'the Branch:' for he shall grow up in his place, and he shall build the Temple of the Lord." Zech. 3:8 also shows us how messianic imagery operated metaphorically as a "branch." "Hear now, O Joshua the high priest, you and your friends who sit before you, for they are men of good omen: behold, I will bring my servant the Branch." In earlier texts we also find full blown messianic allusions attributed the commandment to celebrate the Feast of Sukkot.

Lev. Rabbah 30:16 specifies some messianic themes in the branch rituals required by Lev. 23:40.

> Said R. Berekhiah in the name of R. Levi: In the merit of your fulfilling the commandment to take the palm branch (and the other items) ON THE FIRST DAY . . . Lo, I will appear to you FIRST of all, I will punish your FIRST enemy, I will build for you the FIRST, and I will bring you a FIRST.

The midrashist unpacks this pithy statement in its several assertions and reveals its scriptural underpinnings.

> "*Lo I will appear*" . . . *I will build for you the first*—this "first" means the Temple. It says so in Jeremiah, "The throne of glory is on high, from the *first*, the place of our Temple" (Jer. 17:12). [According to the Targum of Jer. 17:12: punishments will come from God on his throne of glory in the highest heavens from *first*—the place of the house of our Temple.] "*And I will bring you a first*" this "first" means the Messiah. As it says in Isaiah 41:27: "The *first* in Zion behold, behold them, and to Jerusalem I have given a harbinger of good news."

In conclusion, the simple answer why Matt. 21:26 calls Jesus "Son of David" (which no other Gospel does) is because the "King" Matthew mentions in Zech. 9:9 was usually identified as the messiah, David's son. *Tanhuma Vayishlach* s. 1 has no problem in so describing the king in Zech. 9:9. The ancient rabbis readily identify him as Messiah son of David.

> [The one riding on the] "ass" refers to the Messiah, Son of David, as it says: [see, your king comes to you: he is upright and has overcome;] gentle and seated on an ass (Zech. 9:9).

Why should Matthew not have used the same identification of the "king"? The very early common Gospel traditions related Zech. 9—King—and Ps. 118—the one who comes. Accordingly, he is the king, he is the Messiah, he is the Son of David. That the word for "salvation" also happened to be Jesus' name, *Yeshua*, and occupies a key phrase in Ps. 118:21 only clinches the chain of identities. It more than clinches them. It is likely responsible for the entire scene. As such, the art of the Gospels blends the ephemeral ritual and the Christian story into a unit of both biblical imagery and Christian imagination. That Matthew is able to draw on this to allow for the suggestion that, at the last, it will be the gentiles who accept Jesus, and it will be the Jews who ignore him. The gentiles who bless the Son of David are the ones who are blessed. In this moment lies the tension of the ritual pageantry. A glimpse of messiahship over-strewn with the branches and baggage of Jewish hymns and rituals. The scene embodies the salvation history of Israel with the experience of something else, perhaps the glory of non-Israel, glimmering through its leaves. It is possible that in the most Jewishly painted scene of welcoming the Messiah, the King turns out to be the Christian Son of David—the Messiah of the gentile and disadvantaged. After Matthew 21 we will not encounter the term Son of David again. Here are some key usages of "Son of David" in Matthew:

> 9:27: When Jesus passed by from there, two blind people followed, calling out and saying, "Have mercy on us, *Son of David!*"
>
> 12:22-23: Then there was carried to him a blind and mute person possessed by a demon and he healed him, so that the mute person could speak and see. And all the crowds were beside themselves, and said, "Surely, this one could not be the *Son of David?*"
>
> 15:22: Look, a Canaanite woman from those regions came out and shouted, "Have mercy on me, Lord, *Son of David!* My daughter is cruelly possessed by a demon."
>
> 20:30-34: And look, two blind men sitting by the road heard that Jesus as coming by, and cried out, "Have mercy on us, Lord, *Son of David!*" The crowd rebuked them so that they would be quiet, but they cried out louder, "Show mercy on us, Lord, *Son of David.*" Jesus stood and called them: "What do you wish me to do?" They said to him, "Lord, let our eyes be opened." Feeling compassion, Jesus touched their eyes, and right away they saw again, and followed him.

For Jews, the Son of David was to come to redeem Israel from the tyranny of the Roman oppressor, while for Matthew he came to cure the infirm and support the faith of the gentiles. Matthew allows that Jesus, during his ministry, foreshadowed his future role as Son of David—what that future itself would be is never fully revealed by the author of the First Gospel. It is only intimated by the realized coronation of the Son of David in mythic time fading back into conflict with Jewish authorities in Gospel time. And in the end, it will not be the Ark of the Covenant that the throng welcomes at the Close of the Age. For in David's son's resurrection Matthew hears, "All authority in heaven and on earth has been given to me." Indeed, Jesus has replaced the Jewish Messiah, the Jewish Son of David. And Matthew, above all others, can find the subtle shifts of meaning and complex hermeneutics of authentic Jewish tradition with which to anoint his Messiah. In the final analysis, he has misappropriated the Jewish Scriptures, Jewish tradition, Jewish liturgy, Jewish ritual, and the Jewish Messiah and in so doing has created another Scripture, another tradition, another liturgy, another ritual, and another Messiah. Whatever atonement motifs may or may not be present in Matthew, they do not form part of his Messianic picture. Matthew's messiah speaks to a particular community that has revamped genuinely Jewish narratives to create their own Messianic religion.

In sum, the rituals of branches and Hallel psalms mark the entry of the risen Christ in mythic time, not in real time. The Jewish ceremony of palm waving on Sukkot is given Christian meaning. Likely Zech. 9:16 serves as a referent: ("All those nations will make a pilgrimage to Jerusalem to bow low to God and to celebrate Sukkot"). But the Gospel day need not be Sukkot since it is in mythic time The followers are gentiles who recognize Jesus as their savior—the Jews in Jerusalem, as the narrative unfolds in real time, have no idea who Jesus is. Matthew's use of "son of David" reinforces the identification of those who follow him in ritual time (a flash of those who will follow him in future, real time)—gentile worshippers who are on the threshold of redemption from the religion and people of high priests and Pharisees. The ambiguity of Jewish rituals marking a mixture of past redemption and hope for the future is maintained in the passage which combines the Passover and Sukkot Jewish eschatological rituals (activity) with Christian faith (object).

Appendix
Ps. 118:22: Do Early Sources Reincarnate in Later Ones?

It is quite simple to see Matthew's startling exegesis of Ps. 118:22: "The stone [Heb., *even*] which the builders [Heb., *habonim*] rejected was to be the head stone of the corner." The stone refers to the gentile nations in Matt. 21:42, but to Jesus in Mark 12:10, Luke 20:17, Acts 4:11, Eph. 2:20, and 1 Peter 2:7. The obvious reference in the Psalms is the nation of Israel. Neither the New Testament nor the Targum follow the obvious.

The Rabbinic Targum gives us:

> The child [= *talia*] the craftsmen [= *ardikhlayia*] rejected—he was the son among the sons of Jesse and merited to be selected for ruling and governing.

The base of this paraphrased interpretation of the nouns is led by the verbs [*rejected, was, to be*] in Scripture that are rendered literally in this Targum. This brings us to the dream interpretation style of Joseph in Genesis and the kindred *pesher* style of Qumran biblical exegesis. In full form, the ancient interpreters would have said about our verse: "the stone the builders rejected," its interpretation refers to the child of Jesse whom the superintendents refused and he was chosen to be king.

So while perhaps Targum Psalms as a whole is late, maybe even as late as the seventh century, much of the structure, method, and content is arguably ancient. First, Matt. 27:46 gives the Aramaic form of Ps. 22:2, the last utterance of Jesus upon the Cross that has a very slight variance with our Targum, "*lama shabaktani*" compared to, "*metul ma shabaktani*" and Eph. 4:8 cites Ps. 68:19 closer to our Targum: "giving presents" versus Masoretic text's "taking presents." There are other indications of an early base as well to the Targum of Psalms. And quite surprisingly, we have an Aramaic version of Ps. 20:2-6 that was written in Demotic (Egyptian) characters in pre-Chrtistian times.[1] Suffice it to say that it seems likely that our late Targum of Psalms rests on much early material. So the rendition of Matt. 21:42-43 shows us Christian exegesis in the extreme.

> Jesus says to them, Did you never see in the Writings, "The stone which the builders put on one side, the same has been made the chief stone of the building: this was the Lord's doing, and it is a wonder in our eyes" (Ps. 118:22)? For this reason I say to you, *The kingdom of God will be taken away from you, and will be given to a nation producing the fruits of it.*

---

[1] See Charles F. Nims and Richard C. Steiner, "A Paganized Version of Ps. 20:2-6 from the Aramaic Text in Demotic Script," in *Journal of the American Oriental Society* 103 (January-March 1983), pp. 261–274.

PART II

Jewish Rabbinic literature and the New Testament can use the very same ancient, original material to their own purposes. This is true not only of the use of Written Scripture but also of Oral Torah as I shall demonstrate here. Like Judaism and Christianity themselves, these works developed out of a common, earlier, religious matrix and eventually each one went its own, separate direction. I am leaving the issue of dating Jewish texts aside because even when it is clear that materials are patently late, it has happened that a chance discovery shows the materials to be a hundred years earlier, even a thousand years earlier, than had been posited by leading scholars.

Professor Himmelfarb[2] wrote a lengthy refutation of Albeck's "naïve" claims. She insisted that the rabbis had simply adopted the Greek version of the popular document that had been preserved by Christians. Twelve years later, Professor Michael Stone in *Dead Sea Discoveries* volume 3 demonstrated that Moses haDarshan's text closely copied the Qumran text rather than the Greek version. Albeck, in 1939, had been right, Himmelfarb, in 1984, wrong. Indeed, the first century writer, Josephus, records many, many laws that accord with much later rulings given in the literature of the rabbis (2nd c. to 6th c.).[3] Let us drop date and geography and look at the materials themselves.

At the same time, I should like to say, *en passant*, I fall on the side of a minority of scholars in seeing Matthew as a gentile Christian, (or, at most, a self-hating Jew),[4] and whatever genuinely Jewish exegetical traditions survive in Matthew comes from sources apart from the author of that Gospel.

We will show the appropriateness of using some Rabbinic declarations to assess some Jesus sayings. Where two documents share common images and common language and share the same past,

---

[2] "R. Moses the Preacher and the Testaments of the Twelve Patriarchs," in *Association of Jewish Studies Review* 9 (1984), pp. 55–78.

[3] See the listings in Louis H. Feldman and Gohei Hata, eds., *Josephus, Judaism, and Christianity* . . . (Leiden, 1987), pp. 37–40.

[4] See William David Davies and Dale C. Allison's discussion of the various views of Jesus: Jew or Gentile, in *Matthew 1-7: A Critical and Exegetical Commentary on the Gospel according to Saint Matthew* (ICC Critical Commentary Series; London, 2004), pp. 7–30. They argue against those who see Matthew as a Gentile. See the listings in Feldman and Hata.

we can try to understand the meaning of passing references in the one by examining the fuller references in the other. Of course, every saying depends on its immediate context for accurate meaning, and since the contexts of New Testament and Rabbinic literature are very far from each other, the functional meanings cannot be the same. Nevertheless, the precision of the idiom will function the same, the rhetoric and interlocking of the images will be fixed and run the same directions. The technical instruments are the same and the melody will be similar, the meaning of the whole in which it is encased will impose different senses in the different literatures. The antiquity and continuity of Rabbinic modes of thought are to be appreciated and validated by the study of New Testament. We have now to make our case.

We find in Babylonian talmudic passages (B. Ket. 8a, B. Ber. 61a, B. Erub. 18a) a vague teaching concerning God's creation of humankind: "At the beginning God created (them male and female) with the intention they be two but in the end he (Adam) was only created to be one."[5] In the case of the creation of males and females Scripture explicitly attests to such a creation, and it is not clear if the text implies some unfilled intention or just temporary situation. Whatever the case, the major evidence for the wording of our text, whatever it may mean, derives from a tradition recited variously as that of Abbahu or Judah who lived centuries after the New Testament authors. The talmudic homily wants to reconcile verses in which it seems on the one hand that God created *two* humans, both male and female together, and on the other hand it seems he created just *one* human. The resolution: "At the beginning God created them with the intention they be two, but in the end only one was created." But what on earth can this mean? The solution to this problem is the basic thrust of this paper. I claim that both New Testament and the Rabbis wrestled to make sense of these very ancient words.

The preservation of this lesson in the Talmuds is rather poor and the cited biblical verses vary, according to which source is consulted.

---

[5] The words "with the intention they be" likely should be bracketed since they seem to be have been influenced in a very early stage of transmission by another ancient text, poorly preserved in Midrash Aggadah Buber 1:1 and alluded to in Gen. Rabbah 12:15: "At the beginning God created [the world] *with the intention it be* by the power of justice."

It stands to reason that there was an original teaching which was popularly transmitted until the precise references were in doubt. The point was to isolate verses, and parts of verses, that apparently contradict each other. Gen. 1:27, Gen. 5:2-3, and Gen. 9:6 are all candidates respectively. "So God created man in his own image, in the image of God He created *him*, male and female he created them." "When God created man, he made him in the likeness of God; male and female he created *them*." "For God made *man* in his own image." While the Talmuds are not certain which verses prompted the original question, they agree on the answer: "At the beginning God created *them* with the intention they be *two* but in the end only *one* was created." Some later rabbis speculated what this tradition meant, "how were there *two* which became *one*?" No talmudic tractate provides a simple, satisfactory explanation of this homily. Exactly how the exchanges of arguments proceed in the various tractates that cite our passage cannot be easily uncovered, and every commentator pushes things in different directions.

I suggest we recognise that the second Temple origin of this enigmatic passage can be recovered from the Gospels, albeit with some minor uncertainties. Here then are the passages I wish to compare:

Bavli Ketubot 8a
R. Judah raised this problem: It is written *(i.e., in Scripture)*, And God made **Adam** in his own image, and it is written, **Male and female he made them**. How is this [to be understood]? [In this way:] **In the beginning** it was the intention [of God] to make **two** [human beings: male and female], and **in the end [only] one [human being] was made**.

Matthew 19
The Pharisees also came to him, testing him, and saying to him, Is it lawful for a man to divorce his wife for any cause? 4: And he answered and said to them:
   Have you not read *(i.e., in Scripture)* that **he who made** [hoti/ho poiēsas/var. ho ktisas/ap arxes but seems the object missing,—"him," i.e. Adam? In Mark 10:6 rephrased as "beginning of the creation"], **from the beginning** [*min avala?*= In the beginning (Targ Ps. Jon. 1:1)] **male and female he made them**? (Gen 1:27), 5: And said, **Therefore, shall a man leave his father and mother, and shall cleave to his wife: and they—two—shall become one flesh** (Gen. 2:24)!
   6 In this way, they are **no more two, but one flesh**.
   What God has joined together let not man put asunder.

Suggested explication: Matt. 19:4 asks a question about Gen. 1:27: "he made **him;** male and female he made **them,**" so did he make one or two beings? Vs. 5 answers based on another verse: when two are married they become one. Vs. 6 appears to rephrase the answer in terms of some missing or assumed line that must have contained the words "first two then one" and left us wondering how are the two one? By saying, "In this way," the Jesus figure indicates he has solved this puzzle. And his way was to interpolate for emphasis the key words "from the beginning" into Gen. 1:27. LXX already has the key word "two" in its version of Gen. 2:24. "In this way" we can explain how at first there were two who are destined at a later point to become one. Note how this solution follows the Rabbinic rule: two scriptures will contradict each other only until a third comes and reconciles them (see reference below).

Let us now try to analyse the Gospel passage in detail. In Matt. 19:3-9 (and Mark 10:2-12), Jesus claims that God abhors divorce but Moses was forced to make a concession and permit it because of human shortcomings. How do we know God abhors divorce? Jesus begins with a story that has holes in it that we will fill in. "From the beginning God made them male and female." "For this reason shall a man leave his father and mother and cleave to his wife and they shall be one flesh" (Gen. 2:24). And now Jesus concludes. "So they are no longer *two* but *one*." This solves the problem of conflicting Scriptures and he adds triumphantly, "What God has joined together let not man put asunder."

Close reading shows us how pieces of this passage are somewhat fragmentary and require explanation. The components of the passage suggest Jesus is building on an intricate interpretation of Scripture. Why is the text in Matthew so choppy: Have you not read that he who made [?—him? them?] from the beginning male and female he made them? Early copyists, perhaps Matthew, seem to have mistaken the point of the retort. The syntax requires some kind of object to the verb "made." Instead of inserting "them" as most translators do, we do better to insert "him." When Jesus says "God made them male and female" he appears to refer to some verse like Gen. 1:27, or Gen. 5:2 which tells us that God created ONE male but also TWO sexes. Jesus next cites a verse stipulating a coming together of male and female and he concludes the TWO sexes are to become ONE, (and this matches LXX to Gen. 2:24) inseparably one. "So they are no longer TWO but ONE." Why does he say this—to what end? When we compare this to the above Rabbinic passage we are led to suspect the Gospel knew of an interpretation dealing with the conflict in verses in Genesis (man created first in one place, male and female created together in another). And this interpretation was stated in some kind of riddle form, "first two then one." The Gospel seems to respond to this cryptic form and provide a solution to it by adding a third verse to the mix. "For this reason shall a man leave his father and mother and cleave to his wife and they shall be ONE flesh" (Gen. 2:24). We find here an early example of the hermeneutic rule of "Where two verses contradict each other a third will come to reconcile the matter" (Mekhilta Rabbi Yishmael end of *Jethro*, and Sifre Numbers, end of *Naso*). "Male and female he created them" versus "He created him" reconciled by "He shall cleave to his wife and be one flesh." And hence follows the conclusion that claims to have solved the riddle of the Talmudic passage: "So they are no longer two but one."

Having given us his developed sermon with the traditional ending common to both the rabbis and the Gospels, Jesus represents the midrash with its interpretation to make his final point: What God has joined together, let not man put asunder!" He dwells on the solution that God ordained that a man shall be joined to, or cleave to, his wife to draw the lesson that no human should annul this sacred, divine decree. In the first instance God made them male and female but at the end this is no longer the case, they are now one and so, he adds, divorce is not an option. The solution of Matthew's source shows great acumen and credibility to solve the conflict in scriptures. The retort about marriage being eternal is good rhetoric but not compelling. His interlocutors would surely be impressed with the solution to a pharisaic puzzle of early vintage but not necessarily by his conclusion. Yet, they can hardly argue against the faultless commentary to the enigmatic "first two and then one" (and may be based on the LXX reading of Gen. 2:24) that has long perplexed students of Pharisaic teachings.

So, it is the very form of the Gospel homily that suggests we have before us an allusion to a popular, fuller teaching of Pharisees. Jesus, we argue, is pictured as reconstructing a well-known sermon in order to serve his purpose that no one may dissolve a marriage. Both Jesus and the rabbis offer an interpretation to an older puzzle. What did the preacher mean when he said: "at first two then one." Jesus uses his biblical lesson of "first TWO then ONE" to preach against divorce. The Talmud uses it to discuss the need for duplicate blessings at the Jewish Wedding or to discuss if Adam was created with an extra rib or as hybrid male-female. In either case, Eve would be severed from him.

To sum up: On what basis do I make the claim that the New Testament and Talmudic passages complete each other? Since all Jesus wanted to say in the first place was that God decreed marriage why does he dwell on the whole story of God's creating people male and female? He might have just cited the verse that God ordained a man to be joined to his wife. If we look closely at the New Testament passages we will see that there is a definite homily built on the biblical story about the two sexes: namely, that *two* have become *one*. He refers us to Genesis' teaching that male and female are ordained to be one flesh. He ends this solution to an ancient homily with an encouraging flourish, asking his audience to fulfil the divine will by resisting the compromise of divorce. No teacher in extant Rabbinic sources ever used this particular rhetorical feature to forbid divorce, although some rabbis (M. Git. 9:10), like Jesus, did forbid divorce where there was no infidelity. It is not the message that concerns us here but the medium. The passage is best seen as a solution to the meaning of B. Ket. 8a and other talmudic sources. The various twists in the talmudic lessons suggest that the inherited tradition was so ambiguous and amorphous it could serve purposes at hand even if the sense varied from context to context. There was no fixed meaning to the piece.

What was the actual meaning of the ancient midrash? We do not know. It is a fact the Gospels interpret the context of the lesson in light of biblical passages describing the consequence of Eve's creation from Adam's body (Adam seeking to join to "the flesh of his flesh and the bone of his bone") and it is a fact the later rabbis interpret the midrash, however awkwardly, in terms of the separation of Eve from Adam in some fashion or other. It is likely therefore that the original midrash had something to do with the story of the creation of Eve from Adam, but beyond this we cannot know for certain. The solution of Jesus nicely portrays the idea that *two* are made into *one*. The solution of the rabbis nicely deals with the words of dual creations—"He made." The Gospel omits any mention of God's creating something to be one, but explains well how a teacher could have taught: at Creation's end male and female were to be "no longer *two* but *one*." In balance, the Gospel form is illuminated by the Rabbinic midrash but the midrash itself is greatly enhanced by the realization that the Gospels might indeed preserve the original intent of the teaching by introducing Gen. 2:24.

Students of midrash might well ponder the Christian version of the antique midrash as holding the key to the original intent of an early scribal teaching, although they will doubt it was ever used as an argument against divorce. The rabbis cite the same midrash to very different ends in their discussions. Both codifications, Jewish and Christian, can use the original material to their own purposes. Like Judaism and Christianity themselves, these teachings developed out of a common, earlier religious matrix where eventually each one went its own, separate direction. As for us students of the history of midrash, how fortunate to have documents that can help us retrieve early forms of what perplexes us. We also see that rabbis did not invent their lore but built on early foundations. By merging Jewish and Christian textual studies New Testament scholars gain access to fill in what is alluded to but not explicit in various Gospel texts; Rabbinic scholars gain an appreciation into the antiquity of some talmudic texts and their earlier forms.

For the sake of completeness, I add here that in my opinion and that of most others, the Damascus Document (CD 4.20-21) does not at all proscribe divorce as do Matt. 19:6 and Mark 10:9. CD 4.20-21 states: "In unchasity (we include) taking two wives in their lives, while the foundation of creation is 'Male and female he created them' (Gen. 1:27)." The issue in the text is not divorce; possibly, but not likely, it is remarriage (and so might possibly relate to Matt. 5:32). Most scholars today see the reference to be solely polygamy and even irrelevant to the issue of remarriage.[6] The connections between Rabbinic literature and Gospels are much greater than the connections between Qumran literature and either of the others.

---

[6] See D. Harrington, "Jesus and the Dead Sea Scrolls," in Doris Donnely, ed., *Jesus. A Colloquium in the Holy Land*; with James D.G. Dunn, et al. (Continuum, 2001), p. 27–44.

RABBINIC TEXTS IN THE EXEGESIS OF THE NEW TESTAMENT[*]

Miguel Pérez Fernández
University of Granada

I. *Re-Encounter of Jewish and Christian Exegesis*

Current research reveals a renewed appraisal of Jesus' Jewish environment and background (J. Jeremias, M. Smith, D. Flusser, G. Vermes, E.P. Sanders, J. Neusner, etc.), under the simultaneous influence of two reciprocal trends: on one side, Judaism's sincere, almost passionate—and partly non-critical—interest in recovering Jesus for their people (Jesus' re-Hebrewization); and, on the other side, the sincere and cordial interest of Christians in Judaism. Qumranic discoveries, the renewed study of Apocrypha, and the growth of Targumic studies have undoubtedly contributed to this situation. The vision of the Judaism in which Jesus lived has changed in recent years: it is not only that of orthodox Judaism bound to rules, but also Essene, apocalyptic, and Samaritan Judaism, as well as the singular Judaism of the Galileans and that of the diaspora. The *criterion of difference* thus remains uncertain: different from who or what? Jesus is more plausibly conceived within the context of Judaism's internal movements of renewal, and on the basis of prophetic, apocalyptic, and sapient biblical tradition.

The deformed vision of Jesus of some Talmudic texts and medieval compilations[1] remains quite distant. The Jewish sympathetic feeling

---

[*] Reprinted from *Review of Rabbinic Judaism* 7, 2004, pp. 95–120. Translated and revised by the author from a paper presented in September, 2003, at a meeting of the *Asociación Bíblica Española*. The Spanish version has been published in *Estudios Bíblicos*.

[1] Regarding the medieval work *Toledot Jesu*, see J. Klausner, *Jesus of Nazareth. His Life, His Times, and His Teaching* (New York, 1989), pp. 47–54. In Rabbinic literature, Jesus is known as Jesus the Nazarene: B. Sot. 47a, A.Z. 47a, San. 43a, 103a, 107b (cf. A.Z. 6a and Ta. 27b: "the day of the Nazarene"). Some texts follow a tale of Jesus ben Pandera/Panther, referring to Jesus himself: T. Hul. 2:22-24 (parallels in B. A.Z. 27b and Y. Shab. 14d, Y. A.Z. 40d-41a). In other texts, the name is Ben Stada, which, if it is a different character at the beginning, in the end is seen as Jesus: T. Shab. 11:15, B. Shab. 104b, T. San. 10:11 and B. San. 67a. There might be

of modern times towards Jesus is very well reflected in the art of Jewish painter Marc Chagall, where a crucified Jesus appears as a rabbi—with phylacteries and tallit—in representation of the thousands imprisoned in concentration camps.²

II. *Opposing a Seminar of Jewish and Christian Researchers*

In the framework of the congeniality among Jewish and Christian researchers, we come to question the use of Rabbinic texts in the exegesis of the New Testament. Two aspects are to be considered: whether these texts may be used at all and, if so, which methodology should be applied.

In addressing these issues, I refer to a work jointly published last year by Jews and Christians: Bruce Chilton, Craig A. Evans, and Jacob Neusner, *The Missing Jesus. Rabbinic Judaism and the New Testament* (Boston

---

other references to Jesus behind the name of Balaam (M. San. 10:2 and M. Ab. 5:19; but cf. B. Git. 56b-57a and Yalqut Shimoni to Num. 23:7), Heretic (Y. San. 25d), and Bastard (M. Yeb. 4:13). Closely examined, these texts (the most explicit ones are not found in printed editions of the Talmud due to censorship) prove to be late, legendary, confusing, and of no historical value. They are only useful to know as Evangelic traditions, which were not learned directly; they have mingled with legends yielding outrageous stories, and as Jesus' image in Jewish contexts progressively deteriorated, from the Mishnah to clearly medieval texts (the best studies on these texts are by Herford, Krauss, Lauterbach, and Klausner). In these documents, Jesus appears as a bastard (child of an illegitimate union), a heretic who practices magic and idolatrous cult, who brings witchcraft from Egypt, someone who intends to walk on water and is absorbed by the sea, who shares his bread with many and has five disciples, someone who is denounced by hidden witnesses and is hung and lapidated on Easter's eve.

² P. Lapide, *Is das nicht Josephs Son? Jesus im heutigen Judentum* (1976) presents a significant sample of Jewish testimony of the nineteenth and twentieth centuries in which Jesus is vindicated to Judaism, such as that of Leo Baeck (1873-1956), great rabbi of Berlin: "[The Gospel] is a Jewish book, mostly because the fresh air in it, and on which it is inspired, is that of the Sacred Scripture; because it encourages the Jewish spirit; because Jewish faith and hope, Jewish needs and suffering, Jewish wisdom and hope, are all through it. It is a Jewish book amongst Jewish books. Judaism may not go past it without acknowledging it and least of all do without it. It is also in it that Judaism should see its own essence, it must apprehend what belongs to Judaism. . . . In this early Gospel, where the Jewish mark is evidenced in all its lines and signs, we can clearly see a man open to everything pure and good of Judaism, a man that could only germinate in the soil of Judaism, and only from that soil could he obtain such disciples and followers: a man only here, on this Jewish soil, within Jewish trust and reminiscence, could go through his life and death. A Jew amongst Jews. Neither history, nor Jewish thought may be overlooked by him, nor may he take his sight away from it."

and Leiden: Brill, 2002). In it, each report is followed by a reply or annotation from one of the participants. I believe this produces a new point of view in the interpretation of Rabbinic texts, apparently ignoring the classical Christian exegesis of the twentieth century, where Bultmann (its most outstanding representative) is held responsible for linking Jesus directly to the prophets, while showing disdain for what he calls late Judaism. The most frequently quoted researchers—apart from the authors—are Crossan and Mack, Sanders, and G. Vermes. The first two represent the Cynic-Hellenistic hypothesis; the other two are spokesmen for the studies of Jesus within a Jewish context. Let us have a briefly review criticisms of these approaches:

a) The argument against Mack and Crossan[3] affirms that the context in which Jesus may be understood is not Hellenistic-Cynic but also Jewish: the characters surrounding Jesus, the religious and political issues that are set forth, and the style of Jesus' teachings (parables) present Jesus as a Jewish master in a Jewish environment.[4] Contact with the world of Cynics is general and superficial: in a sense, Jesus and the Cynics might be identified as a counter-cultural group, though the type of opposition is quite varied: Cynics despise and ridicule society and have no reform or restoration plan. Crossan's comparison between the Rabbinic structure of Judaism in Jesus' day and the papacy of the Catholic Church[5] is representative of his generalizing tendency. There is an obvious similarity among all rebellious characters in history,[6] but nothing could be more far fetched than identifying

---

[3] The works of B.L. Mack taken into consideration are: *A Myth of Innocence: Mark and Christian Origins* (Minneapolis, 1988); *The Lost Gospel: The Book of Q and Christian Origins* (San Francisco, 1993). From Crossan, the focus is on the work *The Historical Jesus. The Life of a Mediterranean Jewish Peasant* (San Francisco, 1991).

[4] The term "rabbi," which Cynic Jesus promoters try to avoid, is no anachronism, or in such case, it is as much as interpreting the term "messiah" in the apologetic sense of the early Church, or the term "Son of God" in the sense of Nicea's Christology. In Jesus' day, the term "rabbi" was in use (Dan. 2:48; 4:6; 5:11; M. Ab. 1:6, 16; cf. inscriptions in J.P. Kane, "Ossuary Inscriptions of Jerusalem," in *Journal of Semitic Studies* 23, 1978, pp. 268–282.

[5] In my opinion, the most radical critic is Crossan himself, upon his offering of the list of the quoted Rabbinic texts: eight from the Mishnah, nine from the Babylonian Talmud, one from the Yerushalmi, three from the Tosefta, all referring to Honi and Hanina ben Dosa; two quotes from Targum and six from Qumran; no texts from the Midrashim. Do Qumranic and Rabbinic texts really have so little to offer?

[6] The parallels found in Downing's work (the Strack-Billerbeck of Hellenism) are not greater or more important than those found in Rabbinic literature (parallels as well as statistics should be used as part of an experts' method).

Jesus as an antinomic, counter-cultural Cynic or a "Jewish Cynic with peasant status" (Crossan).[7] Placing Jesus in a Cynic context suggests the modernization of Jesus that Christian exegesis has always legitimately pursued; it may have been politically correct for some in the twentieth century (the characterization of Cynics as "hippies in the yuppy world of august times" is quite significant), but it collides with the most immediate evidence provided by the sources. Apart from this, the Christian tendency to remove Jesus from his original Jewish context is understandable, if we take into account that Christianity is presented as a universal religion and introduced to pagans immediately following Jesus' death. Already in the New Testament, Jesus, as the Savior of the Universe, tends to replace Jesus the Messiah of Israel, son of David. This is why exegesis must not avoid a historical and formal point of view in the critical analysis of texts.

b) The image of Jesus as a charismatic Galilean who preaches tolerance of those who disobey the Law, as G. Vermes[8] presents him, is purely speculative. It so happens that the miracle workers mentioned by Vermes are strictly obedient to the law, and so are their donkeys; Honi and Hanina ben Dosa are considered rabbis in later tradition; the image of the charismatic hero leading a revolutionary movement

---

[7] On the other hand, the Cynic hypothesis has a very weak basis: that Jesus might have contacted the Cynic world in Sepphoris is always possible, but, given the facts, it seems pure conjecture, since nowhere in the New Testament is this city mentioned, and it is contrary to Jesus' normal avoiding of large urban centers. The presence of Cynics in Sepphoris is equally possible, but there is no proof of that either. I am surprised at seeing that from a mere possibility, J. González Echegaray asserts: "This is the city in which Jesus spent a good part of his life. His way of thinking, acting, and expressing himself cannot be totally strange to the environment in which he did his everyday work, nor to the people to whom he was related from the time of youth, nor to everything he saw and heard on the streets, nor to the criteria and ways of thinking of a society in which he was inserted" (*Jesús en Galilea. Aproximación desde la arqueología* [Estella, 2000], p. 136). It would more logical to infer that due to the closeness of Bet Shearim—an important Rabbinic center a few kilometers from Nazareth—Jesus became there an expert on the Law (though the city's Rabbinic-Hellenistic growth is later than 135 C.E., it could also be possible to think of a prior pre-Rabbinic center). Even accepting Sepphoris' Cynic coloring, it is not right to define all of Galilee based on that city. Jesus' speech and language belongs to Jewish tradition. His preaching (the Kingdom of God), his parables, his controversies on purity and the Sabbath, his references to the Temple, his teachings to the disciples, etc., are all part of the Jewish world of his time. Crossan himself acknowledges that Jesus did not act in a Cynic manner with his disciples, nor in matters of pureness, nor in his praxis to avoid cities, or in the limitation of his activity to Israel.

[8] G. Vermes' most popular trilogy: *Jesus the Jew* (London 1973), *Jesus and the World of Judaism* (London, 1983), *The Religion of Jesus the Jew* (London 1993).

against a community structure (in the style of Max Weber's charismatic hero) cannot be adapted to Honi or Hanina, or Jesus.

On the other hand, Sanders[9] does not see Jesus as a midrashic or halakhic master using midrash (though this is not consistent with many texts that Sanders himself considers retro-projections of Gospels). What is most debatable in Sanders' method is the use of the criterion of difference, which leads him to deny everything Jewish or Christian as authentically related to Jesus: his denial of the demand for conversion by the historical Jesus is based on the fact that Gospels state that Jesus in fact demanded it![10]

Still, it would be ridiculous not to acknowledge the contributions to the exegesis of the New Testament[11] of each of these positions.

- Even if Jesus was not a pure "Cynic philosopher," there is no doubt he possessed certain characteristics of a rebel in the style of Cynics. The success of Christianity in the Hellenistic-Roman culture was not only due to matters of politics and strength. The Christian message was consistent with what was expected of intellectuals of that time, and it had already become a popular expectation.[12]
- Even if he was not simply charismatic, his attractive personality and radical demands, based on an intimate consciousness of his own closeness with God, should not be overlooked.

---

[9] E.P. Sanders, *Jesus and Judaism* (London, 1985).

[10] B. Chilton writes: "The assumption of Jesus as the great original, heroically dissimilar from his environment, is intrinsic to every application of the criterion that has ever been attempted. Moreover, from Perrin onwards, there has been a willingness to discount what seems Jewish and what seems orthodox, but to embrace as authentic elements which are consistent with Gnosticism and with Greco-Roman philosophical conventions. (Crossan's work, discussed below, is an example of that trend.) Such a bias can only result in the privileging of the Christology of certain wings of early Christianity, the wings within which it was fashionable to see Jesus as magus, as Cynic, and/or as transcendent Redeemer. . . . Sanders's application of the criterion of dissimilarity exacerbates its inherent weakness. He is, of course, in no position to claim that a saying attributed to Jesus contradicts the necessity of repentance. The only index at his disposal to suggest that Jesus did not require repentance is that the Gospels claim he did require repentance!" (in B.D. Chilton, Craig A. Evans, and Jacob Neusner, *The Missing Jesus* [Leiden, 2002], p. 148).

[11] For example, the rabbinization process of Honi and Hanina ben Dosa that Crossan proposes in his chapter VIII ("Magician and Prophet") must be taken into account.

[12] A very prudent appraisal of the contribution to knowing Jesus provided by the "Cynic" thesis may be found in R. Aguirre, "Nuevo Testamento y helenismo. La teoría de Jesús como un predicador cínico," in *Estudios Bíblicos* 61 (2003), pp. 3–25.

- The intention to present Jesus exclusively within the context of pre-Rabbinic (Pharisaic) Judaism ignores the religious variety of the time. For instance, are a number of Jesus' characteristics not found in the Essene world?
- It is likewise evident that his Galilean environment had a decisive influence at the time of his formation: Jesus was a Galilean and that was how he was seen and known; even more so, I would say classified: "'This is the prophet Jesus, from Nazareth in Galilee,' the crowds answered" (Matt. 21:11); Nicodemus' Pharisaic colleagues say to him: "Are you also from Galilee? Study [the Scriptures] and you will learn that no prophet has ever come from Galilee" (John 7:52); during the process, someone addresses Peter: "You, too, were with Jesus of Galilee" (Matt. 26:69); "When Pilate heard 'Galilee' he asked, 'Is this man a Galilean?'" (Luke 23:6). His group of disciples is Galilean and his particularly successful mission took place in Galilee: Gospels are especially careful in emphasizing the Galilean characteristics of the disciples and of the women that accompanied him to the cross (Mark 15:40-41 and parallels). The following is very significant: Mark and Matthew (and John 21) mention a regrouping of the disciples following the death of Jesus in Galilee; Luke mentions nothing in regards to that, thus re-elaborating the information from the sources in benefit of his theology regarding Jerusalem; however, when Luke narrates the ascension of Jesus in Jerusalem in Acts 1:1, he puts the following words in Jesus' mouth: "Galileans, why are you standing there looking up at the sky?" Undoubtedly, Jesus' group was known—before being Christians—as "the Galileans:" "These people who are talking like this are Galileans!" (Acts 2:7). As has been known for a long time now, the polarity Galilee-Jerusalem marks the story of this Galilean who came to be King of the Jews. Researchers now deem Galilean idiosyncrasy highly important, as a product of the climate and human and political geography: it was a particularly Hellenized region, recently reconverted to Judaism by the Maccabees. This region was also homeland to a number of anti-Roman dissident groups (Acts 5:37 mentions Judas the Galilean, and Luke 13:1-2 refers to a killing of Galileans ordered by Pilate).

The above remarks are no obstacle to Rabbinic literature's being acknowledged as the best means of clarifying the exegesis of the

New Testament. The dominant pre-Rabbinic or Pharisaic trend stood behind Paul's formation, and probably Jesus' formation also. It was with this trend that early Christianity also was confronted.

III. *How to Use Rabbinic Texts in New Testament Exegesis*

The first issue is that of historical and methodological legitimacy: the earliest redaction of Tannaitic texts is not prior to the third century C.E. The first haggadic Midrashim appear towards the fourth century. Talmudic studies commenced in the fifth century. Is it possible for such late texts to clarify the New Testament? The answer is: Yes.

This is true, first, because all Rabbinic literature has an oral pre-history and because oralism has never been apart from the texts.[13]

Second, both Rabbinic literature and the New Testament have a common reference in Scripture; in a way, we could say that the New Testament and Rabbinic literature are the oral tradition that always accompanied Scripture. Neither of them, therefore, has been able to avoid taking the other into consideration. That is why the Rabbinic literature is as important to the exegesis of the New Testament as the

---

[13] "Oral traditions always accompany a written text. This has always happened and happens today in every culture. Texts, even after having been written down, are alive through the attached notes and commentaries. Such a live tradition is noticeable in the edited Rabbinic Bibles, where masoretic notes, Aramaic targums, and great classical Jewish commentaries frame the biblical text. The Bible has been always handed down with an oral tradition. 'Tradition—*massoret*—is a fence to the Torah,' R. Aqiba said (M. Ab. 3:13) following the Great Assembly's advice (M. Ab. 1:1). Mishnah—'repetition'—is by definition oral tradition. In Aqiba's representation, the Oral Torah is deduced from the Written Torah. In the more popular representation, the Oral Torah comes from Moses at Sinai. In any case, it deals with the legitimization of the Oral Torah, i.e., the efforts of every generation to update the immutable written text. So it is understandable that different opinions about the halakhah, even those not accepted by the Sages, keep their weight and deserve to be recorded (cf. M. Ed. 2:4-6). The Gospel literature arose in the first century C.E. from a Jewish movement, which accepted the Bible as its reference: for Christians the Bible is also the Word of God. At that moment the Mishnah was not yet written down, but many of its traditions were alive, as is shown by qumranic writings (4QMMT), Flavius Josephus, and New Testament literature. Many halakhic and theological discussions collected in the Gospels could be understood in a similar way to the Rabbinic interpretations in the framework of the Oral Law. Therefore it is not surprising that oral traditions of the Mishnah appear in the Gospels, without necessarily presuming literary dependence in any direction" (M. Pérez Fernández, "Gospels, Oral Traditions of the Mishnah in," in J. Neusner, A. Avery-Peck, and W. Green, eds., *Encyclopaedia of Judaism* (Leiden and Boston, second revised edition, 2005), vol. 2, pp. 892–904.

latter is to coming to know Rabbinic Judaism. We only need to think of what could be known of the Judaism prior to the Mishnah without the New Testament. Would the Qumran scrolls sufficiently reveal first-century Judaism? And what would we know about Rabbinic Judaism based only on the New Testament without resorting to the Mishnah?

Third, targums provide a reference in the consideration of Jesus' use of the Scripture, which some (Chilton) have found enlightening: Targumic studies have shown Chilton that Jesus' use of Scripture is not "midrashic" (even if it "comments" as in the Rabbinic style). Jesus reads Scripture as well as its language and images through the common method of analogy (simple and spontaneous comparison), as becomes evident in the targums[14] (notably, Jesus' use of Scripture is not "technical," for, as we shall see, there is no express reference to the *middot*). The date of the targumim has been debated, even if there is no debate about the date of many of these "translations." Although the extant texts (TgOnq, TgN, TgPsJ, TgF, TgC) may be subsequent to 70 C.E. and include medieval extensions, their contents are older (Qumran).

Fourth, the use of Rabbinic texts in the exegesis of the New Testament has an influence on the subject of parallels. Parallels to the New Testament may be found in worldwide literature of all times. There are plenty of them in Cynic and stoic literature. Sometimes they are trans-cultural borrowings that cross borders inadvertently. In other cases, they are absolutely independent and probably originate in the sapiental and prophetical background common to all cultures and periods. In order to bear significance, parallels must belong to the same context. Isolated parallels, outside a common structure of thought and behavior, are of little use in establishing genetic or historical relations with the texts of the New Testament. It is illustrative that the golden rule of Matt. 7:12 ("Do for others what you would have them do for you: this is the meaning of the Law of Moses and of the teachings of the Prophets"), positively stated in Lev. 19:18, is constantly repeated and restated in Jewish tradition (Tob. 4:15; Aristeas 207; Philo, *Hypothetica, apud* Eusebium, *Praep. Ev.* 8:7.6; Test. Neft. 1:6; PsJ Lev. 19:18; 2 Enoch 61:1-2; B. Shab. 31a), as well as in Hellenistic tradition: Seneca (*Epist. Mor.* 103:3-4), Sextus (*Sententiae* 89), Dio Cassius (51:34.39), Isocrates (*Ad Nicodemum* 49). The ascription of

---

[14] B. Chilton, "Jesus within Judaism," in Chilton, Evans, and Neusner, *The Missing Jesus*, p. 146.

New Testament texts to either tradition depends on the context of the study: is there preference for the Cynic-Hellenistic context or for that of the Hebrew Bible?[15] This is where the importance of determining the context in which Jesus is interpreted becomes evident.

IV. *Texts of the Rabbinic Halakhah in New Testament Exegesis*

John 7:23: *Circumcision on the Sabbath*

In one of the many controversies about the Sabbath found in the Gospels, Jesus argues: "Moses ordered you to circumcise your sons (although it was not Moses but your ancestors who started it), and so you circumcise a boy on the Sabbath" (John 7:22). Indeed, the practice of circumcision on the Sabbath was expressly authorized in the Mishnah, and, as the Gospels show, it as an ancient praxis: "Everything implied by circumcision may be done on the Sabbath" (M. Shab. 18:3; 19:2, 3, 5). "R. Yose[16] says: The marvel of circumcision allows it to displace the most severe precept of the Sabbath" (M. Ned. 3:11). Jesus may then ironically say that no one obeys the Law, with the same argument as that of the synoptic tradition: "Or have you not read in the Law of Moses that every Sabbath the priests in the Temple actually break the Sabbath law, yet they are not guilty?" (Matt. 12:5). The fact is certain and is indicated in the Mishnah itself: M. Erub. 10:11-15 lists a number of activities that may take place on the Sabbath in the Temple but not outside it; M. R.H. 1:4 points out that "when the Temple still existed, profaning [the Sabbath] was allowed on all [new moons] due to the regulation of sacrifices." In T. Pes. 4:13 the debate is whether the precept of observing holidays prevails over that of the Sabbath, and Hillel (somewhat younger than Jesus) resorts to the same argument used in the Gospel:

> "Is it that we only have one holiday in the year that repeals the Sabbath? Throughout the year we have over three hundred holidays that repeal the Sabbath!" To all the courtesans gathered at the Temple he said: "Daily sacrifice is public offering and the holiday is public offering. So if daily sacrifice is public offering and repeals the Sabbath, then the holiday, which is public offering, also repeals the Sabbath . . . ."

---

[15] At this point, Crossan's approach is debatable. Why for Luke 12:22-31 and Matt. 6:24-34 does he refers to Cynic parallels provided by G. Downing, while the one evident from M. Qid. 4:14 is overlooked?

[16] Disciple of Aqiba, from the second half of the second century C.E. (Sepphoris).

This shows that the later halakhah of the Mishnah was applied in the time of Jesus, and this is the halakhah Jesus bases his arguments on. Jesus' dialectics have to be analyzed within the halakhic context we only know through the Mishnah.

Coming back to John's text: Jesus goes on with an argument typical of a *Qal wa-Homer*: "If a boy is circumcised on the Sabbath so that Moses' Law is not broken, why are you angry with me because I made a man completely well on the Sabbath?" (John 7:23). The point is that if circumcision, which affects a small limb, justifies repealing the Sabbath, certainly a procedure that affects the entire man should do so. The Mishnah similarly holds that saving a life displaces the Sabbath (M. Yom. 8:6). In the Mekhilta of R. Ishmael, Jesus' same *Qal wa-Homer* argument appears: R. Eleazar b. Azariah (beginning of the second century C.E.) says: "If circumcision—which affects only one of man's organs—postpones the Sabbath, then all the more so when the rest of the body is affected!" (Mek. to Exod. 31:13; also in T. Shab. 15:16).

It may be inferred from these texts that subsequent rabbis share Jesus' perspective; while it would not make sense to say they copied Jesus' halakhah, it seems likely that their interpretation dates back at least to the time of Jesus. Then is it so that Jesus was confronted with some particularly "wild" Pharisees? This is, in a certain way, H.W. Basser's conclusion:

> Specifically I wish to show that the teachings embedded in the Gospels that portray Jesus as antagonistic to Pharisees are themselves Pharisaic teachings. If what Jesus taught astounded the people, it was not because he set up his authority against the Pharisees but, as the evidence shows, because he had mastered Pharisaic law more than his interlocutors had done and taught properly according to their authority[17]

The diversity of opinions regarding the halakhah of the Sabbath is notorious, and it brings forward a scope of interpretations ranging from rigorous to lax. The most obvious case is that of taking an animal out of a pit on the Sabbath: Matt. 12:10-13; Luke 14:2-6; CD XI:13-16 and 4Q265, 2 i; M. Yom. 8:6; T. Shab. 14 (15):3.[18] Even so, the idea that Jesus was just another Pharisee is as askew as seeing him as an anti-Pharisaic radical. As Chilton has pointed

---

[17] H.W. Basser, "The Gospels and Rabbinic Literature," in Chilton, Evans, and Neusner, *The Missing Jesus*, p. 78.
[18] L.H. Shiffman, *The Halakhah at Qumran* (Leiden, 1975), pp. 121–122, and F. García Martínez, "Interés de los manuscritos del Mar Muerto para judíos y Cristianos," in *El Olivo* 46, pp. 23–44.

out, Jesus' authority is not perceived through his agreement with the most frequently illustrated Pharisaic exegesis but in diverse arguments. That shall be considered in the following.

Mark 2:23-28; Matt. 12:1-8; Luke 6:1-5: *The episode of the ears of corn (Mark 6:27)*

In regards to this episode, Mark's original narration shows Jesus as taking Rabbinic praxis to a radical extreme and leaving casuistry aside; while one of Matthew's typical re-elaborations shows Jesus making argumentations as a rabbi would. In my opinion, Mark's narration is the one that takes us closest to the historical Jesus. What should be emphasized here is the lapidary phrase of Mark 6:27 that has come to symbolize the anthropocentric attitude in Jesus' ethics as radically anti-Pharisaic. "The Sabbath was made for the good of man; man was not made for the Sabbath."

The surprising thing is that we find this same phrase by a rabbi in the second to third century C.E.: at Mekhilta to Exod. 31:14, Simeon b. Menasia interprets this text: "You shall keep the Sabbath *for yourselves* because it is sacred:" "The Sabbath has been granted to you, *you have not been given to the Sabbath*," which is Jesus' same statement, obtained here by exegesis or midrash. The difference is that Jesus does not provide an argument from Scripture, as in the Rabbinic style. His argument is spontaneous and authoritative, based on common sense and on his position regarding the authority of Scripture. The context of the discussion in the Mekhilta is a group of rabbis who interpret Exod. 31:13-17. The fact that one of the interpretations appears in Jesus' words proves that the Pharisaic halakhah was already present in the first century: what is original in Jesus is that he does not need to expressly infer the law from Scripture; I would say that he even refuses to be seen as a teacher of Scripture.[19]

These two examples show the importance of cross-referencing and confronting texts of Rabbinic literature and those of the New Testament; despite the difference in dates, they are both enlightening. At the same time, they suggest another matter that was introduced by Isaac Mayer Wise (1819–1900): "We challenge the whole Christian *establishment* to mention one single teaching by Jesus, universally valid

---

[19] Cf. M. Pérez Fernández, "Lectura del Antiguo Testamento desde el Nuevo Testamento. Estudio sobre las citas bíblicas atribuidas a Jesús en el Evangelio de Marcos," in *Estudios Bíblicos* 47 (1989), pp. 449–474.

to all humankind, which is not found in Judaism." Prof. Basser meets this challenge by placing Jesus in the Pharisaic context. I accept that there are many coincidences between Jesus' halakhah and Rabbinic halakhah. It could also be possible that many of Jesus' controversies might have been transformed by the Evangelists to create a radical opposition, in order to justify severing the Christian community from Pharisaic praxis. However, I cannot overlook some of Jesus' attitudes that were unacceptable to the Pharisaic world, such as his attitude towards the Torah. A few examples suffice to prove the usefulness of resorting to Rabbinic texts in order to understand the Gospels.

V. *Rabbinic Attitudes and Jesus' Attitudes*

Matt. 7:24-27: So, then, anyone who hears these words of mine and obeys them is like a wise man who built his house on rock. The rain poured down, the rivers overflowed, and the wind blew hard against that house. But it did not fall, because it was built on rock. But anyone who hears these words of mine and does not obey them is like a foolish man who built his house on sand. The rain poured down, the rivers overflowed, and the wind blew hard against that house, and it fell. And what a terrible fall that was!

These words have a close parallel in M. Ab. 3:17: "Whom does the one whose learning is greater than his work resemble? He resembles a tree of luxuriant leaves but weak rickety roots. The wind blows and turns it upside down. But whom does the one whose works are more abundant than his learning resemble? He resembles a tree of few branches but with many roots, that would not move even with all the winds on earth blowing at once." Both the Rabbinic author (Eleazar b. Azariah, late first century) and Jesus apply the metaphor of Jer. 17:5-8: "I will condemn the person who turns away from me and puts his trust in man, in the strength of mortal man. . . . But I will bless the person who puts his trust in me."[20] However, there is a substantial difference between the two texts: while Jesus refers to putting his words into practice, M. Abot refers to putting into practice the words of the Torah.[21]

---

[20] Mishnah MS. Kaufmann does expressly quote the text of Jer. 17:6, 8, the exegesis of which underlies the other two texts.
[21] Jesus changes the image from the tree to the house. To J.G. Echegaray, this change reveals Jesus' trade: "and about this I have the knowledge to speak to you for it is my trade" (*Jesús en Galilea. Aproximaciones desde la arqueología* [Estella, 2000], p. 126).

Luke 9:59-62: He said to another man: "Follow me." But that man said, "Sir, first let me go back and bury my father." Jesus answered, "Let the dead bury their own dead. You go and proclaim the Kingdom of God." Another man said, "I will follow you, sir; but first let me go and say good-bye to my family." Jesus said to him, "Anyone who starts to plow and then keeps looking back is of no use to the Kingdom of God."

These words are inspired by the passage in which Elysium follows Elias: "[Elysium] left the ox and as he ran behind Elias he said: Allow me to go back and kiss my father and mother and then I shall follow you. [Elias] replied: Go and come back" (1 Rev. 19:20). But, unlike Elias, Jesus' demand to follow him is so radical that it scandalizes Jewish ears: it rejects not only the precept of honoring one's father and mother but also renounces the act of mercy of burying the dead, so emphasized in Jewish tradition: TgN Gen. 35:9; TgPsJ Deut. 34:6; Gen. Rabbah 8:13; B. Sot. 14a; Ecc. Rabbah 7:2; ARN B 8:4; Semahot 11, Rule 7.[22] In order to enter the Kingdom of God preached by Jesus, it is necessary to join him in disregard of written and oral Law. This is not an isolated saying from Jesus. Also note: "Whoever comes to me cannot be my disciple unless he loves me more than he loves his father and his mother, his wife and his children, his brothers and his sisters, and himself as well. Whoever does not carry his own cross and come after me cannot be my disciple" (Luke 14:26-27; Matt. 10:37-38). It may be possible to find parallels to these sayings about demands and radical ruptures in Cynic and anarchistic literature. But the enlightening parallels share the context of the Scriptures, those of the rabbis.[23]

Mark 2:22: *The Parable of the Wine and Wineskins*

M. Ab. 4:20 discusses whether it is better to learn as a child or as an adult. Three rabbis from different periods are quoted[24] (this is,

---

[22] Cf. M. Pérez Fernández, "Cana's Wedding and the Burial of Jesus (John 2:1-11 and 19:39-40). Two Acts of Mercy in John's Gospel," in *Signum et Testimonium. Estudios en honor del Prof. Antonio García-Moreno* (Pamplona, 2003), pp. 119–132.

[23] Neusner particularly insists on the contextuality of parallels: "Commonly, extra-contextual comparison produces traits in common that prove illusory upon closer inspection" (Chilton, Evans, and Neusner, *The Missing Jesus*, p. 67).

[24] Elisha b. Abuya belongs to the period prior to Bar Kokhba; Yose bar Judah and Rabbi are from the same period, around the second and third centuries.

then, a discussion created by the editor), with each using a different image to support his opinion:

> Elishah b. Abuya said: "He who learns as a child, what is he like? He is like ink on new paper. He who learns as an old man, what is he like? He is like ink on rubbed paper."
>
> R. Yose bar Judah, from the village of Ha-Babli, said: "He who learns as a child, what is he like? He is like the one who eats unripe grapes and drinks wine from the press. He who learns as an adult, what is he like? He is like the one who eats ripened grapes and drinks aged wine."
>
> Rabbi said: "Do not mind the jug, but what is inside it. There are new jugs full of aged wine, and old jugs that do not even have new wine."

Elishah b. Abuya uses the example of writing on new paper, where it is easy to write and read, while writing on old paper becomes blurred. Yose bar Judah believes it is more profitable to learn as an adult: unripe grapes and new wine are bitter, as opposed to ripened grapes and aged wine, which are sweet. Rabbi says it depends on the person: new jugs can contain old wine and vice versa. This kind of parable must have been quite popular. In Mark 2:22 (= Matt. 9:17; Luke 5:37-39) the same comparison appears, although the point is different: "Nor does anyone pour new wine into used wineskins, because the wine will burst the skins, and both the wine and the skins will be ruined. Instead, new wine must be poured into fresh wineskins." It must be understood that changing the simile from M. Abot 4:20 is not fortuitous, nor an error of transcription. Jesus is aware of his rejection of old wine in lieu of new wine, and he prefers new wine and new wineskins. The reference to the old and the new Torah is obvious. Klausner commented as follows on this passage: "John the Baptist, like the Pharisees, thought it possible to keep the old 'bottle' in its old form and even to fill it with new wine, repentance and good works, and so hasten the coming of the Messiah. But this was not possible; a new content requires a new garb. Pharisaic Judaism must be transformed from the root."[25]

It is, then, understandable that when a Jew reads the synoptic Gospels, he may admire Jesus' ethical message, though unavoidably thinking: "how deeply personal is the focus of Jesus' teaching: it is on himself, not on his message." And he may understand that what is really at stake is "Torah as against Christ." And he might feel

---

[25] J. Klausner, *Jesus of Nazareth. His Life, His Time, His Doctrine*, pp. 248 and 275.

surprised and ask Jesus' followers: "And is your master God? For, I now realize, only God can demand of me what Jesus is asking."[26]

VI. *Rabbinic Parables and Jesus' Parables*

Matt. 22:1-14 (= Luke 14:15-24): *The Parable of the Wedding Feast*

J. Neusner[27] has studied this parable in relation to a similar one at B. Shab. 153a. Prior to Neusner, J. Jeremias had referred to them as related.[28] Ecc. Rabbah 9:8 offers a similar version of the Rabbinic parable, with the intention of clarifying certain elliptical Hebrew expressions of the talmudic text;[29] the ascription of the Talmud to

---

[26] Neusner, *A Rabbi Talks with Jesus* (Montreal, Kingston, London, and Ithaca, 2000), pp. 62, 65, 68.
[27] Chilton, Evans, and Neusner, *The Missing Jesus*, pp. 61-65.
[28] J. Jeremias, *Die Gleichnisse Jesu* (Göttingen, 1965), pp. 78-81.
[29] Ecc. Rabbah 9:8: (I) "Always wear white garments and be properly anointed" (Ecc. 9:8). R. Yohanan b. Zakkai said: If Scripture referred only to white garments, would pagans ever lack garments! If Scripture referred only to ointments, would pagans ever lack ointments! Therefore, the reference must only be to precepts, good acts, and the Torah. (II) R. Judah the Patriarch told in a parable: What does this resemble? It resembles a king who organized a feast and invited guests to his house by requesting them: 'Go and bathe and get anointed; wash your garments and get ready for the feast,' although he did not set a time for arriving at the feast. The wiser ones went to wash their garments, got ready for the feast and awaited in front of the royal palace while thinking: How could something be missing in the royal palace? Those who were not so wise paid no attention and disregarded the king's orders. They thought: 'In time we will realize what the king's feast is about. How could a feast be organized without previous preparation or conversation among the parties?' And the bricklayer turned to his bricks, the potter to his pottery, the forger to his ember, and the launderer to his laundry. Suddenly the king ordered: 'Let everyone in for the feast!' Some of them went in radiant, the others untidy. The king was happy for the wiser ones, those who had obeyed his orders and had also honored his palace, and was angry at the less wise, those who had disobeyed his orders and had also degraded a royal palace. So he ordered: 'Those dressed for the feast may come in and eat; those not dressed for the feast may not.' Could they possibly have to go just like that? The king said: 'Better still, those had better sit at the table to eat and drink, and these had better stay standing to watch and suffer.' Likewise, in the coming world, Isaiah's text reads: 'I assure you that my humble servants shall eat, but you shall be hungry . . . I assure you that my humble servants shall rejoice' (Is. 65:13-14). (III) Zevatai said on behalf of R. Meir: Those shall better sit at the table to eat and drink, and these shall better sit at the table also, without eating or drinking, because the torment of the one having to stand is not as much as the torment of being at the table. The one who stands without eating or drinking is like a manservant. The torment of those sitting at the table without eating is twice as hard: his face goes pale. That is the reason the text of the Prophet reads: 'You shall see again the difference between what is fair and what is wicked' (Mal. 3:18)."

Yohanan b. Zakkai is preferable to the ascription of Ecc. Rabbah to Judah the Patriarch; R. Meir's added gloss (he was a disciple of Aqiba, prior to Judah) so implies; but the context is certainly an exegetical comment on Ecc. Rabbah 9:8:

Matt. 22:1-14	B. Shab. 153a

Matt. 22:1-14

1 Jesus again used parables in taking to the people.

(I) 2 "The Kingdom of heaven is like this. Once there was a king who prepared a wedding feast for his son.

3 He sent his menservants to tell the invited guests to come to the feast, but they did not want to come.

4 So he sent other menservants with this message for the guests: 'My feast is ready now; my bullocks and prize calves have been butchered, and everything is ready. Come to the wedding feast!'

5 But the invited guests paid no attention and went about their business: one went to his farm, another to his shop,

6 while others grabbed the menservants, bit them and killed them.

7 The king was very angry; so he sent his soldiers, who killed those murderers and burnt down their city.

(II) 8 Then he called his menservants and said to them, 'My wedding feast is ready, but the people I invited did not deserve it.

B. Shab. 153a

(I) In the Mishnah we have been told that R. Eliezer said: "Convert one day before your death" (M. Ab. 2:10). The disciples asked R. Eliezer: "Is it that man knows the day of his own death?" He answered: "That is the best motive for converting today; in case of dying tomorrow you will find all your days shall be spent in converting." So said Solomon: "Always wear white garments and be properly anointed" (Ecc. 9:8).

(II) Rabban Yohanan b. Zakkai told a parable: It is like the king who invited his humble servants to a feast without setting a date. The wiser ones dressed up and sat at the palace's entrance and said: Might something be missing at the palace [for the feast to take place]? Those more foolish went back to their chores saying: Could it be possible for a feast to take place without preparation?

The king suddenly convoked his humble servants. The wiser ones went before him dressed up, and the more foolish went before him untidy. The king approached the wiser ones with joy and the

9 Now go to the main streets and invite to the feast as many people as you find.'

10 So the menservants went out into the streets and gathered all the people they could find, good and bad alike; and the wedding hall was filled with people.

(III) 11 "The king went in to look at the guests and saw a man who was not wearing wedding clothes.

12 'Friend, how did you get in here without wedding clothes?' the king asked him. But the man said nothing.

13 Then the king told the menservants, 'Tie him up hand and foot, and throw him outside in the dark. There he will cry and grind his teeth.'"

14 And Jesus concluded, "Many are invited, but few are chosen."

more foolish ones with irritation and said: These who dressed up for the feast may sit to eat and drink. These who did not dress for the feast shall stand and watch.

(III) R. Meir's son-in-law explained on his behalf: These also appeared as servants, all seated, but ones eating and the others hungry. Ones drinking and the others thirsty, as it has been said: "The Lord says: And so I tell you that those who worship and obey me will have plenty to eat and drink; but you will be hungry and thirsty. They will be happy but you will be disgraced" (Is. 65:13-14).

(IV) Another interpretation: "Always wear white garments" (Ecc. 9:8) makes reference to the fringes; "And be properly anointed" (Ecc. 9:8): refers to the phylacteries.

The shared motif of the Evangelical and Rabbinic parables is a feast that guests refuse to attend. The comparison can be done based on the objective: the Rabbinic parable is exegetic, a comment on Ecc. 9:8, a sapiental teaching in which death is the inexorable fate, while the Evangelical parable is of the Kingdom of Heaven and does not include any specific quote from any biblical text, following Jesus' style. That is the reason each parable develops in a different manner: the date of the wedding (the day of death) is not determined in the Rabbinic parable, which becomes a call for permanent conversion. The Evangelical parable sets the date of the feast ("the feast is ready") and emphasizes the allegorical elements until it becomes an exaggerated and impossible paradigm: not only the guests' refusal to attend but also the murder of messengers and the king's bloody vengeance; and yet a second call with no discrimination ("good and bad alike"), and an unexplainable expulsion by the king of someone who attended without wedding clothes. While the Rabbinic parable sticks to a simple line of narration that develops within a rational logic with the only objective of inculcating the need to convert permanently towards the "date still not set," the Evangelical parable is an absurd succession of scenes aiming at different objectives: the irruption of the Kingdom (the wedding of the King's son), the guests' refusal (Israel does not accept Jesus), the outrageous vengeance with the death of the guests and burning of the city (the punishment implied by the destruction of Jerusalem), the later invitation without discrimination between good and bad (opening and mission to the pagans),[30] incongruous demand for wedding clothes (dignity is always demanded to enter the kingdom's feast).

Every expert on the New Testament knows that the parallel version of Luke 14:15-24 adjusts more to an original source, and it is considered close to Q: missing are the king, the son's wedding, the killing of messengers, and the king's vengeance, allusion to the mission; the invitation to good and bad is substituted by the invitation to the dispossessed ("poor, handicapped, blind and lame"), and on a second instance to those "from the roads and stockades;" while there is no mention whatsoever of Matthew's tale regarding the "sponger" without wedding clothes. Surely, Luke's text better reflects the words that Jesus must have pronounced.[31] However, the basic direction of Luke is the same as in Matthew: the Kingdom of Heaven is a feast that guests refuse to attend, and it is open to the least expected. Matthew emphasizes the Christological element, and Luke the sociological element in Jesus' message.

How does the Rabbinic parable help? How is the Rabbinic parable enlightened from the Evangelical parable? What we have called "Matthew's tale" (Matt. 22:11-14) provides us with the clue: He who does not wear wedding clothes is the figure representing the ignorant who did not dress up and were condemned to stand and watch, without the chance to eat or drink. In the Rabbinic text, this figure is directly

---

[30] Such is the most obvious interpretation. Cf. I. Gomá, *El Evangelio según San Mateo* (Madrid, 1976), vol. II, p. 380: "The third and last task by the messengers evokes the definitive opening of the Christian mission beyond the limits of Israel. It is, finally, the way to the path of the pagans."

[31] To Fitzmyer, the version of EvTom 64 is the one closest to the words of Jesus: his aim is to warn the rich. Crossan understands the parable as "the open commensals," a characteristic topic of Jesus: Luke 14:12-14.

taken from Ecc. 9:8 (white garments and ointment, characteristic of the preparation of corpses for burial)[32] applied to the conversion necessary for death. In the Evangelical parable it has been taken for participation in the Kingdom's feast. I believe that the basis of Ecclesiastes should be in the original stratum where those dressed up are confronted with those who stained their garments. The excuse of the guests is developed in the version of Ecc. Rabbah, independently from the text of the New Testament, since there is no coincidence in any of the excuses, which comes to prove that it is all about one original parable with diverse developments. The fact that we are faced with parallels within a single context allows us to inquire on the initial topic and its many developments according to the consistency of Jewish and Christian principles: The Evangelical Kingdom of Heaven has a Christological dimension announced and presented by Jesus; for Judaism, the Kingdom of God is in the here and now of everyday life. Differences in the parables are a result of the diverse points of view.

Matt. 20:1-16: *The Parable of the Workers in the Vineyard*

Matt. 20:1-16	Sifra Lev 26:9 (Weiss 111a)
¹The Kingdom of heaven is like this. Once there was a man who went out early in the morning to hire some men to work in his vineyard. ²He agreed to pay them the regular wage, a silver coin a day, and sent them to work in his vineyard. ³He went out again to the marketplace at nine o'clock and saw some men standing there doing nothing, ⁴so he told them, "You also go and work in the vineyard, and I will pay you a fair wage." ⁵So they went. Then at twelve o'clock and again at three o'clock he did the same thing. ⁶It was nearly five o'clock when he	"I will bless you and give you many children . . . I will be with you" (Lev 26:9). They told a parable. What does this resemble? It resembles a king who hired many workers when he already had a worker who had worked with him many days. When the workers went to get their pay, that other worker came with them. The king said to him: "Son, I will be with you. To all these

---

[32] "Qoh. 9:8 . . . is taken to refer to keeping one's body in condition as a corpse, that is, garmented in white, the color of death in the Rabbinic writings, and properly anointed, as the corpse is anointed for burial" (Neusner, in Chilton, Evans, and Neusner, The *Missing Jesus*, p. 63).

went to the marketplace and saw some other men still standing there. "Why are you wasting the whole day here doing nothing?" he asked them.⁷ "No one hired us," they answered. "Well, then, you also go and work in the vineyard," he told them. ⁸When evening came, the owner told his foreman, "Call the workers and pay them their wages, starting with those who were hired last and ending with those who were hired first." ⁹The men who had begun to work at five o'clock were paid a silver coin each. ¹⁰So when the men who were the first to be hired came to be paid, they thought they would get more; but they too were given a silver coin each. ¹¹They took their money and started grumbling against the employer. ¹²"These men who were hired last worked only one hour," they said, "while we put up with a whole day's work in the hot sun—yet you paid them the same as you paid us!" ¹³"Listen, friend," the owner answered one of them, "I have not cheated you. After all, you agreed to do a day's work for one silver coin. ¹⁴Now take your pay and go home. I want to give this man who was hired last as much as I have given you. ¹⁵Don't I have the right to do as I wish with my own money? Or are you jealous because I am generous?"³³ ¹⁶And Jesus concluded, "So those who are last will be first, and those who are first will be last."

men who have done a small task with me, I shall give a small pay. But with you I shall settle a greater debt." Likewise, the Israelis were asking the Almighty their pay, and so were the nations of the world requesting their pay before the Almighty. And the Almighty said to Israel: "Sons, I shall be with you." These nations of the world have done a small task with me, and so I shall give them a small pay. But with you I shall settle a greater debt." That is the reason for saying: "I will be with you."

---

³³ The Semitic character of this idiom is remarkable: cf. Prov. 22:9; 23:6; 28:2; M. Ab. 2:9; 5:13, 19, M. Ter. 4:3; ARN 40; Sifre Deut. 284.

Workers called to the vineyard at different hours all receive the same salary. This brings the complaint by the ones who worked more, and the response by the master in defense of his freedom to be generous. The Rabbinic parable is exactly the same, but with the opposite attitude, which is also more logical: a master pays more to the ones who worked more. These are obvious variations of the same parable, but they include such significant differences that the outcomes may be opposite: the purpose of the Rabbinic parable is to explain the cause for choosing Israel, and this is expressed by showing that the option is neither arbitrary nor gratuitous: Israel has done the greater and better work. On the contrary, Jesus poses his parable in defense of "those who are last will be first" (and so Matt. 20:16 understands it), a slogan that in the words of Jesus expressed the inversion of conventional preferences: rich—poor, Jews—pagans.[34]

One tends to suspect that the Rabbinic parable is the antithetical response to Jesus' parable. However, a prudent consideration may discard that hypothesis. Tannaitic exegesis is truly traditional. Sifra bears the characteristic of performing the exegesis by providing the obvious sense of the text, and the text reads, "I will be with you." In Tannaitic tradition of old times there was always the question of why the chosen people was Israel and not other, and the answer is always "because Israel was committed to obeying the Law even before knowing it (Exod. 24:7: "All that the Lord hath spoken will we do, and obey").[35] What the Evangelical parable tells us is that the Rabbinic version dates back to the first century. Jesus' parable appears in the controversy it arose. This is a clear example for us to view the continuity of Jesus with the Judaism of his time (use of a popular parable), and, at the same time, the discontinuity in his rupture with the closest traditionalism and exclusive attachment to ideas. Both continuity and rupture offer, in this case, a consistent and credible character. While the Rabbinic parable is typically midrashic (exegetic), that of Jesus avoids the use of the Scripture but at the same time deals with the same matter.

The Rabbinic parable also enlightens the discussion of the original sense of the Evangelical parable. J. Jeremias rejects the idea that the

---

[34] It is one of those sayings, always and only in the words of Jesus, applied to the inversion of values implied in his message (Matt. 19:30; 20:16; Mark 10:31; Luke 13:30): in Luke clearly refers to the entry of pagans into the Kingdom.

[35] Mekhilta to Exod. 20:2.

logion "those who are last will be first" belongs to the original parable, the purpose of which was to show the goodness of God with the poor: the last to be hired, as per Jeremias, are guilty of being unoccupied with "a typical oriental indolence" (sic!); "the parable does not describe an arbitrary act, but the fact of a man with a heart, generous and full of compassion for the poor. . . . We are suddenly in a practical situation of Jesus' life, criticized by his treatment of those despised and proscribed; we are constantly being told about the men for which the Gospel is a scandal. Jesus has to justify his behavior at every instant, as well as defend the Good News. So, here also: This is what God is like, so good, so full of compassion for the poor. So he acts now through Me. Do you wish to reprehend me?"[36] I accept that the *logion* "those who are last will be first" might not belong to the original parable. Whether or not Jesus used the *logion* here cannot be known, though we do know that it was one of his characteristic *logions*; the Evangelist used it in a context in which the Rabbinic parable justified the choice for Israel. In my opinion, Jeremias is wrong. Let New Testament specialists judge.

VII. *Rabbinic and Evangelical Haggadah*

Professor Basser finds in late Midrashim to Ps 43:2-3 all the topics of the narration of the transfiguration (Matt. 17:1-8; Mark 9:2-8; Luke 9:28-36). It may then be inferred that such haggadic interpretations were part of the Judaism of the first century. The same evidence is obtained from the well-known midrashic interpretation of Ecc. 1:9: "There is nothing new under the sun:"

> R. Berekhiah said on behalf of R. Isaac that the last Redeemer would be like the first:
> - and so, as it has been said of the first, "So Moses took his wife and his sons, put them on a donkey" (Exod. 4:20), it has also been said of the last: "Your king is coming to you . . . humble and riding on a donkey" (Zech 9:9);

---

[36] J. Jeremias, *Las parábolas de Jesús* (Estella, 1970), pp. 47–48. J. Jeremias knows a later version of the Rabbinic parable: Y. Ber. 2:3, with developments he considers dependent on the Evangelical parable. Sifra weakens this author's argument. The Talmudic text, also found at Ecc. Rabbah 5:11, is nothing more than a development and application of the Tannaitic parable.

- just as the first redeemer dropped manna, as it has been said, "I am going to make food rain down from the sky for all of you" (Exod. 16:4), so the last shall also be able to drop manna, as it has been said, "May there be plenty of corn in the land, may the hills be covered with crops" (Ps. 72:16);
- just as the first redeemer made the water spring pour out, so the last shall make the water spring pour out, as it has been said: "A stream will flow from the Temple of the Lord, and it will water the Valley of Acacia" (Joel 3:18) (Ecc. Rabbah 1:9).[37]

R. Berekhiah is an Amorite of the fifth generation (second half of the fourth century C.E.) who transmits a tradition of Isaac (second century C.E.). The mosaic features of the messiah date back to the oldest Jewish tradition and are present in the Bible itself.[38] The age of the tradition is found through Evangelical narrations. Any Christian with a minimum knowledge of Scripture would believe that he is reading not the midrash of Ecclesiastes but a patristic text: the three associations of Moses with the donkey, the manna, and the water are exploited in the New Testament to present Jesus as "the second liberator:" the scene where young Jesus returns from Egypt to Israel (Matt. 2:13-14.19-21) is a literary copy of Exod. 4:20 (the iconographical tradition of the "flee to Egypt" has added the donkey, taking it from the scene of the Exodus); Zech. 9:9 ("your king is coming to you . . . humble and riding on a donkey") is used by all Evangelists and in an explicit way by John 12:5 to narrate the entry of Jesus in Jerusalem; Jesus is the one who provides the real bread from heaven (John 5-6) and the one who shall make the streams of life-giving water pour out (John 7:37-39).[39] The community of exegetic-haggadic traditions simultaneously shared by Jews and Christians allows for a better understanding of the text of the New Testament and places Jesus in the true context in which his own pretensions, and those of his "biographers," may be enlightened.

---

[37] Translation by María del Carmen Motos López.
[38] Cf. Fernández, *Tradiciones*, pp. 183–198; R. Bloch, "Quelques aspects de la figure de Moïse dans la tradition rabbinique," in *Moïse, l'Homme de l'Alliance* (Paris, 1955), pp. 127–138. Moses' sufferings and death make up in Deutero Isaiah the Servant of Jehovah and leader of the second Exodus. Cf. TgPsJ Deut. 34:5.
[39] Cf. Pérez, *Tradiciones*, pp. 131–135, 189–191.

VII. *Conclusion*

In conclusion, we justify use of Rabbinic texts in the exegesis of the New Testament as follows:

1. Jesus' attitude, as original as it may be, is by all means—and that is how it was understood—a kind of interpretation of the Torah. The attitude of the Church towards the Old Testament shows that it considers Jesus from the perspective of the testimony of the Torah.
2. Rabbinic texts often provide the best context in which to understand the problematical issues and religious vision underlying the text of the New Testament.
3. All Rabbinic texts are subsequent to the New Testament. However, they may be used whenever it may be verified that they represent the crystallization of an oral tradition that dates back to the period of the New Testament, or whenever they present the unfolding of a topic from that period.
4. Therefore, the use of Rabbinic texts requires a historical-critical analysis of the texts themselves. Also, the studies that approach the New Testament from Judaism must accept the critical exegesis of the New Testament.
5. Some features of Jesus' personality go beyond the image of the "Master of the Scriptures" and even contradict it. Cynic and charismatic features are part of Jesus' personality, as most recent critics have shown. Though Jesus' general context is the Judaism of his time, he represented extraordinary characters, not completely assimilated: the *'am ha-arets*, the Essenes, the apocalyptic, the therapeutists, the thaumaturges, the charismatic, the Hellenized, the collaborationists, etc.
6. The parallels in any literature, culture, or sect are more illustrative when they may be presented as belonging to Jesus' context. In this regard, Rabbinic parallels have the privilege of sharing their source with that of Jesus: the Bible and Jewish tradition.
7. It is understandable and logical that Christianity updated Jesus' message to the pagan world to which it was aimed. But a historical-critical exegetic study is bound to search for the original context of Jesus' sayings and facts.

Bibliography

Basser, H.W., "The Gospels and Rabbinic literature," in Chilton, B.D., Craig A. Evans, and Jacob Neusner, *The Missing Jesus. Rabbinic Judaism and the New Testament* (Leiden, 2002), pp. 77–99.
Buchanan, George W., "The Use of Rabbinic Literature for New Testament Research," in *BTB* 7 (1977), pp. 110–122.
Chilton, B.D., *A Galilean Rabbi and His Bible: Jesus' Use of the Interpreted Scripture of His Time* (Wilmington, 1984).
Chilton, B.D., "Jesus within Judaism," in Chilton, Evans, and Neusner, *The Missing Jesus*, pp. 135–156.
Chilton, B.D., "Reference to the Targumim in the Exegesis of the New Testament," in Lovering, Jr., E.H., ed., *Society of Biblical Literature 1995 Seminar Papers* (Atlanta, 1995), pp. 77–81.
Crossan, J.D., *The Historical Jesus. The Life of a Mediterranean Jewish Peasant* (San Francisco, 1991).
Downing, F.G., *Christ and the Cynics: Jesus and Other Radical Preachers in First-Century Tradition* (Sheffield, 1988).
Evans, C.A., "Early Rabbinic Sources and Jesus Research," in Lovering, *Seminar Papers*, pp. 53–76.
Evans, C.A., *Jesus and His Contemporaries: Comparative Studies* (Leiden, 1997).
Evans, C.A., "The Misplaced Jesus: Interpreting Jesus in a Judaic Context," in Chilton, Evans, and Neusner, *The Missing Jesus*, pp. 11–39.
García Martínez, F., "Interés de los manuscritos del Mar Muerto para judíos y Cristianos," in *El Olivo* 46, pp. 23–44.
González Echegaray, J., *Jesús en Galilea. Aproximación desde la arqueología* (Estella, 2000).
Herford, R. Travers, *Christianity in Talmud and Midrash* (London, 1903).
Jeremías, J., *Die Gleichnisse Jesu* (Göttingen, 1965).
Klausner, J., *Jesus of Nazareth. His Life, His Times, and His Teaching* (New York, 1989).
Lapide, P., *Ist das nicht Joesphs Son? Jesus im heutigen Judentum* (1976).
Mack, B.L., *A Myth of Innocence: Mark and Christian Origins* (Minneapolis, 1988).
Mack, B.L., *The Lost Gospel: The Book of Q and Christian Origins* (San Francisco, 1993).
Neusner, J., *A Rabbi Talks with Jesus* (Montreal, Kingston, London, and Ithaca, 2000).
Neusner, J., "Contents of Comparison: Reciprocally Reading Gospel's and Rabbi's Parallels," in Chilton, Evans, and Neusner, *The Missing Jesus*, 45-68.
Neusner, J., *Rabbinic Literature and the New Testament* (Valley Forge, 1994).
Pérez Fernández, M., "Gospels, Oral Traditions of the Mishnah in," in Jacob Neusner and Alan J. Avery-Peck, eds., *Encyclopaedia of Judaism* (Leiden, 2003), vol. V, pp. 2124–2136.
Pérez Fernández, M., "Las bodas de Caná y la sepultura de Jesús (John 2,1-11 y 19:39-40). Dos obras de misericordia en el evangelio de Juan," in *Signum et Testimonium. Estudios en honor del Prof. Antonio García-Moreno* (Pamplona, 2003), pp. 119–132.
Pérez Fernández, M., "Lectura del Antiguo Testamento desde el Nuevo Testamento. Estudio sobre las citas bíblicas," in *Estudios Bíblicos* 47 (1989), pp. 449–474.
Pérez Fernández, M., *Tradiciones mesiánicas en el Targum Palestinnse* (Valencia and Jerusalem, 1981).
Sanders, E.P., *Jesus and Judaism* (London, 1985).
Shiffman, L.H., *The Halakhah at Qumran* (Leiden, 1975).
Vermes, G., *Jesus the Jew* (London, 1973).
Vermes, G., *Jesus and the World of Judaism* (London, 1983).
Vermes, G., *The Religion of Jesus the Jew* (London, 1993).

CHRISTIANITY, DIASPORA JUDAISM, AND ROMAN CRISIS[*]

Robert M. Price

Acts of the Apologists

I first came to the study of the Bible as a would-be theologian, which meant I wanted to take the great menagerie of texts and genres and feed them into a meat grinder that would give me neatly packaged sausages called "theology."[1] It was, as some Postmodernists like to say, "Logocentric," at least an exercise in abstraction. I wanted to press Scripture into the service of so-called Systematic Theology. When I thought I had jumped the track and changed my focus to New Testament and Early Christianity as a descriptive discipline, little did I suspect I was still trying to play the same game. I was trying to construct an abstract template of "Christian Origins," as church historians had always done, and then fit all the data of the New Testament and the Church Fathers into that symmetrical systematic outline. I began with the traditional outline, accepted by Christian historians since Eusebius in the fourth century. According to this schema, Christianity began with Jesus Christ who taught true doctrine to his disciples, the apostles. The sum and substance of this faith was preserved in the Apostles' Creed. The apostles in turn taught the true doctrine to their appointed successors, the bishops, who in turn trained their own successors, the next generation of bishops, and so on down the line. As the official version had it, Satan waited until the last of the original apostles died and then began to train and send out heretics to corrupt the church with false doctrines. Had the devil not done this, there would have been no real diversity of belief or practice among Christians. And since it was the devil's doing, the approach to diversity could not be one

---

[*] Reprinted from *Review of Rabbinic Judaism* 5:3, 2002, pp. 316–331.
[1] Gerhard Lohfink, *The Bible: Now I Get It: A Form Criticism Handbook* (Garden City, 1979), p. 65.

of friendly dialogue. No, it had to take the form of suppression, polemic, eventually of persecution. It was war, not love.

But eventually I began to see the wisdom of more recent scholars like Ferdinand Christian Baur, Walter Bauer, Walter Schmithals, and others,[2] who had redrawn this map. They showed in great detail how the texts of the New Testament and other early Christian writings made much better sense if you pried the traditional puzzle apart, reshuffled the pieces, and started over again. The approach was more inductive, derived from the data read as much as possible on its own, not deductive, trying to make the facts fit a later creed superimposed on them in the name of institutional dogma.[3] History began to be done for its own sake, not to reinforce a party line. It was coming to be real history, not just theology in disguise. Naturally, there is never any complete escape from systematic paradigms as heuristic tools through which to construe the data as data, as Collingwood[4] would remind us: evidence for what? Without some theoretical framework through which to filter raw data, we are left dumbly facing the blooming, buzzing confusion of the undifferentiated manifold of perception, as we do every day until the evening news tries to make sense of it for us.

But the paradigm we employ may arise from our consideration of the data themselves, insofar as we can momentarily shelve our expectations about them and approach them with Zen-like wonder. Or the paradigm can be imposed out of some extraneous interest (and it is this that we hope to avoid). In this sense at least, we

---

[2] Ferdinand Christian Baur, *Paul the Apostle of Jesus Christ, His Life and Work, His Epistles and His Doctrine* (London, 2nd ed., vol. I, 1876, vol. II, 1875); Walter Bauer, *Orthodoxy and Heresy in Earliest Christianity* (Philadelphia, 1971; Walter Schmithals, *The Office of Apostle in the Early Church* (New York, 1969); Schmithals, *Gnosticism in Corinth* (New York, 1971); Schmithals, *Paul and the Gnostics* (New York. 1972); Schmithals, *Paul and James* (London, 1965); Schmithals, *The Theology of the First Christians* (Louisville, 1997); James M. Robinson and Helmut Koester, *Trajectories Through Early Christianity* (Philadelphia, 1971); James D.G. Dunn, *Unity and Diversity in the New Testament: An Inquiry into the Character of Earliest Christianity* (Philadelphia, 1977); Burton L. Mack, *The Lost Gospel: The Book of Q and Christian Origins* (San Francisco, 1993); *Who Wrote the New Testament? The Making of the Christian Myth* (San Francisco, 1995).

[3] Thomas S. Kuhn, *The Structure of Scientific Revolutions* (Chicago, 1962).

[4] R.G. Collingwood, *The Idea of History* (New York, 1956), p. 281: "Nothing is evidence except in relation to some definite question." Cf., Stanley Fish: "something very important about evidence: it is always a function of what it is to be evidence for, and is never independently available;" Fish, *Is There a Text in This Class? The Authority of Interpretive Communities* (Cambridge, 1980), p. 272.

may speak of the "colonialist" perspective of traditional Church History, in that the historical data winds up being wrested from its aboriginal (or at least earlier) meanings and appropriated for new and heteronomous dogmatic agendas. Theologians stand astride the conquered texts, planting the flag of theology where perhaps some other, earlier banner ought to fly. We seek, by contrast, to let the texts speak for themselves if we can. It may be a naive hope. Stanley Fish and others warn us that we will find nothing in the texts but whatever we approach them looking for (the traditional bane of historical Jesus studies, even today), or at least that our "findings" will inevitably be a function of the methodology we adopt and the kind of thing we approach the text looking for,[5] but the advice of Thomas V. Kuhn still holds good as a rule of thumb and a virus-alert against total subjectivity: it is easy enough to recognize "anomalous data," bits of information, signals that conspicuously did not fit well the traditional paradigm but rather ground like sand in its gears.[6] Those were bits that defied the hermeneutical project of "naturalizing the text" (Jonathan Culler).[7] They were not easily assigned a place in the orthodox scheme of things, except by harmonizations and special pleadings that made even apologists for the system guiltily wish for something better. These are the graft points from which a new paradigm may begin to grow. Ideally, it will be able to make new sense of these anomalous data as well as most

---

[5] Stanley Fish: "formal units are always a function of the interpretative model one brings to bear; they are not 'in' the text, and I would make the same argument for intentions" (*Is There a Text in this Class?*, p. 164). "This, then, is my thesis: that the form of the reader's experience, formal units, and the structure of intention are one, that they come into view simultaneously, and that therefore the questions of priority and independence do not arise" (p. 165).

[6] Kuhn, pp. 64–65.

[7] Jonathan Culler, *Structuralist Poetics: Structuralism, Linguistics, and the Study of Literature* (Ithaca, 1976): "what we speak of as conventions of a genre . . . are essentially possibilities of meaning, ways of naturalizing the text and giving it a place in the world which our culture [or, with Stanley Fish, our community of interpreters] defines. To assimilate or interpret something is to bring it within the modes of order which culture makes available, and this is usually done by talking about it in a mode of discourse which a culture takes as natural" (p. 137) "The expectations enshrined in the conventions of genre are, of course, often violated. Their function, like that of all constitutive rules, is to make meaning possible by providing terms in which to classify the things one encounters. What is made intelligible by the conventions of genre is often less interesting than that which resists or escapes generic understanding" (p. 148).

of the data that fit quite well into the old understanding. That, it seems to me, is precisely what Baur, Bauer, Mack, Schmithals, and the other revisionist historians of Christianity have sought to do, and with fabulous success.

A Jungle, Not a Garden

The picture of Christian origins that I accept and seek to build on is much sloppier than the traditional one. It posits no single origin for the Christian religion. If there was a historical Jesus in the first place (something I certainly do not take for granted anymore),[8] even he was no more than one significant factor. Radical critics sometimes say that Judaism was only partly the origin of the Christian faith, that paganism contributed just as much of the original DNA. Indeed, in some ways this reflects the traditional Jewish view of Christianity[9] as far as I understand it: Christianity is a somewhat paganized form of Jewish ethical monotheism and therefore inherently benign, though still heretical. I would agree with this if it weren't possible to get things even a bit more tightly into focus. To twist the scope over a notch, we must recognize with recent scholars[10] that our picture of a single Orthodox Jewish mainstream in the first century, a kind of Eohippus version of Rabbinic Judaism, is a fantasy, at least an exaggeration produced as a piece of apologetics for later Rabbinic

---

[8] Robert M. Price, *Deconstructing Jesus* (Amherst, 2000). In this book I extrapolate form the multiple-root model of Burton L. Mack, derived in part from Jonathan Z. Smith's studies of the diverse forms of the myth and cult of Attis, to a scenario in which, though there may well have been a historical Jesus, such a figure cannot account for all the New Testament Christologies and is required for none of them.

[9] See Jonathan Z. Smith, *Drudgery Divine: On the Comparison of Early Christianities and the Religions of Late Antiquity* (Chicago, 1990), where he tries to understand modern discussions of heresies as pseudo-historical proxy-wars between rival ecclesiastical camps who caricature and condemn each other under the guise of ancient heresies.

[10] Jacob Neusner, William S. Green, and Ernest Frerichs, eds., *Judaisms and Their Messiahs at the Turn of the Christian Era* (Cambridge, 1987); Robert Eisenman, *The Dead Sea Scrolls and the First Christians: Essays and Translations* (Rockport, 1996), esp. chapter 1, "Maccabees, Zadokites, Christians and Qumran: A New Hypothesis of Qumran Origins," pp. 3–110; Norman Golb, *Who Wrote the Dead Sea Scrolls? The Search for the Secret of Qumran* (New York, 1995); Gabriele Boccaccini, *Beyond the Essene Hypothesis: The Parting of the Ways between Qumran and Enochic Judaism* (Grand Rapids, 1998).

Judaism.¹¹ Jewish Orthodoxy as we know it only became any kind of mainstream in the early second century C.E. after the Roman conquest of Jerusalem and the establishment of the Yavneh Sanhedrin. Before that, the religion swarmed like a kaleidoscope with swirling sects and parties including the Pharisees (named, I think, for their considerable theological debt to the Parsees, or Zoroastrians),¹² the Sadducees, the Essenes, the so-called Zealots, or dynasty of Judas of Galilee,¹³ the Masbotheans, Sabeans, Hemerobaptists, Nazoreans, etc. As Norman Golb argues in *Who Wrote the Dead Sea Scrolls?*, the so-called Qumran scrolls may originally have formed the Jerusalem Temple library,¹⁴ and that means there was as yet no orthodoxy, not even any mention in the sacred texts of anything we would recognize from later standards as orthodoxy.

Margaret Barker, in *The Great Angel: A Study of Israel's Second God*¹⁵ and Raphael Patai, in *The Hebrew Goddess*¹⁶ go further and make clear by a survey of lots of usually neglected evidence that not even the cornerstone of Jewish monotheism was secure in the first century C.E. What would later be christened Trinitarianism emerged first from popular, traditional Israelite polytheism, the very ancient belief, interdicted by prophet and king alike, that God was one, eventually the king, of a larger pantheon, a king who had reigned with a divine

---

¹¹ Solomon Schechter, *Some Aspects of Rabbinic Theology* (New York, 1910); George Foot Moore, *Judaism* (Cambridge, 2nd ed., 1954).
¹² T.W. Manson, *The Servant Messiah: A Study of the Public Ministry of Jesus* (Cambridge, 1961), p. 19.
¹³ Contra Richard A. Horsley, *Jesus and the Spiral of Violence: Popular Jewish Resistance in Roman Palestine* (Minneapolis, 1993), pp. 77–89, who tries desperately to make Judas the Galilean/Gaulonite into a pacifistic resistor of Roman taxation. He observes that Josephus says Judas was willing to resist even to the point of shedding blood, and Horsley, who wants to interpret Jesus, too, as a non-violent resistance leader, makes Judas his predecessor by suggesting that all Josephus meant was that Judas was willing to have his own blood shed in martyrdom rather than pay taxes to the pagan empire, like the saintly Eleazar who underwent horrible tortures rather than have a ham sandwich at Antiochus Epiphanes' behest. But then what sort of "fourth philosophy" can it be that Judas founded by whatever action he took? We know good and well from Josephus' subsequent references to various violent revolutionists, like Menahem and the Zealots, who proudly traced their dynastic descent from Judas, something they would scarcely have done had Judas been a pacifist as Horsley wants him and Jesus and us to be.
¹⁴ Golb, chapter 5, "The Copper Scroll, the Masada Manuscripts, and the Siege of Jerusalem," pp. 117–150 and 382–383.
¹⁵ Margaret Barker, *The Great Angel: A Study of Israel's Second God* (London, 1992).
¹⁶ Raphael Patai, *The Hebrew Goddess* (New York, 1978).

queen, who had had a son, or been a son, depending on which God one conflated with which other God. In many or even most ways, early Christianity differed not so much from contemporary types of Judaism as it did from the later paradigm of orthodoxy, whether Jewish or Christian. It was only once Orthodox Judaism consolidated itself after the Roman crisis that Christianity looked so different, because Christianity was a direct cousin of those types of Judaism that had been rejected from the Orthodox synthesis.

This was a process with an ancient pedigree in Israelite religion, as Julius Wellhausen was the first to show. Each major regrouping and standardizing of Jewish traditions led to a retroactive, revisionary view of what had gone before. At first, for instance, anyone might construct an altar anywhere that God had manifested himself (for example, in a dream, Gen. 28:10-22). So stipulates the Book of the Covenant preserved in the J source of the Pentateuch, in Exod. 20:24-26. But after Deuteronomy's centralization of worship, implicitly in Solomon's Temple, the Deuteronomic redactors who compiled Joshua, Judges, Samuel, and Kings made these once-proper shrines into abhorrent "high places," as if they had always been illicit dens of blasphemy. The Priestly Code even makes Moses and Israel centralize worship by carrying the Ark of the Covenant around amid their wanderings. Still later, the Chronicler, who cannot picture Israel without a temple, concocts the mini-temple called the Tabernacle, which must be knocked down and set up again every day in the Sinai Wilderness—not likely. In each case, the current arrangements of orthodoxy were retrojected into the remote past.

The same held good for the very late development of monotheism, the exclusive belief in a single God. It surfaced first with Jeremiah and Second Isaiah, and once it had taken hold among the religious establishment, we suddenly read that Moses himself had commanded monotheism, and so had all the prophets. Where had all the other gods mentioned in Scripture come from? Simple: they must have been illicit adoptions from Canaanite polytheism. As if there had ever been much of a difference between ancient Israelite religion and its cognate forms across the borders in the adjacent postage-stamp kingdoms. In fact, Jehovah had always been little more than Baal-Hadad with a nom-de-plume. He had defeated Leviathan just as they said he had defeated the dragon Lotan across the street where they recounted the same myth with only a difference in accent.

It is exactly in this light that we can start to make sense of the Jewish perception that Christianity began as a straining of Judaism through a filter of pagan assimilations, by pagans who admired Judaism from afar, the so-called God-fearers. It only looks that way once you superimpose onto the history an anachronistic model of Judaism, as if gentile God-Fearers started with an early form of Rabbinic Judaism, stripping off most of the purity regulations and adding odd bits of pagan cult soteriology. Instead, it seems more likely that what they learned as Judaism already had more native content in common with the paganism they had inherited. In turn, this was not because ancient Israel had assimilated forbidden cultic fruit from the Canaanite blasphemers, but rather because ancient Israelite religion originally had quite a bit in common with its neighbor denominations. It is not so much a case of Christianity and Judaism having separated from one another as of emergent Orthodox Judaism, Mishnaic Judaism, excluding from itself the various earlier types of Judaism among which early Christianity belonged.

Suitors and Seducers

What about the challenges of diaspora assimilationism? There surely was such a thing as Jews' taking attractive features of gentile faiths and mixing them with their own. My caveat is just to say that wildly diverse Judaisms already existed back in the Holy Land. And I would say the mythemes later assimilated from Hellenistic Mystery Religions were able to gain entry because they answered to elements already present in Judaism, perhaps all the more attractive once they had become forbidden fruit in the wake of Yavneh. In other words, when the family next door celebrated the death and resurrection of Osiris or Adonis this might appeal to a Jew who was dimly aware that his grandfathers had celebrated pretty much the same rites in honor of Baal, Tammuz, or even Isaac, years before.[17] 2 Maccabees 6:7 tells

---

[17] For Isaac as an echo of a Hebrew dying-and-rising god, see Shalom Spiegel, *The Last Trial: On the Legends and Lore of the Command to Abraham to Offer Isaac as a Sacrifice, the Akedah* (Woodstock, 1993), pp. 57–59, 111–113. On Abel as Baal, see Robert Graves and Raphael Patai, *Hebrew Myths: The Book of Genesis* (New York, 1983), p. 95. In the latter case, the crying out of Abel's voice from the bloody ground is a remnant of the myth in which Anath discovers Baal's fate on the bloody field and resolves to restore him to life.

us that Antiochus converted large numbers of Jews to the worship of Dionysus. One suspects it was no arduous task, given that some Greek writers already considered Jehovah simply another local variant of Dionysus anyway. The Sabazius religion of Phrygia is plainly an example of worshipping Jehovah as Dionysus. The Phrygian Attis was another version of Adam, his mother and lover Cybele a cognate form of Eve. No wonder the Naasene Document identifies the resurrected Jesus with both Attis and Adam. No wonder we have Jewish sarcophagi from this period depicting both the menorah and the symbol of the resurrected Attis.[18]

The temptations and challenges of the diaspora only served to increase the diversity of ancient Judaism, a diversity directly reflected in emerging Christianity, which demonstrably partakes of Jewish Gnosticism,[19] Zoroastrianism,[20] the Mystery Cults, etc. As Rodney Stark has shown, diaspora Jews remained a major and continuous source of new Christian converts on into the fifth century.[21] Christianity would have been, Stark very plausibly surmises, the ideal assimilation vehicle, since the "new" faith allowed one to retain the cherished ethical monotheism of Judaism yet without keeping up the walls of purity rules that separated one (arbitrarily, as it seemed, and as it would seem again to nineteenth- and twentieth-century Reform Jews) from one's neighbors. It seems to me that adherence to Christianity (the "true Israel") would also have been the natural way of clinging to traditional elements of popular Judaism upon which Orthodoxy had frowned but which, as Barker shows, had never died out. I suspect that such Christian-leaning Jews eyed emergent Rabbinic Yavneh Judaism as a modern product and viewed it as most pious non-Pharisaic Jews had always viewed the stricter party of the Pharisees (and the Essenes). It would have been entirely natural for Christianizing Jews, hanging

---

[18] Richard Reitzenstein, *Hellenistic Mystery Religions: Their Basic Ideas and Significance* (Pittsburgh, 1978), pp.123–125, 158, 176–177.

[19] Walter Schmithals, *The Apocalyptic Movement: Introduction and Interpretation* (New York, 1975); Gershom Scholem, *Jewish Gnosticism, Merkabah Mysticism, and Talmudic Tradition* (New York, 2nd ed., 1965), esp. chapter IX, "The Relationship between Gnostic and Jewish Sources," pp. 65–74.

[20] Andrew Welburn, *The Beginnings of Christianity: Essene Mystery, Gnostic Revelation and the Christian Vision* (Edinburgh, 1991), pp. 44–51. The identification of the Nag Hammadi *Apocalypse of Adam* as Zoroastrian in substance has enormous implications.

[21] Rodney Stark, *The Rise of Christianity: A Sociologist Reconsiders History* (Princeton, 1996), pp. 57–64.

on to cherished "underground" mythemes, etc., to have viewed themselves as the real Judaism, the old-time religion. We have, again, been too eager to take the Rabbinic claims to pedigree and originality at face value. Perhaps one more piece of evidence that this is a proper way to view matters is the otherwise odd fact that many Christians continued to attend synagogue for centuries, alongside church, often to the great consternation of their bishops. This implies that the synagogue-attenders viewed the defining label for their religiosity as Judaism, not as a new, split-off religion. Their Christianity was Judaism in their eyes, even if Christian bishops (like Chrysostom) and Jewish rabbis alike bemoaned the fact.[22]

Assimilation Makes an Ass out of I and Him

What happens to a culture that is suddenly and massively challenged by an invasive culture? There are three responses to such a situation. They may be predicted like clockwork. First is cultural-religious capitulation, where the threatened people simply throws in the towel and admits the new, foreign gods must be the ones to worship, since, after all, one's own traditional deities proved unable to turn back their assault. It was to fend off such a conclusion that the prophets had argued that it was the Hebrew God, not the Assyrian and Babylonian gods, who had directed the heathen to defeat Israel. Or one might simply reassure oneself that the new God was just the old one under a different name—as he might well have been! Or think of Philo, who reinterpreted the Torah as an allegory of Plato, rationalizing that Plato had himself derived his thought from reading Moses! Those to the left of Philo reasoned that, since they understood the allegorical meaning of the laws of Moses, there was no longer any need to keep them! What some called apostasy from Judaism, others deemed the rehabilitation of Judaism. No wonder confusion arose among Jewish Christians as to whether Jesus had abolished or fulfilled the Torah! Was it that hard to tell the difference? Ask today's Orthodox and Reform Jew!

Second, one might make a stand, refuse to compromise, and try to fight off the alien culture. Presumably we might see Mattathias

---

[22] Ibid., pp. 66–70.

and his sons in this position, throwing off the yoke of the Seleucid Empire. Whether they fought the fight without compromise is not absolutely clear. After all, the subsequent shape of proto-Orthodox Judaism, with its rabbi-disciple relationship, the institution of synagogues, hermeneutical rules like Hillel's, all come from Greece.[23]

Third, one may recognize that the heathen must be onto something or they would not be so successful, so one selectively adopts and adapts aspects of the enemy to use against him. Perhaps the Hasmoneans belong in this category. A movement like this third type is called a Revitalization Movement.[24] It seeks to save the old ways by making creative compromise with the new. The Ghost Dance religion of the Sioux would be a good example, as would numerous Cargo Cults described by Peter Worsley in *The Trumpet Shall Sound: A Study of "Cargo" Cults in Melanesia*.[25] In the latter group of movements, we find a recurring pattern whereby islanders assimilate at least the pantomiming of Western technology and religion and wind up with a belief that the colonists' Jesus was originally one of themselves, stolen from them, like their other resources, by the Western occupiers, and that he will soon drive out the Europeans and return aboard an airplane or an ocean liner filled with all manner of Western goodies for the faithful. Of course, the inevitable danger here is that one's new product, partaking both of the familiar and the alien, will be perceived (perhaps rightly) as a species of dangerous Modernism scarcely less ominous than the challenge from without. Traditionalists may give up, feeling they are faced only with Scylla and Charybdis. But then this may be the point when an old religion dies and a new one is born, the improbable product of hybridization between the alien and the traditional religions/cultures.

John G. Gager[26] has suggested Christianity began as precisely such a revitalization movement, facing down the twin challenges of Hellenism and Roman domination. But his theory seems to presuppose the traditional picture of a historical Jesus as the single and specific founder

---

[23] Martin Hengel, *Judaism and Hellenism: Studies in their Encounter in Palestine during the Early Hellenistic Period* (Philadelphia, 1981), vol. I, pp. 80–81.

[24] Anthony Wallace, *Religion: An Anthropological View* (New York, 1966), pp. 30–38; Wallace, "Revitalization Movements," in *American Anthropologist* 58 (1956), pp. 264–281.

[25] Peter Worsley, *The Trumpet Shall Sound: A Study of Melanesian "Cargo" Cults* (New York, 2nd ed., 1974).

[26] John G. Gager, *Kingdom and Community: The Social World of Early Christianity* (Englewood Cliffs, 1975).

of the movement, just reinterpreting him a bit, sort of a variation of S.G.F. Brandon.[27] It seems to me that the various depictions of Jesus and the various sayings attributed to him are functions, products, of the various factions of early Christianity, themselves the products of various Jewish and Hellenistic currents. And yet, perhaps, this very insight mitigates the problem with Gager's theory in that the messianic office may need to function only as a banner of faith which, dropped by one fallen bearer, may be taken up by a successor, scarcely missing a beat.[28] Remember how the followers of both men are shown in Mark 6:14; 8:27-28 to have believed Jesus was John the Baptist resurrected from the dead and carrying on for him, just as Jesus himself is shown interpreting John the Baptist as the promised return of Elijah (Mark 9:12-13). Was Jesus' ostensible resurrection similarly his replacement by a successor?[29] One might almost say that the notion of a hero's resurrection is simply a symbol for the continuity between a fallen Messiah and his successor, who is thus perceived as the first Messiah's continuation. It is perhaps the office not the man (though a particular man's name may have become a title of office).[30] So Gager's reconstruction need not necessarily depend on there having been one single prophet-founder.

These three options would have faced Jews in the Holy Land, but Diaspora Jews like Philo also faced them as I have already implied. How best to witness for Judaism? By drawing the lines clearly between oneself and one's non-Jewish neighbor? Or by seeking to translate one's own beliefs and mores into pagan idiom? Many understand

---

[27] S.G.F. Brandon, *Jesus and the Zealots: A Study of the Political Factor in Earliest Christianity* (New York, 1967).

[28] Stephen Fuchs, *Rebellious Prophets: A Study of Messianic Movements in Indian Religions* (New York, 1965), p. 150: "As often in messianic movements, when a prophecy fails to come true it is the prophet, not his prophecy, that is discredited. The failure is his fault. Thus the way remains open for another prophet to come forward with a slightly modified version of the doctrine and claiming that he, and not his predecessor, is the true Messenger of God and Messiah." One early Unificationist (Moonie) missionary from Korea to America said, "Reverend Moon is one of the potential messiahs, because his role has to be fulfilled, and it is not yet fulfilled. So I don't say he is the actual messiah. Whether he will be the one, I can't say yet." Quoted in Frederick Sontag, *Sun Myung Moon and the Unification Church: An In-Depth Investigation of the Man and the Movement* (New York, 1977), p. 49.

[29] In John's gospel, one receives the distinct impression that the coming of the Paraclete is synonymous with the return of Christ, and that the Paraclete is none other than the man who wrote the Gospel of John.

[30] See the excellent and most informative article by Scott D. Hill, "The Local Hero in Palestine in Comparative Perspective," in Robert B. Coote, ed., *Elijah and Elisha in Socioliterary Perspective* (Atlanta, 1992), pp. 37–73.

Paul the Apostle as embracing the latter option as an evangelistic strategy. And his creative "indigenous" theologizing is understood by many as the major entry point of pagan elements into Christianity. I think this is an error. Paul is as much a factional totem with many faces as is Jesus himself. Again, we can speak only of Paulinism as a type (or family of types) of early Christianity.[31] And it seems likely to me that the Pauline trajectory was less a matter of paganizing the Judaism of Jesus than it was of seeking to abstract a cosmic half-philosophical salvation myth from its original Jewish elements.

Paulinism, especially Marcion and the Gnostics in the second century, did this precisely, I am guessing, as a repudiation of emerging Rabbinic Judaism, the Judaism that no longer bore the marks of kinship with primitive Christian sectarianism. This has become crystal clear from the discovery of the astonishing Nag Hammadi texts, which must be understood as the written testaments of living religious conventicles, including Christianized Sethian Jewish Gnostics, Melchizedekians, and Zoroastrians. We cannot leave these writings in a docetic vacuum, as if they were a bunch of science fiction novels spun out of the imagination of some eccentric. Rather, I believe, they will demand a wholesale rewriting of Christian origins once we have studied them enough to surmise how to reshuffle the pieces of the puzzle, now that we have more of them, to compose a much larger and more colorful resultant picture.

Prehistoric Monsters

Marcionism, Gnosticism, Jewish Christianity, and several other kinds of Christianity are now fossils in the theological museum, and for one simple reason. There came a moment of Christian consolidation, again, due to Roman influence.[32] The foundation of Yavneh

---

[31] Hermann Detering, "The Dutch Radical Approach to the Pauline Epistles," in *Journal of Higher Criticism* 3/2 (Fall, 1996), pp. 163–193.

[32] It is remarkable that in both cases of Roman crisis issuing in doctrinal consolidation of the religion, the relevant Caesar came to assume a messianic character. Josephus proclaimed Vespasian the messiah predicted in Scripture, while Constantine viewed himself implicitly as the new Christ, arranging to be buried surrounded by the gathered relics of the twelve apostles (William Steuart McBirnie, *The Search for the Twelve Apostles* [Wheaton, 1973], pp. 19–20). Come to think of it, Cyrus the Persian, patron of Ezra's consolidation of a new Post-Exilic Judaism, had been hailed as God's Anointed in exactly the same fashion (Is. 45:1).

Judaism after the destruction of Jerusalem had its parallel in the establishment of Catholic/Orthodox Christianity under Constantine's heavy-handed patronage. Not Christianity per se, but a particular kind of Christianity attracted his favor (if he had not actually been brought up in it):[33] a combination of the Gnostic Redeemer Myth with the sacramental initiation of the Mystery Cults.[34] Other Christians and scriptures and texts of the New Testament were systematically destroyed as far as the long hand of the Emperor and his favorite bishops reached. And the retrospective understanding of church history I began with was crafted to form the legitimation myth of this Establishment Christianity. The Nicene Creed and the Athanasian New Testament canon were the result.

One caveat: when we speak of Gnosticism as a type of Christianity that was suppressed, we probably ought to think of it (as with Ebionite "Jewish Christianity" and the rest) as more of an ideal type, a collection of spiritual and theo-mythological tendencies abroad in early Christianity, than as a set of discrete organizations with membership lists, as if some would have considered themselves adherents of a movement called "Gnosticism" and others would not have.[35] Distinct social entities corresponding to "Gnosticism" did eventually emerge, namely later congregations of Manicheans, but first- and second-century Gnostics existed, as Irenaeus tells us, as cells within Catholic churches. (Marcionism was an organized denomination from early on, but it was not Gnostic, holding back no advanced course for the elite.) The best analogy would be that of the modern American Pentecostal/Charismatic movements. At the turn of the nineteenth-twentieth centuries, "Pentecostalism," i.e., emphases on empowering Spirit-baptism and the initial evidence of speaking in tongues, began among Holiness Church circles and revivals and quickly spread into Baptist and Methodist congregations. They sought to coexist, but their zeal led to their being excluded, excommunicated, whereupon they had no choice but to organize their own new churches and

---

[33] T.G. Elliott, *The Christianity of Constantine the Great* (Scranton, 1996), chapter 4, "Rome, 312-and Eusebius' Conversion Story," pp. 61–72.

[34] I am afraid I am unable to consider emerging Catholic Christianity as even one of the early types of Christianity. It seems rather to be a secondary development, an amalgam, as I have said, of two earlier types, each with its own theological integrity, plus the popular Hellenistic tradition of Jesus as a wonder-working demigod.

[35] Michael Allen Williams, *Rethinking "Gnosticism": An Argument for Dismantling a Dubious Category* (Princeton, 1996).

denominations, like the Church of God in Christ, the Assemblies of God, the Pentecostal Holiness Church, the United Pentecostal Church. For our purposes it is important to recognize that Gnosticism must have begun and proceeded in somewhat the same manner. That is, the polemics against Gnostic teachings and practices by Irenaeus and Tertullian, like the opposition of Baptist, Methodist, and Holiness hierarchies to Pentecostalism, would have led to a social consolidation of Gnostics into new groups, and this made it possible subsequently for Constantinian bishops to pursue violent persecutions of such publicly visible groups. But if we retroject "Gnosticism" as a social entity back before Irenaeus, we are stumbling into the old familiar pitfall. We are positing an apologetically convenient whipping boy whom we may accuse of insidiously corrupting a hitherto distinct and pure Christianity when in reality it was just a name for a set of tendencies shared throughout Christianity (as in Judaism). In delineating and polemicizing against Gnosticism, Irenaeus and his fellows were not trying to fight off invaders from some other theological world. Instead, they were trying, like Dr. Jeckyll, to exorcise the dangerous tendencies from their own breast, and the result was a veritable Mr. Hyde, a theological bogeyman. Gnostics had thus taken over the role from the ancient Canaanites.

It was in defense of Constantinian Orthodoxy that Eusebius invoked from the (possibly fictive) second-century Jewish Christian historian Hegesippus[36] and his model of the post-apostolic sabotage of pristine Catholicism. I think we can see the real function and nature of this model by observing how easily it is appropriated by a whole series of sectarian groups, all of whom see themselves as the restorers of authentic primitive Christianity. For them, the post-apostolic "Fall of the Church" is the very establishment of Constantinian Orthodoxy! By contrast, the efforts of Alexander Campbell, Joseph Smith, Charles Taze Russell, Mary Baker Eddy, John Nelson Darby, Victor Paul Wierwille, and others were aimed

---

[36] I suspect that "*He-gesippus*" is a garbled version of "Josephus," made into a catch-all pedigree for whatever tradition or belief one wished to retroject into an earlier "apostolic" period; cf., Jacob Neusner, *In Search of Talmudic Biography: The Problem of the Attributed Saying* (Chico, 1984) on the similar problem, in Rabbinic literature, of knowing whether an attribution to a venerable name ever in fact refers to anything earlier in history than the document in which the citation appears.

at voyaging into the apostolic past and recreating the Christianity of those days. All such strategies represent what Jacques Derrida calls "the dangerous supplement," something that poses as a lost original but is actually a later substitute. Other examples would include the Golden Age of primitive communism, the Noble Savage, primitive Matriarchy, the Historical Jesus. All are hypothetical reconstructions seeking to supplant inherited beliefs or institutions which have come to seem unsatisfactory. In all such cases, one is in effect trying to substitute counter-culture for the reigning culture by the device of claiming for one's creation the privileged status of nature, the "real thing" before culture ruined things. The easy and natural sectarian use of the Hegesippean/Eusebian model reveals emergent Catholic Orthodoxy, ironically, as one more sect striving to appropriate the coveted pedigree of apostolic foundation.

Evolution, Not Excommunication

This "classic," "Orthodox" type of Christianity does not look much like Yavneh-Rabbinic Judaism, nor like the varieties of Christianity suppressed for its sake. Thus Christianity as we know it and Judaism as we know it never in fact separated from one another in the manner of, say, Eastern Orthodox and Roman Catholic Christianity in the eleventh century. Rather, each is a finally dominant form at the end of its own branch of the tree of religious evolution. I am denying what evolutionists deny when they correct the popular misconception that humans descended from apes: no, the two are related, but not directly. They merely share remote evolutionary ancestors.

And the same goes for Islam. To glance in that direction, we may suggest that, just as primitive Christianity inherited and/or preserved beliefs excluded by formative Rabbinic Judaism, making them central, so did Islam cherish numerous discarded elements of once-vibrant Christianities rendered "heretical" by Constantine. These would include the belief that Jesus only seemed to die on the cross, the expectation of the Paraclete as a historical individual,[37] the use of

---

[37] "And the figure itself must have originated in a body of opinion, according to which the revelation was not concentrated on one historical bearer, but shared amongst several messengers following upon each other, or repeated in them;" Rudolf Bultmann, *The Gospel of John: A Commentary* (Philadelphia, 1975), p. 567.

apocryphal gospel traditions, and the elimination of the so-called "Writing Prophets" in favor of an esoteric succession of prophets including Adam, Seth, Noah and Enoch.[38] In the same way, Shi'a Islam seems to have preserved and accentuated elements gradually excluded from the Sunni community, eventually spinning off the Druze and Baha'i Faiths. The Shi'ites took up for themselves the fallen banner of messianic expectation, rejecting the Sunni notion of Muhammad as the Final Prophet in all but name, and replacing the Sunni prophetology with a continuing line of Imams inspired by Allah and descended from Ali. As time went by, Orthodox Islamic prophetology was further revoked as the various Imams took their places following Muhammad and his own predecessors (as well as new trajectories of Caliphs, Imams, and Babs) as veritable divine incarnations. The great wave that had once swept Muhammad to his seemingly insurmountable pinnacle had receded and had now thundered back in, carrying a number of others even further in its wake. Theological sea-walls erected to stop the wave's next encroachment only served to increase its power when it came roaring back in.[39] And so it goes. Nothing is lost. The repressed returns. One faith's outgrown heresy becomes the next faith's cherished badge of orthodoxy, just as Buddhist monks donned the shrouds of the dead for their monastic habit.

---

[38] Tor Andre, *Mohammed: The Man and His Faith* (New York, 1960), esp. chapter IV, "Mohammed's Doctrine of Revelation," pp. 94–113.

[39] See the historical deposits of these tidal waves of revelation in Mohammed Ali Amir-Moezzi, *The Divine Guide in Early Shi'ism: The Sources of Esotericism in Islam* (Albany, 1994); Abdulaziz Abdulhussein Sachedina, *Islamic Messianism: The Idea of the Mahdi in Twelver Shi'ism* (Albany, 1981); Fuad I. Khuri, *Imams and Emirs: State, Religion and Sects in Islam* (London, 1990); Farhad Daftary, *The Isma'ilis: Their History and Doctrines* (Cambridge, 1990); Matti Moosa, *Extremist Shiites: The Ghulat Sects* (Syracuse, 1988); Sami Nasib Makarem, *The Doctrine of the Ismailis* (Beirut, 1972); Makarem, *The Druze Faith* (Delmar, 1974); Robert Brenton Betts, *The Druze* (New Haven, 1988).

THE MEDIEVAL PERIOD

NEWTON, MAIMONIDEAN*

José Faur
Netanya College

I

The triumph of the anti-Maimonidean ideology in Spain, bent on eradicating "heresy" from Israel, had a ripple effect as of yet unexplored by Jewish historians and other luminaries. It is not accurate that the anti-Maimonideans were against "assimilation" to non-Jewish ideas, as the magistrates of Jewish wisdom kindly moralize. In fact, the anti-Maimonideans were willing to take a lesson or two from those Christians who condemned men of the stature of William of Conches (ca. 1090–ca.1160), Peter Abelard (1079–1142), and Thomas Aquinas (1224/5–1274). These holy men would not shy away from learning from *any* persecuting ideology, regardless of religion or philosophical persuasion.[1] What they opposed were people like the Maimonideans who were spreading all types of silly, essentially harmful, ideas, like writing that sorcery and witchcraft are "lies and falsehood." There is malice in these fabrications. They were designed to impugn the minds and judgment of those saintly men—the inerrantly pious—who not only witnessed demons but also kept daily contacts with them and other supernatural beings. In fact, all men of sound mind and spirit should reject the Maimonidean folly, especially in light of the unimpeachable evidence provided by "the science of necromancy." As a good and wise doctor at the Sorbonne wrote in 1609 about those feeble souls denying night-flying witches, metamorphoses, etc., magical phenomena are so well attested to that they could be "disbelieved only by those of unsound mind."[2]

The anti-Maimonidean society is, primarily and fundamentally, a persecuting society.[3] It seems that Gresham's law of economics,

---

* Reprinted from *Review of Rabbinic Judaism* 6:2–3, 2004, pp. 215–249.
[1] See José Faur, *In the Shadow of History: Jews and Conversos at the Dawn of Modernity* (Albany, 1992), pp. 9–27.
[2] See José Faur, "Anti-Maimonidean Demons," in *The Review of Rabbinic Judaism* 6, 1, 2003, pp. 3–52.
[3] See Faur, *In the Shadow of History*, pp. 2, 6, 215–217. A telling detail, indicative of the supreme authority exercised by the anti-Maimonideans: throughout the

whereby bad money drives good money out of circulation, applies to political and social leadership as well.[4] A society that accepts magic and the reveries of lunatics as God's True Word would not tolerate rational discourse—least of all the scientific study of nature or an intelligent consideration of Judaism. Thus, creative thinking, let alone scientific knowledge, was no longer tolerated. This explains the sad fact that most of the creative thinking in the sciences, humanities, and literature in Spain, was made by *conversos*. Yet nothing remotely similar was taking place within the confines of the Jewish communities.[5] In this respect, after the Expulsion (1492) things got worse, not better. The few men who preserved some vestige of the old Jewish scientific tradition—I am thinking about such distinguished figures as Rabbis Moses Almosnino (c. 1515–1589), David Gans (1541–1613), Joseph Del Medigo (1591–1655)—were working with medieval concepts, no longer on a par with the scientific outlook unfolding at their time. The few creative minds had to tread carefully. On the instigation of Sabbatean sympathizers, R. David Nieto (1654–1728), rabbi of the Sephardic community in London, was about to be excommunicated for a sermon he pronounced in his own synagogue.[6] R. Israel Moses Hazan (1807–1863), who had been the Chief Rabbi of Rome, Corfu, and Alexandria, was ferociously persecuted by his semi-literate colleagues.[7] R. Elie Benamozegh (1822–1900), Chief Rabbi of Leghorn, one of the most distinguished communities in Europe, was declared a heretic and his books banned, etc.[8] We often forget that Jews were able to produce a Freud or an Einstein not as the result of some

---

communities around the Mediterranean Basin and the Middle East (with the exception of Yemen) is yet to be found a single scroll of the Torah written according to the format prescribed by Maimonides! This is true even in Aleppo, home of the famous codex of Maimonides' *Keter Aram Soba*. Cf. Faur, "Anti-Maimonidean Demons," nn. 23–24.

[4] Cf. Faur, *In the Shadow of History*, pp. 21–22.

[5] Ibid., p. 2.

[6] On the content and significance of this sermon, see José Faur, *Golden Doves and Silver Dots: Semiotics and Textuality in Rabbinic Tradition* (Bloomington, 1986), pp. 19–22.

[7] See José Faur, *Rabbi Yisrael Moshe Hazan* (Heb.) (Haifa, 1978), pp. 15–18.

[8] The impact on his family and personal life was devastating. However, on behalf of the persecuting rabbis one may point out that this was not a case of simple malice. As always, the "heretical" view of the "other" is connected to pecuniary gain. In our case, R. Benamozegh owned one of the largest printing houses of Hebrew books in Leghorn. Declaring him "heretical" meant that the books he printed must be proscribed, regardless of content. Consequently, competing firms, which until now could not enter the market, gained the upper hand. A few years

internal development but simply because universities decided to open their doors to Jews without demanding prior conversion. One can only ponder what the state of Jewish scholarship today would have been (including the fields of Talmud and Rabbinics), if it were not for the "Jewish Studies Programs" at universities world-wide.

It should not be surprising to discover, therefore, that some Jewish thinkers, particularly those professing the kind of religious humanism and pluralism developed by the Maimonidean tradition, chose to share their knowledge and exchange ideas with members of the Christian intelligentsia, many of them distinguished Hebraists in their own rights.[9] One such individual was R. Isaac Abendana (c. 1640–c. 1710), brother of R. Jacob Abendana (1630–1685), Chief Rabbi of Amsterdam. He arrived in England in 1662. Abendana was an extremely talented and accomplished scholar. At the urging of Cambridge theologians he translated for the first time the entire Mishnah into Latin.[10] His book, *Discourses on the Ecclesiastical and Civil Polity of the Jews* (London, 1706; 2nd edition 1709) is the first work written by a Jew in English. While at Cambridge he kept contact with the scholarly community at Oxford. Eventually, he moved to Oxford in 1689 and taught Hebrew at Magdalene College. In a work published in 1710 we are told, "Dr. Abendana assisted Dr. [Thomas] Hyde [1636–1703]. . . . The said Dr. [Abendana] was himself the author of the Hebrew tract (written in a florid style) concerning Chess, published as an old piece by Dr. Hyde."[11]

---

ago in Leghorn, on the one hundred year anniversary of Benamozegh's death, I pointed out that as a result, he no longer would append his full signature to the books he printed and his editorial notes, but only the initials אב"א, standing for Eliahu ben Amozegh.

[9] See the important work of Aaron L. Katchen, *Christian Hebraists and Dutch Rabbis* (Cambridge, MA, 1984). On the impact of Maimonides in particular, see ibid., chapter 3. On the impact of Maimonides on sixteenth and seventeenth century Englishmen, such as Hobbes, Milton, John Smith, John Spencer, et al., see the stimulating note of J.L. Teicher, "Maimonides and England," in *Transactions, Jewish Historical Society of England* 16 (1950), pp. 97–100.

[10] See Israel Abrahams, "Isaac Abendana's Cambridge Mishna and Oxford Calendars," in *Transactions, Jewish Historical Society of England* 8 (1915–1917), pp. 98–121; and idem, "Note on Isaac Abendana," in *Transactions, Jewish Historical Society of England* 10 (1921–1923), pp. 221–224. For some valuable notes on Isaac and Jacob Abendana, see M. Kayserling, "Les Correspondants Juifs de Jean Buxtorf," in *Revue des Études Juives* 13 (1886), pp. 272–276.

[11] Cited by William D. Macray, "A letter from Isaac Abendana," in *Festschrif zum . . . Moritz Steinshneider's* (Leipzig, 1896), p. 89.

Elsewhere I proposed that Abendana was Isaac Newton's (1643–1727) Hebrew teacher.[12] Abendana began teaching Hebrew at Cambridge in 1663, a year after Newton entered Trinity College. Newton was an excellent Hebraist. Although only a small portion of Newton's library was saved (see below section III), several Hebrew Bibles, Buxtorf, *Lexicon Hebraicum* (1621), Robertson, *Lexicon Hebraeum* (1680), as well as many works on Jewish subjects were found in the remains of his library.[13] Newton's knowledge of Rabbinics was simply amazing. In the course of a Rabbinic discussion, Newton records the opinion of R. Aharon ha-Levi (thirteenth century), the supposed author of *Sefer ha-Hinnukh*,[14] and his disagreement with Rashi on the matter at hand. He also refers to the Rabbinic work Sifra as well as to the view of R. Aaron ibn Hayyim (b. ca. 1560), author of *Qorban Aharon* (Venice, 5369/1609).[15] Later on, he examined *Seder Ma'amadot* (the participation of the Israelites in the daily sacrifices) and quoted the opinion of R. 'Obadiah of Bertinoro on M. Yoma 7:1.[16] In a discussion of the apocalyptic conflict of Gog and Magog, he made reference to the Targum to Esther (2:12), to the Rabbinic work Leviticus Rabbah, and to the commentaries of Se'adya Ga'on and Ibn 'Ezra.[17] In his *Chronology of Ancient Kingdoms* (London, 1727), Newton cites Yerushalmi Shebi'it (p. 198) and Seder 'Olam (p. 357).[18] In his work *The Sacred Cubit of the Jews*, published in the *Collected Works* of John Greaves (London, 1738), he alludes to the commentary of R. Obadiah of Bertinoro on M. Erubin 4:5 (s.v. *ella*) (p. 421); he translates the Aramaic version of Ruth 1:6 in conjunction with the distance a Jew is permitted to travel by foot on the Sabbath and holidays (pp. 422–423); cites a passage in the Talmud (B. Erubin 42a) and the note on it in *Shibbole ha-Leqet* (by R. Sidiqiyya ha-Rofe, Venice 5306/1546, #97) (p. 423); and also makes reference to the two cubits that were engraved

---

[12] José Faur, "Newton, Maimonides, and Esoteric Knowledge," in *Cross Currents: Religion & Intellectual Life* 8 (1990), p. 528.
[13] See Richard de Villamil, *Newton: The Man* (London, 1927), p. 67, and ibid., "Supplementary List," p. 105.
[14] There is a book by Johann Heinrich Hottinger, *Juris Hebraerorum* (Zurich, 1655), based on this work.
[15] See Yah. Ms. 13.2, 21b-22a.
[16] Yah. Ms. 13.2, 22b.
[17] See H. McLachlan, *Sir Isaac Newton Theological Manuscripts* (Liverpool, 1950), p. 135.
[18] There is a Latin translation of this work by Gilbert Génébrard, *Chronologia Hebraerorum Maior* (Paris, 1578).

in the city of Shushan (B. Pesahim 86a) (p. 425). There are some Hebrew writings in Newton's own hand[19] as well as extensive passages from the Babylonian Talmud and Yerushalmi in Latin in his own hand.[20] With the exception of Nieto and Abendana, no other scholar in England at the time, Jew or Christian, equaled his mastery of Jewish knowledge.

A copy of Abendana's first edition of *Discourses on the Ecclesiastical and Civil Polity of the Jews* (1706) was found in Newton's library.[21] Indeed, many of the subjects subsequently developed by Newton are found in Abendana's book. From his teacher, Newton must have gotten his keen interest in the Jewish calendar.[22] I would like to call attention to Yah. Ms. 22, a work by Newton on the Calendar, "Considerations about rectifying the Julian Kalendar." On p. 4 of the ms. is a quotation from Maimonides' *Qiddush ha-Hodesh* in the Jewish calendar, taken from Ludovicus de Compiegne de Veille, *Secunda Lex, Tractatus de Conservatione Calendarum* (Paris, 1669)—a favorite topic of Abendana.[23] Again, in line with Abendana's interest in Jewish measurements,[24] there is a detailed investigation by Newton of the Jewish cubit. A short tract by Newton, *The Sacred Cubit of the Jews*, was published in the *Collected Works* of John Greaves (London, 1738), pp. 405–433. From Abendana, too, he must have gotten his keen interest in Maimonides. In addition to four books of Maimonides' Legal Code in Latin,[25] as well as Pococke, *Porta Mosis* (1655) in Hebrew

---

[19] See Ms. Yahuda (at the Hebrew National Library, Jerusalem) 13.2, pp. 5b, 17a–b, 18a, 19a, 22b; Ms. Keynes 2, p. 17a.

[20] See *A Catalogue of the Portsmouth Collection of Books and Papers Written by or Belonging to Sir Isaac Newton*, prepared by H.R. Leard, G.G. Stokes, G.C. Adams, G.D. Liveing (Cambridge, 1888), p. 29 #2; Yah. Ms. Var. 13.2, 18a-22b. On the Latin translations of the Talmud, see Erich Bischoff, *Kritische Geschichte der Talmud-Übersetzunger* (Frankfort, 1899).

[21] See de Villamil, *Newton: The Man*, p. 63.

[22] See ibid., pp. 81 (*Jewish Kalendar*), 87 (Munster, *Kalendarium Hebraicum*), 94 (*Rule for Finding Easter*, &c). In *Chronology of Ancient Kingdoms* (London, 1727), p. 77, he referred to the intercalation of the year of the Jewish calendar, as well as the years of the kings among Jews, ibid., p. 296. By contrast, ibid., p. 298, he made reference "to the vulgar Aera of Christ." On Abendana's Jewish calendars, see "Isaac Abendana's Cambridge Mishna and Oxford's Calendars," pp. 117–121.

[23] See Isaac Abendana, *Discourses on the Ecclesiastical and Civil Polity of the Jews* [henceforth: *Discourses*] (London, 1706), pp. 171–198; and "Isaac Abendana's Cambridge Mishna and Oxford Calendars," pp. 104–107.

[24] See *Discourses*, pp. 198–200.

[25] See *A Catalogue of the Portsmouth Collection*, p. 85.

and Latin found in his library,[26] there are thousands of words copied by Newton from Maimonides' legal writings in Latin.[27] Abendana completed a Latin translation of Maimonides' work on *The Vessels of the Temple*.[28] There are long excerpts of the Latin translation of Maimonides' *De Cultu Divino* in Newton's own handwriting.[29]

II

Newton's religious views affected his scientific writings.[30] David Castillejo (who catalogued the Newton manuscripts in the Yahuda collection at the Hebrew University) noted the remarkable fact that Newton used certain numerological symbolism, particularly the numbers three, seven, and ten taken from the Temple of Solomon to structure his *Opticks*. According to Newton, the Temple was built horizontally in units of ten, and vertically in units of three, seven, and eight. His *Opticks* consists of seven books arranged into three parts. It opens with eight Definitions, eight Axioms, and eight Propositions, a triple row of eights. "It is likely," wrote Castillejo, "that this is only the tip of an iceberg revealing the presence of much more complicated meaning, proportion, and intent in his work."[31]

Newton's interest in Rabbinics and Maimonides was not mere intellectual curiosity. It affected his most intimate religious beliefs and his Christianity. "[T]here was something sinister in his religious beliefs," we are told.[32] Bishop Horsley (1773–1806), who examined

---

[26] *A Catalogue of the Portsmouth Collection*, p. 91.

[27] See, for example, *A Catalogue of the Portsmouth Collection*, p. 29 #2, and p. 30 #16; Yah. Ms. 13.2, 1a–18a. Cf. McLachlan, *Sir Isaac Newton Theological Manuscripts*, p. 16. He seems to have used the translation of Ludovicus de Compiegne Veille, *De Cultu Divino* (Paris?), cf. Newton, "The Language of the Prophets," in Keynes Ms. 5, chapter 2, pp. 9, 10. On the translations of Maimonides' *Mishne Torah* to Latin, see *Christian Hebraists and Dutch Rabbis*.

[28] See W.D. Macray, "A letter from Isaac Abendana," p. 90; and Israel Abrahams, "Note on Isaac Abendana," in *Transactions, Jewish Historical Society of England* 10 (1921–1923), pp. 221–224.

[29] See above, n. 27.

[30] I hope to develop this theme in a forthcoming study.

[31] David Castillejo, "A Report on the Yahuda Collection of Newton's MSS," found in the file on Newton at the Jewish National and University Library at Jerusalem, p. 8.

[32] Louis Trenchard More, *Isaac Newton: A Biography* (New York, 1962), p. 631.

some of Newton's papers on theology, declared them unfit for printing. Sir David Brewster (1781–1868), Newton's famous biographer, believed that bishop Horsley "exercised a wise discretion" in not allowing their publication. In the name of Christian charity, Brewster refused to formally declare Newton a "heretic." Piously, he explained:

> It may be an ecclesiastical privilege to burrow for heresy among the obscurities of thought, and the ambiguities of language, but in the charity which thinketh no evil, we are bound to believe that our neighbor is not a heretic till the charge against him has been distinctly proved.[33]

A cursory examination of some of his theological views published thus far makes it abundantly clear the reason for the horror that they caused. The papers reveal that Newton was a strict monotheist. He saw no need for a new revelation and rebuffed the Christian notion of atonement and salvation. Siding with Rabbinic tradition and *contra* Christian doctrine, he maintained that the Noahide precepts alone suffice for salvation, and thus there is no need for Jesus' expiatory death.[34] In opposition to Christian doctrine, he proposed that the Church derives from the Synagogue—not the Temple—"the name of synagogues being changed to that of churches" by converted gentiles.[35] Therefore, not only does he refer to the Jewish "Church" but also to the Christian "Synagogue."[36] This is consistent with Newton's view that the fundamentals of Judaism and Christianity are the same: "love of God and love of humankind."[37] More grievously, Newton was resolute in his belief that the Law of Moses was not abrogated with the advent of Christianity. Referring to the Gospels, he writes: "It is as much the law of God as the Law of Moses was, and as unalterable."[38]

---

[33] Sir David Brewster, *Memoirs of the Life, Writings, and Discoveries of Sir Isaac Newton* (Edinburgh, 1855), vol. 2, p. 340.
[34] See Richard S. Westfall, *Science and Religion in Seventeenth-Century England* (New Haven, 1958), p. 208.
[35] See McLachlan, *Sir Isaac Newton Theological Manuscripts*, pp. 39–40, cf. pp. 16–17. Cf. José Faur, "Law and Hermeneutics in Rabbinic Jurisprudence: A Maimonidean Perspective," in *Cardozo Law Review* 14 (1993), pp. 1673–1764.
[36] Cf. McLachlan, *Sir Isaac Newton Theological Manuscripts*, pp. 38, 41, etc.
[37] See ibid., p. 28.
[38] Ibid., p. 35.

Therefore, the Christian Scripture must be understood in light of the Hebrew Scripture, and not the other way around:

> [I]f any question at any time arises concerning his [Jesus'] interpretations, we are to have recourse to the Old Testament and compare the places interpreted with the interpretations of the New. As, for instance, in explaining why Jesus is called the Christ or Messiah, the Son of Man, the Son of God, the Lamb of God and the Lord who sitteth on the right hand of God, the God who was made in the beginning with God and by whom all things were made. And by this means the Old Testament will be better understood. So then for the names of Christ we are to have recourse to the Old Testament, and beware of vain Philosophy, for Christ sent his Apostles not to teach Philosophy to the common people and to their wives and children, but to teach what he had taught, taken out of Moses and the Prophets and Psalms concerning Christ.[39]

In full accord with Maimonides,[40] and *contra* the Church, Newton regarded the worship of intercessors as rank idolatry. In a passage discussing the worship of God, Newton writes:

> These things we must do, not to any mediator between him and us, but to him alone, "that he may give his angels charge over us," who, being our fellow-servants, are pleased with the worship which we give to their God. And this is the first and principal part of religion. This always was and always will be the religion of all God's people from the beginning to the end of the world.[41]

Concerning prayers, he wrote: "We need not pray to Christ to intercede for us," adding: "If we pray the Father aright, he will intercede."[42] Worshiping God means, "To love, fear and trust in, and seek unto one but himself immediately."[43] The last term "immediately" is of the essence and underlines the prohibition against saints, deities, etc., functioning as intercessors with God.

---

[39] Ibid., pp. 33–34.

[40] Moses Maimonides, *The Guide for the Perplexed* (henceforth: *Guide*), I, 61, p. 100 (ll. 20-29). All quotations proceed from the Arabic text, *Dalalat al-Ha'irin*, edited with variant readings by Issachar Joel (Jerusalem, 5691 [1930/31]); the translations are mine. Subsequent references are given in the text according to section, chapter, page and line. *Guide*, I, 36, p. 56 (ll. 19-27); *Mishne Torah, 'Aboda Zara*, 1:1; *Perush ha-Mishnayot, Sanhedrin*, X, 1, Foundament V, ed. R. Joseph Qafih (Jerusalem, 1964), vol. 4, p. 212. Cf. *Mishne Torah, Teshuba* 3:7.

[41] McLachlan, *Sir Isaac Newton Theological Manuscripts*, p. 51.

[42] Ibid., p. 57.

[43] Yah. Ms. 15, pp. 1–2.

Newton noticed that in the Hebrew Scripture, God's name is also applied to his angels and messengers.[44] This means that God may be semiotically associated with his creatures. There is, however, a huge distinction between semiotics and worship: although God's name may be connected with one of his creatures, no one may be worshiped except him: one ought to return "thanks to the Father alone . . . we ask of him immediately in the *name* [italics added] of Christ."[45] He incorporated this doctrine as an article of faith:

> Art. 11. To give the name of God to angels or kings is not against the First Commandment. To give the worship of the God of the Jews to angels or kings is against it. The meaning of the commandment is, Thou shalt worship no other God but me.[46]

Newton repudiated Jesus' divinity[47] and regarded Jesus as "a true man born of a woman,"[48] only "the Word or prophet of God."[49] "The time will come," he told Hopton Haynes (1672–1749), "when the doctrine of the Incarnation, as commonly received, shall be exploded as an absurdity equal to transubstantiation."[50] In this connection it would be helpful to consider Newton's explanation of the enigmatic "deity of the *ma'uzzim*" in Dan. 11:38-39. Jewish commentators associate these verses with the rise and spread of Christianity. R. Isaac Abarbanel (1437–1508), interprets *ma'uzzim* as "fortresses." These are the Christian Cathedrals that look as if they were fortresses; the "divinity" within these fortresses is the cult of Jesus.[51] Newton identified *ma'uzzim* as mausoleums, harboring

---

[44] See Exod. 23:21 and *Guide* I, 27, p. 39 (ll. 16–28); I, 64; II, 6; and the explanation given by R. Manasseh ben Israel, *The Conciliator*, trans. by R.E.H. Lindo (London, 1842), vol. 1, pp. 70, 260–261; vol. 2, pp. 12–18. Cf. R. David Qamhi, on Josh. 3:11 and Is. 42:8.

[45] McLachlan, *Sir Isaac Newton Theological Manuscripts*, p. 57.

[46] Ibid.

[47] See Westfall, *Science and Religion in Seventeenth-Century England*, pp. 210–211; More, *Isaac Newton: A Biography*, pp. 640–644.

[48] McLachlan, *Sir Isaac Newton Theological Manuscripts*, p. 54, cf. ibid. pp. 55, 56.

[49] Ibid., p. 56.

[50] Cited in H. McLachlan, *The Religious Opinions of Milton, Locke, and Newton*, (New York, 1972), p. 127.

[51] R. Isaac Abarbanel, *Ma'yane ha-Yeshu'a* (Venice, 5407/1647), XI, 8, 75d. A Latin translation of this work was made by Johannes Henricus Maius, *De haustu aquarum a fontibus salutis* (Frankfurt, 1710).

"the souls of the dead." To make sure that no one would miss the point, he continued:

> All which relates to the overspreading of the Greek Empire with Monks and Nuns, who placed holiness in abstinence from marriage; and to the invocation of saints and veneration of their reliques, and such like superstitions, which these men introduced in the fourth and fifth centuries.[52]

Consistent with the preceding, Newton rejected the Christian interpretation that "the elder of days" (Dan. 7:9, 13) refers to Jesus.[53] "[W]hence are you certain that the Ancient of Days is Christ?"—he asked Locke (1632–1704). In full accord with Jewish exegesis that it refers to God,[54] Newton asked Locke: "Does Christ any where sit upon the throne?"[55] More grievously, Newton rejected belief in the Holy Trinity and submitted that the passages in the New Testament to this effect are interpolations made by the ecclesiastical authorities.[56] It is clear now why such a deeply religious man as Newton did not attend Church.[57]

III

To discredit Newton's religious beliefs it was alleged that by 1692 he had gone mad,[58] although his correspondence with Locke and Bentley at the time show him to be perfectly sane. "[I]t is a gross

---

[52] See Isaac Newton, *Observations upon the Prophecies of Daniel and the Apocalypse of St. John* (London, 1733), p. 191.

[53] For a summary of the Christian interpretation of this passage and the ensuing Jewish criticism, see Abarbanel, *Ma'yane ha-Yeshu'a* VIII, 6, 44a-45c.

[54] On this point, see the incisive remark by the editor, R. Abraham Joseph Wertheimer, R. Isaiah di Trani the First, *Commentary on Prophets and Hagiographa* (Heb.) vol. 3 (Jerusalem, 1978), p. 216, n. 85.

[55] More, *Isaac Newton: A Biography*, p. 360; see ibid. p. 361. Predictably, More, ibid., p. 626, tried to explain this away by claiming that at the "time, Newton was skeptical of Daniel's prophecy as predicting the coming of Christ." And yet at the bottom of the page, More quotes a passage of Newton stating that "to reject his [Daniel's] prophecies is to reject the Christian religion." See McLachlan, *Sir Isaac Newton Theological Manuscripts*, p. 18.

[56] See *Historical Account of Two Notable Corruptions of Scripture*. For a brief discussion of this work, see *Memoirs of the Life, Writings, and Discoveries of Sir Isaac Newton*, vol. 2, pp. 331–337; More, *Sir Isaac Newton: A Biography*, pp. 632–635.

[57] See Gale E. Christianson, *In the Presence of the Creator* (New York, 1984), pp. 257–258.

[58] See McLachlan, *The Religious Opinions of Milton, Locke and Newton*, pp. 162–163. His interest in alchemy is often mentioned as evidence of his alleged madness.

exaggeration to refer to this as 'Newton madness'"—remarked Professor Andrade (1887–1971).[59] The allegation was intended to conceal Newton's "dreadful secret." Lord John Maynard Keynes (1883–1946), who examined these papers, replied:

> Let me not exaggerate through reaction against the other Newton myth which has been so sedulously created for the last two hundred years. There was extreme method in his madness. All his unpublished works on esoteric and theological matters are marked by careful learning, accurate method and extreme sobriety of statement. They are just as *sane* as the *Principia*, if their whole matter and purpose were not magical. They were nearly all composed during the same twenty-five years of his mathematical studies.[60]

To conceal any connection between Newton and Judaism, pious scholars fabricated all kinds of silly theories: from his alleged "madness" to having fallen under the influence of Jacob Boehme (1575–1624).[61] Inventive biographers (moved by ethical virtue, they are the best) piously masked Newton's beliefs by relating them to this or that "heretical" view held by some vague *Christian* denomination. Louis Trenchard More (1870–1944), Newton's best biographer to date, proposed that Newton was a Unitarian or perhaps an Arian;[62] he could also be described as "essentially a Protestant"[63]—although he negated the Holy Trinity;[64] or that his beliefs are those of "extreme

---

We forget that in his time "alchemy" was the equivalent of our "chemistry" and could have a much more scientific connotation than what the term suggests to the modern ear. For a sketchy description of Newton's interest in alchemy, see Edward Neville da Costa Andrade, *Sir Isaac Newton* (Garden City, 1958), pp. 129–132. To the present, there is no serious study of Newton's writings on alchemy. This is the place to point out that on the basis of the chemical and optical data at his disposal, Newton had as much a grasp of atomic theory as could have been possible at the time; see S.I. Vavilov, "Newton and the Atomic Theory," in *The Royal Society Tercentenary Celebrations*, pp. 43–55.

[59] Edward Neville da Costa Andrade, "Newton," in *The Royal Society Newton Trecentary Celebrations* (Cambridge, 1947), p. 16.
[60] Ibid., p. 30.
[61] See McLachlan, *Theological Manuscripts*, pp. 20–21. None of Boehme's works were in his library. More to the point, investigation in this area had shown this to be false. At best, his interest in Boehme may have been peripheral and related to his alchemists' notions alone; see Stephen Hobhouse, *William Law: Selected Mystical Writings* (London, 1938), vol. 4, pp. 346–347.
[62] See More, *Isaac Newton: A Biography*, pp. 630–631.
[63] Ibid., p. 611.
[64] See ibid., pp. 636–637, and Christianson, *In the Presence of the Creator*, pp. 250–255.

Protestants," with the qualification, however, that they exhibit "tenderness towards the Arians."[65] I think that More had in fact clinched our argument!

The only writer who had the fortitude to reveal Newton's "dreadful secret" was Lord John Maynard Keynes—one of those luminous minds with which God graces humanity once in a long, long time. The Director of the Bank of England and father of the "Keynesian Economics," he was the most influential English economist of his time. People familiar with the particulars of his life know that he was a man of extraordinary courage, unyielding to public opinion or to pressure, either personal or social. Keynes had read more of Newton's papers than anyone else, and was eminently qualified to speak with authority on this matter. He was an avid collector of books, and in close contact with the renowned Jewish book dealer Gustav David, who advised him on Jewish material. Although he was not a specialist in Jewish philosophy, Keynes himself was a gifted philosopher and the author of a brilliant book on logic, *A Treatise on Probability* (London, 1921). A Philo-Semite, he was not only personally active in helping individual Jews (the economist Piero Sraffa comes to mind), but he put great efforts in trying to alleviate the lot of Jewish refugees in general. He was also a Zionist, the only non-Jewish member of the advisory committee under the chairmanship of Herbert Samuel that prepared the preliminary draft for a Jewish national home in Palestine.[66]

Although he did not cite the specific documentation, Keynes' testimony is unimpeachable. Precisely because Keynes was not a specialist in Jewish topics, he would not have risked his reputation by associating Newton with Maimonides, unless he had found solid evidence supporting this view:

> Very early in life Newton abandoned orthodox belief in Trinity. . . . It may be that Newton fell under Socinian influences, but I think not. He was rather *a Judaic monotheist of the school of Maimonides* [italics added].

---

[65] More, *Isaac Newton: A Biography*, p. 637. See McLachlan, *Sir Isaac Newton Theological Manuscripts*, pp. 23–25. Newton had no sympathy for Arian doctrines. This is why he did not say a word on behalf of the Arian beliefs of his friend William Whiston; see Christianson, *In the Presence of the Creator*, p. 255.

[66] A fact not noted by his biographers Harrod, Skidelsky, and Hession. Keynes' role acquires particular significance when we bear in mind that "the fiercest opponent of the Zionist" in the British cabinet was none other than the secretary of state for India Edwin Montagu, his close friend and benefactor; see Anand Chandavarkar, "Was Keynes Anti-Semitic?" in *Economic and Political Weekly*, May 6, 2000, p. 1622. I thank my friend Dr. Ranjit Chatterjee for bringing this article to my attention.

He arrived at this conclusion, not on so-to-speak rational or skeptical grounds, but entirely on the interpretation of ancient authority. He was persuaded that the revealed documents give no support to the Trinitarian doctrines which were due to late falsification. The revealed God was one God.[67]

And indeed a Maimonidean he was.[68] His argument for the rejection of the Christian doctrine of *homoousion* ("co-substantiation" of God and Jesus) and thereby the Holy Trinity (leading him to believe that the New Testament had been corrupted intentionally by the scheming powers of the Church) comes from Maimonides. "Homoousion," argued Newton, "is unintelligible. 'Twas not understood in the Council of Nice, nor ever since. What cannot be understood is no object of belief."[69] The argument comes from Maimonides, who postulated that what cannot be intellectually conceptualized cannot be the object of faith. Maimonides illustrates the impossibility of such a belief by pointing to the Christian doctrine of the Trinity.[70] Newton's statement concerning miracles and the impossibility of changing the laws of nature is identical to that of Maimonides.[71] It is plain, therefore, why Newton could not accept the articles of faith of the Church of England and refused the Holy Order. For the same reason, he could not be Master of Trinity College and had to obtain a special dispensation to hold his Fellowship and the Lucasian Chair. The few historians who grasped Newton's ideas were determined to keep his "dreadful secret." Quoting Keynes, again:

> Newton's proverbial fear of controversy, his suspicious attitude and neurotic behavior, his obsession with secrecy, and his eventual departure from Cambridge to an administrative position in London—all

---

[67] de Villamil, *Newton: The Man*, p. 30.

[68] See McLachlan, *Sir Isaac Newton Theological Manuscripts*, pp. 16–17, where Newton's interest in Maimonides is acknowledged. McLachlan failed to appreciate the deep intellectual connection between them, on two grounds. First, he did not have first-hand knowledge of the subject and relied on the standard views of nineteenth century Jewish scholarship, which were trite and shallow at best. Second, he noticed that Newton wanted to keep philosophy and religion apart (cf. ibid., p. 58), whereas Maimonides embraced both. However, at the time of Newton, "philosophy" meant also "science." What Newton was saying is that one should not expect to find in Scripture "philosophical," that is, scientific, descriptions; see José Faur, "Esoteric Knowledge and the Vulgar," in *Trumah* 12 (2002), pp. 187–189.

[69] McLachlan, *The Religious Opinion of Milton, Locke and Newton*, p. 160.

[70] *Guide* I, 50.

[71] More, *Isaac Newton: A Biography*, p. 623, and *Shemona Peraqim*, chapter 8 (= *Porta Mosis*, p. 240); cf. *Guide* II, 29; III, 24.

this, become perfectly clear in light of the dreadful secret he had to hide all his life. But this was a dreadful secret which Newton was at desperate pains to conceal all his life. It was the reason why he refused Holy Orders, and therefore had to obtain a special dispensation to hold his Fellowship and Lucasian Chair and could not be Master of Trinity. Even the Toleration Act of 1689 excepted anti-Trinitarians. Some rumours there were, but not at the dangerous dates when he was a young Fellow of Trinity. In the main the secret died with him. But it was revealed in many writings in his big box.[72]

IV

The foregoing leads us into what in fact is the *only* riddle surrounding Newton's life: the outrage perpetrated against his books and manuscripts by England, a country known for her profound reverence for the book and the written word. The irony of the matter is that while England was sponsoring the removal of the written records of the most recondite cultures of the globe, to be deposited and safeguarded in her libraries and museums, and at the same time that English travelers and savants were encouraged to collect books and manuscripts from all over the world for the motherland, England did not blink an eye while the books and manuscripts of her greatest genius were trashed away. The existence of Newton's library was well known.[73] Yet no efforts were made to save or catalogue it. It almost disappeared completely after his death. The books "were sold in bundles (one bundle being, in fact, composed of two hundred volumes!), as if of no special interest or value, and were sold, in consequence, at rubbish prices." Many of his books were "sent to the pulp mill."[74] His manuscripts were auctioned by order of Viscount Lymington, in July, 1936. They were divided into 330 lots and were sold by auction to thirty-three buyers, mostly dealers. Thus, under the passive (but always vigilant) eye of England, the thoughts of Newton were scattered throughout the four corners of the globe. "The papers were auctioned piecemeal," bewailed a scholar. "It must be regretted that any of them were allowed to leave England."[75] Part of the collection was acquired by Lord Keynes and is now at Kings College, England. Another portion was purchased

---

[72] de Villamil, *Newton: The Man*, pp. 30–31.
[73] See ibid., p. 4.
[74] Ibid., p. 6.
[75] McLachlan, *The Religious Opinions of Milton, Locke, and Newton*, p. 172.

by Professor Abraham Shalom Yahuda (1877–1951) and is now at the National Library in Jerusalem. The rest was scattered all over.[76] England's silence at this outrage is eloquent indeed. Why?

I submit that the failure to preserve Newton's library and manuscripts was the effect of religious bias. Newton himself was aware of the religious prejudices of his contemporaries and opposed the publication of his manuscripts.[77] Efforts were made to prevent the general public from examining his writings. The volume of those writings was huge. There are over 1,300,000 words on religious matters in the Portsmouth collection alone.[78] None of the material had been published or indexed. The few who examined the papers were shocked. To protect Newton's "good name," the importance of the manuscripts was denied. "The Historical and Theological MSS," ascertained the scholars in charge of cataloguing the Portsmouth Collection, "cannot be considered of any great value."[79]

Those who would say that England has no sense of fair play should not judge harshly. England, it seems, is no less frail than the rest of us, plain folk, who find it easier to preach than to teach. Being religiously superior is a serious responsibility, not always easy to discharge. We all like to think of ourselves as open minded, but there is a limit. Those familiar with the recondite paths crisscrossing the English ethos know that English etiquette freely excuses acknowledging favors received, but is unforgiving of naughty behavior. It is inexcusable and boorish not to shell tit-for-tat. Granted, golden boys have privileges, and England's favorite son was entitled to special treatment. True, to a point. But how in the name of good sense and good manners can one explain that a genius, of Newton's rank no less, would prefer. . . . That is inexcusable! As noted by a modern student of Newton, no less than a professor of *History* at a distinguished university:

> His [Newton's] future relationship with God was to be an intellectual rather than an emotional one, in which Christ, the loving and forgiving Redeemer, played a secondary role. It was . . . the omnipotent Creator, harsh Taskmaster, and imperious Judge of the Old Testament, who commanded Newton's lifelong attention and obedience.[80]

---

[76] On the major collections of Newton MSS, see I. Bernard Cohen, "Newton, Isaac," in *ACLS Dictionary of Scientific Biography* (New York, 1974), p. 94.
[77] See McLachlan, *Sir Isaac Newton Theological Manuscripts*, p. 2.
[78] See Andrade, "Newton," p. 21.
[79] *A Catalogue of the Portsmouth Collection*, p. XIX.
[80] Christianson, *In the Presence of the Creator*, p. 248. For other derogatory remarks, see ibid., pp. 252, 255, etc., etc. Cf. *Reflections on Men and Ideas*, pp. 26, 179.

What pearls of wisdom! One can only wonder why such a staggering thought never crossed Newton's wits! The indignation of a superior mind is not surprising. This august scholar could not ignore the fact that Newton had exchanged a religion of "tolerance" for "the jealous Creator of the Old Testament"! Let us hear the full statement. Disposing of the God of Israel simply as Y . . . h (a theological euphemism that nobody is expected to take seriously, and my Jewish upbringing disallows me from spelling) he offered the kind of intellectual probity that only an accomplished historian can pronounce:

> Y . . . h, as the Hebrews so painfully learned, was anything but a God of patient tolerance. Above all else, He had commanded the children of Israel, "Thou shalt have no other gods before me." Nor, despite the moderating influence of a loving Christ's compassionate entry into history, did the record show that the jealous Creator of the Old Testament had experienced a profound change of heart.[81]

There is not a grain of cynicism, let alone hypocrisy. These words capture perfectly the mood and intellectual honesty the academic world cherishes so much! Any one minimally acquainted with history, particularly with the treatment of *conversos*, Native Americans, et al., will surely agree with the above "patient tolerance" and "loving Christ's compassionate entry into *history*" [italic added] exhibited by those untouched by the "jealous Creator of the Old Testament."[82]

V

The Hebrew Tetragrammaton, what the sages of Israel refer to as *shem ha-meforash*, stands for God *ad intra* as He is to Himself.[83] Since Judaism postulates Creation *ex nihilo*, any and all ontological relationships between God and whichever of his creations, must be negated, totally and categorically. Thus, essentially and fundamentally, God's

---

[81] Christianson, *In the Presence of the Creator*, p. 252.

[82] For some insights into the savagery and genocide performed by these good hearted folks, from the perspective of the victims rather than the aggressor, see José Faur, "Jews, *Conversos*, and Native Americans: The Iberian Experience," in *Annual of Rabbinic Judaism* 3 (2000), pp. 95–121.

[83] B. Sot. 38a. For some clarifications on this designation, see Louis Ginzberg's note in Israel Efros, *Philosophical Terms in the Moreh Nebukhim* (New York, 1924), pp. 143–144. Since already in biblical times the Tetragrammaton was regarded as

existence and the existence of every thing else are absolutely dissimilar.[84] God is "a necessary Being."[85] This means—as R. Manasseh ben Israel (1604–1657) explained—"His inherent, absolute and unconditional existence."[86] God's necessary Being stands in syntagmatic opposition to everything else, which is only "a possible being."[87] It is worthy of note that according to Maimonides, the literal meaning of the Tetragrammaton is, He who "necessarily exists."[88] Moses' first mission was to transmit this fundamental doctrine to the elders of

---

too holy to pronounce, after the first Exile it was replaced by *Adonai*. This can be gathered by comparing parallel passages in *Chronicles* and early Scripture. During the Second Temple period it was uttered only by the priests when pronouncing the priestly blessing and by the high priest during Yom Kippur worship. Out of deference, it was no longer pronounced after the destruction of the Temple; instead, *Adonai* was said.

[84] See *Guide*, I, 51, 53, 55, 57, 60, etc. Cf. José Faur, "The Character of Apophatic Knowledge in Maimonides' Guide," in Dan Cohn-Sherbok, ed., *Theodicy* (Lewiston, 1997), pp. 67–74.

[85] *Guide*, I, 57, p. 90 (ll.6-7); cf. ibid., 58, p. 92 (l.6); 63, p. 106 (ll. 20-24). For a definition of "God" as "a necessary Being," see *Mishne Torah, Yesode ha-Torah*, 1:1-4; *Perush ha-Mishnayot, Sanhedrin*, X, 1, Foundation I, vol. 4, pp. 210–211; and José Faur, *Homo Mysticus: A Guide to Maimonides' Guide for the Perplexed* (Syracuse, 1998), p. 101. In Jewish tradition (in opposition to Aristotle, see below and n. 87) it has a double connotation: he is absolutely self-sufficient, depending on himself alone and on nothing else, while everything else depends on him alone. This doctrine is implicit in Seʿadya's rendition of *Shaddai* (Gen. 17:1; Exod. 6:3) as *at-ta'iq al-kafi*, "the Absolute, the Self-sufficient;" cf. *Guide* I, 63, p. 107 (ll.6-9); *Perush ha-Mishnayot*, vol. 4, pp. 211–212; on the term *at-ta'iq*, see ibid. p. 211. Elie Benamozegh, *Em la-Miqra* (Leghorn,1862), vol. 3, 18b-19b, proposed that this concept is explicit in Aqilas's translation cited in *Bereshit Rabba* [XLVI, 1, Teodor-Albeck, ed. (Jerusalem, 1965), vol. 1, p. 461]. In support of this thesis, he cited Natan b. R. Yehiel, *ʿArukh*, s.v. *iqyum*, where he reports that this term was employed by Byzantine Jews to translate *Shaddai*. Benjamin Musafia, ad loc., interpreted that Greek term to mean "self-sufficient." On philological grounds, the editor, Alexander Kohut, *ʿArukh ha-Shalem* (New York, 1878), vol. 1, p. 255, rejected Musafia's interpretation. The value of Musafia's contribution rests, however, on his keen knowledge of the *koine* or regional, colloquial *spoken* Greek, rather than on classical texts and dictionaries. This specialized knowledge is particularly valuable in our case, since the *ʿArukh* emphasized that it was *used* in the *oral* translation of the Torah. To sum up, the idea of God as a "necessary Being" is a primary Jewish concept, already known to Greek speaking Jews. From them it passed somehow to the Arabic of Seʿadya, finally acquiring doctrinal formulation in Maimonides' writings. On the Aristotelian notion of "necessary existence," see Faur, *Homo Mysticus*, pp. 101; 223 n. 59.

[86] *The Conciliator*, vol. 1, p. 104.

[87] See *Guide*, I, 57, p. 90 (ll.4-9); II, Introduction, Axioms 19, 20; chap. 1, p. 172 (ll.14-25); and R. Joseph b. Jehuda, *Drei Abhandlungen*, ed. Moritz Lowy (Berlin, 1879). Cf. Harry Wolfson, *The Philosophy of Spinoza*, 2 vols. (Cambridge, MA, 1934), vol. 1, p. 67; and *Homo Mysticus*, pp. 98–102.

[88] *Guide*, I, 61, p. 101 (l.10). Expressing in a single word the three tenses of the verb "to be" in Hebrew; thus, signifying, continuous, uninterrupted beingness, from ever onto ever.

Israel, under the title "I am that what I am" (Exod. 3:14). The task of the mission was elucidated by R. Manasseh ben Israel:

> Shew them [to the elders of Israel] . . . that my Being is within myself, independent of every other, different from all other Beings, who *are* so alone by virtue [of] my distributing it [existence] to them, and might not have *been* nor could actually *be* such without it.[89]

In Scripture, God is occasionally called *Adon* "Lord," "Master," in the specific sense of possessing "Dominion"—as in "Lord (*Adon*) of the whole earth" (Josh. 3:11, 13; Zech. 4:14, 6:5; Ps. 97:5). From this substantive derives *Adonai*, regularly used in Hebrew as an appellative to "God." In Scripture, God's dominion is related to the root *QaNaH*, which means not only "ownership," "possession," but also "forging," "making," as when Eve said on the birth of Cain, "*qaniti* a person with God" (Gen. 4:2), i.e., "I have forged a person together with God."[90] Bearing this sense in mind, the oath pronounced by Abraham to Melchizedek, "I have raised my hand [in oath] to the Supreme God, *qone* heavens and earth" (Gen. 14:19, 22), acquires precision and depth. God is acknowledged *qone* in the double connotation of Creator/Lord of the universe.[91] It means that God, the Creator, has Supreme Dominion over all by Right of Creation. This doctrine is ripe with implications, both theological and political.

The association Dominion/Creation is explicit in Maimonides. When discussing the title *Adonai* used by the Hebrews for reading the Tetragrammaton, Maimonides explained that it derives from the root *Adon*. The final diphthong *ai* (rather than the suffix *i* as in *Adoni*) indicates the grammatical absolute construct noun. Accordingly, *Adonai* stands for total "Dominion," without condition or encumbrance.[92]

---

[89] *The Conciliator*, vol. 1, p. 103.

[90] See Umberto Cassuto, *From Adam to Noah* (Jerusalem, 1953), pp. 133–135 (Heb.) and Deut. 32:5. Cf. Prov. 8:22, and Se'adya Ga'on, *Mishle*, ed. and trans. Joseph Qafih (Jerusalem, 1976), p. 77. The enigmatic aphorism exhorting that one should "*qene* a friend" (M. Abot 1:5) means "to forge" a friend through amity and comradeship, rather than hope to find one "ready made." Incidentally, the above mentioned verse means that Eve, the first mother of humanity, recognized that parents have only *limited* dominion over their children, subservient to God's, see B. Yeb. 5b; *Mishne Torah, Mamrim* 6:12; unlike pagan society where parents' dominion over children is absolute, cf. below, n. 131.

[91] See *Guide* II, 30, p. 251 (ll.22-25).

[92] *Guide*, I, 61, p. 100 (ll.20-29). Cf. Judah ha-Levi, *Kuzari*, IV, 3, Arabic original, eds. David H. Baneth and H. Ben-Shammai (Jerusalem, 1977), p. 153 (l.5): *ya mawlai*, "O my Lord," in the sense of "supreme sovereign" or "governor," "master;" the Hebrew translation, p. 159 (ll.1-2) misses the point. This is the root used by Maimonides in connection to *qana*; see the quotation below, n. 94.

More cogent for our present purpose is the fact that "Dominion" is a function of *qana* in a double sense: Creator and *thus* Lord (*Dominus*) with absolute Dominion (Gen. 14:19, 22).[93] Here is what Maimonides says:

> Concerning Him it was said to have possession (*qana*) (Gen. 14:19, 22) over them [Heaven and earth], because He, the most High, has dominion over them [His creatures] as a Master has dominion over his slaves. This is why He is called "Lord (*Adon*) of all the earth" and "the Lord" (*ha-Adon*), since one cannot be a Master unless having possession (*qinyan*).[94]

Intimately bound up with the idea of God's absolute Dominion is that "Creation" must be essentially and fundamentally *ex nihilo*. This is why, explained Maimonides, Scripture stipulates that God "*bara* ("created") the whole world, because according to us, it was created out of nothing."[95] To ascertain this overwhelming principle, Jews proclaim in the *Amida* thrice daily, that God is *Qone ha-kol*, "Creator/ Having Dominion over Everything." In this respect, God's Dominion is positively different than that of earthly monarchs. The latter's claim for Dominion is based on violence and the might of the sword. God's Dominion alone is categorical and absolute, since is based on the right of Creation. Concerning this focal principle, Abendana wrote: "Whereas God Almighty is the Lord and Governor of the Universe, as having by Right of Creation the Supreme Dominion over all Creatures."[96] It would be helpful to consider at this point that the Septuagint renders *Adonai* by the Greek legal term *Kyrios*. This, as Professor Bickerman observed, is

> [a] legal term meaning the legitimate master of someone or something, a word which as a substantive was not used in Greek religious language. It is simply a literal translation of the Hebrew appellative *Adonai* (the Lord), which became in the meantime the standard pronunciation of the awe-inspiring Tetragrammaton.[97]

The doctrine represented by the Tetragrammaton standing for God as a necessary Being and the doctrine of God as having absolute

---

[93] See *Guide* II, 30, p. 251 (ll.22-25).
[94] *Guide* II, 30, p. 252 (ll.6-8). Judah ha-Levi, mentioned above, n. 92, refers to the same verse.
[95] *Guide* II, 30, p. 252 (ll.4-5).
[96] *Discourses*, p. 126.
[97] Elias Bickerman, *From Ezra to the Last of the Maccabees* (New York, 1962), p. 66.

Dominion, represented by *Adonai*, are interrelated. The point of the Hebrew Scripture is not merely that God "exists" (as a metaphysical postulate) but that he has absolute Dominion over all Creation. Put differently, only a necessary Being can have absolute Dominion. (Polytheism is the intellectual alternative to the above).[98] Thus, Maimonides opened the *Mishne Torah* with the formulation of these two doctrines (*Yesode ha-Torah* 1:1-5). The first paragraph postulates that God alone exists from eternity and everything depends on him. This postulate constitutes, "The Foundation of Foundations and the Pillar of the Sciences" (1:1). It means that everything depends on him (1:2), but he does not depend on anything else (1:3). Since everything else exists conditionally, Scripture established that he alone exists *truly*: nothing else could partake of *his* level of existence (1:4). These paragraphs are followed by a paragraph stipulating God's absolute Dominion. Paraphrasing the biblical formula (Josh. 3:11, 13; Zech. 4:14, 6:5; Ps. 97:5) quoted above, Maimonides wrote: "That [necessary] Being is the God of the Universe, Ruler of the whole World" (1:5).[99]

Before proceeding I must dispose of a common misconception. Popular wisdom notwithstanding, for Maimonides the first precept (*misva*) of Judaism is not belief in the "existence" of God. As argued by R. Hasdai Crescas (d. ca. 1412), conceptually a *misva* (precept) presupposes a *mesavve* or "authority" issuing the *misva*.[100] In our case, this would lead to the absurdity which, subsequent to believing in the existence of the Supreme Authority God (issuing the *misva*), we are prescribed to believe that he *exists*?! Rather, as per the Arabic original of Maimonides' *Sefer ha-Misvot*, the precept consists in "acknowledging [God's] *ar-rabbubiyya*."[101] Like many such terms, this, too, entered the

---

[98] Cf. Faur, *Homo Mysticus*, pp. 139–142 and p. 235, n. 89.

[99] Maimonides chose the expression "Ruler of the whole Earth" out of stylistic considerations; see the anonymous *Perush* ad loc. printed in the standard editions. It refers to the "*inhabitants* of the earth," and it parallels the liturgical formula "King of the Universe."

[100] This point was raised by Hasdai Crescas, *Or ha-Shem* (Offset Edition, Tel-Aviv, 1963), 3a. R. Crescas did not have the foggiest idea what Maimonides was talking about. In several of my writings I point out that with the triumph of the anti-Maimonidean ideology, Jewish thinkers were closer to Christian theologians than to the rabbis or Scripture.

[101] Maimonides, Arabic text of *Sefer ha-Misvot*, Joseph Qafih, ed. (Jerusalem, 1971), positive precept # 1, p. 58. This term appears once at the beginning of the paragraph, "acknowledging [God's] *ar-rabbubiyya*," and once at the end, concluding that

Arabic religious lexicon via Judeo-Aramaic; in our case the Aramaic *rab* translating the Hebrew *Adon*. Accordingly, the first *miṣva* consists in "acknowledging God's Dominion."[102] For that reason, immediately after formulating the doctrine that God is ruler of the whole world (1:5), Maimonides continues: "And acknowledgement of this [Hebrew demonstrative pronoun, singular: *ze*] matter is a positive precept" (1:6). It may be of some interest to note that in the course of explaining Gen. 28:20, Maimonides' son, R. Abraham (1186–1237) reports in the name of his father: "Far be it from the faithful—even if he would be the lowliest of the children of Jacob—to accept God's Dominion (*rabbubiyyatihi*) only conditionally."[103]

Concerning the biblical basis for the first precept, Maimonides cites "I am God *elohekha*" from the First Commandment (Exod. 20:2). This point deserves to be explained. Rather than simply assuming that *elohekha* is a tautology, as is often done, and translating it "your God" (accordingly, the first message transmitted by God to Israel is a redundancy: "I am God your God"), in Judeo-Arabic tradition this term is translated *rabbak* "your Master," i.e., someone with *ar-rabbubiyya* over you.[104] Bearing this in mind, Maimonides' sense of is clear: the First Commandment does not come to establish "I am God," but, rather, "I am God *elohekha*,"

---

indeed the first commandment consists in "acknowledging [God's] *ar-rabbubiyya*;" see textual variants, n. 6. (Qafih's translation is faulty). It appears also in ibid., Principle IX, p. 32, see below, n. 107. For a further analysis, see José Faur, *Studies in the Mishne Torah* (Jerusalem, 1978) (Heb.), pp. 159–160; and idem, "Intuitive Knowledge of God in Medieval Jewish Theology," in *Jewish Quarterly Review* 67 (1976–1977), pp. 90–110. Cf. below, n. 104.

[102] My friend, the late Professor E.Y. Kutscher, *Words and Their History* (Jerusalem, 1961), p. 31, dismissed the popular association of the Latin *Dominus* with the Hebrew *Adon*. He is only partially correct. For the Romans, *dominus* was semantically and linguistically linked to *domus*, "house, domicile;" see Émile Benveniste, *Indo-European Language and Society* (Coral Gables, 1969), p. 245. The *semantic* field of *Dominus*, particularly as it appears in Christian texts and ecclesiastical Latin (but not exclusively), is not Roman but the Jewish *Ribbon/Adon*. In the form *rab* it stands in Talmudic literature for the title "scholar, master," having *authority* to transmit and render legal decisions (hence the modern "rabbi"). It may be of some interest to Latinists to note that under the influence of the Jewish *rab*, *dominus* was used in Medieval Latin in the sense of "legal expert;" see the texts cited in Herman Kantorowicz and Beryl Smalley, "An English Theologian's View of Roman Law," in *Medieval and Renaissance Studies* (1941), pp. 241, 247.

[103] *Perush R. Abraham*, R.S. Sasoon, ed. (London, 1958), p. 88 (Heb.).

[104] It is important to recall that *eloah* with or without a suffix, e.g., *elohekha*, *elohenu*, is not a mere synonym but one out of the seven appellatives of the God of Israel; see *Mishne Torah, Yesode ha-Torah* 6:1-3, i.e., with a specific and singular

that is, "*rabbak*, "with Dominion over you."[105] God's Dominion is absolute and indivisible.[106] Accordingly, the Second Commandment does not come to prohibit polytheism but, as per Se'adya's translation, to attribute God's *rabbubiyya* to someone else.[107] The apostasy of the golden calf was not because these people believed in another God; they apostatize, rather, because by declaring "This is *elohekha*, O Israel!" (Exod. 32:4, 8)—Se'adya's translation: "this is *rabbak* O Israel!"—they attributed dominion to something other than God.[108] It would be opportune to point out here that the *Shema'* is not merely an affirmation that there is only one God, but, rather, that "God *elohenu* is One God" (Deut. 6:4). In Se'adya's translation: "Hear O Israel, that God *rabbana*—having Dominion over us—is one God," i.e., no one else can claim Dominion but him.[109]

---

connotation. Invariably, when it relates to the God of Israel, Se'adya translates it *rabbak*, see, for example, his translation of Exod. 15:26; 20:2, 6, 9, 11, etc. Lev. 2:13; 18:21; 19:12; 21:8, etc. However, when the verse refers to a pagan deity, he translates it *ma'budak*, "your [object of] worship;" see Gen. 31:32.

[105] The same idea is found in ibn Ezra, *Yesod Mora*, Joseph Cohen and Uriel Simon, eds. (Ramat-Gan, 2002), VII, 10, p. 142 (ll.106-107), who wrote that the first precept is for the individual to accept God as *elohav*, cf. editors' note, ad loc. The source of this definition is Rabbinic. In Y. Ber. 1:10, 3c, the expression "I am God, *elohekha*" in the First commandment is equated with *elohenu* at the beginning of the *Shema'*, the purpose of which, according to the M. Ber. 2:2, is "acknowledging the Kingdom," i.e., Dominion, "of Heaven." This passage appears in *Hilkhot ha-Yerushalmi le-ha-Rambam*, Saul Lieberman, ed. (New York, 1947), p. 21. Lieberman was unaware of the precise connotation of these terms; see his note ad loc., and therefore he could not come to grips with the meaning of the above or the reason why Maimonides needed to include it in his compendium of the Yerushalmi.

[106] And not shared with any creature, cf. David Qamhi, on Is. 42:8.

[107] See Se'adya's translation of Exod. 32:4, 8. Cf. *Sefer ha-Misvot*, Arabic text, p. 181; similarly, ibid., Principle IX, p. 32; Maimonides illustrates an "intellectual sun" as if one were to attribute *rabbubiyya* to someone besides God (Qafih's translation in both places is faulty). Likewise, in his son's commentary, *Perush R. Abraham*, p. 315, the Second Commandment comes to prohibit attributing God's *rabbubiya* to someone else. The source of this interpretation is Rabbinic. According to M. San. 7:4, "acknowledging" (*ha-meqabbel*) an idol or a deity as *eloah* constitutes "'*aboda zara*," even if no ritual was performed; see B. San. 61a, *Mishne Torah, 'Aboda Zara* 3:4; and José Faur, "Performative and Descriptive Utterances in Jewish Law," in Arye Edrei, ed., *Studies in Jewish Law in Honor of Professor Aaron Kirschenbaum* (*Dine Israel* 20–21, 5760–5761), pp. 101–121, especially pp. 108–110 (Heb.).

[108] According to Judah ha-Levi, *Kuzari*, I, 97, pp. 33–36, Arabic original, pp. 29–32, the children of Israel neither worshipped the golden calf nor "negated [God's total] *rabbubiyya*;" Arabic original p. 30 (l.18); cf. ibid., p. 29 (l.18), and IV, 15, p. 168 (l.9); the Hebrew, p. 34 (l.24) is faulty, but ibid., p. 33 (l.24), and IV, 15, p. 174 (l.5) correctly translated: *ribbonuto*.

[109] This is consistent with the rabbis' interpretation of the *Shema'* mentioned above, n. 105.

A semantically cognate term, but not identical to *Adon* and *Ribbon*, is the Rabbinic *manhig*. It has several meanings. As a verb, its primary sense is "to conduce," "to move or keep in motion," a beast (as in M. B.M. 1:2, etc.). It also means to "manage," "to guide," as with the pillar of fire guiding and protecting Israel in the desert (T. Sot. 11:1), and a parent guiding and protecting his child (Y. Qid. I, 7, 61a, etc.). As a substantive, *manhig* stands for "governor," "political leader."[110] Occasionally, the rabbis apply this term to God, in quality of *manhig* of the world.[111] In these two senses Maimonides applies the title *Manhig* to God. First, God conduces and gives motion to the cosmic sphere, *not* as the mechanical prime mover, but as a supreme political leader in charge of all his subjects (Arabic: *mudabbir*, Hebrew: *manhig*).[112] To dispel any suggestion of some point of contiguity (either ontological or spatial) between God, *Manhig*, and the Universe, Maimonides compares God's ruling of Creation to a skipper, but not exactly:

> The relation of God to the Universe is the relation of a skipper to his boat. This, however, is not an exact comparison or true simile. Rather, we only intended to indicate that God guides (Arabic: *mudabbir*, Tibbon: *manhig*) whatever exists. It intends to imply that He awards to it [His creations] contiguity [both spatial and time] and preserves their proper order.[113]

---

[110] *Debarim Rabba* (Lieberman), *Shofetim* IX, pp. 88–89; *Bemidbar Rabba* XX, 4 (Vilna edition), 83d; ibid. XXI, 2, 88d; *Debarim Rabba* V, 8 (Vilna edition), 110c.

[111] See *Bereshit Rabba* XXXIX, 1, vol. 1, p. 365; *Debarim Rabba* (Vilna edition) IX, 9, 117c. Thus, the common Judeo-Arabic expression *Alla yudabber*, "God shall lead," indicating that God, as Supreme leader, will take charge.

[112] Cf. *Teshuba* 3:2. Consistently, Samuel ibn Tibbon identifies the Arabic *mudabbir*, "political leader," in the *Guide* with the Hebrew *manhig*; see *Guide* I, 58, p. 93 (l.22), etc. As with many other technical terms, the Arabic *mudabbir* come from the Judeo-Aramaic, in our case *debar*, "to guide;" see, for example *Targum* on Gen. 2:15, 11:11, 20:14, 31:14, etc. This applies even when an angel, Exod. 14:19, 21, or God, Deut. 20:4, is guiding. As a substantive, *dabbar* means "political leader," see B. San. 8a. (In both cases, as a verb or substantive, the root DBR is connected with the Hebrew DBR, "speech," "word." This is the place to point out that the Hebrew *manhig* indicates, not only someone who guides directly without an intermediate agent or cause, but also someone assuming responsibility and supervising what is taking place; see, for example, *Debarim Rabba* IX, 9 (Vilna edition), 117c. God exercises *his* guidance and providence variously by means of angels and other agents while still remaining absolute Lord and *Adon*; see *Guide*, II, 6. Indeed, "you will not find at all an action executed by God except through an angel," ibid., p. 182 (l.14); see *The Conciliator*, vol. 1, pp. 260–261. Cf. *Guide* II, 10, p. 186 (l.29) ff., and below, n. 114.

[113] *Guide* I, 58, p. 93 (ll.20-23).

This fundamental doctrine was incorporated in the *Mishne Torah* (*Yesode ha-Torah* 1:5): "The God of the Universe and *Adon* of the whole earth is *Manhig* the (cosmic) sphere with a boundless and uninterrupted might."[114] Patriarch Abraham, in Hebrew intellectual tradition, is not the first monotheist, but the first to have discovered that the One and Only God actually is the "*Manhig* moving the (cosmic) sphere."[115] The source is Rabbinic. The rabbis report that given the lack of homogeneity and uniformity of astral bodies,[116] Abraham concluded: "Unless [the celestial bodies] have a *manhig* they could not [move] in this fashion! [Therefore] it would be inappropriate to worship them, rather [we should worship] their *Manhig*!"[117] God/*Manhig* is a key, elementary concept. In the intellectual apparatus of Israel there is no cogent difference between an atheist postulating that "there is no God" and another postulating "that the world has no *Manhig*:" both fall into the first class of *minim* (heretics). Noticeably, to the second class of *minim* belong not those ascertaining the existence of more than one deity but those positing "that there is a *Manhig*, but they are two or more."[118]

The modern emphasis on biblical "monotheism" misses the point.[119] Scripture does not come to teach a metaphysical axiom

---

[114] Cf. M. B.M. 1:2, B. B.M. 8b-9a, and *Mishne Torah, Gezela* 17:5: ownership of a beast goes to the *manhig*, i.e., the person controlling the beast's movements— not to the person mounting or holding it. This is consistent with the first blessing of the evening *Shema'* proclaiming that God *ma'arib 'arabim* by his word, i.e., as a *Manhig*. For the precise connotations of *manhig*, see *Mishne Torah, Shabbat* 20:6, *Kil'ayyim* 9:7; and Faur, "Performative and Descriptive Utterances in Jewish Law," pp. 112–114. Cf. Below, n. 144.

[115] *Mishne Torah, 'Aboda Zara* 1:3 (l.38, and l.34); *Guide* II, 19, pp. 216 (ll.23)–217 (l.5); II, 13, p. 198 (ll.28-30); cf. Se'adya and ibn 'Ezra on Deut. 33:26.

[116] See below, n. 144.

[117] *Medrash Haggadol, Genesis*, M. Margulies, ed. (Jerusalem, 1967), pp. 210–211. In an parallel text, ibid., p. 205 (l. 5): *Adon*. As indicated by the editor, a similar passage is found in the Geniza fragments published by Jacob Mann, *The Bible as Read and Preached in the Old Synagogue*, vol. 1 (New York, 1971), Hebrew Section, pp. 59–60. Obviously this bears on the whole concept of divine providence; see *Guide* III, 17, p. 335 (ll.8-11); 23, especially pp. 360 (l.10)–361 (l.6).

[118] *Mishne Torah, Teshuba* 3:7. Cf. *Guide* I, 75, p. 94 (ll.23-29); III, 17, p. 335 (ll.8-11).

[119] Chiefly on *a priori* grounds and intellectual bias, "Biblical monotheism" is analyzed according to Greek, more specifically Hellenistic, ideology, with the foreseeable results. If one were to add to it the notion of "ethical"—a term antithetical to *misva* and *halakha*—(neither the rabbis lexicon nor Scripture have a semantic equivalent to "ethics"), and then go on to examine "Biblical Ethical Monotheism," the conclusions will be confusing, at best. It is as if one were to assume that "apples" in Judaism are "bananas" and then go on to demonstrate that the biblical concept of this fruit is flawed. See, however, the valiant attempt of V. Nikiprowetzy, in "Ethical Monotheism," in *Daedalus* 104 (1975), pp. 69–90.

but, rather, that the One and Only necessary Existent, Creator of Heaven and earth and everything else has absolute *Dominion* over *his* Creation.[120] It means, that in the quality of absolute Master, he issues *misvot* "precepts"—a series of laws regulating all the aspects of the spiritual and political life of his subjects.[121] To stress this fundamental doctrine, Jewish law requires that a blessing should not only be addressed to "our God," but also should spell out: "King of the Universe."[122] The holidays of *Rosh ha-Shana* and *Yom Kippur* are to remind us that God in quality of King, not only has the right to judge "all the inhabitants of the world"[123] but also to remiss their sins.[124] For the purposes of the present discussion, it may not be superfluous to point out that a most common designation for "God" in Rabbinic literature and Jewish liturgy is *Ribbono shel 'Olam*, "Master" or "Ruler of the Universe." As mentioned earlier, *Ribbon* is the Aramaic translation of *Adon*. Correctly understood, the Hebrew hymn *Adon 'Olam*, sung throughout Jewish synagogues, is a most eloquent testimony of Israel's faith in God's Dominion, both universal and personal.[125] Finally, the eschatological vision of Israel for the universal kingdom of God expresses Israel's hope that eventually the whole of humanity will recognize God as their Supreme King (rather than the king as Supreme God).

Monolatry, the worship of God according to his *misvot*, is the necessary corollary to God's Dominion. The rabbis understood this well. Pointedly, they taught that the purpose of the first portion of the *Shema'*—the most important of all Jewish prayers—is not to *declare* his *existence*—but "to acknowledge the authority of the Kingdom of Heaven." Consequently, the purpose of the second portion of the *Shema'* is "to acknowledge the authority of the *misvot*" (M. Ber. 2:2). The "holiness" that the Jew seeks is not something akin to the

---

[120] Cf. Judah ha-Levi, *Kuzari*, IV, 15, p. 174; Arabic original, David H. Baneth and H. Ben-Shammai, eds. (Jerusalem, 1977), p. 168 (l.9).

[121] Including the Seven Noahide Precepts for non-Jews; see José Faur, "*Sir Isaac Newton*," section III, in Görge K. Hasselhoff and Otfried Fraisse, eds., *Moses Maimonides (1138–1204)* (Würzburg, 2004).

[122] B. Ber. 40b; Y. Ber. 9:1, 11d; *Mishne Torah, Berakhot* 1:5.

[123] See M. R.H. 1:2; B. R.H. 16b; *Mishne Torah, Teshuba* 3:1, 4.

[124] See M. Yoma 8:9 and George Foote Moore, *Judaism*, (Cambridge, MA, 1966), vol. 3, pp. 150–151.

[125] There is a beautiful English translation of this hymn with notes in Joseph H. Hertz, *Daily Prayer Book* (New York, 1963), pp. 556–557. Other hymns were modeled after it, the most popular of which is *Ya Ribbon 'Alam* by Israel Najara.

cosmic sacrality of pagan religions,[126] but, specifically, *qedushat ha-miṣvot* "a sacrality that is awarded by God to the faithful for having *fulfilled* his precepts."[127] To ascertain this principle, upon the performance of a *miṣva* a "blessing" is pronounced.[128] It consists of four small segments. An invocation addressed to God ("Blessed are You God"), followed by an announcement that he is "King of the Universe," i.e., the One having total Dominion over everything. The third segment ascertains that (consequently) he had "awarded us sanctity with his precepts," concluding, "and prescribed us . . . ," spelling out the specific precept about to be fulfilled. Conversely, biblical "idolatry" is not just worshipping idols, as per popular wisdom, but, as taught by the rabbis: *'aboda zara,* an "alien," non-*miṣva* "worship," either because the ritual was not actually prescribed (see Lev. 10:1) or because the individuals performing the ritual were not charged with this responsibility (see Num. 16:17-17:5). This type of "worship" is repudiated totally and absolutely as *'aboda zara* and it constitutes a supreme act of defiance to his Dominion camouflaged as religion.[129]

The biblical ideal of God as Supreme King (instead of king as Supreme God) is more political than theological.[130] We may add that, correspondingly, God alone can claim Dominion over humankind by Right of Creation: *ex nihilo*. Throughout antiquity there were pagan monotheists,[131] some of whom are mentioned in Scripture

---

[126] See Faur, *Homo Mysticus*, p. 3; idem, "Anti-Maimonidean Demons," pp. 46–48. Cf. *Perush R. Abraham*, p. 302.

[127] See *Mekhilta de-R. Shim'on bar Yohai*, J.N. Epstein and E.Z. Melamed, eds. (Jerusalem, 1955), on Exod. 19:6, p. 139 (ll.22-24); and *Sifre Bemidbar*, H.S. Horovitz, ed. (Jerusalem, 1966), #115, p. 127 (ll.7-12). This is what Joseph, B. Shab. 55a, meant when he taught that "sanctity" may not be "absorbed" from the sanctity at the Temple but must be acquired dynamically by fulfilling (*qiyyemu*) the Torah.

[128] The original sense of "blessing" (how could a human *bless* his maker?!) has been lost. For an accurate understanding of the Hebrew "blessing," see José Faur, "Delocutive Expressions in the Hebrew Liturgy," in *Ancient Studies in Memory of Elias Bickerman (The Journal of the Ancient Near Eastern Society)*, vol. 16–17 (1984–1985), pp. 41–54.

[129] See Faur, *Homo Mysticus*, pp. 10–11.

[130] *Medrash Haggadol, Genesis,* p. 205 (ll.15-16); Nimrod tells Abraham: "Don't you know that I am *Adon* of everything there is? That by (my command) the Sun, the Moon, and the stars and constellations move! I created the entire Universe!"

[131] There is an excellent collection of articles on pagan monotheism, edited by Polymnia Athanassiadi and Michael Frede, *Pagan Monotheism in Late Antiquity* (Oxford, 1999). This is why the concept of "Dominion" in pagan lore is paternal or political, but not divine; see Thomas Hobbes, *Leviathan*, chap. 20.

with deference.¹³² However, not a single pagan thinker is known to have expressed the belief that the One and only God has absolute Dominion over his creatures—and not the local monarch!¹³³ A principal corollary of biblical monotheism is rejection of a ruler with absolute sovereignty.¹³⁴ Hence, the gross antipathy towards the God of Israel, peculiar to dictators, megalomaniacs, and aspiring intellectuals.

VI

It has been lamented that "little trace of true Christian feeling" is present in the *Principia*.¹³⁵ In what follows we will show that Newton incorporated the Jewish doctrine of God's Dominion in the "General Scholium" to the *Principia*:

> [W]e admire him (God) for his perfection; but we reverence and adore him on account of his dominion; for we adore him as his servants; and a god without dominion, providence, and final causes, is nothing else but Fate and Nature. Blind metaphysical necessity, which is certainly the same always and everywhere, could produce no variety of things.¹³⁶

Reading the following paragraph in Latin, one would get the impression that somehow Newton was trying to link the concept of *Dominus* (Dominion) with *Deus* (God)—something that linguistically makes no sense.¹³⁷ It seems, however, that although writing in Latin, Newton,

---

¹³² See *Mishne Torah, 'Aboda Zara* 1:2 (ll.30-31); cf. *Perush R. Abraham*, p. 302.

¹³³ Unlike Hananiah, Mishael, Azariah, and countless Jewish victims who said "No!" to their local Pharaoh. The ideology of anti-Semitism is more political than "religious." For some insights, see José Faur, "On Martyrdom in Jewish Law: Maimonides and Nahmanides," in *Memorial Volume in Honor of Prof. M.S. Feldblum* (Ramat-Gan), especially section I (Heb.).

¹³⁴ Some Jews in antiquity rejected all types of authority and refused to acknowledge a human as *despótes* (= *dominus*) "master;" see Josephus, *Jewish Antiquities* (Loeb Classical Library), XVII, 23, vol. 9, p. 22. (Incidentally, there is no connection between the above sect mentioned by Josephus and the M. Yad. 6:7, *in fine*.) Obviously, this will lead to total anarchy and therefore never became part of the political ideology of Israel, which recognizes sovereignty *under* the Law.

¹³⁵ Giorgio de Santillana, "Newton the Enigma," in his *Reflections on Men and Ideas* (Cambridge, Mass., 1968), p. 26.

¹³⁶ *Principia*, tran. by A. Motte and revised by F. Cajory, 2 vols. (Berkeley, 1934), vol. 2, p. 546.

¹³⁷ Naturally, the English translator of *Principia*, p. 544, note at the bottom of the page, assumed that Newton was thinking of the Latin *Deus/Dominium*. Since there is no linguistic relationship between these Latin terms, he suggested that perhaps "the Latin word *Deus* [derives] from the *Arabic du*...which signifies *Lord*."

in the footsteps of Maimonides, was connecting *Adon,* "Lord," with *Adonai.*[138] Here is what Newton wrote:

> [F]or God [i.e., Hebrew *Adonai*] is a relative word, and has respect to servants; and *Deity* is the dominion of God not over His own body, as those imagine who fancy God to be the soul of the world, but over servants. The supreme God is a Being eternal, infinite, absolutely perfect; but a being, however perfect, without dominion, cannot be said to be Lord God; for we say, my God, your God, the God of *Israel,* the God of Gods, and Lord of Lords; we do not say, my Eternal, your Eternal, the Eternal of *Israel*; but every Lord is not a God. It is the dominion of a spiritual being which constitutes a God: a true, supreme, or imaginary dominion makes a true, supreme, or imaginary God. And from his true dominion it follows that the true God is a living, intelligent, and powerful Being; and, from his other perfections, that he is supreme, or most perfect. He is eternal and infinite, omnipotent and omniscient; that is, his duration reaches from eternity to eternity; his presence from infinity to infinity; he governs all things, and knows all things that are or can be done.[139]

According to Maimonides, God's Dominion is inherent to the idea of God as a necessary Being. This doctrine, too, was incorporated in the "General Scholium." All agree, wrote Newton, "that the Supreme God exists necessarily." He then goes on to describe God as "a Being necessarily existing."[140] Given that only God is a necessary Being, nothing could be coeval with him; i.e., "creation" is essentially and fundamentally *ex nihilo*. Maimonides maintained that "causality," "necessity," as well as all the physical laws are the effect, not the source of "creation." Hence, the laws ruling the universe do not apply to God.[141] The preceding precludes identifying God as a force imminent in nature, acting as "the soul" of the world.[142] "This Being," wrote Newton, "governs all things, not as the soul of the world, but as Lord over all."[143]

---

[138] See above, n. 94.

[139] *Principia,* trans. by A. Motte and ed. by Florian Cajori (Berkeley, 1962), vol. 2, pp. 544–545.

[140] *Principia,* vol. 2, p. 546.

[141] See *Guide,* I, 56; cf. ibid., 35 (82); 63, p. 106 (ll.10-13). On the designation of God as "First Cause," see ibid., I, 69, and Faur, *Homo Mysticus,* pp. 89–94.

[142] *Guide,* I, 70, p. 118 (ll.22-26); III, 29, p. 375 (ll.22-25). On this fundamental concept, see Philo, *The Special Laws,* I, 18 (Loeb Classical Library), vol. 7, p. 109.

[143] *Principia,* p. 544; cf. Isaac Newton, *Opticks* (New York, 1952, based on the Fourth Edition, London, 1730), *Qu.* 31, p. 403.

Fundamental to the doctrine of God as a "necessary Being," is the belief that he acts not mechanically but as a *Manhig*, that is, as a willful, free agent. Maimonides pointed to the uneven distribution of celestial matter as well as the dissimilar motions of astral bodies, as an indication of choice and design, rather than necessity.[144] The chain of cause and effect, observed Newton, will eventually lead us "to the very first Cause, which certainly is not mechanical;"[145] the planetary system is "the Effect of choice" exercised by God.[146] Even though God had created a perfectly mechanical universe, he acts as "a voluntary Agent."[147] "[T]he Motions which the Planets now have," wrote Newton to Richard Bentley (1682–1742), "could not spring from any natural Cause alone, but were impressed by an intelligent Agent."[148] Roger Cotes (1682–1716) further developed this theme in the "Preface to the Second Edition" of the *Principia* (1713) and attacked those who deny that the world "was caused by the will of God," attributing it to "some necessity." There is "not the least shadow of necessity" compelling the Creator. "Without all doubt this world," he declared, "could arise from nothing but the perfectly clear free will of God directing and presiding over all." Maimonides discerned in the anatomical and physiological arrangements, evidence of God's exquisite care and providence.[149] God's wisdom and management exhibited "in an ant or a bee," remarked R. Judah ha-Levi (ca. 1071–1141), "is no less wondrous and subtle than his wisdom and management of the sun and its sphere."[150] In the same vein, Newton wrote:

> Can it be by accident that all birds, beasts, and men have their right side and left side alike shaped (except in their bowels); and just two eyes, and no more, on either side of the face; and just two ears on

---

[144] See *Guide* II, 19. Cf. above n. 116. This doctrine is the theme of the first blessing of the Evening *Shema'*; cf. above, n. 114.

[145] *Opticks*, Qu. 28, p. 369.

[146] *Opticks*, Qu. 31, p. 402. Cf. *Guide* II, 20, pp. 218 (l.23)–219 (l.2), and Faur, *Homo Mysticus*, pp. 112–115.

[147] "Letters to Bentley," I, reproduced in I. Bernard Cohen, ed., *Isaac Newton's Papers & Letters on Natural Philosophy* (Cambridge, Mass., 1958), p. 282.

[148] Ibid., p. 284.

[149] *Guide*, III, 12, p. 322 (l.28) ff.

[150] *Kuzari* III, 17, ed. and trans. by Y. Even Shmuel (Tel-Aviv, 1994), p. 112; cf. ibid., I, 68, p. 21; IV, 25, p. 184; and V, 20 (iii), p. 228; see *Guide* II, 6, p. 183 (ll.11-25). The *Kuzari* was translated into Latin by Johannes Buxtorf and published in 1660.

either side [of] the head; and a nose with two holes; and either two forelegs or two wings or two arms on the shoulders, and two legs on the hips, and no more? Whence arise this uniformity in all their outward shapes but from the counsel and contrivance of an Author?[151]

Maimonides saw in the biological designs, particularly the eye, evidence of God's Providence and Guidance. On the basis of *Psalms* 94, he argued:

> ... If [God] would be impervious to the theory of sight, how these instruments which are essential for sight came about? Could one envision that by mere chance it came to pass that a transparent humor was produced, and beneath it another humor similar to it, and beneath it a certain membrane which by mere chance contains a perforation, and that underneath that membrane came about a transparent membrane which [by pure chance] is solid? By way of conclusion: could an intelligent person envisage, that the humors (making up) the eye, the membranes and nervous [system] that as it is well known, are so ingeniously planned—all of which designed to meet a single function [sight]— came about by mere chance? No! But, (then he would propose) necessarily that it is a design of nature, as put forward by every physician and philosopher![152] [But] don't all philosophers agree that nature has neither intelligence nor direction?! [153]

---

[151] *Memoirs of the Life, Writings, and Discoveries of Sir Isaac Newton*, vol. 2, pp. 347–348; cf. McLachlan, *Sir Isaac Newton Theological Manuscripts*, pp. 48–49; cf. *Opticks*, Qu. 31, pp. 369–370.

[152] This is precisely what ancient pagans and atheists argued; see above, nn. 142–143. The modern anti-creationist theory is just a rehash of the old pagan belief in a certain organizing force *inherent* to nature, which organizes and directs. Conceptually, their most important contribution is that instead of referring to it as "spirit" or "soul" (terms denounced as heretical), it is now "scientifically" designated "random." This very notion of "nature" was rejected by Nieto in his famous sermon; see Faur, *Golden Doves*, pp. 19–27. See the following note.

[153] *Guide*, III, 19, p. 346 (ll.11-22). The Jewish position on this matter was cogently formulated by Elie Benamozegh; see José Faur, "The Hebrew Species Concept and the Origin of Evolution: R. Benamozegh's Response to Darwin," in *Rassegna Mensile di Israel* 63 (1997), pp. 43–66. According to the anti-Creationist dogma, positing total randomness (if it is not "total" it could not be "random"), even if a color TV set were found in some remote astral spot, together with instruction in French and English, it would prove absolutely nothing about extra-terrestrial intelligence, since the design of a TV apparatus is infinitely less complex than the design of a single cell. Upon consideration, assuming their theory of total randomness, the papers and works produce by these luminaries could also be regarded the result of blind chance—there is less probability for the random production of a single petal of a rose than for some of the hodgepodge parading under the cloak of "science;" see Jeremy Campbell, *Grammatical Man* (New York, 1982), p. 16; Faur, *Golden Doves*, pp. 18–27, 59–60. For a full examination of this problem, see Ludwig von Bertalanffy, *General System Theory* (New York, 1968).

A similar view was echoed by Newton:

> Whence is it that the eyes of all sorts of living creatures are transparent to the very bottom and only transparent skin and within transparent humors, with a crystalline lens in the middle and a pupil before the lens, all of them so finely shaped and fitted for vision that no artist can mend them? Did blind chance know that there was light and what was its refraction, and fit the eyes of all creatures after the most curious manner to make use of it? These and such like considerations always have and will prevail with mankind to believe that there is a Being who made all things and has all things in his power.[154]

Given that God's existence is utterly different from anything else, Maimonides rejected all manners of anthropocentric theology.[155] Consequently, every form of anthropomorphisms and positive attributes are wrong and illegitimate.[156] The same with Newton:

> Whence also he is all similar, all eye, all ear, all brain, all arm, all power to perceive, to understand, and to act; but in a manner not at all human, in a manner not at all corporeal, in a manner utterly unknown to us. As a blind man has no idea of colors, so have we no idea of the manner by which the all-wise God perceives and understands all things.[157] He is utterly void of all body and bodily figure, and can therefore neither be seen nor heard nor touched; nor ought he to be worshiped under the representation of any corporeal thing. We have ideas of his attributes, but what the real substance of anything is we know not . . . much less, then, have we any idea of the substance of God.[158]

Not only are God's perceptions and actions unlike those of man, but his "knowledge" also is utterly dissimilar to ours. Therefore, Maimonides submitted that God's omniscience and omnipresence are not intrusive to human beings, and we remain free even though God has perfect foreknowledge of our actions.[159] Similarly, Newton

---

[154] *Memoirs of the Life, Writings, and Discoveries of Sir Isaac Newton*, vol. 2, p. 348. Cf. *Opicks*, Qu. 28, pp. 369–370.

[155] See Faur, *Homo Mysticus*, pp. 3–5, 89–90, 121–123.

[156] See *Guide*, I, 51, 53, 55, 57, 60, etc. José Faur, "The Character of Apophatic Knowledge in Maimonides' Guide," in Dan Cohn-Sherbok, ed., *Theodicy* (Lewiston, 1997), pp. 67–74.

[157] On the metaphor of the blind man, cf. Maimonides, *Perush ha-Mishnayot*, *Sanhedrin*, X, 1, vol. 4, p. 203.

[158] *Principia*, pp. 545–546. Cf. *Mishne Torah, Yesode ha-Torah* 2:10. On God's knowledge, see the quotation from Maimonides, in the following note.

[159] *Mishne Torah, Teshuba* 5:5; cf. *Yesode ha-Torah* 1:9, 2:10, and Faur, *Homo Mysticus*, pp. 93–94. On God's ominpresence, see José Faur, "God as a Writer: Omnipresence and the Art of Dissimulation," in *Religion and Intellectual Life* 6 (1989), pp. 31–43.

remarked: "God suffers nothing from the motion of bodies; bodies find no resistance from the omnipresence of God."[160] Given that God's existence is dissimilar to ours, Maimonides concluded that it is impossible to have direct knowledge of him,[161] but only indirectly through his creations.[162] Likewise, Newton wrote that, "We know him only by his most wise and excellent contrivances of things, and final causes."[163] Although it is impossible to have an immediate knowledge of God, Maimonides maintained that one can draw near him through the understanding of his creations.[164] Similarly, Newton wrote that when he developed the *Principia*, "I had an Eye upon such Principles as might work with considering Men for the Belief of a Deity."[165]

VII

Basic to linguistic knowledge is the faculty of syntagmatic opposition between the speaking subject ("I") and the addressee ("you").

Dominion, in Hebrew intellectual tradition, is a fundamental dimension of humankind. Adam, so it seems, was the first humanoid to have been created in "the image of God" (Gen. 1:26). Unlike everything else, this creature alone had the singular ability of self-consciousness. Incisively, the Aramaic version associates this faculty with the linguistic apparatus and speech (Gen. 2:7).[166] Fundamental to the linguistic apparatus is the faculty to structurally connect the signifier (sound-image) with the signified (linguistic concept) and thus create a linguistic sign.[167] Interaction of these signs within the linguistic apparatus, permit humankind to communicate and develop

---

[160] *Principia*, p. 545.
[161] *Guide* III, 20, p. 348 (ll.15-29); cf. I, 57–58.
[162] *Guide* I, 34, p. 50 (ll.8-9); see 71, p. 126 (ll.25-27); III, 51, p. 456 (l.5) ff.
[163] *Principia*, p. 546.
[164] This kind of knowledge, however, does not lead to the ultimate knowledge of God. See *Guide* III, 51, p. 455 (l.28) ff.
[165] "Letter I to Richard Bentley," in *Isaac Newton's Papers & Letters on Natural Philosophy*, p. 280; cf. *Opticks*, Qu. 31, pp. 405–406. Maimonides (as well as the English *virtuosi*) believed that there are no contradictions between physics and Scripture and that the study of science is indispensable for the proper understanding of the God of Scripture; see *Mishne Torah, Yesode ha-Torah* 2:2; *Guide* I, 46; cf. ibid. 71 (end); III, 28, p. 373 (ll.16-22).
[166] See José Faur, "Person and Subjectivity: A Linguistic Category," in *Mentalities* 6 (1990), pp. 15–18.
[167] See Faur, *Golden Doves*, pp. xix, 71.

linguistic knowledge *without* having genuine comprehension of what they speak about. We can appreciate the rabbis' view (I sense a dash of humor in their words) that, in this respect, human beings are superior to angels, since the latter cannot communicate about matters that they don't comprehend fully. The most important function of the linguistic apparatus is to structure a syntagmatic opposition between the speaking subject ("I") and the addressee ("you"). "I"—the very feeling of subjectivity and self-consciousness—is a linguistic creation established by the syntagmatic opposition "I/you." Without a "you" there is no "I," and vice versa.[168] Adam's self-awareness and consciousness comes in stages. At first, he realizes his own differentiation within the animal kingdom, but is not yet conscious of his subjective "I." His own subjectivity he apprehends at a later stage, when realizing the syntagmatic opposition Adam/Adon.[169]

The rabbis reported that before creating Adam, God consulted with the angels:

> [God] asked them: "Shall we make Adam?"
> They replied to him: "This Adam, what type [of creature] is he?"
> God told them: "His wisdom is greater than yours." He then proceeded to parade before them beasts, wild animals, and birds.
> He asked them: "This! What is it called?" But they did not know! "This! What is it called?" And they did not know! He then paraded them [the animals] before Adam.
> He asked him: "This! What is it called?"
> "This is an ox!"
> "This! What is it called?"
> "This is a camel!"
> "This! What is it called?
> "This is a donkey!"
> "This! What is it called?"
> "This is a horse!" . . .
> "And you, what is your name?"
> He [Adam] answered him [God]: "To me it would be fit to call Adam, since I was created from *Adama* (dust)."
> "And what is my name?"
> "To you it would be fit to call *Adon* (Master), since you are the Master of all your creations."[170]

---

[168] See ibid., pp. 41–48.
[169] See Faur, *Homo Mysticus*, pp. 4–5.
[170] *Bereshit Rabba* XVII, 4, vol. 1, pp. 155–156. Cf. above, n. 90. People who don't recognize God's Dominion believe in human dominion, either of their own or of others.

This means, in simple words, that devoid of consciousness of his syntagmatic relation to Adon, Adam will fall short of forging his own "I" and the "image of God" unique to his distinctive individuation.[171]

VIII

R. David Nieto came to London in 1701 and served as the head of the Sephardic synagogue *Sha'ar ha-Shamayim* at Bevis Mark until his death in 1728. Newton came to London to take up his appointment as Warden of the Mint in 1696. He moved several times and finally in 1709 he took up residence in a house at St. Martin's street, not too far from Leicester Square, where he lived until 1724. R. Nieto lived in a house next to the synagogue, about a mile from the Mint (at London's Tower). It is highly probable that Newton heard of Nieto, particularly after the rumpus caused by the sermon he delivered on November 20, 1703, negating the notion of "universal Nature"—a position strikingly similar to Newton's.[172] We should bear in mind that Abendana and Nieto must have known each other well.[173] Not only did they belong to the closely knit circle of Spanish and Portuguese Jews, but more importantly they shared a similar educational background and represented the same intellectual tradition of religious humanism and pluralism. It would not be unreasonable to assume that Abendana had mentioned Newton to Nieto, and then Nieto to Newton. I have no proof that Nieto and Newton ever met. But, why shouldn't they? Nieto was the only Jew at the time who had the scientific background to read the *Principia*. Knowing what I know of Nieto's personality and his interest in science and Torah, it would be surprising if he would not have made some effort to meet Newton. I suppose that Newton, too, would have wanted to meet Nieto. In addition to sharing the same passion for Scripture, Rabbinic thought and literature, the calendar, history, religion, and science, Nieto was the only person (besides Abendana)

---

[171] Cf. Faur, *Homo Mysticus*, pp. 8, 15–16, 127–128, 138–142.

[172] See Faur, *Golden Doves*, pp.18–22, and above, nn. 142–143.

[173] Abendana must have worshiped at *Sha'ar ha-Shamayim* where his brother, R. Jacob, served as rabbi (1680–1685). Nieto knew of Abenadana; see Kayserling, "Les Correspondants Juifs de Jean Buxtorf," p. 272, n. 2; and of his calendars, see H. Graetz, "Wissenschaftliche," in *Monatasschrift* 9 (1860), pp. 29–34; and the note of A. Berliner, *Magazin* 4 (1877), p. 235.

with whom Newton could discuss matters pertaining to his "dreadful secret." At any rate, Nieto relates an event taken place before 1715. It runs as follows:

> A man came to me and said: "I know that you are from the children of Israel and believe that there is a God, Creator, who is from Eternity. But I cannot believe that."
> I asked him: "Why?"
> He replied: "Because I cannot mentally conceive how something can exist without a beginning."
> I asked him: "Then, who created the universe?"
> He replied: "I do not know!"
> I said to him: "There could only be two possibilities. You may either admit that [the universe] is eternal without a beginning or that there is a cause [external to it] that created it, and that cause is from eternity."
> He replied: "I think that [the universe] is from eternity."
> I replied: "You are contradicting yourself! First you stated that you cannot believe that there is a God, Creator, since it is impossible for you to mentally conceive that there can be something from eternity. Now you are ascertaining that the universe has no beginning!"
> For a while he remained speechless. Then he said: "Your question perplexes me. I don't know what to answer."
> I said to him: "You are acknowledging [the existence of] something from eternity. Mistakenly, however, you are attributing eternity to the creation, whereas you should have attributed eternity to the Creator. Now, confess and acknowledge that there is an Eternal [Being] and that that Eternal [Being] is the Creator, in contradistinction to the universe—a creation—which was created."
> Thereupon, he threw himself at my feet, sobbing with great joy. He then kissed me and hugged me and said: "You have bestowed life onto me! For now I know that there is a God, Creator of Heaven and earth, Wise, who Governs and exercises Providence over his creatures. He should bless and multiply you, and increase you in wealth, property, and glory."[174]

Could it be? I don't know and have no support on the matter. But this does not prevent me from imagining (paraphrasing a more publicized but somehow less intellectually charged occasion), "That this might have well turned out to be the beginning of a wonderful friendship."

---

[174] R. David Nieto, *Esh Dat* (London, 1715), II, #134, p. 33b.

MOSLEM, CHRISTIAN, AND JEWISH CULTURAL INTERACTION IN SEFARDIC TALMUDIC INTERPRETATION*

Daniel Boyarin
University of California at Berkeley

For Ze'ev Brinner

The general participation of Iberian Jewry in the scholastic culture of the high middle ages is very well known. Less well known is the continuing influence the Aristotelian tradition had on Spanish and Sefardic Jewish intellectual life in the fifteenth and sixteenth centuries, including its most particularly Jewish of activities, the interpretation of the Talmud. In this period, there appears a new theory and practice of Talmudic hermeneutic, which is called *'iyyun*, "speculation:"[1] Talmudic interpretation as an application of the Aristotelian theory of language.

From the point of view of the history of Jewish culture, one of the most salient aspects of the *'iyyun* is the integration it brings to Jewish culture in two ways, vertically in that it integrates the different branches of intellectual life among Jews in this culture and horizontally in that it integrates Jewish textual practice with the literary culture of the other elements of contemporary society. After discussing evidence for this thesis in the first part of the paper, I will have something to say about its implications for our general modeling of Jewish cultural history.

Two of the most important methodological works of the school of *'iyyun* are *Darkhe hattalmud*[2] by the father of the method, R. Yitzhaq Kanpanton (d. 1493), the last great spiritual leader of Spanish Jewry before the Expulsion[3] and *Kelale Shmuel*, by R. Shmuel Ibn Sid

---

* Reprinted from *Review of Rabbinic Judaism* 5:1, 2002, pp. 1–33.
[1] In the technical sense.
[2] Isaac ben Jacob Canpanton and Shemu'el al-Valensi, *Darkhe Ha-Talmud*, Y. Sh. Langeh, ed. (Jerusalem, 1980). All translations herein are mine.
[3] For the little that we know of his biography, see Abraham David, "On R. Isaac Canpanton, One of the Great Fifteenth Century Scholars," in *Kiryath Sefer* 51, pp. 324–326 (Hebrew).

(d. 1520). Studying these works carefully enables us to discern different scholastic "influences" at work in them, suggesting that the Iberian pattern of interaction between Jewish sages and scholastic philosophy continued up until the *gerush* and even beyond into the sixteenth century. In particular, specific Thomist elements can be detected in the later work.

Kanpanton's greatest achievement was the revival of talmudic learning as an important intellectual pursuit of the Iberian Jewish intelligencia, after a period of close to a century during which this pursuit was not highly regarded. It can reasonably be hypothesized that one of the reasons he was so successful in this endeavor was his ability to express talmudic learning in the language of the scholastic philosophical discourse so highly regarded by that very intelligencia and to show that talmudic logic was in many respects comparable to Aristotelian logic or more specifically Aristotelian linguistic doctrine. His method of interpreting the Talmud became, through his disciples who founded Yeshivot all through the Ottoman Empire, *the* dominant method of study and interpretation in the Sefardic diaspora for the two centuries following the Expulsion. His little handbook for talmudic interpretation, *Darkhe hattalmud [The Ways of the Talmud]* was so influential that it is quoted almost entire in the sixteenth century Polish halakhic classic, *Shnei Luhot Habberit* as an illustration of the way that Sefardim study Talmud and a recommendation to the author's Ashkenazi fellows that they follow its example. *Kelale Shmuel* is an alphabetical encyclopedia of talmudic terminology together with examples of the usage of the terms, drawn from actual texts and some discussion of problems related to the terms and the specific texts cited. As such, it reveals the systematization and scientific method so beloved of the Spanish Jews influenced by scholasticism. However, the most interesting part of the book is the introduction, in which the author sets out a methodology for the study and interpretation of the Talmud, following the theory and practice of *'iyyun*. This introduction is together with *Darkhe hattalmud* itself one of the two most important theoretical documents of the school that are preserved.

1. *Logic and the Perfection of Speech*

Several of the most important aspects of *'iyyun* can be shown to be applications to talmudic studies of ideas about language and semiotics current in the Arabic logical literature from Al-Farabi and on.

One of the key methodological principles of *'iyyun* was to demonstrate that each and every word of the Talmud was necessary. This principle has sometimes been derived by scholars from the talmudic method of interpreting the Mishnah and from the midrashic method of interpreting the Bible.[4] While I do not deny the relevance of these models, the comparisons I will make show that the proximate theoretical sources were rather in scholastic linguistic philosophy. This principle can be organized into several sub-categories, in each case showing the connection with Arabic predecessors.

The key to the method of *'iyyun* was the intimate relation of logic and language in the Middle Ages. This connection lies in the fact that one of the major tasks of the logician, perhaps the first task, is to determine what linguistic signs mean, and in order to do so, one must first have a theory of *how* linguistic signs mean. The dominant theory of meaning in scholastic logic is the theory of *intentio* or mental language. This doctrine has been well summarized by E.J. Ashworth:

> It was held that for a spoken or written proposition to have meaning, it had to be subordinated to a mental proposition, and such properties as synonymy and equivocation were explained by means of the relationships between these three types of proposition. If a spoken or written proposition was equivocal, this meant that its tokens could be subordinated to more than one mental proposition. On the other hand, if two different written or spoken propositions were said to be synonymous, this meant they were subordinated to the same mental proposition. A corollary of these claims was, of course, that no mental propositions could properly be called either equivocal or synonymous. All mental propositions were explicit and distinct from one another. . . . Moreover, any written or spoken proposition was supposed to have some mental analogue.[5]

This doctrine was crucial in forming the interpretive methodology of the *'iyyun*, for it leads to an understanding of interpretation as the determination of the relationships of written language to mental language or intention within a text, and it was this understanding which generated the methodology of *'iyyun*. That this was indeed

---

[4] Israel Ta-Shema, "Tosefot Gornisch," in *Sinai* 48, p. 159.
[5] E.J. Ashworth, "The Doctrine of Exponibilia in the Fifteenth and Sixteenth Centuries," in *Vivarium* 11 (1973), pp. 139–140.

the interpretation of meaning held by the ʿiyyun can be shown by the following quotation:

> Always investigate and search every interpretation which they interpret or explication of a biblical verse or of the language (i.e., the Talmud) to see if it is correct and properly fitting from the aspect of the language or the intention or both, for that is the ideal.[6]

That is to say: the ideal commentary explains the written language in such a way that it fits perfectly with mental speech, i.e., that no elements of the outer speech have been ignored or distorted in arriving at the explication and that nothing need be supplied that is not, in fact, implied by the language. Moreover, the mental discourse thus hypothesized must be coherent. The ideal is, of course, for both of these conditions to be met fully.

The search for an interpretation of a text which shows that there is a perfect fit between outer and inner speech or between written and mental language is implicated in a doctrine that denies that there is systematic redundancy in language. Thus, when Kanpanton introduces his hermeneutic rule that every part and particle of the language must be proven to make an independent non-redundant contribution to the meaning, he does so in the following way:

> A great principle of ʿiyyun is that you must be very exacting with the language and make great effort if there is any superfluous language or duplication of intention, . . . and, moreover, be very exacting with any change in the language . . . from subject to subject [asking] why is it? And you shall investigate and search diligently to bring out meaning from all of the language in such a way that every word and every particle will signify something new not understood from all that came before.[7]

There are, in fact, three types of redundancy listed by Kanpanton here. The first two are self-explanatory. "Superfluous language" must mean linguistic signs within the text, which are apparently unnecessary to signify the intention of the text. "Apparently" is the crucial word here, for, in fact, by the doctrine I have cited above, "any term which appeared in a written or spoken proposition was supposed to have some mental analogue." Therefore, the interpreter must "make great effort" if there appear to be any terms that do not have such analogues, interpreting them as well, and showing how the meaning

---

[6] *Darkhe hattalmud*, p. 57.
[7] *Darkhe hattalmud*, p. 22.

would suffer were they absent. Similarly, when the text seems to repeat itself ("duplicate its intention"), one must find a way to excise the apparent redundancy. So far, so good, but what is the meaning of "be exacting" with any change in the language, and what has that to do with superfluity or redundancy? As we learn from the interpretive practice of Kanpanton's disciples, what is meant here is that when different language is used in different passages apparently to express the same meaning, one must "be exacting" and show that in fact they have differing intentions behind them. That is to say, Kanpanton rejects the possibility of complete synonymy, not only in mental language, but even with regard to written and spoken language, for this would lead to a defect (superfluity) in the linguistic system, which is deemed to be perfect.

The doctrine of non-superfluity in language, on both the discourse and the systemic levels belongs to an important philosophical tradition. Looking just at sources that were probably well known to Kanpanton, we find the fourteenth century Provençal logician, R. Joseph Ibn Kaspi claiming, "In general, nearly all synonyms have a difference in meaning between them, when examined exactingly."[8] Similarly, Kaspi's countryman, R. Moshe Narbonni claims, "Now synonyms are not employed in the demonstrative sciences," and uses this as an exegetical principle, by which he explains that when Al-Gazzali says "ignorance and error" he must mean two different things.[9] In truth, these are slightly different positions, Kaspi denying that there is any synonymy at all, while Narbonni seems to say that it exists but is avoided in scientific writing. Either view is sufficient to explain Kanpanton's doctrine.

The second sort of redundancy too was rejected on sound logical grounds. First of all, as we have already seen, it was a generally held principle that any term in written or oral speech had its analogue in mental speech. Kanpanton refers to this principle when he says, "Every word and every particle must signify something

---

[8] Text cited in Shalom Rosenberg, *Logic and Ontology in Jewish Philosophy in the Fourteenth Century* (Jerusalem Dissertation, 1973), p. 17 (Hebrew). See also Rosenberg, "Logic, Language and Biblical Exegesis in the Writings of R. Joseph Ibn Kaspi," in *Dat Wesafah*, M. Halmish and A. Kasher, eds. (Ramat Gan, 1979), pp. 105–113 (Hebrew).

[9] G.B. Chertoff, *The Logical Part of Al-Ghazali's Maqasid al-Falasafia, in an Anonymous Hebrew Translation with the Hebrew Commentary of Moses of Narbonne* (Columbia University Dissertation, 1952), p. 16.

new."[10] Moreover, it was a commonly held view that logic is a science of language, the function of which is to teach one to use language in an exact manner. Indeed, in Hebrew, before being called *higgayon* (which also means speech), logic was called *hokhmat haddibbur*, literally, *scientia sermocinalis*.

The connection between logic and the perfection of speech is well established in the thought of Maimonides, a major source for Jewish scholasticism. Let us see then how Maimonides defines "*dibbur*," and how he, thereby, relates language to logic:

> The word "*dibbur*" is a homonymous term by imposition of the ancient peoples, which signifies three intentions.
> The first is that faculty, by which man is distinguished, with which he conceives concepts (intelligibles) and learns sciences and distinguishes between the contemptible and the appropriate. This intention is also called "the faculty of speech" or "the speaking soul."
> The second intention is the concept itself, already conceived by the man. This intention is called "the inner speech."
> The third intention is the utterance in speech of the intention (concept) impressed upon the soul. This intention is also called "the outer speech."[11]

We see, according to Maimonides, that language is the product of an innate capacity for articulate speech, "the speaking soul." Now, this innate faculty is, in fact, none other than the faculty of reason, for it differentiates humans and enables them to learn and distinguish what is correct from the incorrect. Moreover, by virtue of this faculty, concepts are "already" conceived in "inner (mental) speech," prior to their formulation in "outer speech," talking and writing. It follows then that "outer speech," a product of the rational faculty, ought to be made so that it will be a perfect representation of logical form. This indeed, according to Maimonides, is the work of logic, "the science of speech:"

> This science gives rules common to all languages, by which outer speech is guided toward what is correct, and guarded from error, *such that what he utters in his speech corresponds to what is in his mind and is equivalent to it, and the utterance does not add to the intention of his soul, nor subtract from it.*[12]

---

[10] *Darkhe hattalmud*, p.

[11] Moses Maimonides, et al., *Maimonides' Treatise on Logic (Makalah Fi-Sina'at al-Mantik) the Original Arabic and Three Hebrew Translations*, Israel Efros, ed. and trans. (New York, 1938), p. 59. This passage is practically a quote from Al-Farabi's introduction to logic, as has been pointed out by Efros.

[12] Ibid.

Maimonides's statements of the nature of language and of its functions are echoed by R. Shmuel Ibn Sid in such a way that we are left with little doubt as to their being a major source for his linguistic philosophy and the interpretive practice of the Sefardic school:

> Now it is well known that words signify intentions in the soul, and if the practitioner of *'iyyun* wishes to express the intention of his soul, *it ought to be by means of words which signify what is in his soul, and there must not be any addition or subtraction*, in such a way that the image in his soul will be well expressed . . . and when there is a discrepancy between them, then we can object, for the *tanna* [the author of the Mishnah] was (seemingly) not exact with his language.[13]

This statement of Ibn Sid's teaches us three things: 1) that the method of *'iyyun* had its roots in the scholastic theory of meaning, particularly in its Maimonidean-Farabian formulation; 2) that *'iyyun* as an interpretive method follows from the assumption that one trained in logic can use outer speech so as to make it a perfect signifier of inner speech, with no extra or missing linguistic signs for the expression of the inner speech; and 3) that the authors of the talmudic texts are such logicians, and therefore one can apply these canons of interpretation to their language.

2. *The Concept of Understanding by Sub-Audition*

One of the outstanding methods of talmudic interpretation developed by Yitzhaq Kanpanton was the method known as *sebara mibbahutz*, which I will translate here, for reasons that will become apparent, "understanding by sub-audition." Here is the rabbi's description of the force of this technique:

> Diligently investigate in any utterance or sentence what you would have thought from your own reasoning or understood from your intelligence before the *tanna* or the *amora* intervened. For you will have a great benefit from this, namely that if you would have understood of your own as he does, then you can ask of him, what has he come to communicate to us. On the other hand, if your own reasoning is opposed to his, then you must investigate to find what forced him to say what he did and what is the weakness or fallacy in what you had thought. And this is what is called *"sebara mibbahutz"* (p. 26).

---

[13] *Kelale Shmuel*, p. 1.

The *sebara mibbahutz* is then that which would have been understood by the commentator from the language of the Torah or of the Mishnah without the necessity for an interpretive intervention on the part of the tannaim or amoraim. The origin of the term, itself, however, is not totally established. I would like to propose that the *sebara mibbahutz* is a calque on an Arabic logical term, ultimately going back to a Greek term in the commentaries on Aristotle. In that literature, we find the Greek term εξωθεν in the sense of that which is not expressed explicitly in language, because it is understood by the intelligence of the hearer or reader without a need for it to be expressed. So we find it used in Ammonius's commentary on Aristotle:

> What is required in a modal proposition is not merely a verb which includes the copula, but the copula itself, either explicit or supplied to the proposition from outside by subaudition (εξωθεν τη προτασει υπακονομενου), for we say: either "It is possible that Socrates will go," or "It is possible that Socrates will be a musician" with the copula expressed. But we can also express these propositions without the copula thus: "Possible that Socrates will go." We hold that in the latter case, the copula is understood.[14]

We find here that Ammonius uses precisely the term "from outside" to refer to a linguistic sign that does not need to be expressed in the language in order for the sentence to be understood. It is not a difficult step to imagine a talmudic thinker inquiring why is it ever used if it need not be. An even more exact correspondence to our usage is found in Al-Farabi, who frequently uses the expression *admarahu wa-fahimahu min kharij*. As Farabi's editor, F.W. Zimmerman remarks, "*min kharij* presumably is an exegetical concept, and as such occurs in a *set phrase* literally rendering the Greek in the glosses of the Baghdad Organon."[15] As Zimmerman further explains:

> The expression *admarahu wa-fahimahu min kharij* [to supply in the mind and understand it from the *outside*] doubly translates (first idiomatically, then literally) εξωθεν τη προτασει υπακονομενου τι an expression frequently found . . . in the Greek commentaries.[16]

---

[14] Ammonius 223.30-4.10, quoted F.W. Zimmerman, *Al-Farabi's Commentary and Short Treatise on Aristotle's De Interpretatione* (London, 1981), p. lxi.
[15] Ibid., p. lxii.
[16] Ibid., p. cxxxi.

In short, the Greek εξωθεν calqued by the Arabic *min kharij* provides an exact source for Yitzhak Kanpanton's uses of *mibbahutz*. The correspondence is even more exact in the case of interpreting a commentator, such as Rashi, for then the question is, given that I would have understood a given point *mibbahutz*, because it is implied in the language, then why did Rashi have to tell me it explicitly. It is, of course, most significant and interesting to see that the term, once appropriated takes on a life of its own and develops several variant meanings, among them some that are used in Ashkenazi *pilpul* as well.[17]

3. *The Use of Falsity as the Royal Road to Truth*

Certainly one of the most understood elements of *'iyyun* already in its own time was the insistence on producing false interpretations of the talmudic text only to disprove them in the end. This was misunderstood by contemporaries and near contemporaries as a type of merely academic show of prowess and roundly attacked by such figures as the author of *Alilot Debarim*.

This method had, however, several sound bases in the logical thought of the later Middle Ages. The first has to do with the very reason that interpretation is necessary in Kanpanton's view. In a key passage, he states (p. 57):

> Alternatively, the commentator will interpret the matter, in order to exclude another opinion or another interpretation, which would be *possible in the potentiality of the language*, for according to the simple meanings of the words and the syntax, it would be *possible to err* and entertain another view, and in order *to guard against it* and repulse it from the minds of the *me'ayyenim*, since in truth it is a falsehood, for that reason he interprets.

The key phrases in Kanpanton's explication are all of them couched in the language of Hebrew scholasticism. The most important phrase is "possible in the potentiality of the language, *bekoah hallashon*, that is to mean, that which we would have understood by ourselves from the language without the necessity for it to be expressed, or for that

---

[17] Incidentally, this explanation strongly suggests that the direction of influence was from the Sefardic scholars to the Ashkenazik ones, since it is hardly likely that Ashkenazim would have had direct access to Arabic logical terminology.

which we would have understood erroneously from the language itself before the commentators disabuse us of our error. This phrase, "potential in the language" is accordingly very similar in force to *sebara mibbahutz*. It can also develop the sense of that which is implied in the language, as in the following usage of Shmuel Ibn Sid, "A Mishnah or baraita which he could have objected from using that which is explicit in the language, but instead used that which is implicit," that is, in the more usual terminology of talmudic scholarship, the *diyyuq*. And indeed, *bekoah* and *bepo'al* are used in both Hebrew and Arabic [*bi-l-kuwwa bi-l-fi'l*] logical writings to mean, "explicit" and "implicit."

As stated above in the quotation from Ashworth, equivocation in the Middle Ages is defined as a single verbal proposition being subordinated to more than one mental proposition. This generally results from the polysemous nature of terms within the proposition. Now, for most medieval semanticists—Bacon is perhaps an exception—the meanings of polysemous or homonymous terms are fixed, that is to say, they have been fixed by an "imposition" or a series of impositions on the part of the ancient peoples. (Remember the explanation of the homonymy of *dibbur* in the above citation from Maimonides.) Therefore, a given proposition in a text has a limited number of possible interpretations, of which the parameters are the various possibilities which are potential in each of its terms. One of the functions of determining possible false readings of the text, then, is to show the necessity for the comment of the interpreter as excluding those false readings which exist in the potential of the language.

Kanpanton's doctrine is explicitly connected (by his terminology) to the scholastic analysis of sophisms or fallacies. His use of the terms "err" and "to guard against" in the above citation point in this direction, for both are terms of art of the Hebrew literature on sophisms. Most revealing, however, is Kanpanton's use of the term sophisms or fallacies *(hata'ot)* to mean the false interpretations of a passage rejected by the canonical commentators. Sophisms were analyzed by Aristotle into two types: "sophisms in speech" and those "out of speech," or in the terminology of Hebrew scholasticism *hata'ot 'asher bammillot* and *hata'ot 'asher ba'inyanim*. Now, it is quite clear that Kanpanton is referring to sophisms of speech, defined as the fallacious acceptance of one of the possible significations of an equivocal expression, when in fact, another is correct. By referring to the incorrect, rejected interpretations as *hata'ot*, he is drawing an analogy between the commentator and logician, whose common job is to teach people to "guard themselves" from the snares of seductive fallacy.

As we have seen, Maimonides, following Al-Farabi, defined the purpose of logic as giving, "rules common to all languages, by which outer speech is guided toward what is correct, and guarded from error *yishmerehu min hatta'ut*." It is hardly surprising, therefore, that what a commentator does is referred to in all branches of *pilpul* by the root *shmr*, e.g., *Rashi nishmar mizze*, and the pilpulistic method of analyzing commentaries is called universally *derek hashshmirot*.

We can see now that the setting up of false interpretations is an integral part of the system of thought and interpretation of R. Yitzhak and his follower. These false interpretations are required both to show why it was necessary for a commentator to comment at all, by showing the sophisms possible in the text, and also to serve as proof for the ineluctability of his interpretation. The lengths gone to to show the plausibility of the false interpretations served the first purpose, for if there be no true *causa apparentia*, there is no true fallacy, hence no need to interpret. Moreover, it is necessary to eliminate all possible sophisms in order to prove that only one interpretation is possible and therefore correct. Dialectical sophistry is thus conceived of as the only way to achieve truth and certainty in exegesis. As Kanpanton remarks, "the truth cannot be known, except through its opposite."

This view was not merely an eccentricity of talmudists. The fifteenth-century Spanish Jewish philosopher and logician, Abraham Shalom, articulates it as well when he says:

> A man is not called a hero of wisdom, until he can demonstrate a proposition two ways, once positively and once negatively, for a matter is only known through its opposite.[18]

It is surely no coincidence that Shalom here uses the term "ways," *derakim*, a technical term of *'iyyun* as well meaning the alternative interpretations possible in the text.

The ultimate seriousness of this philosophy can be shown by citing two contemporaneous texts. The first, by R. Yitzhak Aboab, claims

---

[18] Abraham Shalom, *The Translator's Preface to the De Interpretatione of Marseille*, A. Jelinek, ed. (Vienna, 1838), p. 7.

that God himself uses the method of sophisms to teach humans the truth, i.e., he explains by this principle the age-old question of why the Mishnah enunciates wrong opinions together with correct ones:

> All of them were given by the same shepherd (Eccl. 12) He wants to say that most often we understand a matter well only via its opposite, and we understand it from its opposite; and therefore, the Holy One, Blessed be He, wished to give us the differing opinions, so that when we arrived at the truth, we would understand it clearly.[19]

The necessity of dealing in falsehood, of setting up and knocking down fallacies, is a feature of the human condition. Only one to whom truth is vouchsafed by revelation can escape it. As another of Kanpanton's disciples, R. Yoseph Taitazak, expresses it beautifully:

> The influence of blessed God was so great upon Adam, that he knew the truth without struggle or effort, and everything was before him like a set table. As for primordial Adam, since the truth grew by itself, there was not need to weed out and cut down the false divisions, for they were cut down of themselves.[20]

We see clearly, once more, that a major principle of talmudic interpretation of Yitzhak Kanpanton is simply a basic epistemological principle of his age brilliantly applied to the discipline of talmudic hermeneutics.

4. *"Conception, Judgment and Ordering" in* Kelale Shmuel

In *Kelale Shmuel*, we find also elements that are not derived from Kanpanton but are a direct continuation of much the same cultural pattern. I believe that this document, despite its rather arcane subject matter, is a cultural monument of very great interest, which testifies to the continued fruitfulness of inter-religious intellectual exchange on the Iberian Peninsula in the very waning of Jewish life there, that is, just before the expulsions from both Spain and Portugal at the end of the fifteenth century. Since it was produced in Safed after the expulsions and was enormously influential in the following generations, it testifies as well to the effectivity of that Iberian cultural openness in the intellectual life of the Sefardic diaspora as well.

---

[19] *Meharrerei Nemerim* (Venice, 1509), p. 16 [erroneously paginated 19].

[20] Quoted in Simon Shalem, "The Hermeneutic Method of Rabbi Joseph Taitazak and His Circle," in *Sefunot* 11, p. 121.

Moreover, the Iberian rabbis and their Sefardic descendants were not only open to Arabic influences. Christian scholasticism also had major effects on the development of their philosophy of interpretation. One of the most strikingly specific instances of scholastic influence on Ibn Sid comes right at the very beginning of the work, where he defines *'iyyun* as being composed of three elements, called by him, *tziyyur, 'immut,* and *siddur,* conception, judgment, and ordering (1):

> Know that any *me'ayyen* of any subject which comes to mind must think and be exact in three categories. The first category is with regard to *conception.* The second category is with regard to *judgment.* The third category is with regard to *order.*
> As for the *conception,* it is known that words signify *intentions* which are in the soul. . . . Afterwards you must perform a second investigation into the language with regard to the *'immut,* which is the second category, and you will investigate and think, if the intention in the *tziyyur* of these words is true or false. . . . After you must perform a third investigation with respect to the third category, which is the *siddur* . . . and investigate with regard to order, whether the words are ordered in a true *siddur* [or not].

Now the first two of these terms are very well known from the Hebrew tradition of scholastic logic. They are, as shown by H.A. Wolfson, calques of the Arabic terms, *tatzawwar* and *tatzdiq,* which were also calqued into the Latin scholastic tradition as *conceptio* or *formatio* and *fides, verificatio* and others. Virtually all works of Hebrew logic in the middle ages begin with the statement that the subject of logic is divided into these two parts. To take but one example, thus begins the standard work, *Kol Melekhet Hahiggayyon* (Riva-di-Trento, 1559):

> All theses which one desires to know in all the mental disciplines are in two parts—the *tziyyuri* and the *immuti.* The *tziyyur* is the nature of the thing itself, or rather that which he thinks is its nature, and it is generally asked about with the question "what." . . . . The *'immut* is the proof or disproof of the proposition . . . and it is generally asked about with the question "if."

There is, therefore, no question that the source of Ibn Sid's *tziyyur* and *'immut* are to be found in the general Aristotelian tradition of the Middle Ages. The question is only, therefore, what is the origin of Ibn Sid's third division, *siddur,* "order," namely the investigation of the order of discourse. The answer, it seems, may be found in the Proem to Thomas's commentary on the *De Interpretatione* which opens:

> There is a twofold operation of the intellect, as the Philosopher says in *III De Anima*. One is the understanding of simple objects, that is, the operation by which the intellect apprehends just the essence of a thing alone; the other is the operation of composing and dividing. There is also a third operation, that of reasoning, by which reason proceeds from what is known to the investigation of things that are unknown.

It is clear from the form of this passage that Thomas regarded the third operation, ratiocination, as an innovation with respect to the pure Aristotelian tradition, and, in fact, as mentioned above, so it seems to be. There seems to be, therefore, a clear prima facia case for regarding the three-fold division of investigation or *'iyyun* in Ibn Sid as having been derived or influenced by the Thomistic tradition. However, this identification is not wholly unproblematic, for Thomas is speaking of the process of reasoning from the known to the unknown, while Ibn Sid speaks of the order of words in the sentence and the order of topics in a text as the subject of the third category. We must address ourselves to this difference an attempt to bridge it for our argument of influence to be acceptable. Moreover, through the process of bridging itself we will be able to more adequately define the nature and source of scholastic influence on *'iyyun*.

The first step is that Thomas, himself, in various places, adds to the above description of the third operation, the term *discurrere*, discourse, as in the following sentence from the introduction to his commentary on the *Posterior Analytics*:

> Tertius vero actus rationis est secundun id quod est proprium rationis, scilicet discurrere ab uno in aliud.
>
> The third act of the mind is according to what is suitable to the mind, that is discourse from one thing to another.

Now, while it is clear that Thomas is still speaking of the process of deduction, the issue of the *order of discourse* is more prominent here, already. We have evidence that Thomas was indeed understood thus. In the curriculum of the University of Alcala, we find the study of logic divided into three areas: Simple Awareness, Judgment, and Discourse. It seems, therefore, that in the wake of the Thomists this had become a commonplace of Iberian intellectual culture, and it is this commonplace that is reflected in Ibn Sid's division.

Finally, it may be remarked that Thomas's own definition of this "third operation of the intellect" was too restricted, because of his commitment to an exclusively deductive, Aristotelian discourse. Ibn Sid, who wishes to apply the three-fold division of *'iyyun* to a textual discipline would have found it necessary in any case to redefine the analysis of discourse, as being the study of the movement from one sentence to the next, whether they are the terms of a deductive argument or not. Nevertheless, it must be admitted that his definition of the third operation of *'iyyun* would have been more satisfactory had he included something like the necessary ordering of the refutations and resolutions of the Talmudic pericope, an omission all the more surprising since this type of *'iyyun* is very prominent in all the actual interpretive work of his school.

We are thus left with some question about the formulation of the definition of Ibn Sid's third division, but the fact of its scholastic origin is not, therefore, made less plausible. As a final support for this contention, I should like to adduce a further parallel between his text and Thomas's *De Interpretatione*:

Kelale Shmuel	Thomas
Be careful to precede your *'iyyun* of *tziyyur* first, and then the *immut* and after that the *siddur*, for the necessity of prior knowledge of [one of these] will force the priority of its *'iyyun*, and this is because knowledge of the intention of the language is necessary for knowledge of its judgment, and knowledge of its judgment is a prior necessity for knowledge of its ordering.	The first of these operations is ordered to the second, for there cannot be composition and division unless things have already been apprehended simply. The second, . . . in turn, is ordered to the third, for clearly we must proceed from some known truth to which the intellect assents in order to have certitude about something not yet known.

I believe that this comparison strengthens my argument in three ways. First of all is the coincidence of this placement of this statement of the necessary ordering at the very beginning of the two texts. Secondly, the very incoherence of Ibn Sid's arguments suggests that he is borrowing a topos. For, since his formulation of the operation of *siddur* is that one is studying the order of the topics considered in a text, it is not necessary that it follow upon proof of the truth or falsity of the judgments. In fact, in the actual commentaries of

Ibn Sid's predecessor (and father-in-law), R. Yitzhaq Aboab, this is the first subject treated. Ibn Sid, it seems, has therefore, modified the order of study, in order to conform formally to the topos of the ordering of the three operations of the intellect with respect to each other. Finally, and this is perhaps, most significant, Thomas, himself, is here discussing the order to justify Aristotle's ordering of three of his works one to the other:

> Since logic is called rational science it must direct its consideration to the things that belong to the three operations of reason we have mentioned. Accordingly, Aristotle treats those belonging to the first operation of the intellect, i.e., those conceived by simple understanding, in the book, *Praedicamentorum*; those belonging to the second operation, i.e., affirmative and negative enunciation in the book *Peri Hermeneias;* those belonging to the third operation in the book *Priorum*. . . . And since the three operations of reason are ordered to each other so are the books.

This forms, of course, a perfect parallel to Ibn Sid's requirement that we, "Say, for example, that he might have placed Chapter *Shenaim Ohazim* before Chapter *Elu Metsiot*," and then, of course, demonstrate why this is not so and the present order is proper and necessary. There is no question that Ibn Sid is referring to the same logical tradition which Thomas is using as well, and since this is an aspect of logical theory which does not belong to the common scholastic tradition of Moslems, Christians and Jews but to a particular Iberian Christian Scholasticism, it is equally clear that Ibn Sid and his teachers in Spain were conversant with the best of logical thought of their time and applied it in their theory and practice of talmudic interpretation. This should not, of course, be taken as evidence for a derivativeness in their tradition but rather for their desire to apply the best thought of their times to the study of Torah, both to understand the Torah better and to show that the Talmud is not inferior in its logic to any production of the Aristotelian tradition. We have here in the *'iyyun*, inspired in Spain and carried on in all of the Sefardic diaspora, what may be called without hesitation a truly scientific approach to the study of Written and Oral Torah.

5. *Towards a New Model of Jewish Cultural Poetics*

Most "Science of Judaism" research is carried out under a paradigm of the Jews as a separate cultural entity whose presence in other cultures is abnormal (from the point of view of Jewish existence).

Such interaction between Jewish and circumambient culture as I have documented here can then only be accounted for as influence from the surroundings. This paradigm is a carry-over, I would claim, from a Central and East European cultural situation and is even exaggerated from that perspective. A more appropriate model, certainly for the study of Jewish culture in Mediterranean societies, is that of the polysystem, studying the ways in which specifically Jewish cultural practices, such as Talmud study, interact with other signifying practices in which Jews and others are involved together.

The concept of the polysystem, a product of the "Tel-Aviv" school of poetics sees culture (and the products of culture) not as a closed signifying system but as the interaction at one and the same time of different signifying practices and systems that are all current within the culture.[21] This dynamic is what allows for cultural change and renewal, for the different systems within the culture interpenetrate and modify each other. An excellent example of this process from an area entirely different from what we are studying here would be the way that jazz developed in American culture out of the interaction between American and African musical traditions and ultimately fructified even the practice of "classical" music-making in America, such as in George Gershwin's work. This dynamic is not understood on polysystem theory as a special case but as the typical and ever-present process of cultural creation and development.

Coming closer to home, the examples of such Sefardic giants as the Naggid and Maimonides come quickly to mind. It would be extremely misleading were we to speak in their cases of Islamic or Spanish influences on their work. They are Spaniards contributing to and participating in Ibero-Arabian culture as fully and as importantly as any other figures in medieval Spanish history. At the same time, much of their cultural practice is specifically Jewish in content, whether halakhic, hermeneutic, theological, or poetic. In order for us to see the one part of their work as authentic and Spanish and the other part as Jewish work influenced by Spanish culture, we have to schizophrenize them, split them into two distinct personalities as it were. There is, of course, not the slightest shred of evidence for such split personalities in either the Naggid or the Rambam. Rather, the model of polysystems allows us to see that

---

[21] Itamar Even-Zohar, *Polysystem Studies*, a special issue of *Poetics Today* (1990).

different signifying systems that co-occur within culture interpenetrate each other in entirely expectable (and indeed to a certain extent predictable) ways.[22] This is true, whether the practitioners of the culture are its great figures, as in these two examples, or whether they are lesser or even quite insignificant figures. The continuation of this cultural pattern by the later Iberian Jews as well, and indeed its elaboration into areas of cultural practice that to the best of our knowledge had not been developed by earlier Spanish Jews, should be considered as a survival of the particular polysystemic structure that the Jews participated in in Spain. Moreover, there is no reason to see it as abnormal within Jewish history. All Jewish sub-cultures can be understood as sub-systems of the general cultures where the Jews lived. Of course, there will be a typology of such Jewish sub-cultures as more or less integrated with other sub-cultures, but in any case having just as much right to the name of culture as the others. This is true of any cultural polysystem; the sub-systems will be more or less interactive with each other. One of the most relevant factors in the typology will be the question of language-use. Obviously Jews using the culture-language current where they live will be more integrated in the polysystem than Jews who use Hebrew exclusively as a culture language. Be that as it may, it seems to me that the cultural pattern of Iberian Jewry and late-Iberian Jewry and even into the post-exilic period can fruitfully be adopted as a precursor for our own practice of cultural integration as Jews in Western culture, where our general and Jewish cultural practice interact in similar ways in the university or even in the modern yeshiva.

---

[22] Rina Drory and Itamar Even-Zohar, *Reshit Ha-Maga`Im Shel Ha-Sifrut Ha-Yehudit `Im Ha-Sifrut Ha-`Arvit Ba-Me'ah Ha-`a'Sirit* (Tel-Aviv, 1988).

Appendix
The Introduction to Kelale Shmuel

Said Shmuel Ibn Sidilio: It has entered my heart to make this collection, which contains no novellae for reading, but which I collected for myself, in order to relieve myself of the trouble of searching, and I took from the books, from here and from there, any utterance or principle, which my soul delights while learning it. For after extreme age has descended upon me, and, also, because of my sins, the light of my eyes has left me, I am not able to go and search for that which my heart desires. For this reason, I have collected here principles for the *gemara*, which are a *vade mecum* to the method of *'iyyun*.[23] [Some of] these principles are of the canons by which the Torah is interpreted, which were transmitted at Sinai, and [others are] from joining together places in the *gemara* and in the commentaries to the *gemara* and the rabbis. And in our time, a sage of the *Maghreb* arranged them into sections and chapters, and I have gathered them here to complete the composition and to ease the trouble of searching. Some I have learned from my teachers and some from my pupils, and for what I have collected and labored for this work, I have called on the name of God for help.

KELALE SHMUEL teaches that aside from Him, be He blessed, there is no reality at all.[24] May the reader not be amazed if he find some principle enunciated briefly without a reference to a place in the Talmud. And also may he not be amazed if it be enunciated in unbeautiful language, and also may he not be amazed that I have not extensively analyzed the *gemara* or the principles, for it was my intention to do so and revise it in every possible way, but my sins have interrupted me. They have smitten me and wounded me and made me to sit in darkness, and did not allow me to complete it, as was in my heart. Accordingly, I have become reconciled to the shortcomings, which are in what I have written, for they do not prevent understanding, for not by virtue of a principle being brief

---

[23] This Hebrew term is generally translated "speculation," that is, deductive reasoning. As the term "speculation" is misleading in its modern sense, I have left the term in Hebrew here.

[24] I.e., from studying the Talmud in accordance with the principles of the *'iyyun*, one comes to realize the greatness of God.

or in unbeautiful language will its understanding be confuted, for whether it is without a citation or in unbeautiful language its intention may be clear. And behold! One who opposes a blind man is in error, and after him a voice cries out and protests, whether he be young or a fool?.

INTRODUCTION. Great is the value of the methods of *'iyyun* in the *gemara* and it commentators. In order to increase the understanding, in this introduction I will place before the reader the way in which I would learn the first *Mishnah* of *Chapter Hazzahav*. If the *me'ayyen* [wishes] to enunciate that which is in his soul, it is appropriate that it should be by means of words which signify that which is in his soul, and that there should not be in them any superfluity or lack, in such manner that his *conception* should be enunciated well with words which signify his *intention*. In any other way it is impossible for his *intention* to be enunciated.

This may be either words which signify one *intention* or words which signify many *intentions*. An example of words which signify one *intention* is that in the *Mishnah* which is before us it says "Gold acquires silver," and the *intention* of these words is to make known that physically taking golden coins effects the acquisition of silver coins. To signify that intention, he enunciated "Gold acquires silver." In truth, however, these words do not signify the intention in his soul, for there is a difference between, "gold acquires silver" and "physically taking golden coins acquires silver coins," which is in his soul. Now, since there is a difference between them, we may object that the *tanna* was not exacting with his language, in accordance with that which we have postulated: that one who enunciates his intention must do so with words that signify the intention of his soul, but these words do not signify the intention of his soul.

And now for words which signify many intentions. It is as if you were to say that you wish to know what was the intention of the *tanna* in the Mishnah, and you will say, his intention is to enumerate those things which effect acquisition. And you will wish to make an investigation and thus say, if it is really the intention of the *tanna* to make known those things which effect acquisition, are there any things in the world which effect acquisition that he has not mentioned, or are there no things in the world which effect acquisition except for these which he has mentioned. You must investigate whether the words which he employed are complete, lacking nothing, or did he employ them in an [in]complete fashion, and they are lacking a *division*[25] or *divisions* besides those he has mentioned. And even if we will say that he employed them in complete fashion, and there is nothing lacking in them, it is appropriate to investigate if he added something. For example, if he articulated three subjects, and it would have been enough had he articulated one of them, and from it the others which he mentioned could have been deduced by us.

It has been made clear to you from what we have said that it is appropriate to examine closely every utterance [to establish] that it has no superfluity or lack but is perfect. One must examine closely, therefore, every utterance in regard to its *conception,* whether it contains superfluity or lack in two ways: whether in words or in subjects. "In words" [means] that there are superfluous words for enunciating the intention, or that they are lacking, i.e., that the enunciation does not contain the necessary words. "In subjects" [means] that there is a superfluous subject, i.e., that from the law of one subject, another of them could have been understood and it is not necessary to enunciate it; or that there is another subject which could not have been understood from the law of the subject enunciated, and it was necessary to enunciate it. So we find in the language an objection of *superfluity* and an objection of *lack*. We see that the objections which occur in the *conception* of the language/ or, in the text of the *conception*: *bilshon hatztziyur,* in general are two: either to object that he added what was not necessary or to object that he omitted what was necessary.

If you find the language perfect with regard to its *conception,* having no superfluity or lack, then you must perform a second investigation with regard to the language, with regard to *judgment,* which is the second category. And you must investigate saying, whether the *conception* of these words is true or untrue. And even if is true, it should not be so true that we do not need it to be made known, but that it is appropriate for it to be made known.

---

[25] This is a technical term of *'iyyun*. Subject matters were considered as genera divisible into their *infimae species* by the method of diaresis or division. Each one of the species discovered in this way was called a "division." Since the *tanna* must have performed such an operation in order to determine the sub-divisions of his discourse, the clauses of the Mishnah may also be termed "divisions." For further discussion of this crucial technical term, cf., Daniel Boyarin "Studies in the Talmudic Commentary of the Spanish Exiles, I; The Method of Diaresis," in *Sefunot,* New Series, vol. 2, pp. 165–184 (Hebrew).

And if its making known is necessary, then it is appropriate to investigate; perhaps you will find in it objections of *"why,"* which are in regard to the speaker of falsehood, and this objection includes *lying*[26] because the intelligence contradicts him or because there is a law in another place that is the opposite from a *Mishnah* or a *baraita* or a *memra*, or if he contradicts himself, whether because of what he said in another place or what he said in this place, in which case we can object: "It itself is contradictory."

From this species is the objection: "When he said it, why did he say it?," for, as we have said, he knows the *Mishnah*, and if he said a law which is the opposite of the *Mishnah*, the *gemara* is amazed at him; how come he said thus? Did he not know the *Mishnah* that contradicts him?! And likewise is the *objector* who asks an objection whose refutation is obvious and is known to him, the *gemara* is amazed at him; how come he objected thus? Did he not know the refutation which contradicts him? And it is as if he contradicts his [own] words. And similarly, one who refutes [an objection] in such a way that the objection [deriving from his very solution] is obvious and was certainly known to him, the *gemara* is amazed at him thus: "When he said it, why did he say it?" The principle which emerges is that the objection is on the *speaker of falsehood*, whether by virtue of that which is *in actuu* or *in potentia*, that is a *diyyuq*.

And even if it is true, perhaps you will raise an objection of *"obvious."* And this is in one of two cases; either it is obvious to the intelligence and it is not necessary to make it known, or he has already said it. And if it is because he already said it, it is in two cases; either he already said it in this statement itself or in another statement. And this [may be] whether he mentioned it *in actuu* or *in potentia*, namely via a *diyyuq*.

And if you have found the language perfect, having no objections of *"why,"* nor objections of *"obvious,"* afterwards you should perform a third investigation of the language, with regard to the third category, which is the *order*. Be careful to put your *'iyyun* of the *conception* first, and afterwards the *judgment* and afterwards the *order*, for the necessity of its preceding knowledge will make necessary its preceding *'iyyun*. This is because preceding knowledge of

---

[26] This is the technical term for speaking falsely in scholastic logic and philosophy without regard to the intention of the speaker.

the intention of the language is necessary for knowledge of the *judgment*, and preceding knowledge of the *judgment* for knowledge of the *order*.

And you shall investigate with respect to the *order* whether the words are ordered in a true *order*. And it is fitting that you should pay attention to this in respect to words which signify one *intention*: for example, one might say of "gold acquires silver," that these words are in order. And not in order would be if one would say "silver acquires gold." In respect to subjects, unordered would be if you were to say that he should have enunciated *Chapter Shenaim Ohazim* after *Chapter Elu Metsiot*. And similarly in a *Mishnah* in which there are two clauses, where the *tanna* should have placed the latter clause before the former clause.

The distinction that obtains between poor ordering with respect to words that are about one *intention* and poor ordering with respect to subjects is that when words that signify one *intention* are unordered it is possible for understanding to be confounded, and even if it is not confounded, it will only be known to us after much *'iyyun* and research of great effort, and therefore the words must be ordered in a true order to *guard the me'ayyen from error*.[27] If the poor order is with respect to subjects, however, it will not occasion that its understanding will be confounded, and what will follow from good order with respect to subjects is the broadening of the intelligence of the *me'ayyen*.

The upshot is that for every language which will be investigated, there are only six types of doubts.[28] And even though the objections[29] in the *Gemara* are of many species and all of them can be enumerated by

---

[27] This is an important technical term of medieval logic, specifically in this case of the Farabian-Maimonidean tradition. The former had defined the purpose of logic as teaching universals of language such that the philosopher would be "guarded from error" in his speech, and the latter, in his handbook of logical terminology, followed the great master. [Rambam, *Millot Hahiggayon*, I. Efros, ed., pp. 19–20] This term and concept became one of the great motivating forces in the development of both Sefardic and Ashkenazic *pilpul*.

[28] This is another important scholastic logical term. See, for instance, Judah ha-Levi, *Sefer Ha-Kuzari*, Yehuda Even-Shmuel (Tel-Aviv, 1972), p. 10, and compare *Darkhe hattalmud*, pp. 46–47. Ibn Sid uses it as a synonym (or near synonym) for *qushiot*, the usual Talmudic term. However, it may also have been specified in his usage for precisely those objections generated by the scholastic assumptions about language, as opposed to the normal sort of objections of Talmudic scholiasts.

[29] *Qushiot*, cf., previous note.

the *faculty of division*,³⁰ I have chosen the path of brevity, namely, that under each of these three genera,³¹ there are two [species]. As for the genus of *conception,* they are *superfluity* and *lack.* As for the genus of *judgment,* they are "*why*" and "*obvious.*" And as for the genus of *order,* they are poor order in the words or the subjects that occur in the paragraph of law, which therefore also produces two divisions.

With this you may obtain all of the *doubts* which there can possibly be in the halakhah,³² in this fashion:

> The *doubts* that fall are either by way of *question* or by way of *wonderment.*
>
> And if it is by way of *question,* that is, when the questioner wants to know that which is unknown to him, it is divided into two:
>
> Either the *law* of the subject is unknown to him, or the *reason* for the law is unknown.
>
> Now as for the *reason* for the law being unknown to him, this may not be divided, but if the *law* is unknown, this may be divided into two:
>
> Either the law is totally unknown to him, or he has before him laws which may be [decided] leniently or stringently, and he does not known whether the true law is lenient or stringent.
>
> Now if it is the true law which is unknown to him,³³ this is divided into two possibilities.
>
> Either the law's being lenient or stringent are equal [possibilities to the questioner], and whether the respondent responds with a leniency or a stringency, he will have no further question; or even when he answers, he will still have a question. For example: the questioner asked a question, "What is the true law, lenient or stringent?" If you will answer, "lenient," he will have no further question,³⁴ but if you will answer, "stringent," he will have another question. The first type of question is when the *Talmud* asks one question, and the second type is when the *Talmud* asks many questions, according to the method of

---

³⁰ Ibn Sid's use of the scholastic method of dichotomous division is extensive. Along with many of his generation, he believed that division in its various applications was the royal road to certainty of knowledge. For full discussion of this method and its application in Sefardic (and to a lesser extent Ashkenzic) pilpul, see my "Studies in the Talmudic Commentary of the Spanish Exiles."

³¹ I.e., conception, judgment, and order.

³² In this context, he means the legal portions of the Talmud.

³³ That is the latter of the two possibilities.

³⁴ That is, not in general, but in a specific, hypothetical case, where the questioner has some reason to believe that the lenient option is the correct one (but not definitive, for if it were definitive, he would not have asked). It could just as easily be the opposite, i.e., that the stringent answer would leave him no question.

"If you will be able to say,"[35] as I will write in the second chapter on questions.

And if the *doubt* is by way of *wonderment*, this is an inclusive [category]. {Behold, I have learned this method in the method of *'iyyun*, when I was studying the *Mishnah*.}[36]

The way we can enumerate the objections by means of division is the following:

(One must know, that in any subject which lies before him, obtaining all the interpretations which are possible in it is only possible via the *faculty of division*. And when you begin the division, do not make more than two divisions, and then divide the two divisions each into two more, if they both are divisible. If you begin with three divisions, e.g., if you will say, "It could be this or this or this," it will be impossible for you to obtain all the interpretations which could be in the subject you are investigating.)

And this is the method of *division* of the *doubts*:

The *wonderment* includes all types of objections, for in every type of objection, the *objector* wonders and objects.[37]

Now we will divide the *wonderment* first into two:

Either he wonders at the speaker that he speaks a *lie*, or not.

If he wonders that he speaks a *lie*, this may be divided into two:

Either he wonders at the speaker of a *lie* because the intelligence contradicts him or because there is a *Mishnah* or a *baraita* or a *memra*[38] which contradicts.

If it is a contradiction,[39] this may be divided into two:

Either he objects from that which is *actual* or from that which is *potential* (that is, from a *diyyuq*).

And if he does not wonder because he is speaking a *lie*, this may also be divided into two:

Either he wonders that he has contradicted himself (that is, the objection of "It itself is difficult"[40]), or not.

If he wonders that he has contradicted himself, this may be divided into two:

---

[35] This is a technical term of talmudic dialectic, by which a complex series of branching questions are set up. This technique may, itself, be related genetically or typologically to diaresis, however the question requires a separate study.

[36] This sentence is erroneous here and reappears later in its proper place.

[37] His point seems to be that "wonderment" is an appropriate name for the category that includes all types of objections, because this is the psychological state of the "objector." "Objector" here is, itself, a technical term for one of the two actors in the dialectic, namely the one who is attempting to refute the thesis of the "refuter."

[38] These are terms for authoritative statements from either the Mishnah and related literature or from rabbis of the Talmudic period.

[39] I.e., the latter case of contradiction from a text.

[40] A standard talmudic dialectical term for a text which contains a contradiction.

Either he contradicts himself in one utterance, e.g., the end of his words contradicts their beginning, or he contradicts himself from what he said in another place.

If he contradicts himself may be divided into two:

Either he contradicts himself from that which is *actual* or from that which is *potential*.

If he contradicts himself from that which is *potential*, may be divided into two:

Either the *diyyuq* of the beginning contradicts the *diyyuq* of the end or not.

If not[41] is divided into two:

Either the *diyyuq* of the beginning contradicts that which is actual in the end, or the *diyyuq* of the end contradicts that which is actual in the beginning.

If he does not raise an objection that he [contradicts] himself is divided into two:

Either he objects to the *objector* and the *answerer* that the refutation of him [i.e., the refutation of his objection or his answer to an objection] is obvious, and why did the *objector* raise an objection whose answer is obvious and why did the *answerer* refute with a refutation whose objection is obvious? (and this is the objection of "When he said it, why did he say it?"[42]) or he does not object in this manner.

If he does not object in this manner is divided into two:

Either he raises an objection against the choice, e.g. there is a *Mishnah* which contains a dispute of *tannaim* and of two *amoraim*, one decided like the first *tanna*, and one decided like the second *tanna*, and he wonders why did one choose the first *tanna* and one the second *tanna*, or he does not object in this fashion.

And if his does not object in this fashion is divided into two:

Either he wonders at a *lack*, namely the *enunciator* did not *enunciate* something that is necessary to say, or he objects to that which he did *enunciate*.

If he wonders at a *lack* is divided into two:

He wonders that there is lacking a word or words which it is necessary to say in that subject, or that a subject is lacking, and this is in a case where he did enunciate subjects and left out one that he should have said.[43]

Behold, I taught this method in the method of *'iyyun* when I studied the *Mishnah Hazzahav*, in order to increase the disciples' understanding

---

[41] I.e., if it is not the case that the *diyyuq* of the beginning contradicts the one of the end.

[42] The standard talmudic term for this type of objection.

[43] That is, where the structure of the text indicates that the author wishes to be comprehensive.

of the method of *'iyyun*,⁴⁴ and in order that this method shall be absorbed in the intelligence of the *scholar*, I have taken the trouble to write the objections which fall in *Mishnah Hazzahav*.

And thus which would be this method for any *Mishnah* or *baraita* or *memra*,⁴⁵ to strive in *'iyyun* by means of these objections.⁴⁶ For, in my opinion *verification of the intelligible* is impossible other than by means of objections, for by their means may the truth be apprehended.⁴⁷ Therefore, the *scholar* must seek every possible objection in order to arrive at truth.

In pursuing the objections which occur with regard to the *conception*, as we have prefaced, in the case of words which signify one *intention*,⁴⁸ we have, for example in the Mishnah, "Gold acquires silver," but the *intention* is to say that pulling golden dinars acquires silver dinars,⁴⁹ but this *intention* is not *enunciated* in the words of the Mishnah.

This objection must be before you with regard to any interpreter of a *Mishnah* or a *memra*, or any other text, namely that if the *intention* is as the interpreter has said of the language, why did the [author] not *conceive*⁵⁰ in his language those words which would *signify* his

---

⁴⁴ This may also be translated as "to increase the disciples' understanding [of the Mishnah] by means of the method of *'iyyun*."

⁴⁵ These are technical names for different types of utterances quoted in the Talmud.

⁴⁶ That is, the objections he has detailed above under his rubrics of conception, order, and judgment.

⁴⁷ This statement of Ibn Sid's reflects a basic scholastic epistemological position discussed above that truth may only be achieved through dialectic.

⁴⁸ He is not speaking here of univocity, as we shall see below, but contrasting simple propositions with texts that contain many propositions, the difference being that in this case, what we may ask is whether there are additional or lacking words to communicate the proposition, whereas in the latter case, we may ask whether or not entire categories or subjects are superfluous or lacking, as he will show below.

⁴⁹ According to talmudic law, a sale is executed not when the money changes hands but when the goods change hands. In a sale of gold for silver, therefore, it is important to establish which is the money and which the goods, to determine whether a sale has taken place. When the Mishnah states that "gold acquires silver," it means to say that in an exchange of golden coins for silver ones, the gold is considered goods and the silver currency, and accordingly, taking possession of the golden coins effects the acquisition of the silver one. "Pulling" is the technical term for taking physical possession.

⁵⁰ It would be more idiomatic in English to say "express." However, the verb used is the root which forms the noun for *conception*, as used by Ibn Sid as well, an I wish to capture this in my translation, because it is this polysemy which has encouraged him to formulate his material as he has.

intention, and it is extremely forced to assume that he should have not *enunciated* words which *signify that intention*.⁵¹

Incline your ears to hear a principle in this matter, namely that it is important that you investigate whether the words which the commentator has written with regard to a certain utterance contradict the words that are written in that utterance or do not contradict. If they do contradict, then the objection is strengthened, for the *intention* is the opposite of what he interpreted. But if they do not contradict, then there is room for the commentator to interpret as he did.

In the Mishnah, in which it says, "gold," and the interpreter⁵² wrote "golden dinars," "golden dinars," are not words that contradict the word "gold," for the word, "gold" includes both the minted and the unminted, and when he interprets that the intention of the Mishnah is the minted, he does not contradict the word "gold." But if you will say, in the final analysis, he [the author of the Mishnah] ought to have said, "golden dinars," and not "gold" alone, one may answer if it were impossible to interpret the word, "gold" as referring to minted gold, then your objection would be indeed an objection, for he should have said "golden dinars." But since the force of his words is that one must interpret that he is referring to the minted, one may not object that he ought to have said "golden dinars." I will say to you, moreover, that it is the way of the *tanna* to be brief, and therefore he said, "gold," and did not say "golden dinars," and when something is self understood, brevity is appropriate.

Now, if you will object that if it is *necessary*⁵³ to interpret that which he said, "gold" as referring to minted, then why was the

---

⁵¹ This constitutes, then, an objection against the interpreter. In our case, as we shall see immediately below, it is the commentator, Rashi, who supplied the information that "gold acquires silver," means that "pulling golden dinars acquires silver dinars," and the question is, if that is what the author meant, why did he not say so?

⁵² That is, Rashi, the classic commentator on the Talmud, who may be called, accordingly, "the interpreter."

⁵³ This term refers in the authors of our school to logical necessity. An interpretation which was the only possible one for a given utterance, or which had been proven to be the only possible one in the context was called "necessary," just as the conclusion of a correct syllogism is necessary. Accordingly, in my translation, I will use the word "necessary" only when Ibn Sid uses the Hebrew technical term for logical necessity, and otherwise I will use required or the like. Thus in this passage, the interpreter was not required to write anything because the interpretation of the language is *necessary*.

interpreter obligated to write something that is self-understood? And you may raise this objection in regard to any utterance for which it appears that they words of the interpreter are not required, since the language is self-explanatory (i.e., that it refers to that *intention*). Now you will known and apprehend the answer to this objection, that the situation of the interpreter who comes to interpret is like the situation of one who has sharp vision as opposed to one whose vision is dull, and both of them are looking at a form inscribed.[54] For example, you could say, that the inscriber inscribed a horse on the wall, by means of lines. He did not bring material and stick it to the wall, thus forming it into the shape of a horse, but he brought a tool and with it made lines, and those lines signify a horse, even though he has not put any material inside of the lines, but left the wall as it was. Even so, it is recognizable that it is a horse, but the lines are very fine and unrecognizable to one who has dull sight, and therefore he said there is no form of a horse there. One who has sharp sight perceived that there is there the form of a horse, and in order that the dull-sighted one should perceive that there is there the form of a horse, brought a tool and broadened the lines. And then the dull-sighted one recognized what he had not before when the lines were fine. Similarly, it will happen with one whose intelligence is sharp and one whose intelligence is dull, for the one whose intelligence is dull does not perceive the *intention* of the *enunciated*[55] language, and because of the smallness of his intelligence, he errs in understanding it. The one who is sharp of intelligence interprets it in language that the dull-witted one can understand its *intention*.

In this case, when he has said "gold," one whose intelligence is dull does not understand that it is about golden dinars that he is speaking, but since it says "gold," he thinks that it is unminted gold. From this cause, there will result such a great confusion in his understanding that he will object that the Mishnah contradicts itself from its beginning to its end, for in the beginning it says that, "Gold acquires silver and silver does not acquire gold," but in the

---

[54] The word "inscribed" or "engraved" used here is precisely the same word that Ibn Sid has been using for enunciation. The polysemy of the Hebrew word has certainly contributed to the making of this simile.

[55] I.e., inscribed. Cf., previous note.

end it says "all chattels acquire one another," implying that also silver acquires gold.[56] Accordingly, the sharp-minded one[57] enlightened him that the beginning is referring to minted gold, and there is, therefore, no contradiction between the beginning and the end, and the *Talmud* is full of examples such as this.

As for that which Rashi has written, "*pulling* golden dinars,"[58] the word, "pulling" is *necessary*, for if you will say that there is here no "pulling," how can there be acquisition, since the methods of acquisition are by money, document, or taking possession, as is explained in a few places, and without these there is no acquisition, and the method of acquisition of chattels is by "pulling." Therefore that which he has taught, "gold acquires," is by the method of "pulling," for that acquisition which is by money, document, or taking possession is only for real estate.[59] Now indeed, it should be clear to you when the words *signify one intention*.[60]

Now, if the words *signify many intentions*,[61] that is to say, that the *tanna*[62] wished to make known to us all of the *subjects* in which acquisition is possible, it will be clear after only a little examination, that in this Mishnah there are: gold, silver, copper, invalid and valid coins, tokens and chattels, and it is clear, therefore, that he wished to make us know the methods of acquisition for many subjects.[63] Since this has been established, an investigation becomes relevant,

---

[56] For unminted metal is a chattel like any other.

[57] Rashi.

[58] Having explained why Rashi interpreted that "gold" means "golden dinars," here, Ibn Sid wishes now to explain why it was necessary for Rashi to add the word "pulling," i.e., what ambiguity there is in the formulation as it is in the Mishnah, which would conceivably lead the dull-minded into error.

[59] Ibn Sid's phrasing here is awkward, and he would undoubtedly have corrected it had he revised his work. Nevertheless, his point is clear, namely that we must be talking about "pulling," that is, transferring the goods into the possession of the new owner, since that is the only method of acquisition which is effective with regard to chattels.

[60] That is, it should be clear to you how to proceed in questioning and answering the adequacy of the language to the *conception*, when dealing with a single proposition.

[61] That is, that we have a complex utterance with several propositions, and now the task is to examine the *superfluity* or *lack* of propositions within the category detailed by the author.

[62] Author of the Mishnah.

[63] That is, since the author of the *Mishnah* has included a variety of categories in his utterance, we may reason that the purpose of the utterance is to make known the methods of acquisition in a general way.

i.e., if there are in the world other subjects[64] aside from those he has mentioned. And if there are other subjects aside from them, namely real estate, an objection with regard to the *conception* of *lack* occurs, for the *tanna* did not *conceive* in the words which are required for all of the subjects in which there is acquisition. But perhaps there is no subject aside from the ones he has mentioned, because the *intention* of the *tanna* was not to speak of the acquisition of real estate but only of chattels, which he *divided* into two categories:

> minted chattels and unminted chattels, and he began with minted chattels and said, "gold acquires," and he ended with unminted chattels and said, "all of the chattels."
>
> Since the minted belongs to three metals, gold and silver and copper, and in these metals it can be that the coin is perfect[65] or imperfect, therefore he began with perfect coin and said, "gold etc.,"[66] and ended with the imperfect, and said "invalid coins and tokens."
>
> And it was appropriate to begin with the perfect, for most purchases are with it. And even with the imperfect, he began with the more perfect of it, which is the invalid coins and ended with the least perfect, the token. From this you should learn that in any place where there are many subjects, one should begin with the more perfect of them, for that is the *virtue of speech*.

Now, even if you say that we do not have any subjects other than the ones he has mentioned, there still may be raised the objection of *conception*, that is *lack*, for acquisition by gold is in five situations; gold of silver, of copper, of invalid coins, of tokens, and of chattels. And similarly acquisition by silver[67] is possible in five situations; silver of gold, of copper, of invalid coins, of tokens and of chattels. And similarly the copper has five situations; copper of gold, of silver, of invalid coins, of tokens and of chattels. And likewise the invalid coins have five situations, and likewise the token has five ways, and likewise the chattel. In sum, then, for these six subjects there are thirty possible situations, and the *tanna* did not choose but only five situations alone, and left out twenty-five situations. And accordingly, the objection of *lack* is raised, with regard to his

---

[64] Belonging to this category, of course.
[65] That is, current legal tender.
[66] Meaning golden coins of legal tender.
[67] It is quite unclear to me why Ibn Sid feels it necessary to repeat all of the categories each time.

teaching that "copper acquires silver," and not teaching the law of its acquisition with regard to gold.[68]

And you may also raise an objection of *superfluity*, which is also with regard to the *conception*, i.e., whether there is an unnecessary subject or not,[69] or if there is an unnecessary word. And in any matter that will come before you, if there is an unnecessary subject or an unnecessary *division* of a subject or an unnecessary law[70] or an unnecessary word. And this may be in two ways: either it has been added *in actuu* or it has been added because of a *diyyuq*.[71] And also in the case of *lack*, it may be that there is lacking a subject, or a *division* of a subject, or the law of the subject is missing, as in the example we have mentioned.[72] Or there may be *lacking* a word in the subject.

Similarly, with regard to the *judgment*, you must examine carefully whether he his speaking *lies* by virtue of the intelligence,[73] or by virtue of that which he has said, either in the same place or in another place, and whether the contradiction is by virtue of that which is *in actuu* or that which is *in potentia*, and in this order you should also raise the objection of obviousness.[74]

Similarly with regard to the *order*, you must examine carefully whether the clauses are ordered appropriately and the words.

Behold, this is what it is appropriate to examine carefully whether these deficiencies or some of them appear in the Mishnah, and I did not speak at length with regard to this *Mishnah*, since I only put it before you in order to make known to you the methods of

---

[68] And this is, indeed, a valid objection, for we do not know whether gold was more current legal tender than copper or not, but Ibn Sid does not answer it here, for he is only interested in exemplifying the method and not solving all of the problems of this particular text.

[69] That is, a subject which is already included or implied by another one mentioned.

[70] That is, the subject is necessary, but once having mentioned the law for part of it, the law for another part is implied and, therefore, unnecessary, but he mentions it anyway.

[71] Linguistic implication. See discussion above in body of paper.

[72] That is, the *subject* is mentioned, i.e., we know that there is gold, silver, copper, etc. What is not mentioned is the *law* for part of the subject.

[73] I.e., whether it is common sense that contradicts what he is saying.

[74] That is, that it is obvious by virtue of the intelligence, or by virtue of that which is said here or somewhere else and *in actuu* or *in potentia*.

'iyyun. What I have said is a guide to you for any subject which comes before you to use the *dialectical method*[75] in every way possible. And in every legal passage[76] be careful to search for the objections which may be raised whether with regard to the *conception*, the *judgment*, and the *order*, and let all this be routine in your mouth, for in any legal passage you will require it.

---

[75] Hebrew *pilpul*.
[76] Halakhah, as opposed, apparently, to narrative passages, aggadah.

DON QUIXOTE—TALMUDIST AND *MUCHO MÁS**

José Faur
Netanya College

To the memory of Professor José Mair Benadrete:
Mentor and Friend

For in the beginning of literature there is myth,
as there is also in the end of it.
Jorge Luis Borges, *Parable of Cervantes and the Quixote.*

I

Jews from Moslem Spain played a major role in the transmission of certain literary genres and motifs to Provence.[1] In Christian Spain, Jews loathed Latin. It was the language of the Church—or "la idolatría" as it was known among Jews and *conversos*. It had the odor of death and brought memories of killing and maiming and rape and pillaging and tearing of limbs and plucking of eyes: all done for the love of God.[2] They would rather write in the vernacular. Anyhow, Latin was used for serious stuff, such as theology and philosophy, and thinkers with Jewish blood better tread carefully upon entering holy territory. What happened to Juan Luis Víves (1491–1540) and Fray Luis de León (1527–1591) and countless other thinkers was a warning to all New Christians. This is why *conversos* expressed their unique situation through literature—an area of little importance in the eyes of the Church. Nonetheless, caution was of the essence. Accordingly, camouflaged within the text were configurations of thought and emotion that could only be decoded by a chosen few. Hence the two dimensions of what eventually will be know as "modern literature"—the earmark of Western culture. It must be

---

* Reprinted from *Review of Rabbinic Judaism* 4:1, 2001, pp. 139–157.
[1] See Ramón Menéndez Pidal, *España, Eslabón entre la Cristianidad y el Islam* (Madrid, 1956).
[2] I remember as a child my parents' debating whether to bring a tutor to help me in Latin, the language of *tum'a*, that is, impurity.

written in the vernacular and must contain a message decipherable only by a privileged public. In this precise sense, to be meaningful, literature—like Rabbinic hermeneutics—must be subversive; not by wrecking the normative, but by using it to point out at something beyond the ordinary.[3] (See below, II.)

This could help us understand a phenomenon never explored before Américo Castro (1885–1972). Christian Spain had no Middle Ages.[4] If one were to compare the Latin chronicles produced in Spain from 1000 to 1250 to what was produced in England, France, or Germany, one would discover how meager and insubstantial they really are. Professor Lomax, who studied these chronicles, wrote:

> One looks in vain for any Spanish chronicler to write about his reigning monarch one-tenth as critically as Matthew Paris writes about Henry III, and the contrast is even stronger when one compares the quantity of attention paid to the decade of, for example the 1230s: 1,900 words in Jiménez de Rada, as against 120,000 in Matthew Paris.[5]

These chronicles are notoriously dull, lacking depth and nuance. On the same subject he pointedly added:

> In short, Hispano-Latin chronicles of this period are comparatively dull and lifeless, and even when dealing with the most exciting moments in the Reconquest are capable of hiding the sharp details of real life behind a veil of rhetoric. One of the first lessons learnt by any researcher into the subject is that any Latin chronicler which describes physical appearance, natural scenery or other realistic details can be crossed off, almost automatically, as a Golden-Age forgery.[6]

Spain is the only country in Western Europe that had no Renaissance. It did not participate even in such basic debates as the relation of reason to religion.[7] How then are we to explain the Golden Age of Spanish literature, beginning around the second half of the fourteenth

---

[3] See my *Homo Mysticus: A Guide for Maimonides's Guide for the Perplexed* (Syracuse, 1999), p. 1. On the subversive character of the *derasha*, see my study, "Retórica y Hermenéutica: Vico y la Tradición Rabínica," in E. Hidalgo-Serna, et al, eds., *Pensar para el Nuevo Siglo* (Napoli, 2001, vol. 3).

[4] See Américo Castro, "Castilla sin Edad Media," in *Historia y Crítica de la literatura Española* (Barcelona, 1980), vol. 1, pp. 23–26.

[5] See Derek W. Lomax, "Medieval Spain: Some Evidence on Oath," in *Hispanic Studies in Honour of Geoffrey Ribbans* (Liverpool, 1992), p. 25.

[6] Ibid.

[7] See my *In the Shadow of History: Jews and Conversos at the Dawn of Modernity* (Albany, 1992), p. 49.

century and stretching all the way to the second half of the seventeenth century? The answer to this puzzle—rarely asked by the specialists—lies in the influx of *conversos* resulting from the destruction of the most important *Juderías*, from Gerona and Barcelona in the north to Seville and Córdoba in the south.[8] Trapped by circumstances beyond their control, these New Christians used literature to express their thoughts and emotions. What they contributed became one of the pillars of modern culture. Addressing their literary accomplishment, a distinguished American hispanist penned these golden words:

> . . . what they contributed to the world was nothing less than the possibility of the major literary genre of modern times: the novel. Cervantes and the men that provided him with this tradition—Mateo Alemán, Alonoso Nuñez de Reinoso (Spain's first reviver of the Byzantine novel), Jorge de Montemayor (creator of the first pastoral novel in Castillian), the anonymous author of *Lazarillo de Tormes,* Fernando de Rojas, the "sentimentalist novelist" Diego de San Pedro, and earliest of all, Alonso Martínez de Toledo, who in the *Corbacho* first brought speech into the Castilian prose—were all, although certain scholars fight rearguard battles in individual cases, *conversos*.[9]

II

There are two forerunners to this literature. The first is *El Libro del Buen Amor* written by Juan Ruiz in the first half of the fourteenth century. There is no documentary evidence that he came from a Jewish background. However, Rosa Lida had shown that the model for *El Libro del Buen Amor* are the Hebrew *maqamot* produced in Catalonia in the twelfth and thirteenth centuries.[10] A controlling theme recurring throughout the book is the contrast between the obvious and the real: appearances may be deceiving.[11] When about to strike its victim, the lion raises its paw as if to bless the table. Some nuns and friars are lewd and sensual. In one case, the meeting opens

---

[8] Ibid., pp. 23, 29–32.
[9] Stephan Gilman, *The Spain of Fernando de Rojas* (Princeton, 1986), p. 154.
[10] See María Rosa Lida de Malkiel, *Dos Obras Maestras Españolas* (Buenos Aires, 1983), pp. 37–52. Cf., Sanford Shepard, *Shem Tov: His World and His Words* (Miami, 1978), pp. 24–25.
[11] This was particularly important in *converso* literature to show how ephemeral Spanish "reality" is; cf. *In the Shadow of History*, pp. 61–63.

with one of the lovers declaring: "In the name of God I went to mass this morning." Conversely, occasionally a white rose lies under a black veil and garment, and behind the label "infidel" a genuine bride of the Lord.[12] The second work is that of Rabbi Santob de Carrion, known in Hebrew as Rabbi Shem Tob ben Isaac Ardutiel (ca. 1290–1369). He was an excellent Hebrew poet and liturgist—a long *viddui* (confession) of his forms part of the Yom Kippur afternoon services in the Sephardic Synagogue. He is the author of an outstanding book in Spanish, *Proverbios morales*, known also as *Consejos y documentos al rey don Pedro* (ca. 1355–1360).[13]

An important motif of this work, first introduced by the apostate Pedro Alonso (twelfth century), is that of the "rose and the thorn," namely, that the rose is not reviled because it was born of a thorn.[14] In Rabbi Shem Tob it has a two-fold meaning. First, one should not judge a thing on the basis of appearances alone, more or less like the Rabbinic dictum "don't [just] look at the flask but on what it contains" (M. Ab. 14:26). Thus, an object is to be apprehended in its *totality* rather than each constitutive element separately. Second, excellence, as represented by the rose, *must* originate in a *thorn*. Worth is the effect of a metamorphosis whereby the despised, in our case the Jew, transforms himself into an individual of quality.[15] (The opposite of what the persecuting society does to the individual in Kafka's *Metamorphosis*).

In a profound sense the literary strategy of the *converso* is the opposite of what Rabbinic literature designates *minut*—a term generally

---

[12] See T.A. Perry, "La rosa y el judio: Santob de Carrion y sus críticos," in *Studies in Honor of Gustavo Correa* (Potomac, 1986), p. 155.

[13] For a highly intelligent overview of his life and works, see Sanford Shepard, *Shem Tov: His World and His Words* (Miami, 1978). T.A. Perry, *The Moral Proverbs of Santob de Carrión* (Princeton, 1987), has rendered a fine English translation of these proverbs, accompanied by a highly informative study and critical appraisal of the principal ideas of this work.

[14] Pedro Alfonso, *Disciplina Clericalis*, ed. and tran., Angel Gonzáles Palencia (Madrid, 1948), p. 107, cited in "La rosa y el judio," p. 152. An Arabic proverb introduced by Jews in the Middle East *min al-shawke ward*, "from a thorn (blossoms) a rose"—in the sense that from bad parents occasionally a good person may rise—captures the precise intention of Pedro Alfonso. As a believing Christian, he was now apologizing for his ignoble (i.e., Jewish) background; cf., below, n. 28. Rabbi Shem Tob used it in a different sense.

[15] For a critical, in-depth study of this subject, see "La rosa y el judio," pp. 150–160. The source of this idea is Rabbinic, as taught by the celebrated Rabbi Joshua (first century) to the princess. See B. Ta. 7a-b; cf., *Sifre*, ed. Louis Finkelstein (New York, 1969), #48, p. 111. Excellence is a function of overcoming. Put differently: without a clay flask wine is impossible.

translated "heresy." Maimonides defined the *content* of *minut*.[16] The rabbis, with Christianity in mind, defined the *methodology* peculiar to *minut*. The law stipulates that a Scroll of the Torah written by *minim*— probably Judeo-Christians—ought to be incinerated together with the names of God it contains (because even the Tetragrammaton, representing the holy of holiest, is contaminated with their idolatrous schemes). Addressing this law, they cited the verse: "and behind the entrance at the door-post (*mezuza*) you (i.e., the *minim*) have placed your remembrance" (i e., your idolatrous schemes) (Is. 57:8). Meaning: they are using the *mezuza*—a sacred Jewish object—to package inside it their idolatrous doctrines![17] To put this less ponderously: appearances may be deceiving! The manifest reliance of the *minim* on the Torah and their use of Jewish values are a ploy intended to deceive and corrupt the dull-witted.[18] Through a peculiar type of "hermeneutics," a metamorphosis takes place whereby the original model is not only "dead" but also "deadly." It is clear why the rabbis associated *minut* with (morbid) sexual violation.[19] The *minim* beguile. At best they expose a single aspect of their doctrines, blocking thereby the victim's judgment, thus, driving him or her to do things he or she will lament for the rest of his or her life.[20] A point in case is the lot of the *conversos* who, upon becoming a member of *Corpus Christi*, discovered the reality of Christian love,[21] exquisitely executed through

---

[16] See *Mishne Tora, Teshuba* III, 7.

[17] B. Shab. 116a.

[18] These are the "faulty exegeses" of the Christians, the *derashot shel-dofi* censored by the rabbis. I have touched upon this subject in several articles, "The Limits of Readerly Collusion in Rabbinic Tradition," in *Soundings* 76 (1993), pp. 156–160; "Law and Hermeneutics," in *Cardozo Law Review* 14 (1993), pp. 1676–1677; and "Monolingualism and Judaism," ibid., pp. 1739–1740.

[19] See *Homo Mysticus*, pp. 37–38, and the corresponding note on p. 203.

[20] This type of sex has neither the "dynamic call" discussed by D.H. Lawrence nor the "erotic" excitement involved in the "unveiling of the truth" of Roland Barthes, as the reader embraces the possibilities of the unknown. See my *Golden Doves with Silver Dots: Semiotics and Textuality in Rabbinic Tradition* (Bloomington, 1986), p. 115. Rather, it pertains to the morbid sex poignantly described in D.M. Thomas, *The White Hotel* (New York, 1981). The purpose of this type of "sex" is to agonize the victim, like the *Conquistador* raping Native American wives while having the husband tied under the bed. See my article, "Jews, *Conversos* and Native Americans: The Iberian Experience," in *Annual of Rabbinic Judaism* III (2000), p. 106. On the pathological aspects of the *min* mentality, see my "De-authorization of the Law: Paul and the Odedipal Model," in *Journal of Psychiatry and the Humanities* 11 (1989), pp. 222–243.

[21] See *In the Shadow of History*, pp. 28–29, 32–49. Christianity rejected the Torah because it is the Law. Yet it bases its entire spiritual apparatus, including that

the edicts of *pureza de sangre* and *Autos de Fé*.²² As a consequence, they soon realized, in the words of Américo Castro, that they "had fallen from the pinnacle of well-being and prestige, to the depth of bodily and moral misery."²³

By contrast, the model for the *converso* literature is King Solomon's "Golden apples in a silver mesh, this is a word spoken on its two circles" (Prov. 25:11). This is not the "metaphor" where significance is *transferred* from "its real place to its intimate place."²⁴ Rather, it involves the passage from a level of consciousness available to the general public (silver), to another level only accessible to a privileged public. There are two dimensions to this type of metaphor. First, both faces must be valuable; the inner one, however, must be *more* valuable than the outer face. Second, a principal function of the outer face is to point to the privileged public the course leading to the inner face.²⁵ The aim of *converso* literature is to expose to the privileged public the "real" in contrast to the "evident" Spain. No one has accomplished this better than Cervantes in *Don Quijote*.²⁶

---

of eternal Salvation effected by the incorporation of the individual into *Corpus Christi*—not on another heavenly voice from Sinai—but on a quite prosaic legal concept: Roman law *corporatio*. As a matter of fact and doctrine, Christian love is predicated on, and thus it is conditioned to, the legal structure of Roman *corporatio*. On this fundamental Christian concept and its relation to Roman law *corporatio*, see ibid., pp. 32–36.

²² See *In the Shadow of History*, pp. 34–35, 45–46, and especially pp. 53–57. On the parallel of these laws to the infamous Nuremberg legislation, see the bibliography indicated, ibid., p. 232, n. 12, and pp. 233–234, n. 41.

²³ Américo Castro, *Hacia Cervantes* (Madrid, 1967), p. 139. A similar lot was that of European Jewry who seduced by the promises of "emancipation," entrusted its wellbeing to "the kindness of the State and civil population." See my "Correlation: The Iberian and German Experiences," in *Midstream*, June-July, 1992, pp. 20–22.

²⁴ For a brilliant, critical and sustained discussion of the metaphor in western philosophical discourse, see José M. Sevilla Fernández, "El filósofo es un *decidor*," in José M. Sevilla Fernández and Manuel Barrios Casares, eds., *Metáfora y discurso filosófico* (Madrid, 2000), pp. 109–166. On this point in particular, see ibid., pp. 130–133. On transference of meaning in Maimonides's *Guide*, see *Homo Mysticus*, pp. 58–61.

²⁵ Maimonides, *Guide*, Arab. ed. Munk-Joel, *Dalalat*, Introduction, p. 7. For the exact translation of this verse in Proverbs and an analysis of Maimonides's interpretation, see *Golden Doves*, pp. 114–115. Because Leo Strauss, Shlomo Pines, et al., conceived of the metaphor in terms of *min* literary tradition, they failed to apprehend Maimonides' "Golden Doves," thus confusing spiritual nihilism with Jewish esoterics.

²⁶ See José Ortega y Gasset, *Meditaciones del Quijote* (Madrid, 1956), especially pp. 120–121.

III

Much has been said about the possible *converso* ideology of Cervantes.[27] For some, including the writer of these lines, the reason his application for a post in the Americas was rejected (1590) was his "tainted" lineage, hence making one think the unthinkable. The name "Quixote"—meaningless in Spanish—is luminous and compelling as *qeshot* "truth"—a biblical term popularized in the Sephardic liturgy *Berikh Shemeh*. The pertinent paragraph reads as follows:

> Neither we trust in the Son of God (i.e., Jesus) but in the God of Heaven who is a *Qeshot* God, his Torah is *Qeshot*, and his Prophets are *Qeshot*, and he abundantly makes Goodness and *Qeshot*. In him I trust! And to his glorious name I give praise.

If one were to regard "la Mancha," lit., "the stain"—a place "whose name," as we are told in the opening line—"I do not wish to remember" (I, 1), to be an allusion to a past not pure enough to pass the edicts of "pureza de sangre" for which Spain was famous[28]— rather than a pointless region in Castille—then the title of Cervantes's famous work acquires chilling precision. "Mr. Truth, Man of Tainted Past," solemnly intones the existential dislocation peculiar to *conversos* (past and present). The image of a gentleman alienated to the point of madness, meandering in a hallucinatory world shielded by an armor, "to increase his own honor (*honra*) and for service to his nation" (I, 1), is a harrowing allegory of the *converso* in Spain.

The tension "appearance/reality" is the matrix for the pathos of isolation and moral agony and exile and loss, landscaping the writings of *conversos*. Witness *La Celestina* (16 acts: Burgos, 1499; 21 acts: Seville, 1502) by Fernando de Rojas (d. 1543); *La Lozana Andaluza* (Venice, 1528)

---

[27] On the Erasmism of Cervantes, a typical *converso* phenomenon, see Marcel Bataillon, *Erasmo y España* (México, 1982), pp. 777–801. On Cervantes's mysticism, see Dominique Aubier, *Don Quichotte, prophète d'Israel* (Laffront, 1966). On the specific *converso* character of *Don Quixote*, see Ruth Reichelberg, *Don Quichotte ou le Roman d'un Juif Masqué* (Bourg-en-Bresse, 1989). There is no question that Cervantes was familiar with certain aspects of halakhah. See, for example, *Entremeses* (Madrid, 1975), a collection of short plays. In the first one, "Juez de los Divorcios," dealing comically with cases of divorce presented to a tribunal (for Christians?!), p. 32, one of the participants declared: "There is a law stipulating that a wife may divorce her husband on the grounds of his having bad breath." See M. Ket. 8:10; B. Ket. 77a. Cf., ibid., "Rufián Viudo," p. 51.

[28] See above, n. 22. Cf., above, n. 14 and below, n. 30.

by Francisco Delicado or Delgado (ca. 1475-after 1534); the anonymous *Lazarillo de Tormes* (1554); *Guzmán de Alfarache* (1599), by Mateo Alemán (1547-c.1615); and "Las Soledades"—one of the finest poems in the Spanish language—by Luis de Góngora (1561–1627).[29]

The purpose of the present study is to examine a story in *Don Quixote* II, 45 together with a passage in the Talmud, B. Ned. 25a. It will be seen that both accounts are interrelated, shedding light on each other. In particular, that Cervantes, with virtuosi skill, has peppered the story with trivia and clues designed to simultaneously conceal his source and expand it.

IV

The story takes place in the mythical Island of Barataria, where Don Quixote's faithful companion Sancho Panza was installed as Governor. It is noteworthy, in passing, that an illiterate peasant (II, 43), who happened to have an "Old Christian (*cristiano viejo*) spirit two inches thick all over his soul" (II, 4), gets a chance at such a position, but not Don Quixote. This is particularly telling within the context of *honra* dividing *converso* from *cristiano viejo*.[30] In accordance with local tradition, Sancho had to adjudicate some legal matters. Our story concerns the second case. It is a delightful story, included in Ephraim London famous anthology *The Law* in *Literature* (New York, 1960). The essential facts are these. Someone loaned the sum of ten gold crowns to a friend without witnesses. The borrower admitted the loan but claimed to have repaid it in full. The creditor asks Sancho to put the debtor under oath. Before taking the oath the debtor hands over his staff, in which he had hidden the money, to the creditor. Unabashedly, he then proceeds to swear that he had returned the loan to the creditor. It reads as follows:

> Two old men were next to present themselves before him, one of whom carried a reed by way of staff. It was the one without a staff who was the first to speak:

---

[29] For a detailed analysis of these contributions (except for *Guzmán de Alfarache*), see *In the Shadow of History*.

[30] See *In the Shadow of History*, pp. 66–70, 111–112. This conflict was a determining factor shaping the Iberian policies in the Americas, and explains why Christians of *converso* background were not permitted to immigrate to the New World; see "Jews, *Conversos* and Native Americans," pp. 95–121.

"My lord some days ago I lent this good man ten gold crowns to make him happy and as a good deed (*por hacerle placer y buena obra*), on condition that he should repay me upon demand. A long time went by without my demanding payment, for the reason that I did not wish to cause him an even greater hardship than that which he was suffering when he sought the loan. However, when I saw that he was making no efforts to pay me, I asked him for the money, not once but many times, and he not only failed to reimburse me, he even refused to do so, saying I had never lent him the ten crowns in question, and if I had loaned them to him then he had already reimbursed me. I have no witness of the loan, and naturally there is none of the payment, since no payment was made. Accordingly, I would have your Grace put him under oath, and if he swears that he did pay me, then I will cancel the debt, here and before God."

"What do you say to that, old man with the staff?" Sancho asked.

"My lord," replied the old man, "I admit that he lent them to me; but your Grace may lower that rod, for, seeing that he had me put under oath, I will also swear that I paid him back, really and truly."

The Governor lowered the rod that he held, and in the meanwhile the old man who had spoken handed his staff over to the other one while he took the oath, as if he was embarrassed by it. Then, placing his hand upon the cross of the rod, he once more affirmed that it was true that he had borrowed the ten crowns that were demanded of him but that he had returned them from his own hand to his [that is the other's hand] (*pero que él se los había vuelto de su mano al la suya*), the only thing being that the other old man did not appear to realize it but was all the time asking for his money. In view of this, the great governor then asked the creditor what he had to say in reply to his adversary's statement; whereupon the old fellow who now held the staff replied that his debtor must undoubtedly be speaking the truth, as he knew him to be a worthy man and a good Christian. . . .

The defendant thereupon took back his staff and, with bowed head, left the court. When he saw the defendant leaving in this manner, without saying another word, and when he perceived how resigned the plaintiff was, Sancho . . . remained lost in thought for a short while. Then he raised his head and ordered them to call back the old man with the staff who had already left.

They did so, and as soon as Sancho saw him, he said, "Good man, give me the staff. I have need of it."

"Gladly," replied the old man. "Here it is, my lord." And he placed it in the governor's hand.

Sancho took it and handed it to the other old man, remarking, "Go in peace, for you are now repaid."

"Repaid, my lord? And is this reed worth ten gold crowns?"

"Yes," said the governor, "It is; or if it is not, then I am the biggest blockhead in the world. We will see right now whether or not I have it in me to govern an entire kingdom."

With this, he ordered that the reed be broken and laid open there in the sight of all, and in the heart of it they found the ten gold crowns. They were all greatly astonished at this, looking upon their governor as another Solomon. When they inquired of him how he knew that the crowns were there, he replied that it had come to him when he saw the old man hand the staff to his adversary while he was taking an oath to the effect that he had really and truly paid his creditor, and, then, when he was through, had heard him ask for it back again. . . . Moreover, he had heard the curate of his village tell another case like this one, and if it was a question of not forgetting what he had need to remember, there was not another memory like his own in all the island.

V

A similar story known as *qanya de-Raba*, "Raba's Reed," albeit with significant variation of details to be examined below, appears in the Talmud. Raba (d. 352) is the celebrated Talmudic sage in whose presence the oath was administered. There are two different versions of the story, the "standard" version found in all printed and manuscript editions and an "older" version known from citations. I have used the critical edition, *Tractate Nedarim*, ed. R. Moshe Hershler, *The Babylonian Talmud* (Jerusalem, 5745/1985), vol. 1, pp. 215–217. The variants recorded in the course of this study, as well as the text of the two versions, proceed from its critical apparatus. The standard version reads as follows:

> Someone demanded payment of money (given in loan) from his friend. He (the creditor) came before Raba (demanding payment).
> He (the creditor) said to the debtor: "Pay me!"[31]
> He (the creditor) responded: "I paid him!"[32]
> Raba told him (to the creditor): "If so go and swear to him that you have paid him."
> He went and brought with him a reed where he had put[33] the money inside. He was leaning on it (the reed) and approaching the Court. He told the creditor: "Hold this reed in your hand."

---

[31] As in the critical apparatus.
[32] As in the critical apparatus.
[33] As in the critical apparatus.

> Then he (the creditor) took a Scroll of the Torah and swore that he had paid him all that he owed him.³⁴ In anger, the creditor broke the reed, and the coins fell on the ground. It was discovered that [technically] he (the deponent) had sworn the truth.

The motif of the reed as a tool of deception is already found in *Livius* I, 56,³⁵ but in a completely different context. The story in the Talmud appears in various Jewish recensions.³⁶ Before proceeding to the older version, a few observations are of the essence. Both the Talmud and Cervantes coincide in the four principal motifs of the story: (i) hiding the money in the reed, (ii) leaning on the reed when approaching the court, (iii) handing over the reed to the creditor before taking the oath, and (iv) discovering the money in the reed. The discrepancies are not substantial and pertain to the different setting and purpose of the story. In the Talmud the story unfolds in a Rabbinic Court; therefore the deponent holds the Scroll of the Torah. In Cervantes it unfolds in a Christian Civil Court; therefore he places his hand on the cross. The object of Cervantes is to show Sancho's cleverness, and the reed is broken by his command. In the Talmud the plaintiff brakes the reed in an act of rage. The purpose of the story is to show that it is possible to lie under oath and still not be liable for perjury. (Thus the need to institute a special formula to prevent abusing the law, see below, VI). In the Talmudic society, it was common to use the reed for walking and hiding. Specifically, some, as with the defendant in our case, used it for dishonest purposes.³⁷ This does not seem of have been the case in Spain. To hint that we are dealing with a special kind of staff, possibly with "Hebrew" undertones, Cervantes used *báculo* from the Latin *baculum* of the Vulgate (see below, VIII), rather than a more common term *vara*. Casually, he mentions that both parties were old. This detail permits the audience to believe that payment may have

---

³⁴ As in the critical apparatus.
³⁵ This was indicated by S.A. Lindermann, "Mehqarim," in *Ha-Maggid* XXIII (1879), p. 247.
³⁶ There are some Christian accounts and also a Muslim recension attributing this story to Jews. See the biographical notes in the critical edition and in *Otzar ha-Geonim*, B.M. Lewin, ed., vol. 11 (Jerusalem, 1942), *Nedarim*, p. 25, n. 2.
³⁷ See M. Kel. 17:16; T. Kel., B.M. 7:10; and Maimonides' Commentary ad loc. On the mendacious uses of such a cane, see R. Emanuel Hai Ricchi, *Hon 'Ashir* (Amsterdam, 5490/1730), fol. 154d, s.v. *wu-maqqel*.

escaped the creditor's memory. By assuming that the defendant too was infirm, the reader is lead to believe that that was the reason he needed a walking rod.

VI

There are two serious difficulties with the Talmudic version. Both are resolved in Cervantes' account.

According to the Talmud, the debtor seems to have said under oath that [i] he had paid the creditor, [ii] in full. Concerning the first point, many Talmudists, among them the celebrated R. Solomon ibn Adrete (ca. 1235–1310) raised a powerful objection. The most fundamental aspect of "payment" (*par'e*)—the term used by the debtor in his oath—is delivery of money in fulfillment of an obligation. This presupposes *notice of the fact* to be communicated by the debtor to the creditor. Unable to meet this objection, he amended the text.[38]

The objection is based on a misreading corrected by Cervantes. The commentators assumed that the term "in his hand" in the oath ("paid him [*par'e*] all that he has *in his hand*") refers to *the hand of the debtor*. In Hebrew, the manifest tenor of such an expression would be "that he (the debtor paid) whatever he (the debtor) *owed the creditor*." This being an obvious lie,[39] such a reading is, in my view, mistaken. The correct reading of "in his hand" is, as proposed by Cervantes, in the hand of the *creditor*—not of the debtor! Thus the debtor was swearing that "he had returned (*vuelto*) them (the ten crowns) from his own hand to *his*"—to *the creditor's* hand! *(de su mano a la suya)*. A further note will confirm the wisdom of Cervantes's reading. Primarily, the Hebrew root PR', from where the term *de-par'e* stems, means "to leave," "to abandon."[40] Accordingly, the idiomatic sense of "leaving" money in the hand of the creditor is "to requite," "to replace," Spanish "volver"—as proposed by Cervantes, rather than "to pay" as understood by the commentators.

---

[38] See *Hiddushe ha-Rishba* on B. Ned. 25a, s.v. *ve-yishteba'*. To resolve this problem, R. Yom Tob as-Sibili, *Hiddushe ha-Ritba, Nedarim* 25a, ed. R. Aaron Yafhen (Jerusalem, 5755/1995), col. 257 ascertained that such an action constitutes payment, a view making little sense either in law or in common sense; see ibid., editor's note 328. Cf., below, n. 44.

[39] See R. ibn Adrete in the preceding note.

[40] See Eliezer Ben Yehuda, *Hebrew Thesaurus* (Tel-Aviv, 1949), vol. 10, s.v. *PR'*, pp. 5208–5210.

Indeed, the commentators' error best illustrates the uncanny ability of the debtor and the problem that the Talmudic sages tried to solve. The Talmud cites the story to explain the purpose of a Rabbinic statute, instituting a special formula before administering an oath. The purpose of the formula is to apprise the deponent that the terms of the oath are in accordance to the "mind of the court," rather than the mind of the deponent. The formula reads: "You are forewarned that we are administering this oath not according to your mental reservations but according to our mind and the mind of the Court."[41] That means that the terms of the oath are to be understood according to the semantic field of the cleric administering the oath ("our mind") and that of "the court."[42] Without this formula the deponent could argue that the terms of the oath were according to *his* own particular understanding, like the defendant of our story.[43]

The Talmudic commentators fell into the debtor's trap! They understood *par'e* in the latter, Rabbinic sense of "paid," precisely as the debtor wanted them to understand: that he had fully satisfied *his* obligation to the payee.[44] In case he would be caught, *then* he would claim that he meant to say that he had *left* his own money in the hand of the payee: he thus would be a cheat, but not a perjurer.[45] Since the Spanish *pagado* cannot be subjected to the semantic

---

[41] This is the correct text as preserved by R. Hanan'el, *Shebu'ot* 29a; Maimonides, *Mishne Tora*, *Shebu'ot* XI, 18. In the standard editions the text was changed to "our mind and the mind of God." The change of the text is essential in order to lay down the future grounds for the doctrine that certain rabbis (now exclusively associated with the holier political parties) may, like the biblical Balaam, "know the mind" of God; see "One-Dimensional Jew, Zero-Dimensional Judaism," in *Annual of Rabbinic Judaism* II (1999), p. 45.

[42] See R. Besal'el Ashkenazi, *Shitta Mequbbeset*, on *Nedarim* 25a, s.v. *ve-ada'ta*.

[43] This type of mental reservations was perfectly acceptable in the ancient world; see Giambattista Vico, *The New Science*, trans. Thomas Goddard Bergin and Max Harold Fisch (Ithaca, 1968), #967-968. The rabbis explained Jacob's statement (Gen. 26:19) accordingly. See R. Elie Benamozegh, *Em la-Miqra* (Leghorn, 1862), vol. 1, fol. 87b-88a; and idem, "Exégèse Biblique," in his *Critiqe, Exégèse* (Leghorne, 1897; recently reprinted in Livorno, 2000, under the title, *Elia Benamozegh spiega la sapienze ebraica*), p. 7.

[44] Unable to cope with the text the commentators proposed all kinds of textual emendations and or far fetched explanations, thus falling again in the debtor's trap and missing the point of the story. See above, n. 38.

[45] In modern legal systems "perjury" is extended to any false statement said under oath, even when not made in a judicial proceeding.

manipulations of *par'e*, Cervantes makes the debtor say that he "will also swear that I paid him (*pagado*) back, really and truly." However, at the time of the oath, the master conniver skips the incriminating words, and says: "that he had returned them from his own hand to his"—but not that he had *pagado* the loan!

To charge someone with perjury, one would need to prove that the statement under oath was categorically false. The story of the Talmud unfolds *without* the statute instituting the reading of the special formula. (For the reason, see below, VII). It wants to show the need for such a statute to be able to charge the liar with perjury. Otherwise, although guilty of lying and deception, as the deponent in our story, he could not be charged with perjury. Remarkably, in neither the Talmud nor Cervantes, is the debtor charged with perjury—a most grievous offense in both Rabbinic and Christian law.[46] (See below, VIII)

VII

The second difficulty concerns the administration of the oath. In both the Talmud and Cervantes, handing over the reed is related to the administration of the oath. Generally, Rabbinic law requires the deponent to hold a Scroll of the Torah as he swears. That is why in our story the accused handed the reed to the plaintiff, to free his hands and be able to hold the Torah. There is an exception to this rule. In a case in which the plaintiff offers no evidence through the testimony of a witness, and the accused denies any pending obligation, the law requires the defendant to take an oath (*shebu'at heset*). This oath, however, does not require holding the Scroll of the Torah.[47] Thus, an essential element of the story vanishes. Once there is no need to hand over the reed, the plot collapses.[48]

---

[46] The Talmudic commentators overlooked this fundamental point.

[47] See Maimonides, *Mishne Tora, Shebu'ot* XI, 13.

[48] See R. Besal'el Ashkenazi, *Shitta Mequbbeset*, on B. Ned. 25a, s.v. *ve-ada'ta*. To meet this problem the commentators proposed several answers, none of which fits either the text or the law of the Talmud. To illustrate, *Hiddushe ha-Ritba*, ad loc. cols. 254-255, advanced the view that the law requires holding a scroll of the Torah even in this type of oath, an opinion with no support in Rabbinic sources; see ibid., editor's notes 305 and 322. Cf., R. Menahem ha-Me'iri, *Bet ha-Behira, Nedarim*, Sh. Dikman, ed. (Jerusalem, 5722-1962), p. 110a.

In Cervantes's account, instead of the Torah, the deponent touches the cross at the head of the Governor's staff. Casually, Cervantes remarks that the accused handed over the reed "while he took the oath, as if he was embarrassed by it." Why should this be embarrassing?

There is an older account of the Talmud, preserved in quotations from early sources. According to this account the oath was pronounced not while holding the Scroll of the Torah but while touching a

> chain on which the Holy Name (i.e., the Tetragrammaton) was engraved. [It was believed that] whoever would swear falsely would not be able to stretch his hand and touch the head of the chain. When that man (the debtor) was about to swear to the plaintiff he told him:
> "Come! I will show you that I am swearing the truth." Then he went and stretched his hand and touched the head of the chain. In anger the other (the plaintiff) broke the reed, and the money fell down. . . .[49]

It follows that the story was dealing with an *extra judicial oath* taken in a judicial proceeding *without requirement of the law*. This is why the above mentioned formula forewarning the deponent was not recited. This account coincides with Cervantes in an essential point: the accused *volunteers* to take the oath! In both accounts the defendant touches the head of a venerated object. Accordingly, the reason that the deponent handed over the reed to the plaintiff was not to hold the Scroll of the Torah as in the standard text of the Talmud but to show *deference* for the sacred object. In Rabbinic etiquette, holding a cane is regarded as mundane and implies lack of reverence.[50] Exactly, as explained by Cervantes "as if he was embarrassed by it (*como si lo embarazara mucho*)," in the sense of respect and humility. Naturally, Cervantes transformed a Jewish sacred object into a cross. The change may not have been totally arbitrary. In the Jewish text the chain is designated "*shoshelita*." Jews holding Christological ideologies (and there were plenty of these among *conversos*) probably read

---

[49] Cited in R. Besal'el Ashkenazi, *Shitta Mequbbeset*, on B. Ned. 25a, s.v. *lo le-appuqe; Otzar ha-Geonim*, B.M. Lewin, ed., vol. 11 (Jerusalem, 1942), *Nedarim*, pp. 25–26; Critical Apparatus, ad loc.
[50] See M. Ber. 9:6. Cf. M. R.H. 2:10.

it as "*sheloshita*," as if referring to the Christian Trinity.[51] Probably this was the reason for suppressing the early account and substituting it with a version that, although legally confusing, was theologically less problematic.[52]

There is another item connecting Cervantes with Rabbinic sources. In the Talmud, this chain was associated with King Solomon.[53] Significantly, even before Sancho could explain how he knew the coins were in the staff, the people looked upon him "as another Solomon."

A most telling detail. When Sancho is asked how he knew that the defendant hid the coins in the staff, he said that sometimes God leads even foolish governors into light, adding, casually, "and, what's more, he heard his parish priest tell of an incident much like this."

In the foregoing we tried to document the priest's source (and reveal thereby his true identity).

VIII

We are now in a position to ask a most fundamental question. What moved Cervantes to choose this particular story from the Talmud? To answer this question and bring out the concrete meaning of the story, a few more points must be examined.

After the debtor swore, Sancho asked the creditor if he was satisfied with the oath. Without hesitation he replied that he believed that the debtor was "speaking the truth, as he knew him to be a worthy man and a good Christian (*hombre de bien y buen cristiano*)." The exchange seems superfluous. Obviously, it has no counterpart

---

[51] On the Trinitarian theology of Jewish apostates, see Pedro Alfonso, *Diálogo contra los Judíos* (Huesca, 1996), pp. 309–316. Some of these apostates used to inscribe the letter *Sh* in the middle of the Tetragrammaton to encode Jesus name "YH-Sh-WH." On these inscriptions, see Israel Lévi, *Revue des Études Juives*, VII (1883), pp. 285–286. About Trinitarian Jews, see *In the Shadow of History*, pp. 14–15; and my articles "Two Models of Jewish Spirituality," in *Shofar* 10 (1992), pp. 43–46; and "A Crisis of Categories: *Kabbalah* and the Rise of Apostasy in Spain," in Moshe Lazar and Stephen Haliczer, eds., *The Jews of Spain and the Expulsion of 1492* (Lancaster, 1997), pp. 41–63, especially pp. 54–58. On *conversos* with strong Christological ideology, both in and outside the Iberian Peninsula, see *In the Shadow of History*, pp. 44–46, 47–49.

[52] On the "internal censorship" of controversial Rabbinic texts, see Saul Liebermann, *Shkiin* (Jerusalem, 1939).

[53] B. Git. 68a; cf., *Yalqut Shim'oni* 1 Kings #182.

in the Talmudic version. In fact, as we shall see in the course of our examination, it is a detail of the highest importance, essential for the proper decoding of the story.

In an address made by King Ferdinand to New Christians on September 6, 1493, he called on them to associate with "Christian Catholics," i.e., *cristianos viejos*, to learn how to "be faithful, and Christian Catholics." In what must be described as a monstrous, hideous request, the monarch called on "newly converted" parents not to raise their own children. Rather, they should entrust their offspring to "Christian Catholics," i.e., people not tainted with Jewish blood, "in order to be taught and be indoctrinated by them." This address had been the focus of the *Lazarillo de Tormes*, a work written with a fantastical sense of humor. In a series of interlinked sketches, the author exposes in moving detail and ice-cold wit the knavery and debauchery characteristic of these paragons of virtue, thus providing a powerful portrait of the moral agony and degradation suffered by Lazarillo, a new Christian, who decided to heed the call of the king and associate with the "worthies."[54]

In our story, Cervantes makes sure to point out to the privileged reader that the villain is a *cristiano viejo*, or as they preferred to be known "worthy man and a good Christian (*hombre de bien y buen cristiano*)." By inference, we know who the designated victim is. Thus, the story exposes, with visceral impact, the self-indulgent moralism of those parading as "good Christians." Like the author of *Lazarillo*, Cervantes, too, wants to expose the cynicism and corruption of those supposing to "teach and indoctrinate" the unworthy neophytes with tainted blood. The cheat is a *cristiano viejo*. *Cristianos viejos* were notorious for their insatiable greed and the desire to gain wealth by pillaging the fruits of other, lower human been.[55] Characteristically, this paragon of Christian virtue does not hesitate to defraud someone who, out of the goodness of his heart, lent him money, "to make him happy and as a good deed." As it happened a million times in Spain, and before that throughout Germany and France, the creditor tries to wiggle out of his legal obligation and defraud the lender by all means of deception.[56] Cleverly manipulating the semantic fields of his oath

---

[54] See *In the Shadow of History*, pp. 61–70.

[55] On the peculiarity of this type of greed, see "The Iberian Experience," pp. 98–99.

[56] See *In the Shadow of History*, pp. 22–23.

and promises, the *cristiano viejo* could never be formally charged with perjury. It is true that at the end of our story justice is done. But this can take place only in the mythical Island of Barataria where Don Quixote's companion rules, not in the *real* Spain.

We can now suggest a reason why Cervantes chose *báculo* for "staff" from the Latin *baculum*, rather than a more common term *vara*. It is the term used by the *Vulgate* to designate the walking staff of the patriarchs (Gen. 38:25; Ps. 23:4) and that of a poor pilgrim (Gen. 32:10). Like the typical *min* mentioned earlier (II), the creditor holds symbols of the Hebrew Scripture to sucker his victim.

A final point. At the end of the story, the Talmud says that upon realizing that the money was contained in the reed, "it was discovered that [technically] he (the deponent) had swore the truth." The term used for "the truth" is *be-Qushta*—a variant pattern-form of Don *Qeshot*, Cervantes's hero. A lexical note could help us decode the message. Whereas *Qeshot* is mainly used in the sense of "straightness," "truth," the form *be-Qushta* is used as an affirmative, designed to ascertain the validity of a statement.[57] Put more simply: *Qeshot* designates the "real" truth, whereas *Qushta* designates the evident, conventional truth, something that occasionally, as in our story, could be a patent lie.

Properly decoded, our story is a story of desperation. A muzzled cry. A frightening allegory, disclosing the dark undercurrents dominating *real* Spain.

* * *

The above proves nothing about Cervantes's ancestry. He could have heard the story from a variety of sources, particularly while a prisoner in Algiers (1575–1580). And yet, the detailed analyses, the handling of minutiae and the grasp of sources, points to a level of understanding of the subject that is simply amazing.

—Perhaps . . . ?
—No! That is simply impossible!
—But why?
—Why!? Next they would say that Columbus was a Jew!

---

[57] On the lexical sense of these terms, see Eliia Levita, *Meturgeman* (Isny, 1591), fol. 140a; Marcus Jastrow, *A Dictionary* (New York, 1992), vol. 2, pp. 1429–1430.

THE MODERN PERIOD

TORAH AND CULTURE:
H. RICHARD NIEBUHR'S *CHRIST AND CULTURE* AFTER FIFTY YEARS: A JUDAIC RESPONSE*

Jacob Neusner
Bard College

Does culture express or defy the religious imperative? Do the patterns of the social order realize the divine plan, or do they represent that from which religion must separate itself, upon which religion stands in judgment? Fifty years ago, a thoughtful and profound theological analysis of the relationship, in Christianity, between religion and culture, H. Richard Niebuhr's *Christ and Culture* (New York, 1951: Harper), formed of Christian theological language and traditions a highly systematic response to that question. The inquiry pertains in particular to religions engaged in constructing norms for the social order of the faithful. That matter, then, concerns, in the language of the respective faiths, the relationship between the generative symbol of a religion and the ambient culture that forms the framework in which that religion constructs its holy society. Does culture form a medium of religion or an obstacle thereto—thus Christ and culture?

Religions that speak to, make provision for, communities of the faithful respond to the issue. They further mediate relationships between those communities and the ambient universe beyond their limits—that is, all religions that rise above the utterly idiosyncratic and private[1]—must address the same issue. Niebuhr defines the issue succinctly:

> Christians living with Christ in their cultures . . . are forever being challenged to abandon all things for the sake of God; and forever being sent back into the world to teach and practice all the things that have been commanded them (p. 29).

---

* Reprinted from *Review of Rabbinic Judaism* 5:3, 2002, pp. 403–429.
[1] We know the social from the solipsistic by reference to the language rules that prevail. One can say, "My Judaism," meaning, one's private belief and practice, called, idiosyncratically, "Judaism," which is not uncommon, and "My Torah," which in most contexts of Judaic society would constitute an oxymoron. One can say, "the Torah of Moses," or "the Torah of Rabbi Aqiba," but the only "my" that works with "Torah" in Hebrew, the sole language that is native to Judaism, is God's, as in "It is My Torah, do not abandon it," of the governing liturgy.

> Given these two complex realities—Christ and culture—an infinite dialogue must develop in the Christian conscience and the Christian community. In his single-minded direction toward God, Christ leads men away from the temporality and pluralism of culture. . . . Yet the Son of God is himself child of a religious culture and sends his disciples to tend his lambs and sheep, who cannot be guarded without cultural work (p. 39).

That is, Christ is represented as distinct from culture and in opposition to the world, or he is represented as engaged by culture. In Niebuhr's picture Judaism finds itself represented as an exception, because Judaism is not a "mere religion" but is characterized as "the same thing" as culture, ethnicity, nationalism. Judaism, unlike Christianity—so we are told—cannot differentiate matters of culture from those of religious faith. We should then not anticipate finding a counterpart issue in the native categories of Judaism. When Niebuhr characterizes what he calls "Judaism," it is only to explain why "Judaism" does not enter into consideration. Whether and how that is so remains to be seen.

Quite what people mean, with reference to both Judaism and Christianity, by such allegations is not self-evident.[2] True, unlike Pauline Christianity but like Islam, Judaism does not differentiate law from religion (a.k.a., Torah from salvation and justification), and the Torah legislates for areas of ordinary life deemed secular or neutral by Christianity. The question fits Christianity, with its rich tradition of differentiation between components and institutions of culture and faith, e.g., between emperor and pope or between church and state. But, as I shall presently show, the issues with which Niebuhr struggles work for Judaism. Properly framed, they prove susceptible to translation into the context and circumstances of "the Torah," which functionally and structurally corresponds to Christianity's "Christ." That is not only because "the Torah" certainly knows the difference between holy and profane, religious and secular. It is because the very points of dialectic and tension to which Niebuhr points in Christianity prove comparable to issues native to Judaism. But, it goes without saying, the doctors of the Torah sort out the issues in

---

[2] Perhaps a subtle response to Niebuhr, Wilfred Cantwell Smith, *The Meaning and End of Religion; A New Approach to the Religious Traditions of Mankind* (New York, 1963) argued that distinguishing religion from culture is never plausible. His case is drawn from Islam, but Judaism would supply an equally probative set of examples. Neither religious tradition has a word for "religion" that refers to "religion/not culture."

the Torah's own terms and categories. The challenge, accordingly, is to identify counterparts, in Judaism and its category-formations, to those of Christianity as Niebuhr expounds matters. To begin with, can I show that the dialectics—Torah as embodiment of culture, Torah as critique of culture—adumbrated in the formulation of Niebuhr pertains to Judaism?

I. *Torah and Culture: A Contemporary Debate in the Torah Camp*

Before turning to a brief reprise of Niebuhr's typology, let me set forth a single demonstration that the issue is native to Judaism and not particular to "Christ and culture," even now as—so I shall show in the shank of this paper—it was in the past. How do we know that it faces the faithful, who practice the faith, and is not a merely theoretical issue of theological speculation?

The contemporary question may be framed very simply. It is [1] "Torah along with secular learning" as against [2] "Torah but no secular learning," and that issue is framed in the world of the Orthodox Yeshivot. Proof-texts for both sides derive from the canonical writings of normative Judaism. Indeed, the debate involves Yeshiva University in the U.S.A. and Bar Ilan University in the State of Israel, as against the Yeshiva worlds of Brooklyn and Bene Beraq, respectively: Does the study of Torah prevent the study of any other subject, as the Yeshiva-world maintains, or does the study of Torah encompass all learning, as Yeshiva University and Bar Ilan aver? If the former, then the Torah stands in opposition to, in judgment upon, secular sciences, and if the latter, then the Torah represents the apex and realization of all learning. As to the conflict, between Torah and secular learning, it may be framed very simply. Is it permitted for a pious Jew to study mathematics, biology, or history, or must he devote all of his time and energy to study of the Torah? The curricula of the great Yeshivot, centers of Torah-study, and of the schools that prepare young men for study in those Yeshivot, answer that question. Some accommodate secular studies, others do not.

Now I cannot think of a more blatant formulation of the debate on the interplay of religion and culture than the issue as it is articulated, to begin with, in contemporary Judaic Orthodoxy. In its interior debates on the value of a secular education, the Torah-camp of contemporary Judaism today moreover carries forward a debate that first came to the surface in the formation, in the nineteenth century, of integrationist Orthodox Judaism, which held that study of Torah does not preclude study of secular sciences, broadly construed, including literature, philosophy, and natural science. Is Torah in conflict with culture, or does Torah infuse culture, so that those who study nature enter into the realm of Torah-learning? From the time of Samson Raphael Hirsch in the nineteenth century to the present time in Yeshiva University and Bar Ilan University, the debate has gone forward on whether or not Israelites faithful to the Torah may devote any amount of time to other-than-Torah-learning. That means in practical terms, may Yeshiva-students participate in instruction in subjects other than the sacred sciences? Integrationist Orthodoxy affirmed, and segregationist-Orthodoxy denied, that proposition. The contemporary debate serves only to show how the basic question addressed by Niebuhr *mutatis mutandis* animates interior debate in the Torah-camp of Judaism. In these corresponding terms, the issue addressed by Christianity is not only *not* alien to, but quite commonplace in the debates of, the continuators of Torah-learning in Judaism. Now to consider matters in greater particularity.

II. *Niebuhr's Framing of the Issue of Religion and Culture*

A work of clarity, deep learning and broad perspective, Niebuhr's book surveyed principal participants in the theological tradition of Christianity. He constructed a typology that situated each in relationship to all others. A survey of the typology that he constructed to solve the problem will open the way to a consideration of comparable responses—ways of thinking about the corresponding issues—in the formative canon of Judaism, specifically, the normative Halakhah of the Mishnah, Tosefta, Yerushalmi, and Bavli. A brief précis of Niebuhr's discussion sets the stage for our work.

What exactly does he mean by culture? A summary follows, which invokes the broad range of constituents of culture:

> What do we mean in our use of this word [culture] to say that the Christian church enduringly struggles with the problem of Christ and culture? What we have in view when we deal with Christ and culture is that total process of human activity and that total result of such activity to which now the name *culture*, now the name *civilization*, is applied in common speech. Culture is the "artificial, secondary environment" which mean superimposes on the natural. It comprises language,

> habits, ideas, beliefs, customs, social organization, inherited artifacts, technical processes, and values (p. 32).
>
> It is [first] always social (p. 32), . . . culture, second, is human achievement (p. 33). These human achievements, in the third place, are all designed for an end or ends; the world of culture is a world of values (p. 34).
>
> Further, the values with which these human achievements are concerned are dominantly those of the good for man (p. 35).
>
> Culture in all its forms . . . is concerned with the temporal and material realization of values (p. 36) . . .
>
> Cultural activity is almost as much concerned with the conservation of values as with their realization (p. 37).
>
> The values a culture seeks to realize in any time or place are many in number (p. 38).

So we deal with the continuities of civilization, the givens of the social order. Now the issue presents itself blatantly: how does Christ/Torah relate to the enduring artifacts of human society. Within the framework of the given definition of culture, Niebuhr identifies five answers to the question of the relationship of "Christ and culture;" of these, the first two state the issue in the most acute and radical way, the next three impart nuance thereto:

> 1. The opposition between Christ and culture: "Whatever may be the customs of the society in which the Christian lives, and whatever the human achievements it conserves, Christ is seen as opposed to them, so that he confronts men with the challenge of an 'either-or decision," e.g., "to abandon the 'world' and to 'come out from among them and be separate.'" (p. 40–41)
>
> 2. A fundamental agreement between Christ and culture: "Jesus often appears as a great hero of human culture history; his life and teachings are regarded as the greatest human achievement; in him, it is believed, the aspirations of men toward their values are brought to a point of culmination; he confirms what is best in the past and guides the process of civilization to its proper goal. Moreover, he is part of culture in the sense that he himself is part of the social heritage that must be transmitted and conserved" (p. 41).

So Niebuhr points to the two poles, the segregation of religion from culture, e.g., in monasteries or in Yeshivot, and the integration of religion with culture, e.g., in the very modalities of the social order. He then finds three mediating positions:

> Three other typical answers agree with each other in seeking to maintain the great differences between the two principles and in undertaking to hold them together in some unity. They are distinguished from

each other by the manner in which each attempts to combine the two authorities (pp. 41–42).

3. The third type understands Christ's relation to culture somewhat as the men of the second group do: he is the fulfillment of cultural aspirations and the restorer of the institutions of true society. Yet there is in him something that neither arises out of culture nor contributes directly to it. He is discontinuous as well as continuous with social life and its culture . . . true culture is not possible unless beyond all human achievement. . . . Christ enters into life from above with gifts which human aspiration has not envisioned and which human effort cannot attain unless he relates to men to a supernatural society and a new value-center. Christ is indeed a Christ of culture but he is also a Christ above culture (p. 42).

4. The fourth type: "the duality and inescapable authority of both Christ and culture are recognized, but the opposition between them is also accepted. . . . Christians . . . are subject to the tension that accompanies obedience to two authorities who do not agree yet must both be obeyed. They refuse to accommodate the claims of Christ to those of secular society . . . so they are like the "Christ against culture" believers, yet differ from them in the conviction that obedience to God requires obedience to the institutions of society and loyal to its members as well as obedience to a Christ who sits in judgment on that society. Hence man is seen as subject to two moralities and as a citizen of two worlds that are not only discontinuous with each other but largely opposed. In the polarity and tension of Christ and culture life must be lived precariously and sinfully in the hope of a justification which lies beyond history" (pp. 42–43).

5. The fifth type, and the third of the mediating answers: "There is the conversionist solution. Those who offer it understand with the members of the first and fourth groups that human nature is fallen or perverted, and that this perversion not only appears in culture but is transmitted by it. Hence the opposition between Christ and all human institutions and customs is to be recognized. Yet the antithesis does not lead either to Christian separation from the world as with the first group or to mere endurance in the expectation of a transhistorical salvation, as with the fourth. Christ is seen as the converter of man in his culture and society, not apart from these, for there is no nature without culture, and no turning of men from self and idols to God save in society" (p. 43).

In the shank of the book, Niebuhr identifies various principals of Christian theology with each of these positions. These are arrayed not in historical sequence but phenomenologically, in accord with the logic of the issue at hand, which is realized in cases through time. The first—that one that opposes religion and culture—is represented by monastic orders and sectarian movements, which called on believers living in what purported to be a Christian culture to abandon the "world" (pp. 40–41). In modern times it is represented by those who "emphasize the antagonism of Christian faith to capitalism and communism, to industrialism and nationalism, to Catholicism and Protestantism." That is the theory that corresponds to the formulation of Torah as against the world that characterizes the Yeshiva-universe, with their monastic stance vis à vis the ambient Jewish community (and, if truth be told, the world of Judaism entirely). The second ("agreement between Christ and culture") is represented by those who identify Christianity and Western civilization, or between Jesus and democratic institutions (or similar antinomies). The Judaic counterpart in contemporary terms has already been identified; but there is a much more subtle corresponding Judaic system, which we shall meet at some length.

What about the mediating positions? The synthetic model ("Christ of culture, Christ above culture") third, is represented by Thomas Aquinas, the fourth ("polarity and tension of Christ and cultural life . . . awaiting a justification which lies beyond history") by Luther, and the fifth ("the conversionist solution") by John Calvin. These are ideal types, to be sure: "The method of typology . . . though historically inadequate . . . has the advantage of calling to attention the continuity and significance of the great motifs that appear and reappear in the long wrestling of Christians with their enduring problem" (p. 44). I would not venture to find Judaic counterparts to these positions, but with some thought they can be identified. Rather, let us turn to the formative age of Rabbinic Judaism, portrayed in the canonical documents of late antiquity, where, as I shall show, the issues of Torah in relationship to culture, to the ambient social world beyond the framework of the Rabbinic system and structure, were worked out in categories native to that system.

III. *Torah and Culture*

How do we compare the Christian with the Judaic framing of what I allege is an issue common to both, each in its own native category-formations? The task is to identify in the normative framework of Judaism in its formative age the native-category-formations that comprehend the same choice as Christianity confronts in the formulation, "Christ and culture." Self-evidently, we cannot translate "Christ" into the language and category-formations of Judaism, or "Torah" into the language and naïve categories of Christianity. "Torah" is not "Christ," nor "Christ," "Torah," even though a comparison of the terms will show points of congruity in function and even structure. The one tradition simply presents no counterpart in either function or meaning for the use of the key-word of the other. That is proved by the fact that we cannot translate "Torah" with all its meanings, or "Christ" with all its dimensions, from one system's terms and structures to those of the other. For example, "Bible" in Christianity conveys little of the meaning of "Torah" in Judaism. But, it may be asked, does not "Christ" stand for "Messiah?" "Messiah" in normative, Rabbinic Judaism in fact does not compare in systemic centrality and coverage to "Christ" in Christianity.[3] In undertaking the comparison of theological constructions set forth by contiguous religious traditions, the most difficult task requires finding what, within one structure and system, possesses a counterpart within another structure and system.

But what if we adopt the results of Niebuhr's typology? When we use generic language, that is, instead of "Christ," "the sacred," and instead of "culture," "the profane" or "the ordinary," then we find comparisons and contrasts do emerge. And, still more to the point, when we abandon the effort to formulate in word-choices the comparable issues, and look for corresponding structures and formations, then we find ourselves in an authentic, native, Judaic category-formation within which the very issues framed by Niebuhr for Christian turn out to flourish. For by concentrating on what is at stake for culture, we are able to identify even in the heart of the Torah, in the Halakhah, counterparts to the dialectics, "Christ" in opposition to "culture," or "Christ" realized in "culture." Specifically, we find that the paired opposites, the main antinomies identified by Niebuhr, prove paradigmatic for Judaism as well. And having shown that prevailing paradigm in the two religions built on Scripture,

---

[3] I have shown that fact in my systemic statement of matters: *The Theology of the Oral Torah: Revealing the Justice of God* (Montreal and Kingston, 1999), Chapters Twelve and Thirteen. In the system of Rabbinic Judaism set forth in the Oral Torah's Aggadic documents, "Messiah" is not an irreducible native category at all. And in the Halakhic counterpart, which I lay out in *The Theology of the Halakhah* (Leiden and Boston, 2001), there is no category, Messiah, at all. The Messiah-theme plays a part in both category-formations, the Aggadic and the Halakhic, but it forms a native category, irreducible and generative, in neither.

we confront an analytical problem for Judaism that is suggested by Niebuhr's nuanced relationships, the third through the fifth. But the task of establishing appropriate points of correspondence suffices for the present exercise. But in the present context, I undertake only the fundamental problem of cultural comparison and contrast. I postpone the more subtle exercise of dealing with Judaic counterparts to Niebuhr's nuanced relationships. For the moment, we confront a binary formulation of matters.

IV. *Torah as a Component of Culture as against Torah as the Entirety of Culture*

I shall now show that counterparts to the two positions outlined by Niebuhr at the outset—Christ versus culture, Christ as the realization of culture—take shape within the normative Halakhic framework. There, it is specifically where the role of Torah within the life of man is worked out that the two positions come to articulation. The antinomy is Torah-study versus other demands upon a man's life as against Torah-study encompassing the entirety of man's life.

I can show that the issue is native to Rabbinic Judaism. It is framed in these terms: should a man learn a trade and also study Torah, in which case Torah forms a chapter of life, to be distinguished from other chapters, thus: Torah as a component of culture? Or should he devote his entire life to Torah-study, to the exclusion of all else, thus Torah in opposition to culture? In the former framework, Torah represents a sector of life, differentiated from other sectors, thus Torah and culture, in Niebuhr's terms; in the latter, Torah lays demands upon the whole of life, in opposition to not only making a living but also responsibilities to family and community, thus Torah versus (the rest of) culture, in Niebuhr's typology.

When Torah is a chapter of life, then Torah is integrated into the affairs of the everyday, a component of the whole. When Torah commands the entirety of the human situation, Torah contrasts with all other forms not only of learning but of human engagement. So at issue, as I shall show, is whether Torah is represented as a component of culture, to be sure, hierarchically at the apex of the social order, or Torah is portrayed as the entirety of culture, in competition with the other, competing and also illegitimate demands that culture makes. And the correspondence with the two extremes of Niebuhr's typology, to review, then is clear: Christ/Torah versus culture or Christ/Torah as harmonious with culture.

What I shall now show is that the categorical conflict is native to Rabbinic Judaism. This I do by demonstrating that the debate between these two positions was carried forward in terms of Torah-study within the social order as against Torah-study in contradiction to the social order—not awfully unlike the contemporary debate within Yeshiva-Orthodoxy. The matter is framed in diverse ways. In normative law, the opposition of Torah and culture comes to concrete expression in the conflict between the natural family and the supernatural relationships brought into being by Torah-study.

One aspect of culture is the social reconstruction of relationships, e.g., family. Everyone knows that Christ rejects family but how does Torah impose itself upon familial ties? One way that the Halakhah finds to express the position that the Torah stands against all other (natural, social) relationships is as follows (M. B.M. 2:11):

> A. [If he has to choose between seeking] what he has lost and what his father has lost,
> B. his own takes precedence.
> C. . . . what he has lost and what his master has lost,
> D. his own takes precedence.
> E. . . . what his father has lost and what his master has lost, that of his master takes precedence.
> G. For his father brought him into this world.
> H. But his master, who taught him wisdom, will bring him into the life of the world to come.
> I. But if his father is a sage, that of his father takes precedence.
> J. [If] his father and his master were carrying heavy burdens, he removes that of his master, and afterward removes that of his father.
> K. [If] his father and his master were taken captive,
> L. he ransoms his master, and afterward he ransoms his father.
> M. But if his father is a sage, he ransoms his father, and afterward he ransoms his master.

The point is made explicit at G-H, the master takes precedence over the father, because the master has brought him eternal life through Torah-teachings, so the natural relationships of this world are set aside by the contrasting ones of the world to come, family by Torah.

In the next statement of the same view, social relationships—the hierarchy of the castes—are reframed in the same way. Now the castes are at issue, priest, Levite, Israelite, mamzer (an outcaste, e.g., the offspring of a union that violates the law, for instance, of a married woman and a man other than her husband) and so on down. These are contrasted with disciple of a sage in relationship to one who is not a disciple of a sage but, by contrast, an *am ha'ares* (in context: ignorant man). Here knowledge of Torah overrides the hierarchy of castes and transcends it (M. Hor. 3:8).

> A. A priest takes precedence over a Levite, a Levite over an Israelite, an Israelite over a mamzer, a mamzer over a Netin, a Netin over a proselyte, a proselyte over a freed slave.
> B. Under what circumstances?
> C. When all of them are equivalent.
> D. But if the mamzer [outcaste] was a disciple of a sage and a high priest was an *am ha'ares* [unlettered in the Torah], the mamzer who is a disciple of a sage takes precedence over a high priest who is an *am ha'ares*.

In both contexts, Torah stands over against the social order and disrupts its natural arrangements, both in family and in caste. What about the conflicting responsibilities of devoting time to Torah-study and devoting time to earning a living? The same view predominates when it comes to earning a living: Torah competes with other components of the ambient culture.

Explicit at M. Hor. 3:8 is that knowledge of the Torah does not change one's caste-status, e.g., priest or mamzer or Netin, and that caste-status does govern whom one may marry, a matter of substantial economic consequence. But it does change one's status as to precedence of another order altogether—one that is curiously unspecific at M. Hor. 3:8. Hierarchical classification for its own sake, lacking all practical consequence, characterizes the Mishnah's system, defining, after all, its purpose and its goal! Along these same lines, the premise of tractate Sanhedrin is that the sage is judge and administrator of the community; knowledge of the Torah qualifies him; but knowledge of the Torah does not provide a living or the equivalent of a living. No provision for supporting the sage as administrator, clerk, or judge is suggested in the tractate.

V. *Study a Craft and also Study Torah vs. Study Torah Only*

What about knowledge of Torah as a way of making one's living? Here is a fine occasion on which to say there is knowledge that possesses value but is not part of the Torah. Or only knowledge of the Torah registers. In the former case, study of Torah represents one component of legitimate learning and livelihood, but there are other things to be learned and to be practiced, and these do not come into conflict with Torah-study. In the latter instance, study of Torah competes with, stands over against, study of all other matters, e.g., of trade or commerce. These represent counterparts to Niebuhr's primary category-formations, Christ within culture as against Christ versus culture. The issue is joined in a systematic way in the Halakhic system, where some authorities recognize the value of studying a trade, while others insist that one should study only Torah, which will provide a livelihood through supernatural means.

Just as Niebuhr shows the diversity of Christian opinion in the interplay of religion and culture, so we see in the normative law more than a single viewpoint. In the list of professions by which men make a living we find several positions. That underscores my basic point: within the framework of Judaism diverse positions register, comparable to the diverse positions outlined by Niebuhr. The issue is common to both traditions, but each frames it in its natural language and category-formations. First is that of Meir and Simeon at M. Qid. 4:14:

> F. R. Meir says, "A man should always teach his son a clean and easy trade. And let him pray to him to whom belong riches and possessions.
> G. "For there is no trade that does not involve poverty or wealth.
> H. "For poverty does not come from one's trade, nor does wealth come from one's trade.
> I. "But all is in accord with a man's merit."
> J. R. Simeon b. Eleazar says, "Have you ever seen a wild beast or a bird who has a trade? Yet they get along without difficulty. And were they not created only to serve me? And I was created to serve my Master. So is it not logical that I should get along without difficulty? But I have done evil and ruined my living."

One's merit makes the difference between poverty and wealth, or one's sinfulness. This simply carries forward the curse of Eden: Adam must work because he has rebelled against God, and that is the human condition. A more practical position is that which follows in the continuation of the passage:

> K. Abba Gurion of Sidon says in the name of Abba Gurya, "A man should not teach his son to be an ass driver, a camel driver, a barber, a sailor, a herdsman, or a shopkeeper. For their trade is the trade of thieves."

> L. R. Judah says in his name, "Most ass drivers are evil, most camel drivers are decent, most sailors are saintly, the best among physicians is going to Gehenna, and the best of butchers is a partner of Amalek."

The third view—the counterpart to "Christ versus culture" in Niebuhr's typology, is that of Nehorai, who holds that Torah suffices as a means for making a living, and Torah-study defines all that man should do, in utter rejection of the imperatives of culture, e.g., mastering a trade and earning a living:

> M. R. Nehorai says, "I should lay aside every trade in the world and teach my son only Torah.
> N. "For a man eats its fruits in this world, and the principal remains for the world to come.
> O. "But other trades are not that way.
> P. "When a man gets sick or old or has pains and cannot do his job, lo, he dies of starvation.
> Q. "But with Torah it is not that way.
> R. "But it keeps him from all evil when he is young, and it gives him a future and a hope when he is old.
> S. "Concerning his youth, what does it say? 'They who wait upon the Lord shall renew their strength' (Is. 40:31). And concerning his old age what does it say? 'They shall still bring forth fruit in old age' (Ps. 92:14).
> T. "And so it says with regard to the patriarch Abraham, may he rest in peace, 'And Abraham was old and well along in years, and the Lord blessed Abraham in all things' (Gen. 24:1).
> U. "We find that the patriarch Abraham kept the entire Torah even before it was revealed, since it says, 'Since Abraham obeyed my voice and kept my charge, my commandments, my statutes, and my laws' (Gen. 26:5)."

Precisely why Torah works as it does is made explicit at R: "It keeps him from evil when he is young." That is to say, the position of Meir and Simeon is repeated, only in a fresh way. If I know the Torah, I will not sin. Meir and Simeon concur in denying conflict between earning a living and studying the Torah, and Nehorai sees a choice to be made.

The first apologia for the Mishnah, Tractate Abot, takes the view that one should not make one's living through study of the Torah. One should both practice a trade and also support himself, and there is no conflict between the one and the other. That is made explicit in Torah-sayings of Tractate Abot, where we find explicit rejection of the theory of Torah-study as a means of avoiding one's obligation to earn a living. Torah-study without a craft is rejected, Torah-study along with labor at a craft is defined as the ideal way of life. No one then concedes that one should do the one and not the other: study the Torah but not practice a trade. The following sayings, M. Abot 2:2 and 3:17, make that point quite clearly:

> 2:2
> A. Rabban Gamaliel, a son of Rabbi Judah the Patriarch, says, "Fitting is learning in the Torah along with a craft, for the labor put into the two of them makes one forget sin. And all learning of the Torah which is not joined with labor is destined to be null and causes sin."
>
> 3:17
> A. R. Eleazar b. Azariah says, ". . . If there is no sustenance [lit.: flour], there is no Torah-learning. If there is no Torah-learning, there is no sustenance."

The way of virtue lies rather in economic activity in the conventional sense, joined to intellectual or philosophical activity in sages' sense. The labor in Torah is not an economic activity and produces no solutions to this-worldly problems of getting food, shelter, clothing. To the contrary, labor in Torah defines the purpose of human life; it is the goal; but it is not the medium for maintaining life and avoiding starvation or exposure to the elements. So too, Tosefta's complement to the Mishnah is explicit in connection with M. Gittin 1:7A, "a commandment pertaining to the father concerning the son:" In this regard T. Qid. 1:11E-G states, "It is to circumcise him, redeem him [should he be kidnapped], teach him Torah, teach him a trade, and marry him off to a girl." There clearly is no conception that if one studies Torah, he need not work for a living, nor in the Tosefta's complement to the Mishnah does anyone imagine that merit is gained by supporting those who study the Torah.

Cited in Abot 2:8, Yohanan b. Zakkai speaks of Torah-study as the goal of a human life, on the one side, and a reward paid for Torah study, clearly in a theological sense and context, on the other. That the context of Torah-study is religious and not economic in any sense is shown by Hananiah's saying, which is explicit: if people talk about the Torah, the Presence of God joins them and participates (M. Abot 2:8, 2:16, 3:2):

> 2:8
> A. Rabban Yohanan b. Zakkai received [the Torah] from Hillel and Shammai. He would say: "If you have learned much Torah, do not puff yourself up on that account, for it was for that purpose that you were created."

2:16
- A. [Tarfon] would say: "It's not your job to finish the work, but you are not free to walk away from it. If you have learned much Torah, they will give you a good reward. And your employer can be depended upon to pay your wages for what you do. And know what sort of reward is going to be given to the righteous in the coming time."

3:2
- B. R. Hananiah b. Teradion says, "[If] two sit together and between them do not pass teachings of the Torah, lo, this is a seat of the scornful, as it is said, 'Nor sits in the seat of the scornful' (Ps. 1:1). But two who are sitting, and words of the Torah do pass between them—the Presence is with them, as it is said, 'Then they that feared the Lord spoke with one another, and the Lord hearkened and heard, and a book of remembrance was written before him, for them that feared the Lord and gave thought to his name' (Mal 3:16). I know that this applies to two. How do I know that even if a single person sits and works on the Torah, the Holy One, blessed be He, sets aside a reward for him? As it is said, 'Let him sit alone and keep silent, because he has laid it upon him' (Lam. 3:28)."

Do worldly benefits accrue to those who study the Torah? The rabbi cited at M. Abot 4:5 maintains that it is entirely inappropriate to utilize Torah-learning to gain either social standing or economic gain:

- B. R. Sadoq says, "Do not make [Torah-teachings] a crown in which to glorify yourself or a spade with which to dig. So did Hillel say, "He who uses the crown perishes. Thus have you learned: Whoever derives worldly benefit from teachings of the Torah takes his life out of this world."

This calls to mind the debate I cited at the outset: May Yeshiva-students study biology or computer science, or does Torah-study constitute the whole of the appropriate curriculum in opposition to secular studies? The contemporary issue, corresponding to the typology constructed by Niebuhr, surfaces in comparable terms here. The counterpart to the position of a harmony between Christ and culture, as I see it, is the instruction at hand, which says, Torah-study forms only a chapter in the proper education of a man. It is the simple fact that the bulk of opinion in the Mishnah and in tractate Abot identifies Torah-learning with status within a system of hierarchical classification, not with a medium for earning a living. And learning a trade and earning a living form harmonious obligations with Torah-study.

Admittedly that is not the only position that is represented. The following seems to me to contrast working for a living with studying Torah and to maintain that the latter will provide a living, without recourse to hard labor (M. Abot 3:15):

> A. R. Nehunia b. Haqqaneh says, "From whoever accepts upon himself the yoke of the Torah do they remove the yoke of the state and the yoke of hard labor. And upon whoever removes from himself the yoke of the Torah do they lay the yoke of the state and the yoke of hard labor."

But the prevailing view, represented by the bulk of sayings, treats Torah-study as an activity that competes with economic venture and insists that Torah-study take precedence, even though it is not of economic value in any commonplace sense of the words. That is explicitly imputed to Meir and to Jonathan at M. Abot 4:9-10:

> 4:9
> A. R. Jonathan says, "Whoever keeps the Torah when poor will in the end keep it in wealth. And whoever treats the Torah as nothing when he is wealthy in the end will treat it as nothing in poverty."
> 4:10
> A. R. Meir says, "Keep your business to a minimum and make your business the Torah. And be humble before everybody. And if you treat the Torah as nothing, you will have many treating you as nothing. And if you have labored in the Torah, [the Torah] has a great reward to give you."

Torah-study competes with, rather than replaces, economic activity. That is the simple position of tractate Abot, extending the conception of matters explicit in the Mishnah. If I had to make a simple statement of the situation prevailing at ca. 250 C.E., sages contrast their wealth, which is spiritual and intellectual, with material wealth; they do not deem the one to form the counterpart of the other, but only the opposite.

VI. *Wealth, Material, and Spiritual: Real Estate versus Torah*

The rational disposition of scarce resources forms a chapter of culture, which defines what is rational and determines therefore what constitute scarce resources. If we wish to construct a contrast between Torah and culture, then, we should do so by pointing to a choice between Torah and other valued things and by contrasting two rationalities, that of the Torah and that of other things that people value. Here we have a story that sets the value of Torah into opposition with the value of real estate, which in antiquity was deemed the preferred form of wealth. To be sure, the tale carries forward the view that a man should study Torah to the exclusion of all else, and that action secures his material needs as well. But the conflict between Torah and culture is expressed in more explicit ways here. Wealth in the form of real estate and income derived therefrom, which conventionally defined a secure investment in antiquity, conflict with the value of Torah-study, the source of supernatural riches. So the conflict is between two rationalities, two definitions of what constitute scarce resources. But there is a twist, which I shall point out (Leviticus Rabbah 34:6):

> B. R. Tarfon gave to R. Aqiba six silver *centenarii*, saying to him, "Go, buy us a piece of land, so we can get a living from it and labor in the study of Torah together."
> C. He took the money and handed it over to scribes, Mishnah-teachers, and those who study Torah.
> D. After some time R. Tarfon met him and said to him, "Did you buy the land that I mentioned to you?"
> E. He said to him, "Yes."
> F. He said to him, "Is it any good?"
> G. He said to him, "Yes."
> H. He said to him, "And do you not want to show it to me?"
> I. He took him and showed him the scribes, Mishnah teachers, and people who were studying Torah, and the Torah that they had acquired.
> J. He said to him, "Is there anyone who works for nothing? Where is the deed covering the field?"
> K. He said to him, "It is with King David, concerning whom it is written, 'He has scattered, he has given to the poor, his righteousness endures forever' (Ps. 112:9)."

Instead of defining wealth as land, this story defines land as not-wealth, and something else is now defined as wealth in its place. It would be hard to find a more precise analogy to the antinomy, Christ versus culture, as framed in the Christian monastic tradition, than the very practical counsel attributed to Aqiba.

The transformation from real estate to Torah is made explicit when we are told how we turn real estate into Torah. That transvaluation is worked out, once more quite explicitly, in the statement (Y. Meg. 4:1.

IV.P-Q): "'I can write the whole Torah for two hundred copper coins.' What did he do, he went and bought flax seed worth two hundred copper coins, sowed it, reaped it, made it into ropes, caught a deer, and wrote the entire Torah on the deer hide." The three operative components here are money (capital) converted into land converted into (a) Torah. In context, the ambient culture comes to expression in the definition of real wealth. In the world at large, as I said, that was real estate. So we transform money into land. But then the definition of wealth is shifted, and the symbolic shift is blatant: turn money into real wealth, then real wealth produces the wherewithal of making a Torah. And with that rather stunning symbolic transformation, we find ourselves in a world wholly different from the one in which scarce resources are identified with matters of material, palpable value, and in which economics is the theory of the rational disposition of scarce resources of capital, labor, movables, real estate, and the like. Now Torah is opposed to the regnant rationality of worth, which is real estate, and Torah stands in judgment of real wealth.

Why do I insist on an antimony between Torah and culture, comparable to that between Christ and culture versus Christ vs. culture? The reason is that there are passages that are quite explicit: land is wealth, or Torah is wealth, but not both; owning land is power and studying Torah permits (re)gaining power—but not both. To take the first of the two propositions in its most explicit formulation (Leviticus Rabbah 31:1):

4.
   A. R. Yohanan was going up from Tiberias to Sepphoris. R. Hiyya bar Abba was supporting him. They came to a field. [Yohanan] said, "This field once belonged to me, but I sold it in order to acquire merit in the Torah."
   B. They came to a vineyard, and he said, "This vineyard once belonged to me, but I sold it in order to acquire merit in the Torah."
   C. They came to an olive grove, and he said, "This olive grove once belonged to me, but I sold it in order to acquire merit in the Torah."
   D. R. Hiyya began to cry.
   E. Said R. Yohanan, "Why are you crying?"
   F. He said to him, "It is because you left nothing over to support you in your old age."
   G. He said to him, "Hiyya, my disciple, is what I did such a light thing in your view? I sold something which was given in a spell of six days [of creation] and in exchange I acquired something which was given in a spell of forty days [of revelation].

H. "The entire world and everything in it was created in only six days, as it is written, 'For in six days the Lord made heaven and earth' [Exod. 20:11].

I. "But the Torah was given over a period of forty days, as it was said, 'And he was there with the Lord for forty days and forty nights' [Exod. 34:28].

J. "And it is written, 'And I remained on the mountain for forty days and forty nights' (Deut. 9:9)."

5.
A. When R. Yohanan died, his generation recited concerning him [the following verse of Scripture]: "If a man should give all the wealth of his house for the love" (Song 8:7), with which R. Yohanan loved the Torah, "he would be utterly destitute" (Song 8:7). . . .

C. When R. Eleazar b. R. Simeon died, his generation recited concerning him [the following verse of Scripture]: "Who is this who comes up out of the wilderness like pillars of smoke, perfumed with myrrh and frankincense, with all the powders of the merchant?" (Song 3:6).

D. What is the meaning of the clause, "With all the powders of the merchant"?

E. [Like a merchant who carries all sorts of desired powders,] he was a master of Scripture, a repeater of Mishnah traditions, a writer of liturgical supplications, and a liturgical poet.

The sale of land for the acquisition of "merit in the Torah" introduces two principal systemic components, merit and Torah.[4] For our purpose, the importance of the statement lies in the second of the two, which deems land the counterpart—and clearly the opposite—of Torah.

Now one can sell a field and acquire "Torah," meaning, in the context established by the exchange between Tarfon and Aqiba, the opportunity to gain leisure to study Torah. That the sage has left himself nothing for his support in old age makes explicit the material meaning of the statement, and the comparison of the value of land, created in six days, and the Torah, created in forty days, is equally explicit. The comparison of knowledge of Torah to the merchandise of the merchant simply repeats the same point, but in a lower register. So too does the this-worldly power of study of the

---

[4] In a well-crafted system, of course, principal parts prove interchangeable or closely aligned, and that is surely the case here. But the successor-system is far more tightly constructed than the initial one, in that the politics and the economics flow into one another, in a way in which, in the initial, philosophical system, they do not. The disembedded character of the Mishnah's economics has already impressed us.

Torah make explicit in another framework the conviction that study of the Torah yields material and concrete benefit, not just spiritual renewal. Thus R. Huna states (Pesiqta deRab Kahana VI:III.3.B), "All of the exiles will be gathered together only on account of the study of Mishnah-teachings."

I portray the opposition as a matter of culture, expressed through economic theory. But the conflict between Torah-study and all else cuts to the bone. For the ultimate value—Torah-study—surely bears comparison with other foci of value, such as prayer, using money for building synagogues, and the like. It is explicitly stated that spending money on synagogues is a waste of money, while spending money supporting Torah-masters is the right use of scarce resources. Further, we find the claim, synagogues and school houses—communal real estate—in fact form the property of sages and their disciples, who may dispose of them just as they want, as any owner may dispose of his property according to his unfettered will. In Y. Sheqalim we find the former allegation, Y. Megillah the latter:

> Y. Sheqalim 5:4.II:
> A. R. Hama bar Haninah and R. Hoshaia the Elder were strolling in the synagogues in Lud. Said R. Hama bar Haninah to R. Hoshaia, "How much money did my forefathers invest here [in building these synagogues]!"
> B. He said to him, "How many lives did your forefathers invest here! Were there not people who were laboring in Torah [who needed the money more]?"
> C. R. Abun made the gates of the great hall [of study]. R. Mana came to him. He said to him, "See what I have made!"
> D. He said to him, "'For Israel has forgotten his Maker and built palaces'! (Hos. 8:14). Were there no people laboring in Torah [who needed the money more]?"
>
> Y. Sotah 9:13.VI:
> C. A certain rabbi would teach Scripture to his brother in Tyre, and when they came and called him to do business, he would say, "I am not going to take away from my fixed time to study. If the profit is going to come to me, let it come in due course [after my fixed time for study has ended]."
>
> Y. Megillah 3:3.V:
> A. R. Joshua b. Levi said, "Synagogues and schoolhouses belong to sages and their disciples."
> B. R. Hiyya bar Yose received [guests] in the synagogue [and lodged them there].
> C. R. Immi instructed the scribes, "If someone comes to you with some slight contact with Torah learning, receive him, his asses, and his belongings."

D. R. Berekhiah went to the synagogue in Beisan. He saw someone rinsing his hands and feet in a fountain [in the courtyard of the synagogue]. He said to him, "It is forbidden to you [to do this]."
E. The next day the man saw [Berekhiah] washing his hands and feet in the fountain.
F. He said to him, "Rabbi, is it permitted to you and forbidden to me?"
G. He said to him, "Yes."
H. He said to him, "Why?"
I. He said to him, "Because this is what R. Joshua b. Levi said: 'Synagogues and schoolhouses belong to sages and their disciples.'"

Not all acts of piety, we see, are equal, and the one that takes precedence over all others (just as is alleged at M. Peah 1:1) is study of the Torah. But the point now is a much more concrete one, and that is, through study of the Torah, sages and their disciples gain possession, as a matter of fact, over communal real estate, which they may utilize in any way they wish; and that is a quite concrete claim indeed, as the same story alleges.

No wonder, then, that people in general are expected to contribute their scarce resources for the support of sages and their disciples. Moreover, society at large was obligated to support sages, and the sages' claim upon others was enforceable by Heaven. Those who gave sages' disciples money so that they would not have to work would get it back from Heaven, and those who did not would lose what they had as Y. Sotah 7:4.IV makes clear:

F. R. Aha in the name of R. Tanhum b. R. Hiyya: "If one has learned, taught, kept, and carried out [the Torah], and has ample means in his possession to strengthen the Torah and has not done so, lo, such a one still is in the category of those who are cursed." [The meaning of "strengthen" here is to support the masters of the Torah.]
G. R. Jeremiah in the name of R. Hiyya bar Ba, "[If] one did not learn, teach, keep, and carry out [the teachings of the Torah], and did not have ample means to strengthen [the masters of the Torah] [but nonetheless did strengthen them], lo, such a one falls into the category of those who are blessed."
H. And R. Hannah, R. Jeremiah in the name of R. Hiyya: "The Holy One, blessed be he, is going to prepare a protection for those who carry out religious duties [of support for masters of Torah] through the protection afforded to the masters of Torah [themselves].
I. "What is the Scriptural basis for that statement? 'For the protection of wisdom is like the protection of money'" (Ecc. 7:12).
J. "And it says, '[The Torah] is a tree of life to those who grasp it; those who hold it fast are called happy'" (Prov. 3:18).

Such contributions form the counterpart to taxes, that is, scarce resources taken away from the owner by force for the purposes of the public good, that is, the ultimate meeting point of economics and politics, the explicit formation of distributive, as against market, economics. Then what is distributed and to whom and by what force forms the centerpiece of the systemic political economy, and the answer is perfectly simple: all sorts of valued things are taken away from people and handed over for the support of sages.

That extends to freeing sages from the obligation to pay taxes, e.g., for the defense of the city. I cannot imagine a more extreme claim than to say that not walls but sages and their Torah-study form the strongest defense for the city. Therefore sages should not have to pay for the upkeep of the common defense. Since people took for granted that walls were the best defense, Torah here confronts the common culture with its uncommon claim.

So it is alleged that sages are the guardians of cities, and later on that would yield the further allegation that sages do not have to pay taxes to build walls around cities, since their Torah-study protects the cities (Pesiqta deRab Kahana XV:V.1):

1.
   A. R. Abba bar Kahana commenced discourse by citing the following verse: "Who is the man so wise that he may understand this? To whom has the mouth of the Lord spoken, that he may declare it? Why is the land ruined and laid waste like a wilderness, [so that no one passes through?' The Lord said, It is because they forsook my Torah which I set before them; they neither obeyed me nor conformed to it. They followed the promptings of their own stubborn hearts, they followed the Baalim as their forefathers had taught them. Therefore these are the words of the Lord of Hosts the God of Israel: I will feed this people with wormwood and give them bitter poison to drink. I will scatter them among nations whom neither they nor their forefathers have known; I will harry them with the sword until I have made an end of them] (Jer. 9:16)."
   B. It was taught in the name of R. Simeon b. Yohai, "If you see towns uprooted from their place in the land of Israel, know that [it is because] the people did not pay the salaries of teachers of children and Mishnah-instructors.
   C. "What is the verse of Scripture that indicates it? 'Why is the land ruined and laid waste like a wilderness, [so that no one passes through?'] What is written just following? 'It is because they forsook my Torah [which I set before them; they neither obeyed me nor conformed to it.]'"

2.
A. Rabbi sent R. Yose and R. Ammi to go and survey the towns of the land of Israel. They would go into a town and say to the people, "Bring me the guardians of the town."
B. The people would bring out the head of the police and the local guard.
C. [The sages] would say, "These are not the guardians of the town, they are those who destroy the town. Who are the guardians of the town? They are the teachers of children and Mishnah-teachers, who keep watch by day and by night, in line with the verse, 'And you shall meditate in it day and night' (Josh. 1:8)."
D. And so Scripture says, "If the Lord does not build the house, in vain the builders labor" (Ps. 127:1).

7.
A. Said R. Abba bar Kahana, "No philosophers in the world ever arose of the quality of Balaam b. Beor and Abdymos of Gadara. The nations of the world came to Abnymos of Gadara. They said to him, 'Do you maintain that we can make war against this nation?'
B. "He said to them, 'Go and make the rounds of their synagogues and their study houses. So long as there are there children chirping out loud in their voices [and studying the Torah], then you cannot overcome them. If not, then you can conquer them, for so did their father promise them: 'The voice is Jacob's voice' (Gen. 27:22), meaning that when Jacob's voice chirps in synagogues and study houses, The hands are not the hands of Esau [so Esau has no power].
C. "'So long as there are no children chirping out loud in their voices [and studying the Torah] in synagogues and study houses, The hands are the hands of Esau [so Esau has power].'"

The reference to Esau, that is, Rome, of course links the whole to the contemporary context and alleges that if the Israelites will support those who study the Torah and teach it, then their cities will be safe, and, still more, the rule of Esau/Rome will come to an end; then the Messiah will come, so the stakes are not trivial. That claim, contrary to the intuited givens of the common culture, places Torah over against that culture, and does so in an extreme manner.

What we see are two distinct positions, Torah-study within the framework of the culture of economics, Torah-study as against the culture of conventional economics. There is no harmonizing the two. Economics deals with scarce resources, and the disenlandisement of economics has turned upon its head the very focus of economics: scarcity and the rational way of disposing of what is scarce. To land rigid limits are set by nature, to the Holy Land, still more narrow ones apply. But to knowledge of the Torah no limits pertain. So we find ourselves dealing with an economics that concern not the rational utilization of scarce resources, but the very opposite: the rational utilization of what can and ought to be the opposite of scarce. In identifying knowledge and teaching of the Torah as the ultimate value, the successor-system has not simply constructed a new economics in place of an old one, finding of value something other than had earlier been valued; it has redefined economics altogether. It has done so, as a matter of fact, in a manner that is entirely familiar, by setting forth in place of an economics of scarcity an economics of abundant productivity. Disenlandising value thus transvalues value by insisting upon its (potential) increase as the definition of what is rational economic action. The task is not preservation of power over land but increase of power over the Torah, because one can only preserve land, but one can increase one's knowledge of the Torah.

VII. *The Harmony of Torah and Culture*

So much for the position that recognizes only conflict between Torah and culture. Is there no view that finds culture in the Torah, that identifies the Torah as the source of culture? Just as Niebuhr is able to show how the several positions on the relationship of Christ and culture inhere within the logic of Christian theology and its dialectics, so I can show how the identification of Torah and culture comes to expression in the same documents as contain the opposite theory of matters. The aspect of culture that is identical to Torah is what we should call natural science. The Torah is represented as fully realized by the creation of the world, so that, by extension, the study of creation carries us deep into the mysteries of the Torah as the record of creation. This view I find in a classic, famous passage, Genesis Rabbah I:I, which alleges in so many words that God created the world by looking into the Torah. Then creation comes about by reference to the design set forth in the Torah. That bears the message: creation forms a guide to the fullness of the Torah, and all natural science forms a chapter in the revelation of the Torah that creation realizes. No. 2 below states that proposition in so many words:

    1.
        A. "In the beginning God created" (Gen. 1:1):
        B. R. Oshaia commenced [discourse by citing the following verse:] "'Then I was beside him like a little child, and I was daily his

delight [rejoicing before him always, rejoicing in his inhabited world, and delighting in the sons of men]' (Prov. 8:30-31).
C. "The word for 'child' uses consonants that may also stand for 'teacher,' 'covered over,' and 'hidden away.'
D. "Some hold that the word also means 'great.'
E. "The word means 'teacher,' in line with the following: 'As a teacher carries the suckling child' (Num. 11:12).
F. "The word means 'covered over,' as in the following: 'Those who were covered over in scarlet' (Lam. 4:5).
G. "The word means 'hidden,' as in the verse, 'And he hid Hadassah' (Est. 2:7).
H. "The word means 'great,' in line with the verse, 'Are you better than No-Ammon?' (Nah. 3:8). This we translate, 'Are you better than Alexandria the Great, which is located between rivers.'"

2.
A. Another matter:
B. The word [for child] in fact means "workman."
C. [In the cited verse] the Torah speaks, "I was the work-plan of the Holy One, blessed be He."
D. In the accepted practice of the world, when a mortal king builds a palace, he does not build it out of his own head, but he follows a work-plan.
E. And [the one who supplies] the work-plan does not build out of his own head, but he has designs and diagrams, so as to know how to situate the rooms and the doorways.
F. Thus the Holy One, blessed be He, consulted the Torah when He created the world.
G. So the Torah stated, "By means of 'the beginning' [that is to say, the Torah] did God create . . ." (Gen. 1:1).
H. And the word for "beginning" refers only to the Torah, as Scripture says, "The Lord made me as the beginning of his way" (Prov. 8:22).

The matter is explicit: the Torah forms the key to the creation of the world, and, working back from nature to the Torah, man penetrates the mysteries of the Torah by investigating the traits and properties of nature. Botany, biology, physics, chemistry—these form media of revelation of God's plan and will, as much as does the Torah in its specific formulation. Here in the terms of Niebuhr's typology, Torah forms a harmonious union with culture. In that capacious vision, one cannot distinguish secular from sacred science, for all learning, all chapters of culture, embody God's plan and program for creation, which to be sure comes to its most authentic expression in the words of the Torah itself.

VIII. *Why the Persistence of the Dialectics?*

If I have succeeded in showing how, within its native category-formations and language, Judaism struggles with the dialectic of the relationship of religion and culture just as does Christianity, I also have to ask, why does this particular dialectics characterize both religious traditions? The answer cannot derive from the history of the two traditions, since the several possible positions do not emerge in temporal order or sequence. From the very beginning to contemporary times, the relationship of Christ and culture has come to expression within a range of models not bound to a particular circumstance or occasion. And along these same lines, in ancient, medieval, and modern times the issues of Torah and culture have come to expression, the details subject to variation, but the main point always the same. As Niebuhr lays matters out, the inner logic of Christianity persistently counterpoises religion and "the world," or "culture," and explores the two possible relationships, harmony and opposition, and the intermediary ones as well. And as I see matters, Rabbinic Judaism concurs on the issue and its resolution.

If I had to hazard a guess on what consistently generates the binary opposites, I should point to the conception of God characteristic of both monotheisms: immanent and transcendent, both with us and wholly other. The same God who makes himself known and hides his face, who shelters his prophet in the cleft of the rock as his glory goes by, is the God who is both at home in humanity and different from humanity. In that setting, why should culture differ? Culture both embodies the faith, reminiscent of God's immanence in the world, and is contradicted by it, recalling God's transcendence over the world. It is hardly surprising, then, that culture is to be abandoned by the faithful and also to be shaped as their primary medium. The generative theology not only sustains but precipitates the dialectics that comes to expression, too, in the conception of Torah as part of culture and separate from culture, why some Yeshiva-masters counsel studying mathematics and astrophysics along with Torah, and many do; and advise studying only Torah, and many more do.

That is what I learn upon rereading *Christ and Culture* fifty years after my first encounter with that exemplary framing of the fundamental issues of Judaic existence, too.

FIVE TYPES OF JUDAISM?
REFLECTIONS ON THE INNER LOGIC
OF JUDAISM AS REVEALED BY NIEBUHR'S
PHENOMENOLOGICAL TYPOLOGY*

Evan M. Zuesse

H. Richard Niebuhr's *Christ and Culture* is a remarkable work, a kind of summing-up, in 1949, of many decades of theological reflection, by one of the leading Christian thinkers of the last century (Niebuhr lived from 1894 to 1962).[1] It takes the form of a brilliant phenomenological assessment of what it calls the five basic and recurring types of Christianity, analyzing each in terms of its relationship to wider culture and society. Each type is discussed with a sympathetic but also critical balance, in an unpretentious style, clearly reflecting a life-time of reading and reflection on Niebuhr's own religious tradition and his dialogues with other Christian theologians. One does not have to share the author's religion or theoretical assumptions, nor even his specific conclusions, to admire the learning and wisdom of his observations.

As Jacob Neusner remarks, Niebuhr's overview calls out for a similar reflection on Judaism. But this immediately evokes some caveats, too. I have been asked to comment as a phenomenologist on Neusner's account of the Rabbinic evidence, not Niebuhr's theory itself. However, Niebuhr's study is naturally a deeply Christian work. This is so not merely in its explicit affirmations and sympathies but also in its founding definitions and implicit assumptions, the things it takes for granted and hardly discusses at all. Just these things may lead us astray if we wish to apply Niebuhr's schema to other religions, so I am forced to consider certain of Niebuhr's own claims before going on to apply them to the Jewish evidence.

---

* Reprinted from *Review of Rabbinic Judaism* 5:3, 2002, pp. 430–451.
[1] H. Richard Niebuhr, *Christ and Culture* (London: Faber and Faber, Ltd., n.d.), reproducing in expanded form the series of lectures the author gave at Austin Presbyterian Theological Seminary, Austin, Texas, in January, 1949. All page references in the text below are to this first edition.

As so often when dealing with Christian thinkers, how Judaism is treated in Niebuhr's book takes us quickly to the heart of the matter, giving crucial clues to some of the basic problems with his general analysis even of Christianity itself. This essay will therefore first briefly discuss some of the problems with Niebuhr's conception of Judaism, which reflect and even are sources of his basic definitions of religion and culture, so as to liberate us for a more fruitful modification and application of his phenomenological typology to Judaism.

Redefining Judaism and Therefore "Culture"

According to Niebuhr, the basic antithesis of "Christ" and "Culture" was established by Jesus in his confrontation with Jewish culture (p. 18). For support, Niebuhr quotes the Jewish scholar Joseph Klausner's assertions that while Jesus was a product of Jewish culture and said nothing that cannot be found elsewhere in Jewish writings, nevertheless he "imperiled Jewish civilization" by his otherworldly conception of the Kingdom of God and "by abstracting religion and ethics from the rest of social life" (loc. cit.). As Niebuhr cites Klausner, "Jesus came and thrust aside all the requirements of the national life" (p. 19): instead of reforming society he ignored it or sought to abolish the connection between religion and national culture. Instances of this are Jesus' refusal to judge adulterers, prohibition on divorce, praise of celibates, and even advocacy of the "toilless life exemplified by birds and lilies" (loc. cit.). Since Judaism is "a national religion," in which religion and culture are identified, Jews inevitably rejected Jesus, according to Klausner and Niebuhr (pp. 19, 20, 54). If Niebuhr has any reservations about the simple either-ors of Klausner he does not expand on them but moves on to Christian ambivalent relations with pagan cultures.

In a later discussion of Paul, Niebuhr asserts that "all cultural institutions were relativized" for the Apostle,

> including trust in the Torah, whether it stressed ritual observances or the keeping of ethical laws. Both the knowledge that found its basis in reason, and the one that looked to revelation for its foundation, were equally remote from the knowledge of the glory of God in the face of Jesus Christ. Christ destroyed the wisdom of the wise and the righteousness of the good, which had rejected him in different ways but to the same degree (p. 165).

So it appears that Christ, as authentically experienced through Paul, did not trust the Torah and destroyed the revelatory path it delineated: all that was merely human wisdom and goodness, far from true knowledge of God. Other quotes confirm this conclusion, that for Niebuhr "Judaism" and Torah itself are a "culture" which are essentially like the other cultures "Christ" relativizes.

To all this one may pose a number of objections, both historical and theoretical. First, contrary to Niebuhr and the source he has chosen to cite, Klausner, the Jews did not reject Jesus, and Jesus did not imperil Jewish culture. The crucifixion was a Roman punishment, and Caiaphas a Roman appointee subordinate to Pontius Pilate. The Gospels got the Romans off the hook by shifting the blame to Jewish authorities generally or simply to "the Jews." Furthermore, the actual historical Jesus (so far as we can discover him from the Gospels) championed Jewish culture and religion: he is quoted repeatedly as explicitly endorsing both Moses's and Pharisaic authority even in the midst of criticizing Pharisaic behaviors (Matt. 23:1-3, Luke 11:42), and as insisting that because the Torah was God's revelation, total obedience to its commandments was obligatory (Matt. 5:17-19, 23:23, also Matt. 19:17, Lk. 16:17, 18:18ff., Mark 10:17ff.). We certainly know that Jesus' most devoted and knowledgeable immediate disciples continued on undeviatingly as a thoroughly Jewish and even Pharisaic sect in Jerusalem under James, Jesus' brother. The supposed tension between Jesus and Jews/Judaism is an artifact of Paulinian theology and the gentile Christian church, polemically written into the Gospels by a later generation.

This is not merely a historical matter. If Jesus was not opposed to Torah, and *expressed* Jewish culture, it affects our understanding of what "culture" means as well, forcing us to reconceptualize both poles in the Christ-Culture antithesis.

A second major objection is that Torah Judaism is not merely to be defined as "culture." There have in fact been many different Jewish cultures that have held fast to the Torah and its God as their transcendental center, both within Rabbinic Judaism's at least two thousand year history and outside it, e.g., as Biblical Judaism, Ethiopian Judaism, or Karaite Judaism.[2] Torah, as God-given revelation or just

---

[2] For a clarification of the distinctions between Torah as "normative Judaism" and the various historical cultures that stem from it, see my article "Phenomenology of Judaism" in Jacob Neusner, Alan J. Avery-Peck, and William S. Green, eds., *The Encyclopaedia of Judaism* (second edition, Leiden and Boston, 2005), vol. 3, pp. 1968–1986.

as archetypal Judaism, presents itself as apart from culture as human artifice; Sinai stands over against the Tower of Babel. It therefore more properly belongs on the same side of the polarity that Niebuhr puts "Christ." It actually is striking that Niebuhr completely overlooks that if there is any prophetic culture-critical and reformist element in Christianity at all, it is entirely due to Judaism, where culture-critical prophetic consciousness is clearly part of the Sinai revelation as described in the Mosaic Torah, creating an outlook that has persisted to the present time. Ethical and social criticism, including criticism of "us," is one of the most salient Jewish cultural traits even today. From a Jewish perspective, that prophetic reformist consciousness has if anything been radically weakened in its Christian versions (see below). When we phrase things this way, we discover that there has been a long history of tension between Torah and culture that can be sorted into the very same general fivefold typology that Niebuhr posits for Christ and culture. As Neusner remarks, Torah covers a partly different range of phenomena than does "Christ" (and so does "Culture"), and this is inevitable since Judaism and Christianity are quite different religions.

Or if we redefine "culture" to include Torah, so as to accept as much as possible of Niebuhr's definitions, we must do just the same with "Christ." After all, all human affairs occur within the medium of culture more broadly understood, even our internal monologues, for culture shapes even the development and specific shape of infants' nervous systems just as particular types of socialized activities shape the outward body into a human body rather than a four-footed "wolf-child." Put bluntly, the nature of human nature is to be cultural. Even our most "private" self-identity is constructed from our earliest history of encounters with specific others. Jesus as a human being, and "Christ" as a concept or faith-experience, are both socio-cultural constructions. They are constituted by and cannot exist without those contexts. To eliminate culture from them would simply cancel them out.

Thirdly, these remarks force us inexorably to a redefinition of "culture." Niebuhr's definition is quoted by Neusner in his article. Niebuhr begins by insisting that "culture is the 'artificial, secondary environment' which man superimposes on the natural" (p. 46, in my edition). We have seen that this attempted dichotomy is superficial. The division between "artificial" and "natural," "secondary" and primary, is itself artificial and secondary and serves what it supposedly leads to, the division of "Christ" and "Culture." Seen more closely, culture is variously sensed by us as something "natural" ("Everybody does that; everybody thinks like that!") and something "idealistic," imposed or unnatural ("To sacrifice yourself for your country is heroic"), so "natural" and "artificial" intertwine and can even change places, but both are essential parts of human nature and society. In any case Niebuhr goes on to characterize his externalized and secondary "culture" as "always social," by which he means involving permanent social groupings, as "human achievement," and as expressive of "values" oriented to human benefit. So culture is concerned with "the temporal and material realization of values" (p. 50). Note the materialistic and deflationary implications of this definition, so as to remove spiritual or idealistic elements from it.

But at least we can build on the hints in Niebuhr's definition that culture has both descriptive and prescriptive aspects, and acknowledge that it describes the entire world of human beings, shaping and valuing all significant items, processes and ideas in that world, and prescribing how those things should be actualized. There is both "is" and "ought" in culture. Furthermore, every culture recognizes diverse gradations in the range of applicability of cultural values: some values are merely etiquette, others matters of ultimate good or evil, so they differ in intensity and obligatoriness. In general we can distinguish the cultural sphere that chiefly relates to the individual and to personal life-style, another one that involves wider social practices and values of the local group or regional society, while the broadest applies to all proper human beings or the entire universe. As is evident even from this, the "oughts" of culture are diverse and often conflicting, as when warrior values conflict with family obligations. Religion, in this reading of "Culture," must be seen as that sphere that specifically engages with ultimate and source realities, which describes basic cosmic and social structures and orders the widest range of values and the most binding "oughts." But even here there are bound to be conflicts both internally and with other cultural values or priorities. Even religious ideals can clash with each other.

So there will always be a multiform tension between ideality and reality in every culture—this is the human condition—and the fivefold resolution of this tension that Niebuhr spells out for Christianity can probably be found, in one way or another, not only in Judaism but in most other cultures and religions. They can be identified, for example, also in the pagan Greek and Roman culture Christianity confronted. Even more pointedly, many of the characteristic forms of the Christian response were basically indebted to their pagan antecedents, especially where the Christian model deviated from the Jewish one. The very ideas that the "spiritual" was antithetical to the "material," and that salvation was solely otherworldly and personal, that we must either patiently endure the cruelties of this world or opt out of it entirely, were pagan ideas. The worldly indifferent "spiritual" option was deeply shaped by neo-Platonism. Outright monasticism and institutional world-rejection drew on pagan ascetical cults and practices. The somewhat more positive Stoic indifferentism was formative for Church ethics and politics. And so on. So the five-fold Christian response to pagan "Culture" turns out in significant part to reflect a complex pagan cultural universe that itself had five-fold responses to culture.

However, even if the five types can be found in most religions, each religion will no doubt have its own characteristic emphases and unique forms of these types, emphasizing as more "typical" and elaborately articulated one or another of those possibilities, and perhaps leaving less "typical" forms disvalued or in merely vestigial condition. It will even define each type differently. For example, essential aspects of the prophetic element that was and is still so crucial to Judaism seem weaker or missing entirely from the mainstream forms of Christianity, even though that religion is so indebted to Judaism and claims solely to continue the prophetic emphasis. This weakness did not only come from the triumphalism of the basic Christian claim to have completed religious history, and to constitute the perfected Israel and messianic kingdom. It was even more the result of a redefinition of basic concepts. For biblical prophecy did not base itself on the separation of the supernatural and salvific "spiritual" from the natural sinful "worldly" that justified the separation in Catholicism and Eastern Orthodoxy of "church" and "state" or that underlay the distinction in Lutheranism between inward faith and outward works. Quite the opposite, prophecy focused on the imperative penetration of society by Torah teachings, first, by the abolition of idolatry, and then even more importantly by the actual conformation of the whole society to the full sweep of the commandments of everyday life, justice and mercy. A thoroughly revamped society was the goal. This was the definitive task of "the

Children of Israel" as an actual people and nation seeking the Kingdom of God. The new Christian community opposed to this its own claim to be a non-national "Spiritual Israel," effectively a cult claiming perfectionism but in fact accepting in non-prophetic fashion a wide variety of societies and moral-social practices, traits which made it attractive to Roman emperors seeking to unify their disintegrating realm. The continuance of gladiatorial games in the Roman Empire for centuries after that empire became Christian, the medieval "divine right" of cruelly oppressive despots to rule, or both the Catholic and the Lutheran teachings about the state and society that so crippled those churches' response to Nazism, will serve to illustrate the point.

As these instances suggest, it is largely because a downplaying of the imperative prophetic integration of religion and society (reflecting the basic repudiation of the commandments as "the Law" that Christ allegedly overcame and supplanted), that mainstream Christianity, whether Catholic, Orthodox or Lutheran, has seen a gulf between Christ and secular culture, between Church and ordinary society. This gulf was then conceptualized into Hellenistic ontological antinomies, essentially opposed spheres, along the lines of "spirit" versus "flesh." Judaism both in spiritual doctrine and in political theory characteristically differs in stressing process and interconnectedness rather than ontological opposites. It bridged together spirit and flesh, Torah and secular society, heaven and earth and sacred and profane, with "the Law." The mutuality of all these things was established by harmoniously differentiated action, modes of sanctification. This, when constantly repeated, built up a universe of dynamic gradations and holy transformations of ordinariness. The central role of the commandments in all this, and their orientation to an entire people and society, cannot be ignored. The prophetic imperative is condensed into the commandments. This is the heart of the Torah message.

A basic struggle with non-Torah-centered culture went on for centuries in Jewish religious history, and according to tradition only the reforms associated with Ezra and Nehemiah finally achieved the "circumcision of the heart" that was the prophetic goal, namely the enduring transformation of everyday Jewish community and domestic life into Torah life. By the Roman period, the Rabbis could even assume as common knowledge that idolatry had been extirpated among Jews, certainly at any rate in Judea (e.g., B. Yom. 9b).[3] As a consequence, the Jewish version of Niebuhr's five types would henceforth be significantly different from the Christian version.

The Five Types When Applied to Judaism

That being said, let us apply Niebuhr's categories to the tensions between Torah and culture. I understand the five different ways of relating Christ/Torah and culture, according to Niebuhr's schema, as follows:

1. Opposition: the either-or
2. Fundamental agreement, in which Christ/Torah is the apex of a single cultural system, one in which cultural mores and ideals are indistinguishable from "real" Christianity/Judaism, and culture has the final word.
3. Participation but also transcendence: Christ/Torah fulfills culture but is above and outside of it, sits in judgment on it.
4. Christ/Torah and culture are opposites, both of which are needed. Each should be kept apart, but affirming the other. Thus one should support the laws and institutions of general society, and be in but not of that society. "Hence man is seen as subject to two moralities and as a citizen of two worlds that are not only discontinuous with each other but largely opposed."
5. Christ/Torah and culture are opposites, and culture must be ceaselessly brought into submission to Christ/Torah: the evangelical option.

The Christian examples of each position are: 1, monasticism, but also the separatist sect; 2. the worldly church or Christ as a conservative Christian gentleman or secular liberal; 3. Aquinas; 4. Luther; 5. Calvin.

Niebuhr tends to view each of these types in terms of a static, even ontological configuration, in harmony with the Christian tendency to ontological thinking and because the prophetic force of "the Law" which bridges Christ and Culture has been so suppressed. But in the Jewish case, the prophetic imperative is clearly the burning heart

---

[3] Cf., George Foote Moore, *Judaism* (Cambridge, 1966), vol. 1, pp. 363f., with the notes thereto.

and motor animating the types and bridging their poles of Torah and Culture, and we easily see that the types are actually different versions of the same dynamic, depending on circumstances. The types are on a continuum of transformations. This is true also for the Christian versions.

Type 5 is most obviously prophetic, although culture need not be termed religion's "opposite" if it is brought into conformity to revealed norms. In that case, in fact, after Type 5 advocates have successfully reformed society at least basically, some of those advocates might well move to Type 3 attitudes. On the other hand, and interestingly, if a prophetically oriented group is thwarted from actualizing norms within the wider society, it might well be motivated to create its own separate society, as for example the early Calvinists did in Geneva, a move that would place it in the sectarian separatist Type 1 category. (In effect, then, monastic asceticism, which rejects natural bodily and social life as such, and sectarian communities which seek to recreate natural and social life in restricted scale, are probably wrongly lumped together in Type 1: they are very different phenomena and probably should be separated, with sectarianism labeled Type 6.) So from a prophetically oriented point of view, the only types that would seem to be unacceptable would be the ascetical form of Type 1, since it explicitly rejects ordinary human life and society as such, Type 2, in which revelation takes second place to secular culture, and Type 4, in which revealed religion and secular culture are kept apart but still actually affirm each other, producing two moralities, not one. We would expect these to be atypical and de-emphasized in the history of the Jewish religion, and they are.

Neusner's analysis almost immediately demonstrates both the similarities and the differences between the Christian form of the "Five Types" and the Jewish form. He is of course most concerned to demonstrate the similarities, so as to confirm the usefulness of Niebuhr's typological phenomenology for Jewish Studies. And he does show persuasively that by Niebuhr's definitions without modification we can find at least partial versions of Types 1 and 2 in the Rabbinic sources spanning the first three centuries C.E. Type 1 sources insist on separating Torah-centered life from general (Jewish) work-oriented lives. Type 2 may be said to apply to those sages who argue that Torah-study must be integrated into regular work-lives.

So where are the differences? Well, we notice immediately that both "types" are in fact found in the same literature and are thus available in the same social grouping, that is, among the Rabbinic sages themselves. This must already alter fundamentally the Jewish version of both. For the Christian types are focused on personal cultural-spiritual attitudes, each elaborated into a specific social and cultic group, and each justified by distinct theological literatures, producing rival and often warring sects. But as we find them in Rabbinic literature, the types are not so radically opposed, since the society and values they juxtapose to Torah is already a Jewish society that accepts the authority of Torah. Such a society can only endorse Torah observance, and the Torah, in turn, endorses and prescribes for that whole society. So neither full separatism nor monastic asceticism as understood in Niebuhr's Type 1 would be probable options in Rabbinic literature. Denial of marriage and family life, as is well known, is very rare indeed in Jewish religious history. The one sage mentioned in the Talmud who refused to marry because he wanted to devote himself wholly to Torah study (Simeon b. Azzai) is quoted as saying he could not help himself, he so loved Torah study, but he added that in general one who abstained from procreation was as if he shed blood (B. Yeb. 63b). Ben Azzai was admired for his mystical fervor but none of his conclusions could be used for halakhic guidance, thus obviating much of his study (some say he was never ordained as a rabbi, perhaps because he died too young, and he is never described as one of the sages, but rather as a disciple). And on the other hand schism and sectarian separatism were disapproved of by the sages, at least within observant Jewish communities. Hillel is said to have remarked, "Do not separate yourself from the community" (M. Abot 2:5; the "community" in question is traditionally understood to be the community of at least nominally observant Jews, not a community of blatantly idolatrous Jews), and as a matter of fact the very content of Torah study, as pursued by the Tannaitic and Amoraic sages (and as presented in the Torah itself), was how God's commandments applied to the entire Jewish people, creating the forms of Jewish national-religious life ranging from the Temple and state to the home. The different cultural "types" are therefore really different personal cultural lifestyles within a common observant religious community, based upon membership in the people Israel and adherence to a shared Torah. We have to do with different "cultures," but the same Torah and therefore the same society.

But if the actual society is the same, then the real question in dispute between those sages who wish to concentrate on Torah study without working and those who wish to combine the two, is how to position sagely preoccupations within an at least nominally observant Jewish society. The Type 1 adherents who would rather not be diverted from Torah by too much outside work (we note that most of the passages cited by Neusner do not call for the utopian repudiation of all work, just of work that consumes a lot of one's time), are not necessarily saying that general Jewish society or ordinary work-life is degenerate, sinful, or impermissible for truly spiritual persons, as would Christian Type 1 adherents. Nor are Rabbinic Type 2 adherents, for their part, necessarily teaching that sages must accept the primacy of Graeco-Roman secular and assimilatory values, nor even that secular Jewish culture should determine Torah understanding. Far from it. Actually, it can be maintained that the real Types 1 and 2 in Second Commonwealth Judaism are the Qumraners/Essenes and the (Sadducean) Hellenizers, respectively. The Pharisees and certainly their Rabbinic disciples, the Tannaim and Amoraim, predominantly represent other options, strongly repudiating radical sectarianism and its opposite, assimilationism, for more subtle and sophisticated alternatives.

So we need not be surprised that, unlike Christian Type 1, not all the justifications offered by those defined by Neusner as Rabbinic Type 1 adherents turn out to reject ordinary society. Let us take for example the first citation offered by Neusner for a Rabbinic Type 1 outlook, M. B.M. 2:11. Torah masters take precedence over even one's own father in certain circumstances. The instance is given of ransoming captives: "He ransoms his master, and afterward he ransoms his father. But if his father is a sage, he ransoms his father and afterward ransoms his master." The natural relationships and obligations are not set aside, in short, only placed in a graduated scale of obligations. Fathers must still be ransomed: family ties remain valid, important and binding. Other citations show the same insistence on graduated responsibilities or rights, with Torah mastery given primacy even over caste structures: in other words, society should be such that caste distinctions do not sum it up, not even as definitive markers of status, for Torah has supremacy, is open to all and is the justification for any Jewish society at all. Torah crowns the society it brings into being and does not replace it.

A sharper antithesis seems to be implied, however, by some of the passages cited that oppose Torah study to learning a craft and working. Some passages even suggest that Torah study should replace work for a livelihood, because Torah study helps assure personal salvation while mere work or worldly wealth does not. Here there certainly seems a Type 1 outlook, even if it is not representative of the Rabbinic consensus. Behind such passages seems to be the assumption that others—family, local community, wealthy benefactors—will support the students through charity, a Torah value, that the society, in short, is not an absolute antithesis to Torah but rather is the sort of society that would sustain such unworldly Torah scholars.

Not all the cited passages make use of the salvation theme, moreover: at least some reaffirm service to the entire people Israel. For example, at one point Neusner cites a number of *Yerushalmi* passages, and from the *Pesiqta deRab Kahana*, to the effect that in a proper Jewish community Torah scholars and students ought not to have to spend too much time working for a livelihood and ought not to be forced to serve in defense forces nor even to pay taxes, for when they devote most of their time to study and teaching, they assure divine protection for the entire Jewish community. As Neusner summarizes this argument, "If the Israelites will support those who study the Torah and teach it, then their cities will be safe, and still more, the rule of Esau/Rome will come to an end; then the Messiah will come, so the stakes are not trivial. That claim, contrary to the intuited givens of the common culture, places Torah over against that culture, and does so in an extreme manner."

However, the common culture assumed by the cited sages, as already pointed out, is a Jewish one, which is to say it values Torah. The sayings seem to assume furthermore that everyone in this common culture would or should agree that the whole purpose of Jewish societal existence, true Jewish culture, is precisely to sustain Torah values and to live by its guidance, and therefore it is incumbent on all Jews in it to support Torah scholars (and learn from them). Those who study Torah and guide its application exemplify and perfect Jewish culture, and are actually doing this on behalf of all Jews, according to the citations. The Torah itself informs us that humanity was created by God, and then Israel, for this very task. Furthermore, as the cited passages emphasize, God has promised that Israel will flourish only to the degree that it perseveres in actualization of the Torah. The passages therefore signify that Torah scholars crown not only the Jewish people's covenantal task, and more largely Jewish culture rightly understood, and therefore assure

God's blessings for Israel, but they have a more cosmic or universal role, sustaining the hopes of humanity as such for righteousness and peace by bringing about the messianic era.

If this account is correct, then the sayings in question assume that Jewish culture rightly understood is not only not opposed to Torah but is only justified and fulfilled through it. Torah as God's revelation transcends actual Jewish culture, to be sure, but it is at the same time the true guide that orients proper Jewish culture, so there should be a continuity between Torah and Culture. Precisely this is why Jews should make it easier for scholars to study and disseminate Torah, so that Torah learning will act like a leaven in the entire society. All these assumptions and explicit arguments support the conclusion that we probably have to do here with sages visualizing a Type 3 graduated and dynamical interaction of Torah and Culture, not a Type 1 radical opposition. General Jewish society is not at all to be rejected as evil per se. On the contrary it is at least minimally observant and can reasonably be called upon to privilege Torah study by specialists even possibly to the point of painful community self-sacrifice. In fact, this theory of organic interrelatedness and mutuality can in the consensus formulation of Yavneh sages affirm that the worker's role is just as needed and holy as the scholar's, even though they are properly distinct, as long as both direct their heart to heaven (cf., B. Ber. 17a).

The basic paradigm echoes the biblical prophetic role: the prophets were called by God to separate themselves from everyday life and society, some of them even joining wandering bands of ecstatics, for the express purpose of conveying God's word back to everyday Jews and persuading them to reform and renew their society. Separation was followed by re-integration, like Moses spending forty (120!) days up in the mountain but then returning to the B'nai Israel with the Tablets. But the sages cited by Neusner seem to visualize themselves more like an elite near to Moses up the mountain than down among the turbulent people of Israel: they argue for a retiring and quietistic role for the Torah scholar. It is enough to study Torah, raise up disciples, and teach students, thus quietly disseminating Torah observance, and this in itself already fulfills at least something of Israel's God-given role and thereby sustains non-studious, more mundane Jewish society.

The ideas that a Torah-centered life has invisible "priestly" effects rippling in gradations far beyond itself, that "the merit of the righteous" can sustain and inspire the less righteous who cling to them (exemplified in the "shield of Abraham" appealed to in the Amidah-prayer), and that these invisible effects even extend to rectifying the cosmos, are frequently encountered in Rabbinic haggadah. Such ideas seem to give a rationale for the passages in question, which would be otherwise inexplicable. It recalls the justification that some fourth century Palestinian sages offered for the existence of Israel per se: "R. Yudan said: The world was created for the sake of [lit. because of the merit of] the Torah. R. Joshua b. Nehemiah said, for the sake of the tribes of Israel" (Gen. Rabbah 12:9). Or again, "If sand is not put into the lime, the lime will not last. Thus, if it were not for Israel, the gentiles could not last. But for Joseph, the Egyptians would have died of hunger; but for Daniel, the wise men of Babylon would have perished. Though Israel is like dust trampled underfoot, without dust there would be no trees, and no produce from the earth; so if it were not for Israel, the gentiles would not exist, for 'in thy seed shall all the gentiles be blest' (Gen. 22:18)" (Pesiqta Rabbati 45b).

But it is not Israel per se that most powerfully has this role, only Israel when it is righteous. For on a yet more basic level, we read that the universe as a whole is only kept in existence because of the righteous persons in it, e.g., Lev. Rabbah 23:3; B. Yom. 38b, B. Shab. 30b. These statements assume a hierarchical but organic interconnectedness of everything following a Torah pattern woven into the universe, so while every person and group have their appointed tasks, the righteous persons, or Israel as a Torah-centered community, stand forth in a pivotal and unifying role like priests in a temple: they synthesize the world and perfect it, and represent all humanity in elevated state before God. In this way they keep a living bond between God and creation, and thereby maintain the entire universe in existence.

As we can see, the Torah scholar within Jewish society, perhaps even especially if it is a halakhically observant one, or Israel as a priestly people among the nations, can have this engaged role without necessarily doing anything directly in those wider contexts. The engagement can then be defined in mystical and quietistic ways, even if the scholar raises up disciples and teaches other Jews as well. This is a Type 3 mentality. If the engagement goes beyond this and is understood to extend to active political and legislative involvement in wider (Jewish) society to reform its practice (as we certainly do find in the Rabbinic sources), then we have Type 5, the more aggressive "evangelical" option.

If, on the other hand, we have the view that the mores of Jewish society are hostile to Torah values but cannot be changed, so that Torah-observant Jews must retreat from the wider prophetic attempt to integrate Jewish society and Torah and reconcile themselves to living on two planes, then we have Type 4. I do not know of any Rabbinic sources from the Talmudic period that take a thoroughgoing Type 4 view, though there are all sorts of statements suggesting that particular commandments should be interpreted leniently or even should be suspended temporarily because they are too far out of line with observant practice (such pronouncements are much cited by Reform, Conservative, and Modern Orthodox today in their programmatic analyses). But these sayings presume that the Jewish society around them is still thoroughly Torah-observant, with Torah as its defining core and practical guide. It is not an assimilatory, idolatrous, or evil society, merely an all-too-human one. The burden of particular commandments can be adjusted, then, all the better to maintain and heighten the overall community observance. But this leniency does not apply to the core ethical or ritual mitzvot or the basic commitment to Torah itself. So this is only partly a Type 4 mentality. The prophetic impulse, and the Talmudic sages' confidence in their contemporary Jewish society, are too strong.

In modern times, however, as Jewish society has merged with ambient non-Jewish cultures and lost its Torah-centeredness, many Orthodox have come painfully to take a more sectarian view, impotently condemning as "gentile" the rest of Jewish society and restricting the prophetic societal demand only to their own group. They therefore have either withdrawn into their own separate communities, which produces a Type 1 sectarian option (as we find in the Meah Shearim section of Jerusalem, let us say), or accepted a Type 4 division of their lives into two moral worlds, the wider secular one, and the personally observant one, along the lines first argued for philosophically by Moses Mendelssohn and developed among the "neo-Orthodox" inspired by Samson Raphael Hirsch.

So it appears that Jewishly speaking the essential factor determining whether Torah-observant Jews advocate Type 1 (6), Type 3, Type 4 or Type 5 is how far (in their view) general Jewish culture is Torah-centered. The same Torah-committed person in different kinds of societies will probably advocate different types of responses.

Three Different Levels of "Culture"

A number of times in the above analysis we have found ourselves sliding from one level of "Culture" to another, and it is necessary at this point to clarify "Culture" further. There are three levels of Culture that can be usefully distinguished. The first is predominant in Neusner's analysis, which is related to one's personal life-style and attitude to the immediate demands of surrounding (Jewish) society. In this case, we can focus directly on attitudes to work and family as opposed to attitudes to Torah study and observance, as Neusner has done. If Torah is taken to oppose "Culture" in this sense, we get the other-worldly ascetical option. If this asceticism is made the basis of a distinct community, then we get radically separatist societies such as the Qumraners and Essenes.

There is another level of culture that is more usually considered as "Culture," which we can term socio-cultural worldview, namely art, philosophy, political thought, and science, and in general the "secular" realm as such. Here it would be relevant to consider the various attitudes within the Jewish tradition, from biblical times through the Talmudic period to the present, to government and political power, to reason and the secular sciences as opposed to revelation, etc. When we juxtapose Torah to Culture in this sense, the question can be phrased as a larger communal-prophetic one: whether the specially dedicated religious community can or should involve itself in philosophical, political and wider social issues affecting the Jewish people, and seek reform and change in the entire (Jewish) society so as to bring it into conformity with Torah values, or on the contrary should conform Torah values to secularly prevalent ones.

In both of the above "levels," we have been dealing with issues internal to Jewish society. But there is also another level or dimension of culture, in which attitudes to non-Jewish culture(s) and humanity as such are in question. This has been a very important issue even within Jewish communities, since not only was the Torah shaped within a historical environment in which other cultures closely impinged on the Jewish nation, but since the Babylonian Exile most Jews have lived as a minority within a wide variety of other cultures. The question in this case is whether Jews should focus on preserving their own distinct community and religio-cultural identity over against surrounding cultures, assimilate to them or take some middle paths of reform and outreach, to change humanity more generally.

The three levels of "Culture" can certainly relate variously to each other. Just to take the first two levels as an example, the Qumraners extended their ascetical personal rejection of ordinary work-lives to a bitter rejection of the rest of Jewish society. So there was a straight congruence between personal style and social outlook. Such sectarianism and Qumran-type communities are extremely rare in Jewish religious history. But as already mentioned, in biblical Israel there were bands of prophets who, it seems, were not engaged in ordinary work-lives but consecrated themselves to the ecstatic life; nevertheless, they considered themselves sent to the wider community and involved themselves in social and political issues, sometimes challenging political authorities, the people's behavior, or the choices of foreign policy. Here a more complex cultural logic applies an exclusionary personal style to an integrationist social outlook. This is far more common, as we have seen the Rabbinic sources reflect such opinions, and their analogue can be found among Jewish groups even today.

For example, most Haredi or Agudah Orthodox in Israel nowadays argue that yeshiva students should not be forced to work, and even less to serve in the Israeli army. The reason given is that their studies preserve the heritage of Judaism, the essence of Jewish existence, which most ordinary workers neglect and soldiers defend in a merely physical way. It is therefore the yeshiva students who provide the spiritual justification for the secular state of Israel, and who are the hope for the future of Jewry. We therefore do not have to do with fully sectarian or separatist movements, since we often find these students, and their Haredi supporters, taking overt political action in wider Jewish society to pursue a variety of "Torah issues" affecting other Israelis (education, Sabbath observance, kashrut, who is a Jew?, etc.). Secularist Israelis might even find their political pressure to increase Jewish observance and spread Torah values a major irritant. In such a case, we have something like a Type 5 modality allied with the prophetic orientation, except that the active reform and missionizing of society is generally not as important as the effort to preserve Jewish tradition at least among an elite. Another Haredi option, however, is to take separatist elitism so far that there is an absolute opposition and enmity between the Torah-centered yeshiva world and that of secular Zionism (as in the case of the Satmarer Hasidim and Neturei Karta). This reminds us of the ancient sectarian model of the Qumraners. Here again we have a full-blown Type 1 (or rather 6) opposing Torah and Culture. (Of course, in such a case there are really two "cultures," namely the secular Jewish culture and the Torah-centered culture; it is assumed that each requires full-time dedication and so a choice must be made; only the second can have an ongoing binding prophetic renewal of Torah observance.)

However, as Neusner's analysis shows, even in Tannaitic times the strongly dominant majority view was that one should and could combine general social engagement, work and family life with Torah study. After all, Torah gives the blueprint of (Jewish) society, so most sages did not abandon society when they studied Torah. In terms of the modern Israeli scene, such views explain the outlook of most "Modern Orthodox" or "Centrist Orthodox" religious Zionists (as in the Mizrahi party) that there is a duty for religious students to serve in the Israeli army.

The Second and Third Levels of Culture

So much for the first level of "Culture." But we understand this level best when we consider it in relation to the second level, involving secular culture as such. For example, it is a notable fact about Jewish history that despite a momentous split on these issues during the "Maimonist controversy" of the thirteenth century, diverse and independent philosophical and scientific thought has in general been much more hospitably accepted in Jewish culture than in either Christian churchly or Muslim cultures.[4] It is also interesting to survey the various political theories developed by Jewish thinkers; they almost all seek to integrate Torah directives and consensus values into their political theory, and tend to avoid the "two worlds, two moralities" Type 4 approach of most Christian and Muslim jurists, which justify

---

[4] The Renaissance had its roots in the Muslim freeing of Hellenistic literature and thought from Byzantine monastic suppression. But despite the diverse philosophies that flourished under the relatively secular and un-pious rulers of the "Golden Age" of Islam up to the twelfth century, when Muslim religious authorities finally took unchallenged authority in society and determined the only correct philosophy, they equated "submission" (*Islam*) to God with the Ash'arite philosophy that removed all freedom or autonomy from creatures and gave it all to God. The result was a freeze both on independent thought and political rights from which the Muslim world has still not recovered. The comments of Lenn E. Goodman, *Judaism, Human Rights, and Human Values* (New York, 1998), pp. 68–70, are particularly penetrating both on Muslim thought and the dissenting "Rabbinic humanism" of medieval Jewish thinkers.

unrestrained authoritarianism while preserving religious communities to the side. Goitein has famously referred to the medieval Jewish communities of the Muslim world as "religious democracies," and recent scholarship on biblical and Rabbinic political thought has shown how important for moderating tyrannical uses of power have been requirements for community consensus and acceptance of multiple perspectives legitimating diverse, cross-cutting hierarchies of authority (e.g., the "Three Crowns" of Torah, Kingship, and Priesthood).[5]

This immediately brings us to the question of the prophetic function that Jewish leaders and the Torah itself should or should not play in Jewish communities. In the modern period, following the "Emancipation" and "Enlightenment," Jewish society is no longer distinct from gentile society; in fact secular Jewish culture and gentile culture are largely the same. Level two of "Culture," referring to Jewish culture, and level three, referring to non-Jewish cultures, have largely merged. This makes the prophetic function much more problematic than ever before. A demand to conform (Jewish) society to Torah norms can now seem like a direct assault on general gentile values and association and a repudiation of "Emancipation" as such, something unacceptable to most modern Jews, so that the prophetic impulse of Judaism can be hamstrung. Some sectarians refuse to accept this, and radically oppose the status quo on behalf of Torah Judaism, like many Haredim, for whom Torah should control everything. If other Jews do not agree, then to preserve a strictly-Torah-true community there must be a radical separation from the insufficiently observant. Historically, a major impetus was given this highly sectarian approach by the "Hatam Sofer" and certain sectors of early nineteenth century Hungarian Jewry. The resulting "Ultra-Orthodoxy" conforms to Type 1 (6).

Other Jews advocate a kind of secular Jewish identity, indiscriminately accepting almost all modalities of contemporary society. Or they might affirm the idea that the Torah provides ideals that can spur

---

[5] On the varieties of Jewish political thought, see Michael Walzer, et al., eds, *The Jewish Political Tradition, Vol. One: Authority* (New Haven and London, 2000). For Goitein's characterization, see S.D. Goitein, *A Mediterranean Society: The Jewish Communities of the Arab World as Portrayed in the Documents of the Cairo Geniza, Vol. 2: The Community* (Berkeley, 1971), p. 5 et passim. On the "Three Crowns," see Stuart Cohen, *The Three Crowns: Structures of Communal Politics in Early Rabbinic Jewry* (New York, 1990), and Daniel J. Elazar, ed., *Kinship and Consent: The Jewish Political Tradition and Its Contemporary Uses* (New Brunswick, 1997).

some reform of society, in a genial fashion. A distinct Jewish community and society however is an embarrassment. "Society" means general secular society. Many secular and Reform Jews hold this view. Since Culture is the dominant pole, this is Type 2 (assimilation).

The third, fourth and fifth ways of interrelating Torah and Jewish culture are harder to attach to specific groups in the modern period, since we can find representatives of each in each of the major religious movements of Reform, Conservatism, and Orthodoxy. It is evident that this is the mainstream Jewish range of response, because of this shared focus. The same "Lubavitch Hasidim," "Centrist Orthodox," "Modern Orthodox," "Conservative," and "Reform" groups that affirm some form of participation in general Israeli or diaspora Jewish cultures will often seek to persuade those cultures to submit to Jewish religious norms (as defined by the specific group) as far as possible, for example in relation to such issues as abortion, heightened Jewish observance or promotion of more Torah study. How much they are willing to concede to popular secular culture or to modify "traditional" Torah practices differentiates the groups from each other. In general Conservative and some Reform Jews are comfortable with Type 3, while more Orthodox Jews want a more thorough-going displacement of secular values by Torah teachings and observance, Type 5.

But in fact a Type 4 "two moralities" attitude is as a practical matter also quite common in the same groups, sometimes merely as a personal attitude (perhaps polemicized against by their religious authorities), and sometimes officially endorsed. Since Jewish everyday culture nowadays really means general gentile culture and society, Type 4 attitudes perhaps can be seen as a development of the Rabbinic precedents for relating diaspora Jewish societies to majority gentile society. The sages did not recommend that Jewish communities agitate within their host societies for religious, political and social reform, but rather that they keep a low profile, maintaining their own community while submitting to general gentile authority. We recall the usual Talmudic justification for accepting some non-Jewish practice, that it is "for the sake of peace," and also the rule *Dina de-Malkhuta Dina* ("The law of the land is law;" B. Ned. 28a, B. B.Q. 113a, B. B.B. 54b-55a). Moses Mendelssohn, as already mentioned, pioneered a far-reaching Type 4 philosophy during the Enlightenment, which has found many imitators in recent generations. In regard to gentile culture, most Torah observant groups do not endorse a prophetic Type 5 mentality. The closest analogues might be the involvement of Liberal Jews in political movements, generally as individuals rather than as a community, and, on the other hand, Lubavitch campaigns to inform gentiles about the Noahide commandments.

In any case, almost all groups seek some positive interaction between Torah and (Jewish) Culture, both internal to their own group and to Jews more widely. Even most Haredim have a kind of outreach, supporting charities and Torah educational institutions in Jewish communities or in Israel, for the sake of the Jewish people as such.

In ancient times the options were a little clearer, with the first and second types represented by the Qumran community and the Hellenizers, respectively. Perhaps most Sadducees might also affirm the genial assimilatory option. The third and fifth options were again the Jewish mainstream, encompassing different wings of the Pharisees and later rabbis, with a more militant version of the fifth also including the Zealots, who were apparently extremist Pharisees and Sadducees. Some say the Qumran community was also such an extremist militant messianist Saducean Zealot group. The fourth option seems less well documented, perhaps because in the nature of things at the time it was a fugitive, individual path, a kind of double life. Interestingly, the Apostle Paul seems to have followed it (both in his allegedly "Pharisaic" phase, unwillingly, and more openly and boastfully in his Christian phase, cf., Rom. 7:15ff., 1 Cor. 6:12, 9:19ff.), and early Christianity developed it further.

If, on the other hand, we consider the Torah vs. Culture opposition to be explicitly about the Jewish relationship to other cultures, the third level of "Culture," then in the modern period Type 1 (6) means Jews must look to themselves alone, Type 2 means they should assimilate to other peoples, with perhaps a Liberal/Reform leaven of ideals, Type 3 suggests a distinct Liberal/Reform practice and community, or more especially some Conservative views, Type 4 involves Conservatism and modern Orthodoxy, and there is no fifth sector in modern Jewry seeking conversion of non-Jewish cultures to Torah observance. But whether basically Type 2, 3, or 4, many activist Jews involve themselves in secular political reform movements with the justification that they are fulfilling Torah prophetic mandates to extend justice in society.

As Neusner's essay demonstrates, and hopefully this essay as well, Niebuhr's brilliant five-fold phenomenology of Christianity has much to teach us about the inner logic of Judaism when properly modified. For example, it has highlighted for me the absolutely central role of prophetic culture-criticism in Judaism, not only in the Judaism of the biblical and Talmudic periods, but right up to the present. I had not seen the commandments so clearly before as the condensed form of the prophetic imperative, applied to an entire society, nor appreciated the far-reaching result of this characteristic of Judaism on its history and forms, until I had to reflect on Niebuhr's typology, its logic, sweep, and limitations. A book that systematically developed this typology in terms of Jewish religious forms, Rabbinic and other, and which pulled together discussion of how Jewish responses to political thought, philosophy, science, and non-Jewish cultures have typically been articulated, and how they in turn have differed from or are similar to Christian and Muslim responses, would be an interesting and very valuable contribution.

THE AGENDA OF *DABRU EMET**

Jon D. Levenson
Harvard Divinity School

One of the most remarkable cultural developments over the past half-century has been the growth of inter-religious dialogue. Members of religious communities that had, on principle, long avoided courteous communication with each other are now in regular discussion characterized by mutual respect, and the discussions not infrequently involve precisely the points of theological difference that had so long precluded dialogue. These conversations are, of course, symptomatic of a new understanding of religious identity characteristic of modernity, at least in democratic lands. But they have also played a major role in bringing that new relationship into existence and strengthening it, as the participating bodies have spread the new insights and revised images to their membership through liturgical reform, preaching, and teaching.

Inter-religious dialogue, needless to say, is not without inner tensions. The most important of these concerns the very goal of the enterprise. Given the history of religiously inspired animosity and contempt to be overcome if dialogue is to develop and continue—a history that includes unspeakable acts of violence from some parties—it is tempting to adopt a model of conflict resolution or diplomatic negotiation as the basis for the conversations. The goal in this case would be to come to agreement, rather in the manner of two countries seeking to bury the hatchet or of a couple going into marriage counseling in hopes of replacing a contentious relationship with one characterized by empathy and mutual support. When this is the model, the

---

* Reprinted from *Review of Rabbinic Judaism* 7, 2004, pp. 1–26. A shorter variant of this essay appeared as "How Not to Conduct Jewish-Christian Dialogue," in *Commentary* 112:5 (December, 2001), pp. 31–37. I thank the editors of *Commentary* for permission to republish sections of that article here. An extended discussion with critics and supporters of the article appears as "Controversy: Jewish-Christian Dialogue," in *Commentary* 113:4 (2002), pp. 8, 10, 12, 14, 16–21. A largely *ad hominem* response, based on a misquotation, appears in David Novak, "Instinctive Repugnance," in *First Things* 123 (May, 2002), pp. 12–14. See the ensuing letters in *First Things* 125 (August/September, 2002), pp. 8–11.

commonalities will be stressed and the differences minimized, neglected, or denied altogether. For the latter are correctly seen as sources of division, and division is then viewed as dangerous. Transposed into the world of religion, Rodney King's plea, "Can't we all just get along?" can thus (at least in the minds of the less subtle or the less theologically committed) quickly become "Aren't we all just saying the same thing?"

When the answer is affirmative, the dialogue may seem to have reached its goal, but the expense is deceptively great, so great that the whole enterprise is, in fact, imperiled. For dialogue on these terms quickly turns into a monologue, as each side simply phrases in its distinctive idiom what is, in fact, the common belief of all involved. Religious difference, once a matter of the deepest beliefs about the most important and universal truths, is thus rapidly downgraded to a matter of mere vocabulary. In this way, conflicting truths can all be held to be valid, only for different communities, so that everybody is right, no mutual critique is possible, and good relations will obtain—at the expense, of course, of the theological core of each community. This assumption is rarely articulated, to be sure, but it does underlie the practice of inter-faith dialogue in more than a few instances.

Fortunately, there is an alternative to this self-defeating model based on conflict resolution or diplomatic negotiation.[1] The alternative, too, seeks good relations and requires each community to confront its misunderstandings of the other and the often-grievous results that these have had. At the same time, however, it also insists on the importance of the theological core of each tradition and requires both dialogue partners to reckon with the full import of the other's theology, even when it not only contradicts but also critiques one's own. In this model, in other words, the differences, no less than the commonalities, must be brought to the fore, for without them the full truth of the individual religious traditions and the relationship

---

[1] The theory of dialogue to which I adhere is laid out excellently in Leora Batnitzky, "Dialogue as Judgment, Not Mutual Affirmation: A New Look at Franz Rosenzweig's Dialogical Philosophy," in *Journal of Religion* 79 (1999), pp. 523–544, esp. 537–540. Contrary to what she suggests, however, I do not adhere to the position that "it is best not to engage in dialogue on theological issues" (p. 540). My view, rather, is that we deeply compromise such dialogue when we make reconciliation or mutual affirmation its objective.

between them will remain concealed. In this more traditional and more theological understanding of dialogue, failure to come to an agreement need not mean the dialogue has failed. It may mean that it has succeeded.

I

Most Christians and nearly all Jews accept that one of the most positive consequences of interreligious dialogue has been a dramatic reversal in Christian teaching about Judaism and the Jews over the past several decades. The classical view, which has roots in the New Testament, portrayed Judaism as, at best, a preparation for the full and final truth that is the Christian gospel. In rejecting the gospel, the Jews proved unable to recognize the import of their own scripture and took upon themselves the role of enemies of the God who authored it. The ultimate example of this enmity was the Jews' unjust killing of their own messiah, a crime for which they must pay throughout their generations. "His blood be on us, and on our children," cries the Jewish crowd to Pontius Pilate, the Roman prefect, in the Gospel according to Matthew (27:25). Their payment entailed not only the loss of God's favor (and their corollary replacement by the new chosen people, the Church), but also the destruction of the Temple in Jerusalem (held to have been prophesied by Jesus himself) and exile from the promised land into the realms of the gentile nations. Indeed, at least from the time of St. Augustine (early fifth century C.E.), the continued existence of the Jews in a state of degradation served as a proof of Christianity. "The Jews, against whom the blood of Jesus Christ calls out," Pope Innocent III wrote in 1208, "although they ought not to be killed, lest the Christian people forget the Divine Law, yet as wanderers they ought to remain upon the earth, until their countenance be filled with shame."[2]

In the process, Judaism, so the classical Christian view would have it, had become obsolete, superseded by the Christianity to which it had always pointed. Its adherents, missing the meaning of their

---

[2] Quoted in Malcolm Hay, *Europe and the Jews: The Pressure of Christendom on the People of Israel for 1900 Years* (Boston, 1950), p. 81.

own practices, concentrated fruitlessly upon external rituals that had lost whatever efficaciousness they had once had, at the expense of the genuine faith of their ancestors. Seeking salvation in their own works rather than in the mysterious grace of God, they became ever more deeply entangled in petty legalism and lacked the means to draw closer to the God who had sent his only begotten son, Jesus Christ, for their salvation—and the salvation of the entire world. The Jews read their scripture according to its literal, that is, carnal sense and persistently failed even to glimpse the spiritual sense, the sense altogether fulfilled in Jesus and the Church.

The relationship between the theological teachings only roughly sketched above and the treatment of the Jews in Christendom over the centuries is highly complex. On the one hand, the Church generally took a dim view of violence against the Jews, as suggested by Pope Innocent III's remarks. On the other hand, persistent accusation, recrimination, and defamation took their toll, one paid, in this case, in blood. The bridge between theology and violence is chillingly evident in Martin Luther's pamphlet, *Of the Jews and Their Lies* (1543):

> First, their synagogues or Churches should be set on fire, and whatever does not burn up should be covered or spread over with dirt so that no one may ever be able to see a cinder or stone of it. And this ought to be done for the honour of God and of Christianity . . . Secondly, their homes should likewise be broken down and destroyed. For they perpetrate the same things there that they do in their synagogue. For this reason they ought to be put under one roof or in a stable, like gypsies. . . .[3]

The difference between what Luther here advocates and what his German compatriots put into action in the Holocaust four centuries later (with considerable success) must not be overlooked. Whereas traditional Christian theology inspired the Protestant Reformer's remarks, so that the hoped-for result was violent religious persecution, modern racism motivated the Nazis, so they sought not conversion as the punishment of the Jews, but their unqualified annihilation. The intended victims' beliefs were irrelevant to the genocidal campaign, and it would be simplistic in the extreme to refer to the Holocaust

---

[3] Quoted from Martin Gilbert, *Exile and Return: The Emergence of Jewish Statehood* (Philadelphia and New York, 1978), p. 20.

as religious persecution. But it would also strain the historical imagination to claim that nearly two millennia of Christian demonization of Jews and Judaism played no role in laying the groundwork for the Final Solution.

In the wake of the Holocaust, many (but not all) Christian communions have engaged in a soul-searching reexamination of the teaching of contempt that was so long dominant in their thinking about the Jews. The result has been a series of statements that reverse, or at least severely limit the classic theology. In most cases, these statements affirm the family connection of Judaism and Christianity, graciously acknowledging both the Church's indebtedness to Judaism (especially for the set of scriptures it received from the Jews) and the continuing validity of the older tradition even after Jesus. In some instances, apologies are proffered for the history of persecutions, including, explicitly or implicitly, the Holocaust. Especially moving was the image of Pope John Paul II—who stood in line of succession to Innocent III and a long line of ancient, medieval, and modern despisers of the Jews—politely visiting the Great Synagogue of Rome and praying at the Western Wall in Jerusalem under Israeli sovereignty.

It was inevitable that the changes in Christian attitudes toward Judaism would alter the very fabric of relations between the two communities. To the extent that Jewish attitudes toward Christianity were premised upon Christian animosity, these attitudes could not but be affected by the new situation (except, of course, among those Jews who live in self-enclosed communities opposed to change as a point of religious principle). Furthermore, it is understandable that Christians, having undergone a painful critical reevaluation of their own traditions (including their scriptures and even the presentation of Jesus in them), would want to know the Jews' reactions to all this. Are the regrets accepted, or do the Jews still hold them responsible for past persecutions? Do Jews acknowledge that the two communities are members of the same larger spiritual grouping, or do they see Christians as a religiously alien group, no closer to them in belief and practice than Hindus and Buddhists? And for those Christians for whom interfaith dialogue is an important part of their missionary agenda (for such Christians, as we shall see, do indeed exist, and in very high places), it would be eminently important to learn whether any softening in Jewish attitudes toward the Church and its gospel were taking place.

II

In the early 1990s, the Institute for Christian and Jewish Studies in Baltimore assembled a group of professors of Jewish Studies to pursue the question of a Jewish understanding of Christianity (the same organization had already been involved in the reverse project, the reassessment of Judaism by Christian scholars). Out of these consultations there emerged in September, 2000, "A Jewish Statement on Christians and Christianity" entitled *Dabru Emet* ("Speak the truth," after the words of the prophet Zechariah [8:16], "Speak the truth to one another."). Four able and highly regarded academics authored the statement,[4] and hundreds other scholars and rabbis signed it. Published in the *New York Times* and numerous other venues, it attracted vast attention, most of it extremely positive.[5]

Dabru Emet essentially consists of eight theses of one sentence apiece (each of which is then followed by a brief explanatory paragraph):

- *Jews and Christians worship the same God.*
- *Jews and Christians seek authority from the same book—the Bible (what Jews call "Tanakh" and Christians call the "Old Testament").*
- *Christians can respect the claim of the Jewish people upon the land of Israel.*
- *Jews and Christians accept the moral principles of Torah.*
- *Nazism was not a Christian phenomenon.*
- *The humanly irreconcilable difference between Jews and Christians will not be settled until God redeems the entire world as promised in Scripture.*
- *A new relationship between Jews and Christians will not weaken Jewish practice.*
- *Jews and Christians must work together for justice and peace.*[6]

The claim that "Jews and Christians worship the same God" is more daring and more innovative than appears at first glance. Historically, it

---

[4] Tikva Frymer-Kensky (University of Chicago); David Novak (University of Toronto); Peter Ochs (University of Virginia); and Michael Signer (University of Notre Dame).

[5] Not long after the statement was issued, there appeared a supporting volume edited by its four authors and David Fox Sandmel, *Christianity in Jewish Terms* (Boulder, 2000).

[6] Ibid., pp. xvii–xx. All citations from *Dabru Emet* in this article are taken from these pages.

would not, to be sure, have met with much dissent among Christians. However much they have believed Jewish modes of worship to be literal, carnal, and obsolete, Christian orthodoxy early on anathematized the belief that theirs was a higher (and thus different) God from that of the Jews and their scriptures. But here—as generally in Jewish-Christian relations—asymmetry reigns, and simple reciprocity is a dangerous course indeed. For historically, Jews have not always been convinced that Christians worship their God. Maimonides, for example, the great Sephardic legal authority and philosopher of the twelfth century, explicitly classifies Christianity as idolatry, thus forbidding contact with Christians of the sort permitted with practitioners of other, non-idolatrous religions.[7] In the medieval Ashkenazic world as well, some authorities interpreted the monotheistic affirmation of the *Shema'*, the mandatory daily declaration of Jewish faith, as an outright denial of the Christianity doctrine of the Trinity.[8]

Here, the issue is even more basic than the familiar questions of whether Jesus was the messiah and of whether the Torah is still in effect or superseded by the gospel: It is a question of the identity of God himself. For Orthodox Christianity sees Jesus not only as a spokesman for God, in the manner of a Jewish prophet, but also and more importantly as an incarnation—nay, the definitive and unsurpassable incarnation—of the God of Israel. In the words of the Nicene Creed (recited liturgically in Eastern Orthodox, Roman Catholic, and many Protestant Churches to this day), Jesus is "true God from true God, begotten, not made, of one being with the Father. Through him all things were made." *Dabru Emet*, like most participants in Jewish-Christian dialogue, speaks as if Jews and Christians agree about God, but disagree about Jesus. It overlooks the key fact that in one very real sense, orthodox Christians think Jesus *is* God. For in the traditional Christian theology, God was *always* trinitarian, three-personed from all eternity to all eternity, and did not become so only when the Second Person (the Son) became incarnate in Jesus of Nazareth.

One would never guess this from *Dabru Emet*, which lacks any reference to the doctrines of Trinity and Incarnation. In an essay

---

[7] Commentary on the M. A.Z. 1:1.
[8] See Jacob Katz, *Exclusiveness and Tolerance: Studies in Jewish-Gentile Relations in Medieval and Modern Times* (Springfield, 1961), pp. 18–19.

in the supporting volume, however, one of its authors, Peter Ochs, does address the issue. In essence, he argues that Christianity overlaps with Judaism but also adds to it points that "belong to a religion other than Judaism and are incompatible with what it means for a Jew to live according to the dictates of Jewish tradition." These additions do not, in his judgment, have "behavioral consequences that would violate Jewish beliefs or the Noahide laws [which Judaism expects all gentiles to obey]."[9]

Even if we concede Ochs' point, however, we still must ask about the ensuing implications for the unqualified claim that "Jews and Christians worship the same God." Surely, if God is known from his biblical story, those who want to understand the God of Christians can never relegate the New Testament (which is also unmentioned in *Dabru Emet*) to the status of a set of harmless superfluities.[10] Rather, they must openly acknowledge that the additions that that testament makes to Jewish tradition are indispensable to the Christian concept of God, for, without them, God is less fully known—or so the logic of Christian belief dictates. To do that, however, *Dabru Emet* would have to reckon openly and honestly with the key doctrines of Incarnation and Trinity that it studiously neglects.

As it happens, it is precisely that traditional Christian theology that enabled some Jewish authorities already in the Middle Ages to exonerate Christians of the accusation of idolatry that others had preferred against them. Thus, twelfth century French authorities ruled that a Jew could accept the validity of the oath of Christians because even though the latter mention Jesus, this is not the name of an idolatrous god:

> For they mean the Maker of Heaven, and although they associate the Name of Heaven [i.e., God] and something else, we do not find it is forbidden to Gentiles to make such an association.[11]

Like *Dabru Emet*, this position (which grew in influence over the centuries, generally eclipsing the alternative) acknowledges "Jews and

---

[9] Peter Ochs, "The God of Jews and Christians," in Frymer-Kensky, *Judaism*, pp. 60–61.

[10] See Michael Goldberg, "God, Action, Narrative: Which Narrative, Action, God?" in *Journal of Religion* 68 (1988), pp. 39–56. Note also his book *Jews and Christians, Getting Our Stories Straight: The Exodus and the Passion-Resurrection* (Nashville, 1985).

[11] Tosaphot to B. San. 63b. See also Katz, *Exclusiveness*, pp. 34–36, and David Ellenson, "A Jewish View of the Christian God: Some Cautionary and Hopeful Remarks," in Frymer-Kensky, *Judaism*, pp. 72–75.

Christians worship the same God." But unlike *Dabru Emet*, it takes seriously the aspects of Christian theology that had led other authorities to classify Christianity as idolatry, and, what is more, it explains why, in the words of *Dabru Emet*, "Christian worship is not a viable religious choice for Jews." The explanation lies precisely in the whiff of idolatry to which *Dabru Emet*, with its unqualified and a-historical affirmation of "the same God," makes no allusion. The issue is not about a viable choice versus one that is less viable. It is about religious truth. It is about the nature of the God of Israel.[12]

The eminent Protestant theologian Wolfhart Pannenberg sees in the first thesis of *Dabru Emet* a repudiation of the traditional Jewish theology of the "association" (*shittuf*) and a welcome (to him) concession on the part of the Jews that "the trinitarian doctrine of God is no longer considered a violation of biblical monotheism."[13] In my view, he correctly identifies the tendency but gives the statement too much credit, since, as I have been at pains to point out, it nowhere mentions the doctrines that Pannenberg find it to repudiate boldly. A statement that either faithfully upheld the traditional idea of the *shittuf* or explicitly opposed it would have been more defensible than the studied ambiguity of *Dabru Emet*. Either alternative would have taken Christianity more seriously.

Partial and misleading as *Dabru Emet* is on God/Jesus, it altogether neglects to mention the personage whom hundreds of millions of those orthodox Christians (principally in the Eastern Orthodox and Roman Catholic Church) call the "Mother of God"—the Virgin Mary. Indeed, the divinity of the human Jesus was so important to the fathers of the Third Ecumenical Council (431) that they placed an anathema on anyone who failed to confess that "the Holy Virgin is the Mother of God."[14] One can see why *Dabru Emet* avoids Mary altogether: If "Jews and Christians worship the same God," then why do the Jews neglect his mother when so many Christians venerate and serve her? And if the Jews are right that in no sense

---

[12] It is significant that Tosaphot here does not use the term "God of Israel," as *Dabru Emet* does, but restricts its language to the term "Maker of Heaven." I thank Rabbi Joel Poupko for bringing this to my attention.

[13] Wolfhart Pannenberg, in "A Symposium on *Dabru Emet*," in *Pro Ecclesia* 11:1 (Winter 2002), p. 8.

[14] Heinrich Denzinger, *The Sources of Catholic Dogma* (St. Louis and London, 1957), p. 50.

whatsoever does God have a mother, what does that say about the doctrines of Trinity, Incarnation, and Mary that the early Church councils were so careful to define and protect? Again, it will not do to say that Jews and orthodox Christians worship the same God but respectfully disagree about Mary. For, according to the orthodox Christian theology, what is unique about Mary is precisely that she is the Mother of God.

What are we to make of the fact that "A Jewish Statement on Christians and Christianity," as *Dabru Emet* is subtitled, takes no account of doctrines central to historic Christianity and very much alive among hundreds of millions of contemporary Christians as well? Whatever its authors' and signatories' intentions, the statement leaves the clear impression that it is directed only at those Christians for whom (whatever their ecclesial affiliations) the classical creedal statements about Christology and Mariology have lost their theological centrality, perhaps even their fundamental credibility. Christians for whom the ancient doctrines are not so important or are an outright embarrassment are hardly likely to protest their omission. Indeed, they are likely to be happy to see an external group, rabbis and Jewish scholars to boot, confirming that what their version of Christianity really is authentic. As for Christians for whom the classic doctrines remain important, many of them seem happy to find that the Jews have, without the slightest hint of reservation, at last accepted a claim that orthodox Christians have made for millennia, "Jews and Christians worship the same God."

A similar partiality of vision, a similar tendency to neglect rather than reassess historic points of discord, informs the second thesis of *Dabru Emet*:

> *Jews and Christians seek authority from the same book—the Bible (what Jews call "Tanakh" and Christians call the "Old Testament").*

The awkward parenthetical gloss already points to the problem. Jews do not consider the New Testament to be the "Bible," and Christians do not refer to the Old Testament alone as the "Bible."[15] In fact, the very equation the gloss makes between the "Tanakh" and the

---

[15] On the theological import of the terminology, see Jon D. Levenson, *The Hebrew Bible, the Old Testament, and Historical Criticism: Jews and Christians in Biblical Studies* (Louisville, 1993), especially pp. 1–32.

"Old Testament" is a half-truth. The Old Testament of the Roman Catholic and Eastern Orthodox churches includes Jewish books that never attained canonical status in Rabbinic Judaism (and, in one case, a book that the rabbis seemed to have removed from the canon). The order of the Tanakh and the Old Testament is also different in revealing ways. The Tanakh, in its current form (the order of some biblical books was notoriously unstable into Talmudic times) ends, for example, with the Persian emperor Cyrus' decree in Chronicles that Jews may return to their homeland, where God has charged him to rebuild the Jerusalem Temple. This is an unmistakable anticipation of the passion for return to the Land of Israel that has characterized Jewish thought. The Old Testament, in contrast, ends with the prophet Malachi's prediction that God will send the prophet Elijah "before the coming of the awesome, fearful day of the Lord." The latter arrangement makes a nice bridge to John the Baptist's heralding of Jesus in the New Testament.[16]

We must also reckon with the different priorities with which Judaism and Christianity have traditionally interpreted those scriptures that they hold in common. From the onset, Christians have been especially attentive to two books in particular, Psalms and Isaiah, priorities that can still be detected to this day.[17] In traditional Jewish thought, however, everything after the Pentateuch results from a lower order of revelation and exercises a lesser authority, so that Leviticus, for example, commands more attention than Psalms and Isaiah combined. (Even when the rabbis turn their exegetical skills toward the non-Pentateuchal books, they often interpret them as commenting on the Pentateuch). This, too, renders the claim that "Jews and Christians seek authority from the same book" highly problematic.

But even if we assume that Jews and Christians have "the same book," the second thesis of *Dabru Emet* still skirts over essential points. For the Tanakh and the Old Testament are, in major ways, subordinated to other elements in their respective traditions. In Christianity, there is, as we have noted, a tradition, extending back to the origins

---

[16] See especially Luke 1:8-17.
[17] See Jon D. Levenson, "Is Brueggemann Really a Pluralist?" in *Harvard Theological Review* 93 (July, 2000), pp. 292.

of the new faith itself, that the true meaning of the Jewish scriptures is revealed in and by Jesus, and the Jews thus misread their own Bible. Paul could not be more explicit:

> Therefore, since we have such hope, we act very boldly and not like Moses, who put a veil over his face so that the Israelites could not look intently at the cessation of what was fading. Rather, their thoughts were rendered dull, for to the present day the same veil remains unlifted when they read the old covenant, because through Christ it was taken away. To this day, in fact, whenever Moses is read, a veil lies over their hearts, but whenever a person turns to the Lord the veil is removed.[18]

Paul does indeed cast his argument as an exegesis of the Jewish scriptures, but he does not simply "interpret the Bible differently," as *Dabru Emet* blandly puts it. Rather, he delivers a broadside against the very way the Jews (and perhaps their Christian sympathizers) read that Bible, that is, non-christologically. The supporting assertion of *Dabru Emet* that "we each take away similar lessons" from our Tanakh/Old Testament is not false. It simply omits to mention that on certain fundamental points, the lessons we take away are not only different, but also mutually exclusive. To be sure, it can be salutary to draw attention to the similarities between religious traditions, for this can help diminish misunderstandings, some of them potentially fatal. But it is the differences, indeed the mutually exclusive truth claims, that are the challenge for interreligious conversation, and it is the differences that *Dabru Emet* consistently neglects. Its respect for Christianity is directly proportional to the extent to which Christianity can be made to look like Judaism.

In its paragraph about the Bible, *Dabru Emet* also passed up an opportunity to correct one of the most common Christian misconceptions about Judaism, that its sole authority is the Old Testament. Had the statement taken a different and more accurate tack, however, pointing to the importance of the Oral Torah (i.e., Mishnaic and subsequent Rabbinic teaching), it would have undermined its claim that the two communities have "the same book," from which they "take away similar lessons." In fact, some affirmations of the

---

[18] 2 Cor. 3:12-16. Unless otherwise noted, all references to the New Testament are from the New American Bible.

importance of the Oral Torah parallel Christian claims for the greater importance of the gospel:

> When the Holy One (blessed be He) said to Moses, "Write down [these commandments, for in accordance with these commandments I make a covenant with you and Israel]," Moses asked that the Mishnah be put into writing. Since the Holy One (blessed be He) foresaw that the nations of the world would translate the Torah, read it in Greek, and say, "We are Israel," and up to this point the scales are equally balanced [between the Jewish and the Gentile claimants to the status of Israel], the Holy One (blessed be He) said to the nations, "You say that you are My children. What I know is that those who have My secret with them—They are my children. And what is it? It is the Mishnah [i.e., teaching] which was given orally."[19]

Here, the key element is not the common scripture, but the element that is *not* shared, God's "secret," the means, that is, for arbitrating between the different readings of the same text. In sum, much of what Judaism and Christianity share in the matter of their common scriptures is a rivalry over how they should be read and who is now the "Israel" that is central to them and bears the indefectible promise they repeatedly make. Were it not for the commonality, the rivalry could not develop. But to speak only of commonalities, ignoring the rivalry or degrading it to the level of mere "differences,"[20] is to miss essential aspects of scripture reading and interpretation in the two related traditions.

Consider as an illustration one of the "similar lessons" that *Dabru Emet* thinks Jews and Christians derive from their common "Bible:" "God established a covenant with the people Israel." That covenant is first announced to Abraham in Genesis 15, following a report that the childless future patriarch trusted in God's unlikely promise to grant him innumerable progeny. The key verse here reads, "And because he put his trust in the Lord, He reckoned it to his merit."[21] Two chapters later, God again announces the covenant

---

[19] Tanh. *ki-tissa'* 33.

[20] Thus *Dabru Emet*: "Jews and Christians interpret the Bible differently on many points. Such differences must always be respected." See also Ellenson, "A Jewish," p. 76, who counsels Jews to "search . . . to affirm elements of commonality that mark these two faith traditions."

[21] Gen. 15:6. Unless otherwise noted, all translations are from the *Tanakh* (Philadelphia, 5748/1988).

with Abraham, only this time ordaining that it shall have a sign, the mandatory circumcision of males of the covenant people. And only several generations later is a covenant made with Israel at Mount Sinai under the leadership of Moses.

Early in his career, Paul, the "apostle to the Gentiles," who had never known Jesus personally, found himself confronted by Jewish adherents of the new religion who had, and who insisted that Gentile men entering it must undergo circumcision and carry out other commandments of the Torah—not an unreasonable demand, given the example of Jesus himself, a Torah-observant Jew. For Paul, seeking to oppose this position, the chronology of covenants in the Torah was a godsend. He understood Gen. 15:6 to mean that God reckoned Abraham as righteous purely on the basis of his faith, even before he became circumcised. Faith, in other words, could substitute for the commandments of the Torah, or, in Paul's own words at the end of his career, "It was not through the Law that the promise was made to Abraham and his descendants that he would inherit the world, but through the righteousness that comes from faith."[22]

At first glance, this may look like an intramural Christian quarrel of only peripheral relevance to Judaism, since the immediate issue concerns circumcision and Torah-observance, neither of which Judaism requires of outsiders. On this reading, we simply see two different religions, related, to be sure, and with a common origin—even "the same book"—but with no need to critique each other or to challenge the other's reading of the shared scriptures. And just so have some New Testament scholars interpreted the situation. The rub is that in Paul's theology, Abraham serves as a model not only for Gentiles, or for Christians but also for all who wish to belong to Israel:

> For not all who are of Israel are Israel, nor are they all children of Abraham because they are his descendants; but "It is through Isaac that descendants shall bear your name" (Gen. 21:12). This means that it is not the children of the flesh who are the children of God, but the children of the promise are counted as descendants.[23]

Just as it is faith rather than circumcision that enables a man to attain the lofty status of Abrahamic descent, so it is faith rather

---

[22] Rom. 4:13. Departing from the New American Bible, I have capitalized "Law" to bring out the fact that Paul is speaking about the Torah.

[23] Rom. 9:6-8, quoting Gen. 21:12.

than birth that determines who truly belongs to Israel (Paul sometimes vacillates on this). And the faith of which Paul speaks is not some vague existential stance, but precisely the faith in Jesus, the very thing that his Jewish kinsmen, to his great disappointment and annoyance, have not accepted, preferring instead their Torah and its commandments:

> What then shall we say? That Gentiles, who did not pursue righteousness, have achieved it, that is, righteousness that comes from faith; but that Israel, who pursued the law of righteousness, did not attain to that law? Why not? Because they did it not by faith, but as if it could be done by works. They stumbled over the stone that causes stumbling, as it is written:
> "Behold, I am laying a stone in Zion
> that will make people stumble
> and a rock that will make them fall,
> and whoever believes in him shall not be put to shame."[24]

Here Abraham, today often called the common father of Jews, Christians, and Muslims, serves a key role in advancing the claim that the Gospels have replaced the Torah (which, properly interpreted, always pointed to it and partook of its nature) and that the Church has replaced the Jewish people, the natural descendants of Abraham. This is, to be sure, a theology from which Paul backs away in a few places and one that Christians involved in dialogue with Jews are usually (but not always) exceedingly eager to renounce. For to the extent that the main outlines of Paul's theology remain in force, Christianity and Judaism become not simply different members of the same family (as *Dabru Emet* would have it), but rather, in the words of the late historian Jacob Katz, "conflicting exponents of the same tradition"—a tradition correctly interpreted by the Christians and profoundly misinterpreted by the Jews.[25]

Not surprisingly, much of the traditional Jewish theology of Abraham moves in a very different—in fact, opposite—direction. Two centuries before the emergence of Christianity, the idea had already appeared that Abraham observed norms only disclosed later, in the time of Moses, thus practicing Sinaitic religion even before Sinai.[26] As the

---

[24] Rom. 9:30-33, quoting Is. 28:16. I have retained the New American Bible translation of the latter verse, which fits better with Paul's particular exegesis.
[25] Katz, *Exclusiveness*, p. 4.
[26] See Jubilees 21, e.g.

Mishnah, compiled about 200 C.E., would later put it, "We find that our father Abraham carried out the whole Torah before it had been given."[27] Whether by design or not, this view undercuts the Pauline use of Abraham as an object lesson in the sufficiency of faith at the expense of the specific norms of the Torah (Paul was not opposed to good works in general or reluctant to characterize those he thought lacking in them). For in this interpretation of the first Jew, the very difference between the Abrahamic and Mosaic dispensations dissolves. Elsewhere in Rabbinic literature, we find the idea that Abraham did not observe all 613 commandments that the rabbis found in the Torah, but only the seven basic norms known to Noah (and incumbent upon all humanity, Jewish and Gentile), as well as the commandment of circumcision enjoined upon him in Genesis.[28] In this case, however, the point is often that the Mosaic is the highest dispensation, higher than the Noahide and higher than the Abrahamic upon which Paul (and later Christians) built as much. In making this evaluation, Rabbinic thought inverts the Pauline model, giving fullest praise to the Mosaic or Sinaitic mode of spirituality and placing the observance of commandments (rather than faith, grace, spirit, or the like) first in importance. (Given this move, the total absence in *Dabru Emet* of the words "law" and "commandment" is deeply disappointing, but, as we shall see, not without explanation).

But what does all this say about the claim in *Dabru Emet* that among the "similar lessons" that Jews and Christians derive from their common "Bible" is the idea that "God established a covenant with the people Israel"? We have already seen that the classic Christological pronouncements render the Christian concept of "God" problematic for Jews in ways of which *Dabru Emet* seems unaware. As for "covenant," the two traditions differ markedly even on so fundamental a question as to what commandments, if any, that relationship requires. They also differ on the worth and viability of that covenant (the New Testament Epistle to the Hebrews claims Jesus mediated a "new covenant" vastly superior to the old one, which was of only temporary duration anyway).[29] And what of "Israel"?

---

[27] M. Qid. 4:14.
[28] See B. Yoma 28b and Pes. Rab. Kah. 12:1. I have given these issues a fuller treatment in Hindy Najman and Judith H. Newman, eds., *The Idea of Biblical Interpretation* (Leiden, 2004), pp. 3–40.
[29] Heb. 8:6, 8, 13.

Surely, we must take note that for all their striking similarities, the two sets of ancient normative books, the New Testament and the Oral Torah, often present diametrically opposed understandings of that all-important term. For the Church early on claimed (with very few exceptions) not to share the status of Israel with the Jews, but to have supplanted the Jews in the role of God's chosen people, and, until rather recently, Christian tradition was all but unanimous in seconding (and even hardening) that ominous judgment. Similarly, Rabbinic Judaism was adamant that whatever spiritual dignity the nations could achieve (and many rabbis thought they could achieve much indeed), "Israel" comprised only the Jews—an extended natural family whose males, whether born or converted into that people, are marked by the covenantal sign of circumcision. Gentiles who "have a place in the world-to-come," to use the Rabbinic terminology, are still gentiles and not "Israel."

This dispute between Christianity and Judaism in antiquity could take place only because the two communities worked from common scriptures that reported that "God established a covenant with the people Israel," in the words of *Dabru Emet*. The commonality served, however, not to minimize opposition, but to make dispute possible, and it now serves—and appropriately serves—to make Jewish dialogue with Christians vastly more encompassing and interesting than the dialogue with adherents of other religions with which Jews have less in common and therefore also less to challenge. Much of what is at stake theologically in a dialogue grounded in these ancient sources disappears when the two disputants are depicted as simply different and therefore out of each other's way. When *Dabru Emet* affirms in a later paragraph that "Christians know and serve God through Jesus Christ and the Christian tradition. Jews know and serve God through Torah and the Jewish tradition," it achieves the desired comity by a kind of demarcation of spheres of influence: Jesus Christ for the Christians, Torah for the Jews. In the process, however, it has radically changed the meaning of both "Jesus Christ" and of "Torah."

In the decades since the Holocaust, to be sure, many Christians have been courageously reassessing and even altering their theology so as to give a positive evaluation to Judaism and Jewish survival. In some instances, the result has been a theology of two covenants of equal worth, one for Jews and one for Christians, and this seems to be the model for *Dabru Emet*'s bold affirmation of both "Jesus Christ" and "Torah" as ways to "know and serve God." The affirmation is, however, in serious tension with the prior affirmation of a common "Bible." For however else they may differ, the Tanakh and the Old Testament know of only one Israel, only one chosen people in covenant with God, or to put it in more biblical language, only one son with the status of the firstborn. Ironically, to the extent that the two traditions turn either to their putatively common Bible or their distinctive post-biblical traditions, they raise problems for the dual covenant theology. So, for all the appeal to common roots, the paramount and governing claim of *Dabru Emet* is on behalf of a modern theology that relativizes Judaism and Christianity in ways that those ancient sources do not accept.

The third of the eight affirmations of *Dabru Emet* tells us that "Christians can respect the claim of the Jewish people upon the land of Israel." No surprise there: Since many Christians respect the Jewish claim (as the paragraph later states), who would deny they "can"? Rather, it looks as though the statement really wants to tell Christians that they *should* do so. Thus the supporting paragraph states that "[a]s members of a biblically based religion, Christians appreciate that Israel was promised—and given—to Jews," and it applauds those "who support the State of Israel for reasons more profound than mere politics." The alternative position—that the Jews forfeited the land promise by not accepting the Church's claims about Jesus—is, as we have seen, the traditional one. It is also very much alive and well today, even in some evangelical quarters. Here is an excerpt from a recent statement issued by Knox Theological Seminary and signed by hundreds of evangelicals:

> The entitlement of any one ethnic or religious group to territory in the Middle East called the "Holy Land" cannot be supported by Scripture. In fact, the land promises specific to Israel were fulfilled under Joshua. The New Testament speaks clearly and prophetically about the destruction of the second temple in A.D. 70. No New Testament writer foresees a regathering of ethnic Israel in the land, as did the prophets of the Old Testament after the destruction of the first temple in 586 B.C. Moreover the land promises of the Old Covenant are consistently and deliberately expanded in the New Testament to show the universal dominion of Jesus. . . .[30]

---

[30] Cited in Richard John Neuhaus, "The Public Square," in *First Things* 134 (June/July, 2003), p. 66. Knox Theological Seminary is associated with the Presbyterian Church in American (not to be confused with the Presbyterian Church USA).

As biblical exegesis, this contemporary restatement of the classic supersessionist theology is not without its problems, of course. After all, the God of the Old Testament does repeatedly assign the land to the descendants of Abraham, Isaac, and Jacob/Israel "to possess forever," as Exod. 32:13 puts it, and not only until the time of Joshua or some still later dispensation. But so to argue is to miss the larger claim of the Christian theology underlying the Knox statement, the claim that the New Testament supersedes the Old, fulfilling and reassigning its promises. It stands to reason that Jews would object to this move, and, in fact, much Jewish-Christian dialogue has long consisted of Jews' trying to persuade their Christian interlocutors to give more weight to the Old Testament and less to the New. And such an entry into an intramural argument among Christians is precisely what *Dabru Emet*, for all its rhetoric about "a dramatic and unprecedented shift in Jewish and Christian relations," is undertaking here: It is taking a stand in favor of one Christian theology over another. The favored theology is, to be sure, both much more congenial to Judaism and upheld by millions of Christians, evangelical and other. But does *Dabru Emet* really maintain that Religion A should change its theology simply because members of Religion B find it unworthy of belief or offensive? If so, what should Jews do with Hindu or Buddhist reservations about Jewish monotheism, to give only two of dozens of similar cases facing *them*?

It must not be missed that supersessionist theology is not necessarily incompatible with the belief that God's gift of the Land of Israel to the Jews is still in effect (which the Knox statement denies). In this connection, I think of those Christians (hardly few in number) who support Israel because they see the ingathering of the Jewish exiles as a necessary prelude to the second coming of Jesus and the conversion of all Israel to Christianity. Should Jews applaud these Christians for "support[ing] the State of Israel for reasons far more profound than mere politics," or is there something deeply problematic in their theology that Jews (and Christians as well) need to face? On this, *Dabru Emet* is strangely silent.

It is on more secure ground when, in its next thesis, it affirms that *"Jews and Christians accept the moral principles of Torah."* All one has to do to see the degree of moral commonality of Jews and Christians in bold relief is to compare the traditional ethic of the two religions to the materialism, and egocentrism, not to mention the narcissistic body culture, of secular America. But "the moral principles of Torah" is an odd phrase in this context, since Judaism has not maintained that Torah obligates non-Jews or that Torah (as opposed to wisdom) is found among them. The phrase is similarly problematic from the other side, for exceedingly few are the Christians who ask of themselves, "Are my morals in line with Torah?" Instead, they are more likely to ask, "What would Jesus do?" (hence "WWJD" on bracelets, pens, bumper-stickers, T-shirts, etc). Indeed, a tradition of Christian thought that goes back nearly two thousand years sees Jesus' moral principles as higher and better than those of the Torah, an improvement or a radicalization and not just a restatement.[31] What this indicates is that there is a moral debate alongside the theological debate between Jesus and Christians, and that historically Christians have usually seen Jesus as instituting a new ethic at odds to one degree or another with that of the Old Testament. In addition, they have not infrequently been critical of commandments themselves as the vehicles of moral imagination, preferring love or the Spirit in their stead, the laws written upon heart, as the Epistle to the Hebrews puts it (following Jeremiah),[32] over those written in the Torah. And so, even when the substantive morality is the same, the principle of derivation often is not, again rendering the last two words in the phrase "the moral principles of Torah" in *Dabru Emet* highly problematic.

A more appropriately worded thesis would have invoked the "seven commandments of the descendants of Noah," those basic norms that the Talmudic rabbis thought incumbent upon Jews and Gentiles alike.[33] To the extent that Christianity promotes adherence to those commandments, a longstanding Jewish tradition maintains it aids its believers in attaining a proper relationship with God (which is very much open to Gentiles and not just to Jews).[34] Or in Rabbinic parlance, it helps them merit "a share in the world-to-come." Amazingly, "the seven commandments of the descendants of Noah" go unmentioned in *Dabru Emet* (unless the "moral principles of Torah" are a garbled reference to them). Had the statement followed a traditional line of thinking, it could have powerfully affirmed the spiritual and

---

[31] E.g., Matt. 5:21-48.
[32] Heb. 8:10, after Jer. 31:33.
[33] B. San. 56a-56b.
[34] See David Novak, *The Image of the Non-Jew in Judaism: An Historical and Constructive Study of the Noahide Laws* (New York, 1983).

moral integrity of Christianity while simultaneously avoiding the (Jewishly) highly inappropriate affirmation of "Jesus Christ" as a way "to know and serve God," alongside Torah. In so doing, it could have built on a long history of medieval and early modern Jewish authorities who rendered highly positive evaluations of Christianity without subscribing to Christian beliefs, resorting to a two-covenant theology that has no basis in the classical Jewish sources (whatever the case in Christianity), or falling into outright relativism.

A similar refusal to face the full measure of difference between Jews and Christians appears even in the finely crafted and delicately balanced statement on the Holocaust, which merits quotation in full:

> *Nazism was not a Christian phenomenon.* Without the long history of Christian anti-Judaism and Christian violence against Jews, Nazi ideology could not have taken hold nor could it have been carried out. Too many Christians participated in, or were sympathetic to, Nazi atrocities against Jews. Other Christians did not protest sufficiently against these atrocities. But Nazism itself was not an inevitable outcome of Christianity. If the Nazi extermination of the Jews had been fully successful, it would have turned its murderous rage more directly to Christians. We recognize with gratitude those Christians who risked or sacrificed their lives to save Jews during the Nazi regime. With that in mind, we encourage the continuation of recent efforts in Christian theology to repudiate unequivocally contempt of Judaism and the Jewish people. We applaud those Christians who reject this teaching of contempt, and we do not blame them for the sins committed by their ancestors.

On the one hand, we here find a forthright acknowledgement that not only individual Christians, but also Christianity itself played a role in making the Holocaust possible. On the other, we see an ungrudging recognition that some Christians resisted the Nazis at the time and many since then, both as individuals and as churches, have repudiated the traditional anti-Semitism out of which Nazism, for all its romanticization of Nordic paganism, partly grew. The problem, rather, comes with the speculation, reported as something much more certain, that, "If the Nazi extermination of the Jews had been fully successful, it would have turned its murderous rage more directly to Christians." Here again, the statement assimilates Jews and Christians much too readily.

The intended "Nazi extermination of the Jews" was, as we have noted, based in racism. Whether the victims believed in Judaism in any sense was not pertinent to their murderers' plan. People of

Jewish ancestry who were altogether secular or who had converted to Christianity were sent to their deaths alongside their more observant kinsmen. In the case of Christians without Jewish ancestors, no such motivation obtained, and it was possible to stay out of the Nazis' way and even (if one's convictions allowed) to support them in full vigor.

Had *Dabru Emet* acknowledged this critical difference, it would have touched upon the subject of a major Christian critique of Judaism. Here, I refer to the fact that Judaism, though it accepts converts, is in the first instance the religion of a kin-group. According to traditional Jewish theology, the Jews are a natural family with a supernatural mission. They are not in the first instance a church, that is, an association of unrelated persons who join together on the basis of shared theology. Especially since the Enlightenment, Christians have often thought of this difference as that between tribalism (Judaism) and universalism (Christianity) and have not been shy about citing Paul's words that "in Christ Jesus . . . there is neither Jew nor Greek"[35] against Judaism. That this is a misreading of Paul, and of the whole question of universalism and particularism,[36] need not detain us here. The point is that by assimilating the nature of membership in the Jewish people to the nature of membership in the Church, *Dabru Emet* once again purchases a false commonality at the expense of an honest and frank confrontation of the differences and what they mean.

Dabru Emet not only fails to acknowledge the racist character of the Nazi understanding of the Jews; it compounds the problem by imagining that the Nazis planned a Holocaust-like fate for Christians as well once they succeeded with the Jews. This would, of course, have entailed annihilating about 95% of the European population, something that the Nazis, in fact, never contemplated. It is also to miss the well-known fact that the Nazis had support aplenty in the churches, especially in university theology departments, including a number of influential scholars.[37] The effect of *Dabru Emet*'s unsupported claim is to make Christians, too, victims of the Holocaust. It presents the

---

[35] Gal. 3:26, 28.
[36] See Jon D. Levenson, "The Universal Horizon of Biblical Particularism," in Mark G. Brett, ed., *The Bible and Ethnicity* (Leiden, 1996), pp. 143–69.
[37] See Doris L. Bergen, *Twisted Cross: The German Christian Movement in the Third Reich* (Chapel Hill, 1996).

Nazi failure to sponsor anti-Christian violence (except in the case of those few believers who spoke out against the regime) as accidental. In short, the Nazis were not, in the first instance, anti-Semitic: They were *anti-religious*. In the face of the historical record, *Dabru Emet* once again conveniently puts Jews and Christians in the same boat—or, to be more precise, on the same train to Auschwitz.

A similar flaw can be seen in the next thesis: "The humanly irreconcilable difference between Jews and Christians will not be settled until God redeems the entire world as promised in Scripture." In this case, the effect is to make Christianity a participant in the events of the last days, events that the two traditions have historically envisioned in ways that are not only different but also incompatible. Why should Jews affirm that the Church will survive at least until God initiates the final redemption? I am very far from suggesting that it will not or that the world would be better off without it. The question, rather, is why should Jews affirm that God has a commitment to the Church that shall endure until he "redeems the entire world"?

The reverse question is easy to answer—and provides a clue why the drafters of *Dabru Emet* have made the dubious assumption that underlies this thesis. The prologue of this Jewish statement notes that its recent Christian counterparts "have declared . . . that Christian teaching and preaching can and must be reformed so that they acknowledge God's enduring covenant with the Jewish people. . . ." The prime basis for this reform in the New Testament is Paul's insistence that "God has not rejected his people," who remain, in fact, "beloved because of the patriarchs (i.e., Abraham, Isaac, and Jacob). For the gift and the call of God are irrevocable." This affirmation (by no means Paul's only position on this, as we have seen) is pro-Jewish but not pro-Judaism. Its point is that God bears with the Jews despite the failure of so many of them to become Christians. "A hardening has come upon Israel in part," the apostle writes, "until the full number of the Gentiles comes in, and thus all Israel will be saved."[38]

In response to the recent concentration on these ideas on the part of some Christians (by no means only the liberal ones, incidentally) and the efforts to make them the basis for a positive evaluation of

---

[38] Rom. 11:1-2, 25, 28-29.

Judaism, it is readily understandable that the Jews would feel the need to reciprocate. The problem is that the relationship is not symmetrical. For classical Judaism (for all its capacity to evaluate Gentiles and Christianity positively) knows of no specific covenant with the *Church*, no parallel, that is, to Paul's belief in the irrevocable call of the Israelite patriarchs. Without that, the Jewish claim that the Church will survive until God finally redeems the world seems like a thin imitation of the Christian doctrine contrived for the purpose of the dialogue. In many areas of life, reciprocity is a wise policy. In the pursuit of theological truth, however, it represents a dangerous temptation because it presupposes a false symmetry—as does *Dabru Emet* in general.

The penultimate paragraph of the statement, alone phrased in the negative, strikes an oddly defensive note:

> *A new relationship between Jews and Christians will not weaken Jewish practice.* An improved relationship will not accelerate the cultural and religious assimilation that Jews rightly fear. It will not change traditional Jewish forms of worship, nor increase intermarriage between Jews and non-Jews, nor persuade more Jews to convert to Christianity, nor create a false blending of Judaism and Christianity. We respect Christianity as a faith that originated within Judaism and that still has significant contact with it. We do not see it as an extension of Judaism. Only if we cherish our own traditions can we pursue this relationship with integrity.

Given the position *Dabru Emet* has already articulated, however, the worries it here dismisses require a more convincing response. The risk of amalgamation—whether through syncretism or intermarriage—is especially great if Jews and Christians really do stand in the relationship that *Dabru Emet* describes in its other paragraphs. For the thrust of the statement is to make Judaism and Christianity look very much alike, indeed two peas in the same Judeo-Christian pod. They have, after all, "the same God"—"the God of Israel," "the same book—the Bible" (from which they "take away similar lessons"), and the same "moral principles"—in fact, "the moral principles of Torah." Moreover, both religions now appreciate God's gift of the Land of Israel to the Jews—or at least "can" do so, and, in principle (though not in the deed), both were the targets of the Nazis' "murderous rage." Although the statement mentions differences a few times and asks that they be respected, overall it leaves the impression that Judaism and Christianity represent minor variations on a common theme. The truth is that it is hard to come away from *Dabru Emet* without the sense that nearly two thousand years of Jewish-Christian disputation have been based on little more than the narcissism of small differences. What other conclusion can we draw from a statement in which a Judaism without law and commandments puts an unqualified seal of approval on a Christianity without New Testament, Incarnation, Trinity, and Mary?

If the commonalities really are so basic and encompassing, many Jews will rightly wonder why intermarriage, conversion to Christianity, and "a false blending of Judaism and Christianity" are (as their own tradition used to tell them) to be strenuously avoided and counteracted (what sort of "blending" is not "false," *Dabru Emet* does not tell us). Indeed, the same decades that have witnessed the remarkable rapprochement of Jews and Christians have witnessed a soaring intermarriage rate and a novel and striking acceptance of intermarriage on the part of many Jewish organizations.[39] This is not at all to imply that interreligious dialogue has caused the increase of intermarriage and assimilation. It is to say, however, that the strategy *Dabru Emet* takes—stressing (or inventing) commonalities at the expense of mutually exclusive structures and truth-claims—makes syncretism and conversion seem much less dangerous. That need not have deterred the signatories of *Dabru Emet* from speaking the truth about the relationship of Jews and Christians as they see it. But it ought to have given them pause about the claim that doing so poses no risks to Jewish practice and identity. For one teaching common to Judaism and Christianity that *Dabru Emet* omits to mention is that truth-telling on profound issues is not risk-free.

Wolfhart Pannenberg, the eminent Protestant theologian, finds confirmation of the risk-free scenario that *Dabru Emet* puts forth in the "emergence of 'messianic Jews,'" i.e., "Jews who confess their faith in Jesus the Messiah without leaving the Jewish community and a Jewish way of life." "Sooner or later Christian-Jewish dialogue will have to take notice of this fact," he notes, gently chiding the Jewish statement.[40] Why did *Dabru Emet* not do so? In fact, it did, but to make a point diametrically opposed to Pannenberg's. "Christian worship is

---

[39] See Jack Wertheimer, "Surrendering to Intermarriage," in *Commentary* 111:3 (March, 2001), pp. 25–32.

[40] Pannenberg, in "A Symposium," p. 9.

not a viable religious choice for Jews," it remarks, in a subordinate clause in the paragraph about our worshiping the same God. In other words, those Jews who combine Judaism with Christianity have indeed abandoned the Jewish way of life, and what Pannenberg sees as proof that the new closeness is risk-free *Dabru Emet* sees as a defection from Jewish authenticity. What the Christian views as positive, the Jews view as negative. But, whereas he is willing to recognize it and has a theology that can reckon with it, they simply deny the problem exists, whistling in the dark.

The last of the eight theses of *Dabru Emet*, finally, affirms that "Jews and Christians must work together for justice and peace." This gutsy stand has doubtless provoked unimaginable consternation in the camp that advocates that Jews and Christians work separately for injustice and war.

III

What then is the agenda of *Dabru Emet*? In its own formulation, it is "to reflect on what Judaism may now say about Christianity" in light of the fact that "Christianity has changed dramatically." The change to which the statement refers is the new respect for Judaism and the discarding of supersessionist theology in a number of Christian communions, large and small. There is, however, another change in Christianity to which *Dabru Emet* responds, a reformulation of Christian faith that removes, or at least emasculates, the elements that put it into conflict with Judaism. I hope to have now demonstrated that the Christianity that this Jewish statement presupposes is, in fact, a Christianity amazingly like Judaism. It is a monotheistic faith based in the Hebrew Bible, respecting the Jewish claim on the land of Israel, adhering to the moral principles of Torah, giving inevitable offense to Nazi murderers, lasting until the final redemption, and in no way challenging Jewish identity and practice. What the Christianity of *Dabru Emet* lacks is the notion of a God who is triune and not simply one, who was definitively incarnate in Jesus Christ, gave a new and more complete revelation in the New Testament, including a basis for morality at odds with the Judaic focus on law and commandments, and called into existence a new Israel, a community not based on genealogy (and therefore immune to genocide, though not to martyrdom, of course) nor promised any particular real estate. The real agenda of *Dabru Emet* is thus not one of dialogue at all. It is one of negotiation. The Jews are making Christians an offer: If you change your religion so as to make it look more like Judaism, we will, without reservation, affirm it alongside Judaism as our fraternal twin. Indeed, we will present Judaism so that it closely resembles the Judaized Christianity that you have produced.

This is an offer that some Christians, whose beliefs *Dabru Emet* accurately reflects, happily accept. For Jews to enter into constructive dialogue with them is exceedingly easy. The challenge of constructive dialogue with the other sort of Christian is much more formidable and more profound. *Dabru Emet* altogether avoids it.

INDEX OF NAMES

Aaron ibn Hayyim, 130
Abarbanel, Isaac, 135
Abba bar Kahana, 238, 239
Abba Gurion, 228
Abba Gurya, 228
Abba Saul, 59
Abbahu, 77
Abelard, Peter, 127
Abendana, Isaac, 129, 131, 132
Abendana, Jacob, 129
Aboab, Yizhaq, 173, 178
Abraham Shalom Yahuda, 141
Abun, 236
Aha, 237
Aharon Ha-Levi, 130
Alemíen, Mateo, 199, 204
Al-Farabi, Abu Nasr, 164, 168, 170, 173
Al-Gazzali, Abu Hamid, 167
Ammi, 239
Ammonius, 170
Aqiba, 59, 89, 91, 98, 217, 233, 235
Ardutiel, Shem Tob ben Isaac, 200
Augustine, 21, 22, 24, 267

Bar Kokhba, 95
Bar Qappara, 19
Ben Pandira, 24
Ben Stada, 24, 83
Benamozegh, Elie, 128, 143, 156, 209
Bentley, Richard, 155, 158
Berekhiah, 71, 104, 237
Brewster, David, 133
Buxtorf, Johannes, 155

Campbell, Alexander, 122
Castillejo, David, 132
Castro, Américo, 198, 202
Cervantes, Miguel de, 199, 202, 203, 204, 207, 208, 210, 211, 212, 213, 214
Chrysostom, 21, 23, 117
Constantine, 3, 13, 57, 120, 121, 123

Darby, John Nelspon, 122
de Rada, Jiménez, 198
Delicado (Delgado), Francisco, 204

Eddy, Mary Baker, 122
Eleazar b. Azariah, 92, 94, 230
Eliezer, 18, 98
Elisha b. Abuya, 95
Ephrem the Syrian, 21, 23

Flavius Josephus, 89
Fray Luis de León, 197

Gamaliel, 17, 230
Gans, David, 128
Greaces, John, 130, 131

Hama bar Haninah, 236
Hanina ben Dosa, 85, 86, 87
Haninah b. Teradion, 231
Hannah (rabbi), 237
Hasdai Crescas, 146
Haynes, Hopton, 135
Hillel, 24, 62, 91, 118, 230, 231, 252
Hirsch, Samson Raphael, 220, 257
Hiyya bar Abba (Ba), 234, 237
Hiyya bar Yose, 236
Hiyya, 18, 234, 236, 237
Hobbes, Thomas, 129, 152
Honi, 85, 86, 87
Hoshaia the Elder, 236

Ibn Ezra, Abraham, 148
Ibn Kaspi, Joseph, 167
Immi, 236
Irenaeus, 121, 122
Isaac (patriarch), 12, 13, 14, 26, 27, 115, 278, 283, 287
Isaac (rabbi), 104, 105

Jeremiah (prophet), 16, 27, 72, 114, 284
Jeremiah (rabbi), 237
Jerome, 21
Jonathan, 232
Joshua b. Levi, 236, 237
Joshua b. Nehemiah, 256
Judah ha-Levi, 3, 144, 145, 148, 151, 155, 185
Judah the Patriarch, 18, 97, 98
Julian, 20, 22, 23
Justin Martyr, 16, 21

Kafka, Franz, 200
Kanpanton, Yitzhaq, 163, 169
Keynes, John Maynard, 131, 132, 138

Levi, 71, 236, 237
Luther, Martin, 268

Medigo, Joseph Del, 128
Meir, 17, 97, 98, 99, 228, 229, 232
Mendelssohn, Moses, 257, 262
Milton, John, 129
More, Louis Trenchard, 132, 137
Moses, Israel, 128

Narbonni, Moshe, 167
Nehorai, 229
Nehunia b. Haqqaneh, 232
Newton, Isaac, 130, 142, 153–158, 160–161
Nieto, David, 128, 160, 161

Obadiah of Bertinoro, 130
Oshaia, 236, 240

Paris, Matthew, 198
Paul, 7, 42, 48, 89, 110, 120, 244, 245, 276, 278, 280, 286–288
Philo, 90, 117, 119, 154
Pope Benedict XVI, 7
Pope John Paul II, 4, 269
Pope John XXIII, 4

Raba, 206
Rashi, 16, 130, 171, 190, 192
Ratzinger, Joseph, 8
Ruiz, Juan, 199
Russell, Charles Taze, 122

Sacks, Jonathan, 4, 8
Sadoq, 231
Samson son of Abraham, 63
Samuel, Herbert, 138
Se'adya Gaon, 130
Shammai, 62, 230
Shmuel ibn Sid, 163, 169, 172
Sidiqiyya ha-Rofe, 130
Simeon b. Eleazar, 228
Simeon b. Gamaliel, 17
Simeon b. Menasya, 17
Simeon b. Yohai, 238
Smith, John, 129
Smith, Joseph, 122
Solomon ibn Adrete, 208
Spencer, John, 129

Taitazak, Yoseph, 174
Tanhum b. R. Hiyya, 237
Tarfon, 56, 231, 233, 235
Thomas Aquinas, 127, 223
Troeltsch, Ernst, 40, 41, 42, 43, 45–50, 53, 55, 57

Vives, Juan Luis, 197

Wierwille, Victor Paul, 122
William of Conches, 127
Wise, Isaac Meyer, 93

Yohanan b. Zakkai, 97, 98, 230
Yose, 91, 239
Yose bar Judah, 95, 96
Yudan, 256

Zeira, 19
Zevatai, 97

INDEX OF ANCIENT SOURCES

HEBREW HIBLE

Genesis
1:1, 241
1:26, 158
1:27, 78, 79, 82
2:7, 158
2:15, 149
2:24, 78, 79, 80, 81
4:2, 144
5:2, 78, 79
5:2-3, 78
8:22, 17
9:6, 78
11:11, 149
14:1-22, 27, 144, 145
14:19, 22, 144, 145
15:1-17, 277
15:6, 277, 278
15:18, 20
16:6, 27
17:1, 143
18:1-8, 27
18:1-33, 26, 27
20:14, 149
21:12, 278
22:1-14, 27
22:18, 256
24:1, 229
24:1-64, 27
26:5, 229
27:22, 239
28:10-22, 144
31:14, 149
32:10, 214
38:25, 214
49:10, 18, 22, 24

Exodus
3:14, 144
4:20, 104, 105
6:3, 143
14:19, 21, 149
15:26, 59, 148
19:6, 152
20:2, 147, 148
20:6, 148
20:9, 148
20:11, 148, 235

20:24-26, 114
23:21, 135
24:7, 103
31:13-17, 93
32:13, 283
32:4, 148
32:8, 148
34:28, 235

Leviticus
2:13, 148
10:1, 152
18:21, 148
19:2, 37
19:12, 148
19:18, 37, 90
21:8, 148
23:40, 63, 66, 70, 71
26:1-46, 44
26:9, 101

Numbers
11:12, 241
16:17-17:5, 152
23:7, 84

Deuteronomy
6:4, 148
9:9, 235
20:4, 149
32:5, 144
33:26, 150
33:1-34:12, 44

Joshua
1:8, 239
3:11, 135, 144, 146
3:13, 144, 146

1 Samuel
1:16, 16

2 Samuel
7:11, 18
7:12-16, 15
7:13, 22
23:5, 15

1 Kings
8:20, 22

2 Kings
23:11, 20

Isaiah
5:13-14, 97, 99
28:16, 279
35:6, 23
40:31, 229
41:27, 72
42:8, 135, 148
58:12, 23
60:20, 19
66:31, 25

Jeremiah
17:5-8, 94
17:12, 72
31:33, 284
31:34-36, 16
33:20-21, 16

Ezekiel
28:25-26, 23
33:24, 27
37:8, 23

Nahum
3:8, 241

Zechariah
3:8, 71
4:14, 144, 146
6:5, 144, 146
6:12, 71
8:16, 270
9:9, 70, 72
9:16, 74

Psalms
2:10, 22
19:6-7, 15
20:2-6, 75
22:2, 75
23:4, 214
28:1, 16
43:2-3, 104
68:19, 75
72:1:20, 16
78:69-70, 22
89:4-5, 15

89:29-38, 15
89:37, 19
92:14, 229
97:5, 144, 146
114:1, 62
118:1-29, 63, 65, 72
118:9, 70
118:21, 61, 66, 72
118:22, 67, 68, 70, 75
118:25, 70
118:26, 61, 62
127:1, 239
132:11, 15

Song of Songs
3:6, 235
8:7, 235

Proverbs
3:18, 237
8:22, 241, 244
8:30-31, 241
25:11, 202

Lamentations
4:5, 241

Job
4:19, 16
9:26, 16

Ecclesiastes
1:9, 104
7:12, 237
9:8, 98, 99

Esther
2:7, 241

Daniel
2:48, 85
4:6, 85
5:11, 85
9:24-27, 22
11:38-39, 135

1 Chronicles
16:1-43, 63, 64
16:33, 63

2 Chronicles
33:13, 59

INDEX OF ANCIENT SOURCES 297

NEW TESTAMENT

Matthew
1:1, 69
5:17-19, 245
5:21-48, 284
5:32, 82
6:24-34, 91
7:12, 90
7:24-27, 94
9:17, 96
10:37-38, 95
12:1-8, 93
12:5, 91
12:10-13, 92
17:1-8, 104
19:1-28, 78
19:3-9, 79
19:4, 78
19:6, 82
19:17, 245
19:30, 103
20:1-16, 101
20:16, 103
21:1-46, 61, 66, 67, 68, 72
21:5, 70
21:9, 61, 62
21:11, 88
21:26, 72
21:42, 75
21:42-43, 75
21:42-45, 68
22:1-14, 97, 98
23:1-3, 245
23:23, 245
24:1-2, 22
26:69, 88
27:25, 267
28:19-20, 69

Mark
2:22, 95, 96
2:23-28, 93
6:14, 119
6:27, 93
8:27-28, 119
9:2-8, 104
9:12-13, 119
10:17ff., 245
10:2-12, 79
10:9, 82
10:31, 103

12:10, 75
15:40-41, 88

Luke
5:37-39, 96
6:1-5, 93
9:28-36, 104
9:59-62, 95
11:42, 245
12:22-31, 91
13:1-2, 88
14:15-24, 97, 100
14:26-27, 95
16:17, 245
18:18ff., 245
19:1-48, 69
19:14-15, 70
19:37-38, 70
20:17, 75

John
2:1-11, 95
7:22, 91
7:23, 92
7:52, 88
12:1-50, 69
12:13, 70
21:1-25, 88

Acts
1:1, 88
2:7, 88
4:11, 75
5:37, 88

Romans
4:13, 278
7:15ff., 263
9:6-8, 278
9:30-33, 279
11:1-2, 25, 28–29, 287

1 Corinthians
6:12, 263
9:19ff., 263

Galatians
3:26, 286
3:28, 286
4:22-31, 26

Ephasians
2:20, 75
4:8, 75

Hebrews
8:6, 280

8:8, 280
8:10, 284
8:13, 280

1 Peter
2:7, 75

APOCRYPHA AND PSEUDEPIGRAPHA

2 Enoch
61:1-2, 90

Jubilees
21, 279

1 Maccabees
13:51, 64

2 Maccabees
10:6-7, 64

Sirach
45:15, 17
47:11, 18

Testament of Naphtali
1:6, 90

Tobit
4:15, 90

MISHNAH

Berakhot
2:2, 148, 151
9:6, 211

Peah
1:1, 237

Terumot
4:3, 102

Shabbat
18:3, 91
19:2, 91
19:3, 91
19:5, 91

Erubin
4:5, 130
10:11-15, 91

Pesahim
10:5, 62

Yoma
8:6, 92
8:9, 151

Rosh Hashanah
1:2, 151

1:4, 91
2:10, 211

Yebamot
4:13, 84

Gittin
1:7, 230

Qiddushin
4:14, 91, 228, 280

Baba Metsia
1:2, 149, 150
2:11, 226, 253

Sanhedrin
7:4, 148
10:2, 84
11:1-2, 58

Abodah Zarah
1:1, 271

Horayyot
3:8, 227

Eduyyot
2:4-6, 89

Abot
1:1, 89
1:5, 144
1:6, 85
1:16, 85
2:2, 230
2:4, 52
2:5, 252
2:8, 230
2:9, 102
2:10, 98
2:16, 230

3:2, 230
3:13, 89
3:15, 232
3:17, 94, 230
4:5, 231
4:9-10, 232
4:20, 95, 96
5:13, 19, 102
5:19, 84

Kelim
17:16, 207

TOSEFTA

Shabbat
11:15, 83
13:5, 56
14(15):3, 92
15:16, 92

Pesahim
4:13, 91

Qiddushin
1:11, 230

Sanhedrin
10:11, 83

Hullin
2:22-24, 83

Kelim
B.M. 7:10, 207

MIDRASH

Sifra
26:9, 101

Sifre Deuteronomy
284, 102

Genesis Rabbah
1:1, 240
8:13, 95
12:9, 256
12:15, 77
13:12, 17
34:11, 17
83:5, 24

Exodus Rabbah
31:10, 25

Leviticus Rabbah
30, 63
30:16, 69, 71
31:1, 234
34:6, 233

Lamentations Rabbah
Proem 23, 19

Ecclesiastes Rabbah
1:9, 105
5:11, 104, 105
7:2, 95
9:8, 97

Abot D'R. Nathan
40, 102
B 8:4, 95

Mekhilta
20:2, 103
31:14, 93

Pesiqta d'R. Kahanah
12:1, 280
15:5, 238

Pesiqta d'Rabbi Eliezer
88, 18

Pesiqta Rabbati
45b, 256

BABYLONIAN TALMUD

Berakhot
17a, 255
61a, 77

Shabbat
31a, 90
55a, 152
104b, 24, 83
119b, 24
153a, 97, 98

Erubin
18a, 77
42a, 130

Rosh Hashanah
16b, 151
25a, 18

Yoma
9b, 24, 250
28b, 280

Taanit
27b, 83

Yebamot
63b, 252

Ketubot
8a, 77, 78, 81

Nedarim
25a, 204, 208, 210, 211
28a, 262

Sotah
14a, 95
38a, 142
47a, 83

Gittin
56b-57a, 84
68a, 212

Baba Qamma
113a, 262

Baba Metsia
8b-9a, 150
106b, 17

Baba Batra
54b-55a, 262

Sanhedrin
5a, 24
8a, 149
43a, 24, 83
56a-56b, 284
61a, 148
67a, 83
76a, 24
103a, 83
107b, 24, 83

Abodah Zarah
6a, 83
27b, 83
47a, 83

Semahot
11, 95

JERUSALEM TALMUD

Berakhot
2:3, 104

Peah
2:6, 24

Shabbat
14d, 83

Sheqalim
5:4, 236

Megillah
3:3, 236
4:1, 233

Nedarim
1:2, 19

Sotah
7:4, 237
9:13, 236

Sanhedrin
25d, 84

Abodah Zarah
40d-41a, 83

Printed in the United States
By Bookmasters